POOR JACK

POOR JACK

*The perilous history of
the merchant seaman*

RONALD HOPE

CHATHAM PUBLISHING

LONDON

Frontispiece:
Drawing of a cherub atop a mast by R G Leslie taken from
Old Sea Wings, Ways and Words in the Days of Oak & Hemp.

First published in Great Britain in 2001 by
Chatham Publishing,
an imprint of Gerald Duckworth & Co Ltd,
61 Frith Street,
London W1D 3JL

Editorial offices: Chatham Publishing,
99 High Street, Rochester, Kent ME1 1LX

British Library Cataloguing in Publication Data
A catalogue record for this book is available from the British
Library

ISBN 1 86176 161 9

Typeset by Dorwyn Ltd, Rowlands Castle, Hants
Printed and bound in Great Britain by The Cromwell Press,
Trowbridge, Wilts

Contents

1 The Birth of Poor Jack — 1

2 The First Millennium — 10

3 Medieval Times 1000–1440 — 24

4 Outward Bound 1440–1505 — 37

5 Round the World 1505–1561 — 50

6 The First Elizabethans 1561–1581 — 60

7 Momentous Years 1581–1589 — 74

8 Privateers 1589–1596 — 86

9 The Gorgeous East 1596–1617 — 103

10 A Larger Prison 1617–1642 — 115

11 The Professionals 1642–1669 — 126

12 Seaman and Surgeon 1669–1689 — 137

13 The Manila Ship 1689–1709 — 150

14 A Cruise on the Spaniards 1709–1735 — 165

15 A Golden Time 1735–1750 — 174

16 The Transit of Venus 1750–1785 — 188

17 God Help Sailors! 1785–1815 — 203

18 Lucky for Some 1815–1835 — 223

19 Sail and Steam 1835–1860 — 241

20 Fiddler's Green 1860–1885 — 253

21 The Last of the Windjammers 1885–1910 — 276

22 All Cargo and no Comfort 1910–1935 — 294

23 War and Peace 1935–1960 — 316

24 The End of Poor Jack 1960–2000 — 341

Notes — 358

Index — 369

*To all those from whom I have borrowed
I dedicate this book.*

CHAPTER 1

The Birth of Poor Jack

Shipman, seaman, sailor, mariner; poor Jack or jolly Jack
– jolly whenever opportunity offered, which was seldom; poor on all but pay-days, when he became inordi-
nately generous – the merchant seafarer of the western
world who sailed on the deep ocean remained substantially
the same for most of the first 2000 years of the Christian
era and, indeed, for the 2000 years before that, which is
when we first learn of him.

In the 2000 years before Christ the evidence for this
from seafarers themselves is slight, but it is implied by the
knowledgeable writers of the day. The first undoubtedly
authentic voice of the seaman is heard much later, in the
Anglo-Saxon poem, *The Seafarer*, much of which may be
read in translation below.

From medieval times the direct evidence becomes
increasingly available, from the Judgments of Oléron,
drawn up in the twelfth century to guide those in command, and which themselves derive from laws drawn up in
the island of Rhodes before the birth of Christ, to the writ-
ings of serving seamen, which become abundant after 1500.

The bulk of this book is to be found in words put down
between 1500 and 2000. Poor Jack himself was never much
of a writer, though it is surprising how eloquent he
becomes when he tries. What he had to say in these years
is eked out with the words of others, all either at sea or

directly related to it, not least those who have come up through the hawse-pipe, that is those ratings who have achieved officer status, and perhaps command of a ship, after starting as cabin-boys or ordinary seamen. This was, indeed, what most mercantile marine officers did before the middle of the nineteenth century, and what more than half of them continued to do for many years after that. If the Royal Navy intrudes into these pages here and there, it is only because poor Jack was commandeered by his sovereign when necessity demanded, though in that sovereign's service he was rarely well looked after.

Joseph Conrad encapsulates much of what I have had in mind when compiling this book on the last page of *The Nigger of the 'Narcissus'*. After a long and sometimes dangerous voyage in sail to the East Indies the crew of the *Narcissus* pay off – receive their pay – in the shipping office near London Dock. But, after a few celebratory drinks, they appear both lost and doomed among the landsmen on Tower Hill. Conrad, however, evokes the great joys and sorrows of the past, 'the fighting prototypes of these men; press-gangs; mutinous cries; the waiting women by the riverside, and the shouts of men welcoming victories'. And the sun shines down on these victims of greed and selfishness, these castaways, like a gift of grace. 'I never saw them again', writes Conrad. 'The sea took some, the steamers took others, the graveyards of the earth will account for the rest.' But ashore and afloat, in good times and in bad, Conrad concludes that they were 'a good crowd'. This is the accolade.

In a time of great uncertainty, suggested Thomas Hobbes, the life of man is nasty, brutish and short. Hobbes had life in time of war particularly in mind and, had he been describing a different life which suffered great uncertainty, that of the merchant seaman, he might have amended one of his adjectives. As the psalmist reminds us, they that go down to the sea in ships, that do business in great waters, these see the works of the Lord and his wonders in the deep. Sailors cannot but be impressed thereby and many merchant seamen, perhaps most, have been ennobled by the experience. The average life spent in the merchant navy was never more than seven years, and it often ended abruptly, so 'short' was an appropriate adjective with which to describe it. No one who reads these pages will doubt, either, that the seaman's life was often also brutish. But 'noble, brutish and short' would seem a more appropriate description than Hobbes's of this uncertain life, for self-sacrifice features frequently as well.

Charles Dibdin, the eighteenth-century songwriter, may have had some understanding that this was so when he wrote, 'There's a sweet little cherub that sits up aloft, to keep watch for the life of poor Jack'. The cherub was never over-diligent, but poor Jack and his fellows themselves kept watch and, the account given of St Paul's shipwreck notwithstanding, their concern was never only for Number One.

Fifty years ago in Britain at least one family in sixty depended directly upon the deepsea sailor, and since the time of the first Queen Elizabeth his productivity had increased a thousandfold. Nevertheless, by 1980 the shipowners had decided that he had priced himself out of the market, and by the end of the twentieth century he had virtually disappeared from the western world. From that sea which, proverbially, is made of mothers' tears, poor Jack (the cowboy of the Western Ocean, as he was said to be when proving obstreperous in the 1950s) has now passed away – flown, no doubt, to that garden of delights which he knew as Fiddler's Green and whose location is given as 'seven miles to loo'ard of Hell'. There the drinks and smokes are logged or tallied, but the bill need never be paid. Few mourn his passing, and most have never noticed it. But those who knew him intimately may think that something has been lost, a spirit of adventure, and an

3

ability to put up with anything for the sight, smell and taste of a distant land. There was never any pot of gold at the end of the rainbow, or over the horizon, but you did not know it if you did not look.

Whatever may be said about sailors' yarns, the professional seafarer is normally a very matter-of-fact witness who tells the truth. He has to be in order to go again safely where he has been before, and he keeps his logbook accordingly. The first recorded sailor's yarn dates from about 2000 years before Christ.[1] Cast upon an island, this man – perhaps a Phoenician, perhaps an Egyptian – was the sole survivor from his ship, and a touch of authenticity is given to the story because he relates that he found cucumbers to eat. They were always a favourite item of diet around the top of the Red Sea and along the eastern Mediterranean coast.

The true western seaman is found in Crete a couple of hundred years later, but he left only pictures of the wonders of the deep, and the written record does not begin until after 1000 BC. The predecessors of Apollonius of Rhodes, who wrote of the Argonauts in the third century BC, told of the first exploration of the Black Sea, made perhaps about 1200 BC, and Homer describes exploratory voyages made at about the same time westward of the Greek homeland. Some sailors of these times felt homesick as soon as they sailed, and they had much to endure at sea, but there were compensations in strange places, exotic customs and food, with all the nice – and not so nice – girls loving a sailor, and a wife to be found in almost every port. The pangs of parting were, of course, severe when the ship sailed again, at any rate until the seafarer was seized with what English sailors call 'the Channels', namely the mad desire to be ashore and home once the home coast hove in sight.

In the Sea of Marmora the Argonauts were delayed by the familiar wind that blows from the north, as later sailors were so often delayed in the English Channel by the prevailing westerlies. At the entrance to the Black Sea the *Argo* stuck on rocks, just as Drake did when sailing round the world. On both occasions the sailors sought divine help, but they also helped themselves when opportunity offered – in Drake's case by jettisoning cargo.

After escaping with their lives and entering the Black Sea, the Argonauts came across a people in Turkey who fornicated in public. Nearly 3000 years later Francesco Carletti reported similarly of Japan, a Land of Cockaigne, or imaginary land of idleness and luxury, to the Portuguese sailors of the sixteenth century.

For many years after the Argonauts sailors did not cheerfully lose sight of land, which makes Ulysses' achievements the more impressive. The wind that held up the Argonauts when they tried to enter the Black Sea drove Ulysses, after he had sailed from Troy, south across the Mediterranean to the land of the Lotus-eaters. (It was, no doubt, a land where the natives ate dates while inhaling the smoke of burning cannabis.) A similar fate befell an aircrew who ditched in the sea in these same waters in the Second World War. They, like Ulysses, landed in North Africa. Trying to reach Greece again, Ulysses was later marooned for seven years in Ogygia, which might have been Malta, where he was consoled for a time by the ardent Calypso. One can imagine that Ulysses, having found his Maltese beauty infinitely desirable at the age of fourteen or fifteen, became somewhat disenchanted by the time she was twenty-two, after she had filled out on her pasta diet. However that may be, like many another shipwrecked sailor, he built himself a boat and sailed away. Nowadays, small-boat sailors lash themselves to their craft and thus, usually, avoid Ulysses' fate of being shipwrecked yet again when the sea grew rough.

The sweet little cherub, however, looked out for the wily Ulysses, who divested himself of his clothes and swam towards the land, ending up on a Corfu beach in the arms of the delicious Nausicca.

On reaching home and his ever-loving wife at last, Ulysses' thoughts reverted, perhaps, to the advice he had received from old Tiresias. The suggestion has recurred to many a mariner since. It was that, on reaching home, he should march straight inland until someone asks him what his duffle-bag – or some other item of a sailor's gear – is, and there he should settle.

In the sixth century BC the legendary Scythian prince Anarcharsis is said to have observed that there were three kinds of people, 'the living, the dead and those that sail in ships'. Herodotus suggests that it is a time when Phoenician sailors may have circumnavigated Africa, though the evidence proves only that this adventurous crew must have been south of the Tropic of Cancer in summer. 'These men', writes Herodotus, 'made a statement which I do not believe myself, though others may, which suggests that as they sailed on a westerly course round the southern end of Libya, they had the sun on their right hand – to the north of them.' However this may be, Hanno of Carthage at about this time voyaged southwards from the Straits of Gibraltar along the coast of Africa, and the Guanches reached the Canary Islands. Himilco, another Carthaginian, turned north out of the Straits of Gibraltar and brought back tales of skin-boats and the tedium and danger of navigation in what must have been the Bay of Biscay. Such sailors' reports were often doubted and, like Herodotus and the sun to the north, Strabo, writing in about AD 20, did not credit tales which the Greek Pytheas had circulated over 300 years before describing a frozen or 'curdled' sea north of Britain and an island called Thule which was six days' voyaging away. Like that first shipwrecked sailor who found cucumbers to eat, Pytheas told the truth and Iceland did exist.

About 360 BC a galley captain complained that many of his crew jumped ship abroad, as did many more in later times, in the hope of higher wages and a better life. The shortage of skilled seamen – often a complaint in the years ahead – led to a change in galley design: an unskilled oarsman was coupled with a skilled man on the same oar and thus the trireme was born.

From this time on many Greek poets wrote of the sea.

> Poor Cleonicus, trading from Syria,
> Was over-anxious for bright Thasos
> And sailed at the setting of the Pleiades.
> He and the Pleiades
> Sank together.

The Pleiades sank below the horizon early in November, thus marking the end of the sailing season. But Antipater of Thessalonia suggested that there were things worse for sailors than the winter sea. More than the setting of the Pleiades, he wrote, he dreaded the teetotaller who remembered everything you said in your cups.

Pirates were rife in the Mediterranean (they have not yet disappeared in Africa and the Far East) and in the first century BC some made the mistake of seizing Julius Caesar while he was on his way to Rhodes to study maritime law. Before being ransomed he good-humouredly promised to return after his release to hang them all. Actually he crucified them but, because they had treated him rather decently during his captivity, he allowed their throats to be cut before nailing them to the cross.

Later in life, Caesar gave a graphic description of the Veneti, seafarers who traded across the English Channel.

> ... they knew more about the handling of ships and the science
> of navigation than anyone else thereabouts; and their control of
> the few scattered harbours which offered refuge from those

violent storms so characteristic of the open sea enabled them to levy tolls on nearly all who used those waters.

The poets were still at work as a new era dawned with the birth of Christ and perhaps Isidorus of Aegae was the first to be inspired by the declaration that most seafarers heard a shipmate make at some time when they were aboard a ship: 'Who'd sell a farm to go to sea?'

> I am Eteocles
> Who sold a farm to sail
> Upon the Tyrrhenian Sea.
> A quick sharp squall
> Sank both my ship and me.
> A different wind ruffles the threshing floor
> From that which blows at sea!

Two thousand years later the unpredictability of a ship in a seaway inspired a nineteenth-century sailor to list the reasons why a ship was like a wayward mistress: there was always a bustle about her, and usually a gang of men; she had a waist and stays; it took a lot of paint to keep her good-looking, and it was not the initial expense that broke you but the cost of upkeep; she was all decked out, and it took a good man to handle her; she showed her topside and hid her bottom, and when going into port she always headed for the buoys.

But sailors had not changed much. Philip of Thessalonika, who flourished before St Paul set out to spread the gospel, saw a ship not merely as a mistress but as a whore. He declared that the ship he wrote of was its master's partner in those profitable trades where the crew that was collected were Aphrodite's maids. The poem continues,

> My bottom on the billow deep
> Might thus the Goddess please –
> A product of the trade ashore

A-bobbing on the seas.
My rig befits a courtesan:
My linen dainty white,
And a winsome wedge of seaweed
Between my timbers bright.
Come sailors you can board me now
And take me from astern.
Innumerable brave oarsmen
Will help my bread to earn.[2]

CHAPTER 2

The First Millennium

Although the seafarer, and the life he led, remained much the same for 4000 years, the recorded evidence for the first 2000 years, as we have seen, is sparse. Fifty or sixty years after the birth of Christ, however, we have what seems to be an unedifying picture of sailors painted in the Acts of the Apostles when St Paul was shipwrecked in Malta, where Ulysses had preceded him.

> When the fourteenth night had come, as we were drifting across the sea of Adria, about midnight the sailors suspected that they were nearing land. So they sounded and found twenty fathoms; a little farther on they sounded again and found fifteen fathoms. And fearing that we might run on the rocks, they let out four anchors from the stern, and prayed for the day to come. And as the sailors were seeking to escape from the ship, and had lowered the boat into the sea, under pretence of laying out anchors from the bow, Paul said to the centurion and the soldiers, 'Unless these men stay in the ship you cannot be saved'. Then the soldiers cut away the ropes of the boat, and let it go.

But this evidence is by no means conclusive of the sailors' malignity. It was perfectly good seamanship to lay out the anchors from the bow, and the sailors, no doubt, meant what they said. It did not make sense, in any case, to let the ship's boat go.

Rome, the city to which Paul was bound, could not be fed without its grain ships, the bulk carriers of their day, and in the second century AD Lucian provides a description of one of these 1200 ton vessels, which was blown off course to Piraeus while on passage from Alexandria. The North Atlantic did not see a ship of this size until 1845.

What a size this ship was! One hundred and eighty feet in length, the ship's carpenter told me, the beam more than a quarter of that, and forty-four feet from the deck to the lowest point in the hold. And the height of the mast, and what a yard it carried, and what a forestay they had to use to hold it up! And the way the stern rose up in a gradual curve ending in a gilded goose-head, matched at the other end by the forward, more flattened, sweep of the prow with its figure of Isis, the goddess the ship was named after, on each side! Everything was incredible: the rest of the decoration, the paintings, the red topsail, even more, the anchors with their capstans and winches, and the cabins aft. The crew was like an army. They told me she carried enough grain to feed every mouth in Athens for a year. And it all depends for its safety on one little old man who turns those great steering oars with a tiller that's no more than a stick! They pointed him out to me; woolly-haired little fellow, half-bald; Heron was his name, I think.[1]

Despite frequent disasters, boys from all over the Mediterranean left their villages to go to sea, as they would do for centuries to come. This is the first letter home to survive, sent by an Egyptian boy after he had joined a Roman ship.

Dear Father,
First, I hope you are all well and will always be well and prosperous, together with my sister and her daughter and my brother. I thank the God Serapis that when I was in danger at sea he saved me. On arrival at Miserium I received from the government three gold pieces for travelling expenses.

Everything is well with me. Please write, Father, first to tell me that you are well, second that my sister and brother are well, and third so that I may kiss your hand, because you gave me a good education and because of it I hope to obtain a speedy promotion, if the gods are willing. Give my love to Capiton and my brother and sister and Serenilla and my friends. I have given Euctemon a picture of myself to bring to you. My [Roman] name is Antonius Maximus, my ship the *Athenonice*. Goodbye. PS Agathodaemon's son Serenus sends his regards, and so does Turbo, Gallonius' son.[2]

Ashore, as always, there were those who made their profit from poor Jack, even though they too might take risks of enormous proportions. One such was Petronius' famous character Trimalchio, the ex-slave who became a multimillionaire.

I built myself five ships, loaded them with wine – which was worth its weight in gold at the time – and sent them to Rome. Every single one of them was wrecked, that's the God's honest truth; Neptune gulped down a cool thirty million in one day. I built myself some more, got another cargo of wine, added bacon, beans, a load of slaves ... the little woman sold all her jewels to raise the cash. I netted a cool ten million on that one voyage.[3]

By this time the sailors from the eastern Mediterranean were sailing to and from India with the monsoon winds, much as the Portuguese traded in the Indian Ocean in the sixteenth century, though they did not sail round Africa. When Alaric the Goth agreed not to sack Rome in AD 408, part of the price paid was three thousand pounds of pepper imported from Indonesia.

In the west Celtic seafarers were venturing into the rough Atlantic. Inspired by a fellow monk, who had preceded him, St Brendan (c484–518) may have visited Iceland and even North America. The evidence, such as it is, is presented in Wynkyn de Worde's *Golden Legend*. The sailors are promised that they will be shown a place 'where is ever day, and never night', which would certainly describe Iceland in the height of summer, and the volcanic nature of that island may be indicated by the following passage.

And then they sailed forth, and came soon after to that land, but because of little depth in one place, and great rocks in another, they cast about and at last went upon an island, thinking themselves safe, and made thereon a fire on which to prepare their dinner, but St Brendan remained in the ship. And when the fire was right hot, and the meat nigh done, then this island began to move; whereat the monks were afraid and fled anon to the ship, and left the fire and meat behind them and marvelled at the moving.

The Celtic saints may have had their share of Irish blarney, and it is difficult to sort truth from embroidery, but the passage below recalls the vines of Vinland or Wineland recorded by the Vikings at a later date. It is unlikely that these seafarers would confuse this unknown land with, say, Gascony, for they were thoroughly familiar with the overland routes through France to the Mediterranean, where they received much of their education.

And then the angel of the Lord ordained all things that were needful to St Brendan and to his monks, in victuals and all other things necessary. And then they thanked our Lord for the great goodness that he had often shown them in their great need, and then sailed forth in the great sea ocean abiding the mercy of our Lord in great trouble and tempests. And soon after came to them a horrible fish which followed the ship a long time, casting so much water out of his mouth into the ship that they expected to have been drowned. Wherefore they devoutly prayed to God to deliver them of that great peril. And anon after came another fish greater than he, out of the west sea, and fought with him, and at last clove him in three pieces, and then returned again. And then they thanked meekly our Lord for their deliverance from this great peril; but they were in great heaviness because their victuals were nigh spent. But by the ordinance of the Lord there came a bird which brought to them a great branch of vine full of red grapes by which they lived fourteen days; and then they came to the little island wherein were many vines full of grapes, and there they landed, and thanked God, and gathered as many grapes as they lived by forty days after, always sailing in the sea in many a storm and tempest.[4]

It sounds like the North Atlantic! And the gales (and further experience) had blown legend away by the time the Irish monk Dicuil flourished, in about 825.

It is now thirty years since I heard this story from the monks who had been to the Island (Iceland) and who had stayed there from the first of February until the first of August. Not only at the summer solstice itself, they told me, but also during the days before and after it, when evening came the setting sun hid itself from them just as if it were passing behind a small hill. Even during that space of time, it never grew dark at all, a man could do any job he wished just as easily as when the sun was with them – could even see perfectly well to remove lice from his shirt! ... One day's sailing northward ... brought them to the sea that was frozen hard.

There is a large number of other islands in the ocean to the north of Britain, which can be reached in two days' and nights' sailing from the north British islands with a consistently favourable wind to fill the sails. A certain father of the church related to me how he landed on one of them after sailing in a two-benched ship for two days and the intervening night. Some of these islands are very small indeed, and at the same time almost all are divided from each other.

For almost a hundred years, hermits from our own Scotland sailed to them and lived there. But just as the islands had always been deserted since the world's creation, so now – on account of the Norse pirates – there are no hermits there, only countless sheep and innumerable birds.[5]

The Celtic seafarers went north before the Vikings came south, and it seems probable that from the Celts the Vikings learned how to navigate on the ocean and what to look out for. But the Celts were not the only inhabitants of the British Isles at sea in the eighth century. By Saxon law, between an earl and a freeman came the thane – later a baron or a knight – and a merchant who financed three successful foreign voyages in his own ships (so Hakluyt tells us)[6] became a thane automatically. 'Be content with what you have', advised a Saxon proverb. 'Remember, a little ship in shallow water is safer than a big ship in deep waters.'[7] Modern seafarers may aver that little knowledge of the sea is displayed here. Nevertheless it is from this period that we have the Anglo-Saxon riddle which describes an iceberg and that remarkable and much-translated poem *The Seafarer*, for part of which I offer a prose translation.

I will sing you a true song of my travels. I have worked hard for hours on end, and suffered much while afloat on the sea, in the roll of the waves. Often in the night watches I have been desperately cold, my feet frozen when on watch in the prow of the ship, the ship pitching beneath the cliffs. At such a time I have been full of cares, hungry, afraid, and weary of the ocean. Those fortunate enough to live on land know nothing of the terrors of an ice-covered sea or even of the freezing voyage towards it. I have often felt lonely, away from my family, lashed by the hail and with icicles in the rigging. All I could hear then was the ocean's roar, the crash of the freezing waves, and the scream of the gull. The chatter of gannets was my only company. No laughter, no drinking – just the seamen singing a chanty. Little does anyone who lives in a city understand about the life of a seaman. The city dweller's hardships are trivial. Worn and weary, the seaman waits on the ocean, darkness falls, and snow comes down from the north.

And yet there is within me, deep down in my heart, a yearning for the sea, the desire to test its strength, and to wander the wide world over. Far from my native land I want to seek out foreign places. No man with a curious mind, a healthy body, a great soul, and a daring nature can resist the call of the ocean, the desire to make a voyage to sea and find what God has in store for him. Such a man has no joy in his harp, no joy in his treasure, no wish for a wife, nor for what the world calls happiness. He wants nothing but the curl of the rolling wave and the longing to sail over it.[8]

Seafarers everywhere would feel that they know this Saxon sailor, the chap who has a chip on his shoulder, who 'drips' (to use the naval slang of the Second World War) and yet who, like Laurence Binyon's John Winter, cannot keep away from the sea. But where did he gain his experience? No doubt in whaling in the Arctic Sea, for that is where the Norwegian Ohthere went, round about 890, for he described a voyage round the North Cape into the White Sea to King Alfred.

He took his voyage directly north along the [Norwegian] coast, having upon his starboard always the desert land, and upon his larboard the main ocean: and continued his course for the space of three days. In which space he was come as far towards the north, as commonly the whale hunters use to travel. Whence he proceeded in his course still towards the north so far as he was able to sail in another three days. At the end whereof he perceived that the coast turned towards the east ... thence he sailed plain east along the coast still so far as he was able in the space of four days. At the end of which time he was compelled again to stay till he had a full northerly wind, forsomuch as the coast bowed thence directly towards the south ... so that he sailed thence along the coast continually full south, so far as he could travel in five days; and at the fifth day's end he discovered a mighty river, which opened very far into the land. At the entry of which river he stayed his course, and in conclusion turned back again, for he durst not enter thereinto for fear of the inhabitants of the land ... The principal purpose of his travel this way, was to increase the knowledge and discovery of these coasts and countries, for the more commodity of fishing of horse-whales [walruses], which have in their teeth bones of great price and excellency: whereof he brought some at his return unto the king. Their skins are also very good to make cables for ships, and so used. This kind of whale is much less in quantity than other kinds, having not in length above seven ells [about seven yards].[9]

Late In the tenth century the Saxon monk Aelfric wrote a revealing schoolbook in which the teacher quizzes a number of people, including the fisherman who preferred fishing in the river.

Teacher: Why do you not fish in the sea?

Fisher: I do sometimes, but not often, for it is a long way down to the sea.

Teacher: What do you catch there?

Fisher: Herrings and salmon, porpoises and sturgeon, oysters and crabs, mussels and periwinkles, cockles and flat fish, flounders and lobsters and many other kinds.

Teacher: Have you ever caught a whale?

Fisher: No.

Teacher: Why not?

Fisher: Because it is far too dangerous for me. It is much safer to row up the river in my boat than to go with a fleet hunting whales.

Teacher: How so?

Fisher: I prefer to catch fish which I can kill and not fish which can kill me. Why, with one blow of its tail, a fish that size could send me and my companions to the bottom, or maim us for life.

Teacher: Yet many do kill whales and escape all harm. They gain much money thereby.

Fisher: That's quite true, but for my part I admit I have not the courage.

The next interview is with a merchant.

Teacher: What do you say, trader?

Trader: I say that I am fit to be an alderman. I am necessary to the king, the wealthy folk and to everyone else.

Teacher: How?

Trader: I go on board my ship with my cargo and I row to all lands. I sell my goods and buy precious things not known in this country. Then with much danger I transport my purchases over the sea to you here in England. Sometimes I endure shipwreck and the loss of all my goods, not to mention the risk of losing my life.

Teacher: What things do you bring me?

Trader: Purple garments and silks, gems and gold, cleverly made suits of armour, spices, wine and oil, ivory and brass, copper and tin, sulphur and many other things.

Teacher: Do you sell these things here for the same price which you paid for them?

Trader: Certainly not. For if I did, what would be the profit of all my labour? I sell them here for a greater price than I paid, so as to get enough profit to keep my wife and my little son.[10]

By this time the Vikings were sailing the Atlantic, Eric the Red's expedition to Greenland being made in about 982.

That summer Eric set out to colonise the land which he had discovered, and which he called Greenland, because, he said, men would be more readily persuaded thither if the land had a good name.[11]

In the year 994 Eric's son Leif the Lucky sailed west from Greenland to a point on the coast of North America, possibly Nova Scotia, which he named Vinland, the land of grapes. Among others, Leif's sister Freydis and his brother-in-law Thorvald sailed to Vinland later on.

They went ashore and looked about them. The weather was fine. There was dew on the grass, and the first thing they did was to get some of it on their hands and put it to their lips, and to them it seemed the sweetest thing they had ever tasted ...

They took on a full cargo of timber; and in the spring they made ready to leave and sailed away. Leif named the country after its natural qualities and called it *Vinland*.

They put out to sea and had favourable winds all the way until they sighted Greenland and its ice-capped mountains. Then one of the crew spoke up and said to Leif, 'Why are you steering the ship so close to the wind?'

'I am keeping an eye on my steering,' replied Leif, ' but I am also keeping an eye on something else. Don't you see anything unusual?'

They said they could see nothing in particular.

'I am not quite sure,' said Lief, 'whether it is a ship or a reef I can see.'

Now they caught sight of it and said it was a reef. But Leif's eyesight was so much keener than theirs that he could make out people on the reef ...

Leif rescued fifteen people in all from the reef. From then on he was called Leif the Lucky. He gained greatly in wealth and reputation.[12]

Although much of the saga concerning Freydis in Vinland is concerned with events on shore, the adventures of this Amazonian female have the ring of truth and she is unique in seafaring literature.

Now there was renewed talk of voyaging to Vinland, for these expeditions were considered a good source of fame and fortune.

In the summer that Karlsefni returned from Vinland, a ship arrived in Greenland from Norway, commanded by two brothers called Helgi and Finnbogi. They spent the winter in Greenland. They were Icelanders by birth and came from the Eastfjords.

One day, Freydis, Eric's daughter, travelled from her home at Gardar to visit the brothers Helgi and Finnbogi. She asked them if they would join her with their ship on an expedition to Vinland, sharing equally with her all the profits that might be made from it. They agreed to this. Then she went to see her brother Leif and asked him to give her the houses he had built in Vinland; but Leif gave the same answer as before – that he was willing to lend them but not to give them away.

The two brothers and Freydis had an agreement that each party should have thirty able-bodied men on board, besides women. But Freydis broke the agreement at once by taking five more men, whom she concealed; and the brothers were unaware of this until they reached Vinland.

So they put to sea, and before they left they agreed to sail in convoy if possible. There was not much distance between them, but the brothers arrived in Vinland shortly before Freydis and had moved their cargo up to Leif's houses by the time Freydis landed. Her crew unloaded her ship and carried the cargo up to the houses.

'Why have you put your stuff in here?' asked Freydis.

'Because,' the brothers replied, 'we had thought that the whole of our agreement would be honoured.'

'Leif lent these houses to me, not to you,' she said.

Then Helgi said, 'We brothers could never be a match for you in wickedness.'

They moved their possessions out and built themselves a house further inland on the bank of a lake, and made themselves comfortable there. Meanwhile Freydis was having timber felled for her cargo.

During the ensuing winter there was further trouble between Freydis and the brothers, but early one morning

Freydis went to see Finnbogi, who was inclined to stay in Vinland, and agreed to exchange his ship, which was the larger of the two, with hers. Freydis then walked back home.

When she climbed back into bed her feet were cold and her husband Thorvald woke up and asked why she was so cold and wet. She answered with great indignation, 'I went over to see the brothers to offer to buy their ship, because I want a larger one; and this made them so angry that they struck me and handled me roughly. But you, you wretch, would never avenge either my humiliation or your own. I realise now how far I am away from my home in Greenland. And unless you avenge this, I am going to divorce you.'

He could bear her taunts no longer and told his men to get up at once and take their weapons. They did so, and went straight over to the brothers' house; they broke in while all the men were asleep, seized them and tied them up, and dragged them outside one by one. Freydis had each of them put to death as soon as he came out.

All the men were killed in this way, and soon only the women were left; but no one was willing to kill them.

Freydis said, 'Give me an axe.'

This was done, and she herself killed the women, all five of them.

After this monstrous deed they went back to their house, and it was obvious that Freydis thought she had been clever about it. She said to her companions, 'If we ever manage to get back to Greenland I shall have everyone killed who breathes a word about what has happened. Our story will be that these people stayed on here when we left.'

Early in the spring they prepared the ship that had belonged to the brothers and loaded it with all the produce they could get and the ship could carry. They had a good voyage and reached Ericsfjord early in the summer.[13]

The formidable Freydis apart, the Vikings were a tough lot. One more quotation from the Vinland Sagas will serve to complete this sketch of poor Jack's lot in the dark age of northwest Europe. Bjarni Grimolfsson's story, besides providing what is probably the first description of the activities of *Teredo navalis,* the wood-boring mollusc which helped to destroy many ships, also suggests a standard of behaviour which many shipmates were to follow, even without prompting, in the centuries that followed.

Bjarni Grimolfsson's ship was blown into the Greenland Sea. The crew found themselves in waters infested with maggots, and before they knew it the ship was riddled under them and had begun to sink.

They discussed what they should do. They had one ship's-boat which had been treated with tar made from seal-blubber; it is said that shell-maggots cannot penetrate timber which has been so treated. Most of the crew said they should fill this boat with as many people as it would hold; but when they tried they found that the boat would not hold more than half of them.

Then Bjarni said that the people who were to go should be chosen by lot, and not by rank.

... they agreed to this suggestion of drawing lots for places [in the boat]. When the lots were drawn it so happened that Bjarni himself, along with nearly half the crew, drew a place, and these all left the ship for the boat. When they were in the boat one young Icelander who had been Bjarni's companion said, 'Are you going to leave me here, Bjarni?'

'That is how it has to be,' replied Bjarni.

The Icelander said, 'But that is not what you promised when I left my father's farm in Iceland to go with you.'

'I see no other way,' said Bjarni. 'What do you suggest?'

'I suggest we change places; you come up here and I shall go down there.'

'So be it,' said Bjarni. 'I can see that you would spare no effort to live, and are afraid to die.'

So they changed places. The Icelander stepped into the boat and Bjarni went back on board the ship; and it is said that Bjarni and all those who were on the ship with him perished there in the maggot sea.

Those in the ship's boat sailed away and reached land.[14]

CHAPTER 3

Medieval Times

1000–1440

The Mediterranean, the Baltic and the seas around western Europe as far as Iceland and northern Norway were all well known to medieval seafarers. Overland from the East to the Mediterranean, and thence by sea, spices and silks were brought to the kitchens and wardrobes of the rich. Herrings caught at the entrance to the Baltic were pickled in brine, and cod caught in Icelandic waters was dried: both were exported by sea, some as far as Italy. Timber and grain were brought from Scandinavia to Britain, and wine came from France. From England, wool, cloth, coal and tin went to the Continent. Governments attempted to establish rules to govern sailors and commerce but, after the fall of the Roman Empire, the western world was poor, states were fragmented, and ships were small, mostly well under 100 tons. Contact by sea with India had been lost and, with a deterioration in the climate in Greenland, the colonies there died out and North America was no longer visited. Not until the last quarter of the thirteenth century did vessels over 100 tons and with more than one mast, carracks and galleys, venture into the Atlantic from Genoa and Venice. For self-protection some ships travelled in convoy, but wrecks were frequent, seafarers from rival ports often preyed upon one another, and piracy was rife.

In Norman times trade between England and Norway was of some importance and it is in this trade, in 1074, just a few years after the Norman Conquest of England, that we find the first recorded stowaway – Turgot, an Angle hostage in Lincoln Castle.

Obtaining by money a mitigation of his imprisonment, he at great risk privily made his escape to the Norwegians, who were then loading a merchant vessel at Grimsby for Norway. In this vessel also certain ambassadors, who King William was sending to Norway, had procured a passage; and now when the ship in full sail was out of sight of land, lo! the King's runaway hostage emerging from the hold of the vessel in which the Norwegians had concealed him, astounded the ambassadors and their companions. For when a diligent search had been everywhere made, the King's inspectors had examined this very vessel, but the cunning of the concealers baffled the observation of the searchers. The ambassadors then insisted that they should lower the sails, and should somehow or other take back the ship with the King's fugitive to England. This the Norwegians sharply resisted, as a voyage so well begun would carry the vessel forward prosperously. Such a quarrel of the parties ensued that they betook themselves to arms on both sides; but since the force of numbers was with the Norwegians, the insolence of the ambassadors was soon repressed, and the nearer they approached the land the more submissive did they become. When they arrived there, the young refugee by his modest and discreet behaviour rendered himself agreeable to the nobles and the gentry.[1]

Half a century later, Prince William, only legitimate son of Henry I, was drowned at sea, and his death has been celebrated in Dante Gabriel Rossetti's poem *The White Ship*. Although he died in an attempt to save his sister's life after shipwreck, he was no Bjarni Grimolfsson, and he was not much of a sailor. The same may be said of the gangster king Richard Lion Heart who travelled overland as far as he could. However, he inspired 4000 volunteers to sail from England at their own expense on the Third Crusade in

1188, probably the first substantial convoy ever to go by sea in either direction through the Straits of Gibraltar, for there is no earlier evidence of considerable traffic, even in Roman times, and Phoenicians trading by sea to Cornwall are a myth. The following regulations – probably drafted by Richard's man of business, Hubert Walter, Archbishop of Canterbury, who led the fleet – governed the voyage.

He who kills a man on shipboard, shall be bound to the dead man, and thrown into the sea; if the man is killed on shore, the slayer shall be bound to the dead body and buried with it. Anyone convicted by lawful witnesses of having drawn his knife to strike another, or who shall have drawn blood of him, he is to lose his hand. If he shall have only struck with the palm of his hand, without drawing blood, he shall be thrice ducked in the sea. Anyone who shall reproach, abuse or curse his companion, shall for every time he is convicted thereof, give him so many ounces of silver. Anyone convicted of theft shall be shorn like a champion, boiling pitch shall be poured on his head and he shall be set ashore at the first land the ship touches.[2]

The wine trade between Bordeaux and England was the training ground for many English sailors – from Roman to modern times French wines have been brought by sea to the immediate neighbourhood of the Tower of London – and the Judgments of Oléron were drawn up about 1194 to regulate this trade. As has been seen already, Julius Caesar went to the island of Rhodes to learn law, and the law of the sea was an important part of the training. The first quotation below is from the Mediterranean *Consulat de la Mer* which continued in the Rhodian tradition, and the Judgments of Oléron which follow are also on the Rhodian model. What is given here is by no means complete. The Judgments as a whole are a mixture of sound business sense, what appears to be reasonable, democratic, and even humane, practice, and what may strike the modern reader as unspeakable cruelty. The cruelty, it may be conjectured, is inspired by fear combined with the difficulty of catching and punishing any transgressor.

A sailor must not undress except in a port of wintering; if he does so, let him be ducked three times in the sea from the yard-arm on each occasion; and after the third repetition of the offence, he is to forfeit his wages and all his property on board.[3]

When a ship is in harbour and awaiting a favourable moment to leave, the captain must not sail without consulting the ship's company, and should say to them. 'Gentlemen what do you think of the weather?' If some of them answer, 'The weather is bad,' and others, to the contrary, say, 'The weather is fine and favourable', the captain ought to be guided by the opinion of the greater number; for if he does otherwise, and the ship is lost, he is liable to indemnify the owners of the ship and cargo as far as he has the wherewithal.[4]

A master hireth his mariners, and ought to keep them peaceful, and offer to be their judge, and if any say that his fellow lieth, having bread and drink at the table, ought to pay fourpence; and if any belieth the master, to pay eightpence; and if the master smite any of the mariners, the mariner ought to abide the first buffet be it with the fist, or flat with his hand, but if he smite more he may defend him; and if a mariner smite the master to pay five shillings or lose his fist.[5]

It may be wondered how many of those guilty of the last offence chose to become 'hands' in the singular sense. It was also decreed that if a pilot swore 'by his head' to take a ship safely into port and then lost her or ran her into peril, he could lose the head thus foresworn. 'If the captain or any of the sailors or any of the merchants should cut off his head, they are not liable to any penalty; but before killing him it is always well to find out whether he has the means of making amends.'[6]

That sailors pray to God in times of emergency is no new revelation in history by this time, and there is other evidence that God listens more readily to princes than to poor Jack, Charles Dibdin notwithstanding. On the occasion recorded below, the prince involved was the somewhat arrogant Edward, later King Edward I of England, who was on his way home after a crusade in the thirteenth century.

> Storms suddenly arose at sea so that imminent destruction threatened the whole structure of the vessel. The sailors could do no more and gave up all hope of rescue, so in terror they prayed loudly to God and the passengers decided each to vow to God whatsoever the Holy Spirit should prompt. All did this devoutly but still the storms did not abate but went on increasing in force. In the face of death everybody on board with one accord begged the prince with tears, as he had not made a vow with the others, to deign to make a vow pleasing to the Lord that he might speedily rescue them from their present peril.
>
> The prince yielded and humbly promised to God and the Virgin that if the Lord should save him and his and theirs and bring them unharmed to shore, he would then forthwith found a monastery of white monks of the order of the Cistercians in their honour within England. He would endow it so richly that it could support one hundred monks for ever. God's strength in saving his people was at once revealed for hardly had the most Christian prince stopped speaking when the storm was quite dispersed and there was calm.[7]

Aphrodite or Venus, a goddess who was born of the sea, always had a special significance for sailors, but was supplanted in due course by the Virgin Mary, often poetically called the Star of the Sea or Stella Maris (the planet Venus), which star was thought of as a lantern shining for voyagers on the sea of evil. (In later times Stella Maris was the name given to a Roman Catholic missionary society devoted to seafarers.)

A real lantern shining for voyagers on the real sea appeared on a staff in the stern of the admiral's ship at least as early as the reign of King Richard II, for it is to be seen on the medieval seal of Sir William Hylton, who was described as the Admiral of the Humber towards Scotland. In the *Black Book of the Admiralty*, which codified the law of the sea in 1336, we find a reference to the admiral's lantern as well as to a sailor's security scheme intended to support those no longer able to follow their profession – a kind of beacon ashore – though it may be doubted whether Poor Jack ever obtained value for money. Later, Drake's Chatham Chest was to follow in its tradition, a fund set up in 1590 for the relief of sick and aged mariners. To finance the scheme then sixpence a month was deducted from the wages of able-seamen serving in the Queen's fleet, but the fund fell victim to corruption. In the Middle Ages, of course, there was no distinction between merchant ships and the sovereign's ships except the use to which they were put.

> And because that the admiral is governor of the mariners and ought to rule them and uphold them in all their laws and cus-toms, and defend them from all injuries against all persons, and if need be to sue for their wages and cause them to be paid the same, he shall have and take out of each pound paid for the wages of the mariners fourpence, for which fourpence the admiral shall in the nighttime, all the while that the fleet is at sea, carry at the top of his mast two lanthorns, to the end that all the masters of the fleet may know and perceive by the light and the admiral's course what course they shall steer.[8]

Hakluyt, the Elizabethan collector of the accounts of voyages, makes the first reference in literature to the whirlpool which no doubt inspired Edgar Allen Poe's *Descent into the Maelstrom*. He refers to priests who were sent to Norway and to the islands between Britain and Norway by King Arthur and attributes the following account to one Giraldus Cambrensis who flourished in 1210.

Not far from these islands (namely the Hebrides, Faroes, etc.) towards the north there is a certain wonderful whirlpool of the sea, whereinto all the waves of the sea from far have their course and recourse, as it were without stop: which, there conveying themselves into the secret receptacles of nature, are swallowed up, as it were, into a bottomless pit, and if it chance that any ships do pass this way, it is pulled, and drawn with such violence of the waves, that eftsoons without remedy, the force of the whirlpool devoureth the same.[9]

Poe puts the maelstrom somewhere above the Arctic Circle between the Lofoten islands and the Norwegian mainland, but this was, no doubt, poetic licence. The Pentland Firth might be a more likely spot, and one better known to Sir Patrick Spens and to Geoffrey Chaucer's shipman.

A poem of this period suggests that a wise man would forbid his son from going to sea because the prospects of survival were slim, and Sir Patrick Spens, in the well-known ballad, complains bitterly of his commission to take the King of Scotland's daughter to Norway in the winter of 1270 or thereabouts, for winter was still a time of year when any sensible seaman laid up his vessel altogether. Sir Patrick was presumably a merchant venturer exporting and importing goods to and from Scandinavia who had been knighted for his services to the government. The verses below have been anglicised.

> 'Oh who is this has done this deed
> And told the king of me,
> To send us out at this time of year
> To sail upon the sea?'

It is on the way home from Norway that tragedy occurs.

> They had not sailed a league, a league,
> A league but barely three,
> When the sky grew dark, and the wind blew loud,
> And stormy grew the sea.

The anchors broke away, the topmast sprang,
It was such a deadly storm:
And the waves came o'er the broken ship
Till all her sides stove in ...

'Go fetch a roll of silken cloth,
Another of the twine,
And thump them into our ship's side,
And let not the sea come in.'...

Oh loath, loath were our good Scots lords
To wet their cork-heeled shoes,
But long before the play was o'er
They wet their hats as well.

And many was the feather bed
That floated on the foam,
And many were the good lords' sons
That never more came home.

Chaucer, a much travelled customs official who at some time had a house at Aldgate in the City of London, probably lived from 1344 to 1400. In a passage in his *Canterbury Tales* he tells us more of fourteenth-century seafaring and seafarers than any other evidence available from his time. Put into contemporary English, what he says is as follows.

Among the pilgrims to Canterbury was a bearded sailor who came from the west of England, probably from Dartmouth. He rode upon a horse, rather clumsily, dressed in a knee-length tunic, a dagger hanging by a cord round his neck and tucked under his arm. The hot summer had tanned him thoroughly, and he proved a good companion. Bringing wine home from Bordeaux, he had often stolen a flask from the barrels on board while the merchant trader slept. His conscience was easy. If he fought at sea and gained the upper hand he threw his enemies overboard. But you could not teach him anything about seamanship or navigation. He knew his tides, his currents and the dangers in the sea, his harbours, the phases of the moon, and his pilotage. Navigating from Hull to Carthage none was his equal. He was hardy, but a cautious seaman who had survived many a tempest. He knew every harbour from Gotland (in the Baltic) to Cape Finistère, and every creek in Brittany and Spain. His ship was called the *Magdalen*.

The *Magdalen* would have been a small vessel of no more than 60 tons.

During the reign of Henry V (1413–22) or soon thereafter – perhaps about 1436 – an unknown author, who could be Adam de Moleyns, wrote *The Libel of English Policy*.[10] This long poem refers to the merchant Richard of Whitingdon, better known as Dick Whittington, one-time Lord Mayor of London, who died in 1423. The moral of the verses for the English nation is that the English should nurture their exports, and to facilitate this they need to control the English Channel. After describing the exports of Portugal and Brittany, the author condemns the latter's piratical sailors:

> And of this Brittany, who so truth loves,
> Are the greatest rovers and the greatest thieves,
> That have been in the sea many a year:
> That our merchants have bought full dear.
> For they have took notable goods of ours,
> On this side sea, these false pelours
> Called of St. Malo, and elsewhere:
> Which to the Duke no obeisance will bear:
> With such colours we have been hindered sore.
> And feigned peace is called no war herefore.

Things had been better, the poet tells us, in the reign of Edward III (1312–77), for in those days the English had forced the Duke of Brittany to exercise proper authority. After describing Scottish and Lowland trade, the author goes on to tell us that

The Genoese come in sundry wises
Into this land with divers merchandises
In great carracks, arrayed without lack
With cloth of gold, silk and pepper black.
...

The great galleys of Venice and Florence
Be well laden with things of complacence,
All spicery and of grocers' ware:
With sweet wines all manner of chaffare [trade].

The poet complains that these great ships brought inessentials to British shores but took away valuable cloth, wool and tin. This first of the Mercantilists considered that the purpose of trade was to accumulate gold and thus to augment state power. Interestingly he tells us that British seafarers had long navigated with the compass to fish for cod though it is a trade that is not of much interest to him.

Of Iceland to write is little need,
Save of stock fish [dried cod]: yet forsooth indeed
Out of Bristol, and coasts many [a] one,
Men have practised by needle and stone [compass]
Thitherwards within a little while,
Within twelve years, and without peril
Gone and come, as men were wont of old
Of Scarborough unto the coasts cold.

By these times Compostella, in Northern Spain, had long been considered the depository of the remains of St James and, in consequence, it possessed a Christian shrine third in importance only to those of Jerusalem and Rome. This was a great place of pilgrimage and St James' symbol, the scallop shell, was not without its seafaring significance, for Aphrodite was born from the sea and borne by the scallop shell. In the fifteenth century it was not unknown for more than two thousand pilgrims a year to be carried from England to Compostella by sea, and one of the most famous of all fifteenth-century poems describes the voyage.

> Men may leave all games
> That sail to Saint James.
> For many a man it grames [grieves]
> When they begin to sail.
>
> For when they have took the sea
> At Sandwich, or at Winchelsea,
> At Bristol, or where e'er it be,
> Their hearts begin to fail.
>
> Anon the master commandeth fast
> To his shipmen in all haste,
> To dress them soon about the mast,
> Their tackling to make.
>
> With 'Ho! hissa!' then they cry,
> 'What, hoist! Mate thou standest too nigh;
> Thy fellow may not haul thereby';
> Thus they begin to crake.
>
> A boy or twain anon up-sty,
> And overthwart the sail-yard lie;
> 'Y ho! taylia!' the remnant cry,
> And pull with all their might.
>
> 'Bestow the boat, boatswain, anon,
> That our pilgrims may play thereon;
> For some are like to cough and groan
> Ere it be full midnight.'
>
> 'Haul the bowline! now, veer the sheet!
> Cook, make ready anon our meat;
> Our pilgrims have not lust to eat,
> Pray God give them rest.'
>
> 'Go to the helm! what, ho! no nearer!
> [ie steer no nearer to the wind]

Steward, fellow! a pot of beer.'
'Ye shall have, sir, with good cheer,
Anon all of the best.'

'Y ho! trussa! haul in the brails!
Thou haulest not, by God; thou fails.
O see how well our good ship sails!'
And thus they say among.

'Haul in the wartake!' [warp] 'It shall be done.'
'Steward! cover the board anon,
And set the bread and salt thereon,
And tarry not too long.'

Then cometh one and saith, 'Be merry;
Ye shall have a storm or a pery [danger]'
'Hold thou thy peace! thou canst no whery,
Thou meddlest wondrous sore.'

Thus meanwhile the pilgrims lie,
And have their bowls fast them by,
And cry after hot Malmsey,
'Thou help for to restore.'

And some would have some salted toast,
For they might eat neither boiled nor roast,
A man might soon pay for their cost,
As for one day or twain.

Some laid their books upon their knee,
And read so long they might not see;
'Alas! my head will cleave in three!'
Thus saith another certain.

Then cometh our owner like a lord,
And speaketh many a royal word,
And dresseth him to the high board
To see all things be well.

Anon he calleth a carpenter,
And biddeth him bring with him his gear,

35

To make the cabins here and there,
With many a feeble call.

A sack of straw were there right good
For some must lie down on their hood;
I had as lief be in the wood,
Without meat or drink.

For when that we shall go to bed
The pump was nigh our beddë's head:
A man were as good to be dead
As smell thereof the stink.

That the ship to which this poem refers was seaworthy is
clearly indicated by the last verse: the bilge water stinks,
and so the ship does not leak too badly.

CHAPTER 4

Outward Bound

1440–1505

The Hanseatic League, an organisation established in the thirteenth century by the north German ports of Lübeck, Bremen and Hamburg, was set up to protect their mutual trading interests, basic to which was the export of pickled herrings. In 1441 the Council of the Hanseatic League complained that 'Sailors are daily found to be disobedient to their captains, which has caused great damage to the merchants' goods and may be to their prejudice in the future unless something is done about it.'[1] But by 1441 the Middle Ages have ended and the best days of the Hanseatic League are past.

In the first half of the fifteenth century, while British seafarers were following in the wake of Pytheas and the Celtic saints and exploring northern waters, the Portuguese, inspired by Prince Henry the Navigator (who was the grandson of John of Gaunt), were following in the wake of Hanno the Carthaginian and going south of the Straits of Gibraltar. By 1444 black Africans, who were claimed to be 'outside the law of Christ' and who could therefore be disposed of in any way that suited their captors, were being sold in the market of Lagos in Portugal, the first of the twelve million black slaves who were forcibly removed from their native lands – as many again being killed in the process.

On the next day ... very early in the morning, by reason of the heat, the seamen began ... to take out those captives and to carry them on shore, as they were commanded. And these, all placed together in that field were a marvellous sight ... But what heart could be so hard as not to be pierced with piteous feelings to see that company? For some kept their heads bowed and their faces bathed in tears, looking one at the other; others stood groaning very dolorously, looking up to the heights of Heaven, fixing their eyes upon it, crying aloud, as if asking help of the Father of Nature; others struck their faces with the palms of their hands, throwing themselves at full length upon the ground; others made their lamentations in the manner of a dirge, after the custom of their country. And though we could not understand the words of the language, the sound of it right well accorded with the measure of their sadness. But to increase their sufferings still more, there now arrived those who had charge of the division of the captives, and who began to separate one from another, in order to make an equal partition of fifths, and then it was needful to part fathers from sons, husbands from wives, brothers from brothers. No respect was shown either to friends or relations, but each fell where his lot took him.[2]

About this same time, in 1445, a seaman's guild, fraternity or friendly society was being formed in Bristol because 'the craft of mariners is so adventurous that, daily being in their voyages sore vexed, troubled, diseased and distressed, the which [by] good means of prayer and good works might be graciously comforted.' But prayers were not always on a sailor's lips. In May 1449, a Devon worthy named Robert Winnington met with a fleet of a hundred vessels – Flemish, Dutch and Hanseatic – on their way to the Bourgneuf salt works. 'I came aboard the Admiral and bade them strike in the King's name of England, and they bade me shit in the King's name of England.'[3] Nevertheless, Winnington is reported to have captured the fleet.

This was five years before the Venetian adventurer Alvise Cadamosto or Alvise da Mosto passed Cape Verde in the service of Henry the Navigator. He landed and met a chief with a hundred slaves. 'As soon as he saw me, he gave me a young girl of twelve to thirteen years of age, pretty for all that she was black, and said that he gave her for the service of my bedchamber. I accepted her and sent her to my ship.'[4]

Many European sailors were now outward bound and it is from these years that the first known pilot book, or rutter in the English language, dates. The author is unknown but the extant manuscript is the work of William Ebesham, a scribe active in the reign of Edward IV (1461–83). Part of the direct route across the Bay of Biscay is described as follows.

> You come out of Spain and you are at Cape Finistère. Then steer north, north-east. When your dead-reckoning suggests that you are two-thirds the way across, and if you are bound to the Severn estuary, you must steer north by east till you come into soundings. If soundings are 100 fathoms or else 80, then steer north until you sound 72 fathoms and pick up fair grey sand. That is the ridge that lies between Cape Clear and Scilly. From there go north till you come into soundings of ooze, and then follow your course east-north-east or else east by north ... If you reckon you have crossed the Bay and you are bound for the Channel, steer north, north-east and by north until you come into soundings of 100 fathoms. If the ground is streamy, you are between Ushant and Scilly at the entrance to the Channel. Continue on your course until you strike 60 fathoms, then steer north-east.[5]

Going the other way, freebooters from England, Flanders and Spain were already encroaching on West Africa, which the Portuguese regarded as their preserve. Round about 1475 one Portuguese chronicler wrote of the members of a Fleming expedition,

> As they did not fear the heavy excommunication of the Holy Fathers ... and as they did not fear the prohibitions of the

Holy Mother Church, God gave them a bad end; for on their return voyage from Mina [Elmina, about 100 miles west of Accra in Ghana] ... they anchored in 25 fathoms; but as the bottom all along this coast is full of rock it cut through their hawser during the night, and a wind blowing up from the sea drove their ship onto the beach, where it was wrecked. The negroes there ate the 35 Flemings who formed the crew.[6]

It is reported by a later chronicler that in 1488 the Genoese Christopher Columbus was at the Portuguese court when Bartholomew Diaz made his report to King John, and Columbus noted that Diaz had reached a promontory which the King named Cabo di Boa Esperanca or Cape of Good Hope.

Bartholomew Diaz and his company, because of the perils and storms through which they passed while doubling it, bestowed upon it the name of Tormentoso [stormy]; but King John, when they arrived in the kingdom, gave it a more illustrious name, calling it 'Cape of Good Hope', for that it promised the discovery of India that was so much wished for, and sought over so many years.[7]

In 1492 Columbus himself sailed west in the service of Spain, to the prayers of his sailors.

After sunset, and before the first night watch was set, all hands were called to evening prayers. The service began with a boy whose duty it was to light the binnacle lamp singing

> God give us a good night and good sailing;
> May our ship make a good passage,
> Sir Captain and Master and good company.

All hands then said the Lord's Prayer, the Creed and the Ave Maria, and concluded by singing the Salve Regina.[8]

And so, from Columbus, we obtain the first, somewhat romanticised, description of what he called the Other World.

Its lands are lofty and in it there are very many sierras and very high mountains, to which the Island Centrefrei [Tenerife] is not comparable. All are most beautiful, of a thousand shapes, and all accessible and filled with trees of a thousand kinds and tall, and they seem to touch the sky; and I am told that they never lose their foliage, which I can believe, for I saw them as green and beautiful as they are in Spain in May, and some of them were flowering, some with fruit, and some in another condition, according to their quality. And there were singing the nightingale and other little birds of a thousand kinds in the month of November, there where I went. There are palm trees of six or eight kinds, which are a wonder to behold on account of their beautiful variety, and so are the other trees and fruits and herbs; therein are marvellous pine groves, and extensive champaign country; and there is honey, and there are many kinds of birds and a great variety of fruits. Up-country there are many mines of metals, and the population is innumerable. *La Spanola* is marvellous, the sierras and the mountains and the plains and the champaigns and the lands are so beautiful and fat for planting and sowing, and for livestock of every sort, and for building towns and cities. The harbours of the sea here are such as you could not believe in without seeing them, and so the rivers, many and great, and good streams, the most of which bear gold.[9]

Of the native inhabitants he wrote,

Of anything they have, if you ask them for it, they never say no; rather they invite the person to share it, and show as much love as if they were giving their hearts; and whether the thing be of value or of small price, at once they are content with whatever little thing of whatever kind may be given to them. I forbade that they should be given things so worthless as pieces of broken crockery and broken glass, ... and I gave them a thousand good, pleasing things which I had brought, in order that they might be fond of us, and furthermore might be made Christians and be inclined to the love and service of their

Highnesses and of the whole Castilian nation, and try to help us and to give us of the things which they have in abundance and which are necessary to us.[10]

Almost the entire Taino race, of whom he wrote, was exterminated within half a century, but not, according to some, before its members had made one gift to Europe – *Spirochaeta pallida*, the spirillum of syphilis.

While Columbus was exploring the West Indies, Bristol seafarers were following in the wake of the Vikings and it was in 1494, according to John Dee, that Robert Thorne and Hugh Eliot of that city discovered Newfoundland. Robert Thorne's son wrote later,

> I reason that as some sicknesses are hereditary and come from the father to the son, so this inclination or desire of discovering I inherited of my father, which with another merchant of Bristol named Hugh Eliot were the discoverers of New Found Lands, of the which there is no doubt (as now plainly appeareth), if the mariners would then have been ruled and followed their pilot's mind, the land of the Indians from whence all the gold cometh had been ours: for all is one coast, as by the card appeareth.[11]

Navigation remained rudimentary, and in 1496 Columbus had problems reaching home at the end of his second voyage.

> After a month at sea all hands were put on a short allowance of six ounces of cassava bread [also known as manioc and yuca; tapioca is a derivative] and a cup of water per diem. About this time, providentially, they caught a westerly breeze south of the Azores, but hunger increased daily. Some Spaniards proposed eating the Indians, starting with the Caribs, who were maneaters themselves; thus it wouldn't be a sin to pay them in their own coin! Others proposed that all the natives be thrown overboard so that they would consume no more rations. Columbus, in one of his humanitarian

moods, argued that after all Caribs were people and should be
be treated as such. The debate was still undecided on June 8th
when they made landfall on the Portuguese coast about 35
miles north of Cape Saint Vincent, where the Admiral intended. There were several pilots on board and all thought
they were still hundreds of miles from shore and hundreds of
miles north of their actual position.[12]

After an abortive attempt in this same year of 1496, John
Cabot and his son Sebastian, who may have been born in
Bristol, were among the leaders of the expedition which, in
1497, took possession of Newfoundland or some other
part of North America (the exact location is uncertain) in
the name of King Henry VII. In December of that year
Raimondo de Raimondi de Soncino wrote to the Duke of
Milan,

> Perhaps amid the numerous occupations of your Excellency,
> it may not weary you to hear how his Majesty here had gained
> a part of Asia, without a stroke of the sword. There is in this
> Kingdom a man of the people, Messer John Cabot by name,
> of kindly wit and a most expert mariner ... He started from
> Bristol, a port on the west of this Kingdom, passed Ireland,
> which is still further west, and then bore towards the north, in
> order to sail to the west, leaving the north on his right hand
> after some days. After having wandered for some time he at
> length arrived at the mainland, where he hoisted the royal
> standard, and took possession for the king here; and after tak-
> ing certain tokens he returned.
>
> This Messer John, as a foreigner and a poor man, would not
> have obtained credence, had it not been that his companions,
> who are practically all English and from Bristol, testified that
> he spoke the truth ... Before very long they say that his
> Majesty will equip some ships, and in addition he will give
> them all the malefactors, and they will go to that country and
> form a colony. By means of this they hope to make London a
> more important mart for spices than Alexandria. The leading

43

men in this enterprise are from Bristol, and great seamen, and now they know where to go, say that the voyage will not take more than a fortnight, if they have good fortune after leaving Ireland.[13]

Peter Martyr tells us of this same expedition.

I will not omit a sport which the said Sebastian Cabot mentions having seen with all his companions, to their great delight, namely that many bears which are found in that country came to hunt these codfish in this fashion: near the shores are many tall trees, the leaves of which fall into the sea, and the cod come to feed on them in shoals. The bears, which eat nothing but these fish, stand in ambush on the shore, and when they see the approach of the shoals of these fish, which are very large and shaped like tunny, they rush into the sea, linked with another of their kind, and striking their claws under the scales, do not let them go and try to pull them on shore: but the cod which are very strong, turn round and plunge into the sea, so that, these two creatures being grappled together, it is a great sport to see now the one under the water and now the other on top, splashing the foam into the air; and in the end the bear pulls the cod ashore and eats him. For this reason it is thought that such a large number of bears are no detriment to the men of the country.[14]

It was also in the summer of 1497 that the cruel and high-handed Vasco da Gama, a man of ungovernable temper, sailed from the Tagus. Arriving off Mombasa in 1498, like Ulysses in the land of the Laestrygonians, he anchored outside the harbour.

Its whitewashed stone houses had windows and terraces like those of the [Iberian] Peninsula – and it was so beautiful that our men felt as though they were entering some part of this Kingdom [of Portugal]. And although everyone was enamoured of the vista, Vasco da Gama would not permit the pilot to take the vessels inside as he desired, for he was already suspicious of him and anchored outside.[15]

An Arab pilot led da Gama across the Indian Ocean to Calicut, which had been described by European sailors in a pilot book called the Periplus of the Erythraian Sea 1400 years earlier, and the Samorin or ruler wrote to the King of Portugal,

> Vasco da Gama, a gentleman of your household, came to my country, whereat I was pleased. My country is rich in cinnamon, cloves, ginger, pepper and precious stones. That which I ask of you in exchange is gold, silver, corals, and scarlet cloth.[16]

Vasco da Gama returned home in 1499, the year in which Amerigo Vespucci had charted part of the South American coast. The following year Pedro Cabral led a second expedition to India, discovering Brazil on the way and losing Bartholomew Diaz at sea.

> Suddenly appeared a black cloud in the air, which the sailors of Guinea call *bulcao,* on the appearance of which the wind died down as though those black clouds had engulfed it all within themselves ... but only to spew it forth more furious than ever. Then the hurricane swept down in an instant, bursting so furiously that it gave no time to furl the sails, and sank four of which the captains were Aires Gomes da Silva, Simao di Pina, Vasco de Taide, and Bartholomew Diaz, to whom, having suffered so many perils by sea in the discoveries which he made, and above all the Cape of Good Hope, this fury of the wind dealt his end, and to the others, casting them into the abyss of that great ocean sea.[17]

The expedition yielded a profit of 100 per cent, nonetheless.

Vasco da Gama embarked upon his second voyage to India in 1502 and at Connamore he awaited the arrival of the native ships from Mecca, to which place they already carried Moslem pilgrims.

After some days an Arab ship, the *Meri,* was sighted coming from the west. It was a vessel belonging to a brother of Khoja Kassim of Calicut on its return voyage from Mecca. In addition to a cargo of merchandise it carried [between 200 and] 380 passengers, men, women, and children, mostly people returning from a pilgrimage to the holy city to their homes in Calicut. The Portuguese commander gave chase and quickly overhauled the Arab ship, which surrendered without resistance, as it would have been futile against such overwhelming numbers. Gama ordered the cargo to be handed over and all arms surrendered. The Arabs thereat denied possessing anything of value. Thereupon the admiral had two of them thrown into the sea, whereat the others confessed that they did carry some valuable cargo. The best of this was loaded on the ship of Diogo Fernandes Correa for the king, and the rest was distributed among Gama's crews. The transfer of cargo occupied two days. The admiral suspected that much was still concealed by the Mohammedans and that perhaps all the weapons had not been handed over. Thereupon, though he had met no resistance and had pillaged a peaceful ship of a country with which he was not at war, ... he ordered the passengers to be locked in the hold of the *Meri,* the ship to be set afire, and all on it burned to death.[18]

It took him four days and four nights to destroy the ship and those on board. In the meantime, Columbus, on his fourth voyage, was anchored off Puerto Limón in Costa Rica where he made friendly contact with the Talamanca Indians.

The usual roles were reversed, the natives eager to do business and the Spaniards somewhat coy. First, the Indians swam out to the caravels with a line of cotton jumpers and ornaments of *guanin,* the gold and copper alloy that Columbus had found in Paria on the Third Voyage. Evidently *guanin* was regarded in Spain as a poor substitute for pure gold, and Columbus would have none of it, but gave the would-be traders some presents to take ashore. Next, to break down 'sales resistance', the Indians sent on board two virgins, one about eight and the other about fourteen years old; 'they showed great courage', recorded [Columbus' son] Ferdinand (who was then about the same age as the elder), 'exhibited neither grief nor sorrow but always looked pleasant and modest; hence they were well treated by the Admiral, who caused them to be fed and clothed and sent them ashore.' (Columbus, on the contrary, wrote that they behaved so immodestly that 'more could not be expected from public women'...)[19]

The continence of the Spaniards astonished the natives, but self-control was requisite when they were subsequently marooned in Jamaica.

On June 25th the wretched vessels, their decks almost awash, entered Saint Ann's Bay, Jamaica, which Columbus had named Santa Gloria on the Second Voyage. He ran them aground side by side on a sand beach and shored them up to keep on an even keel. High tides rose almost to their decks, upon which palm-thatched cabins had to be built for the people. And there they stayed for a year.

These 116 Spaniards marooned on Jamaica were fairly well situated for defence; the ships' hulks made a dry home and no mean fortress. A large and friendly Indian village lay near by. Columbus, who knew by bitter experience that the natives would not long remain friendly if his people were allowed to make contact with them, ordered all hands to stay on board, and allowed nobody to go ashore without his permission.

The first thing that needed attention was the food supply. Columbus sent Diego Méndez and three men on a foraging expedition. They travelled almost to the east end of the island, purchased a dugout canoe, loaded it with native provisions, and returned to Santa Gloria in triumph; and, to ensure a continuing supply, Méndez drew up a tariff agreement with the neighbouring Indians to sell a cake of cassava bread for two glass beads, two of the big rodents called hutía for a lace point, and a great quantity of anything, such as fish or maize, for a hawk's bell. Why these Spaniards and Genoese could not fish for themselves or plant their own cornfields has never been explained; it is clear that if the Indians had not fed them, they would have starved to death.[20]

By this time it was spring 1503 and Vasco da Gama had set off home from India.

On March 5th we set our course to the southeast [from Connamore to Mozambique], 100 miles out at sea. On March 29th we had sailed at sea some 1,200 miles ...; and we began to lose sight of the Great Bear, and the sun was over our heads, so that on April 2nd we could see no ghost or shadow of anything, nor any constellation. In this sea we saw fish with wings to fly so far that they could be shot at with the cross-bow, and they are as large as a mackerel, a herring, or a sardine. And for a space of about 300 miles we saw seagulls, black with white breasts, and they had tails like swans, and are larger than wild pigeons. They catch those flying fish even as they go flying by. On April 11th we had travelled so far ahead that at mid-day on the bridge we saw the sun toward the north. At the same time we saw no constellations of which we could avail ourselves, only our compasses and our charts.[21]

By 1505 the captain of an outward bound Indiaman was already complaining about his raw and rustic crew who

could not distinguish between starboard and port until he tied a bunch of onions to one side of the ship and a bunch of garlic to the other, ordering the helmsman to 'onion' or 'garlic' the helm ... throughout the three centuries of the *carreira* complaints abounded that tailors, cobblers, lackeys, ploughmen and 'ignorant boys' of all kinds were entered as able seamen, gunners and even (as it was alleged in 1652) as pilots. This last seems hardly credible until we recall the well-attested fact that the pilot of the galleon *Nazaré* in 1650 made the West African port of Luanda under the impression that he was off the coast of Malabar in southern India.[22]

CHAPTER 5

Round the World

1505–1561

By the beginning of the sixteenth century the Indies, both east and west, were familiar to European sailors, but no one had yet been round the world. In 1513 the Spanish conquistador Balboa crossed the isthmus of Panama and saw the Pacific Ocean. In 1520, through the Strait named after him, the Portuguese Ferdinand Magellan, in the service of Spain, took three ships, *Trinidad*, *Concepción* and *Victoria*. 'We reached 54° beyond the Line, where day and night are the same, at which point we found a channel which led into the sea between the territory of Your Majesty and India. This channel was one hundred leagues in length.'[1] Of the new ocean, Magellan's Italian supernumerary, Antonio Pigafetta, wrote, 'Well was it named the Pacific, for during this time we met with no storm'. But crossing it was grim nonetheless, for it took nearly a hundred days and food ran short.

We ate biscuit, but in truth it was biscuit no longer, but a powder full of worms, and in addition it was stinking with the urine of rats. So great was our want of food, we were forced to eat the hide with which the main yard was covered. These hides, exposed to the sun, rain and wind, had become so hard we were first obliged to soften them by putting them overboard for four or five days, after which we put them on the embers and had them thus. We also used sawdust for food and rats became such a delicacy that we paid a ducat a piece for them.[2]

Magellan and others were killed in the Philippines and one ship was destroyed at this stage, but those who survived to land in Borneo lived it up, as sailors will when they are able.

We partook of the flesh of various animals such as veal, capons, fowls, peacocks, and others, with different sorts of fish, so that of flesh alone there were 32 different viands. We supped on the ground on a palm mat; at each mouthful we drank rice wine from a little china cup the size of an egg. We used spoons like our own, but these were made of gold.

From these Indonesian waters only the *Victoria*, under the command of the Basque navigator Juan Sebastian de Elcano, returned to Europe.

Your Majesty should know that, sailing to these Islands of Maluco, we found camphor, cinnamon, and pearls. When we wished to leave these Islands to return to Spain, we noticed a big leak in one of the two ships, which could not be repaired ...

When we had left the last island behind, we subsisted for five months on nothing but corn, rice and water, not going near any land, for fear of the King of Portugal, who had left orders in all his territories for the capture of our fleet, so that Your Majesty should never again hear anything of it.

On this course twenty-two men died from hunger; the lack of means of subsistence compelled us to stop at Cabo Verde. The Governor of the island took from us our skiff with thirteen men, and wanted to send me, with the entire cargo, to Portugal, in a ship which had come laden with spices from Calicut; he declared that no one except the Portuguese should venture thither to explore the Spiceries. With the object of overpowering us, he armed four ships. With my company I determined to die rather than fall into the hands of the Portuguese. It so fell to us, overstrained at the pumps, working at them by day and night, and more exhausted than men had ever been before, that with the help of God and the Blessed Virgin Mary, we continued under sail, and after voyaging for three years, ran into the harbour of San Lucar.

I ask your Majesty now to ensure the liberty of the thirteen men who have for so long served Your Majesty, to claim them as being needed. They will count it as their gain to know that we have given practical proof that the earth is a sphere; having sailed round it, coming from the West, we have come back through the East.[3]

When he wrote to the King of Spain, on 7th September 1522, Elcano, the world's first circumnavigator, dated his letter the 6th. In some way that he did not understand he had gained a day in sailing round the world to westward.

In 1524 Vasco da Gama sailed again for India to become Viceroy. Just before weighing anchor off Belém in northern Brazil the admiral,

both for their souls' sake and on account of quarrels and plots, ordered proclamations to be made on shore, and posted as well at the foot of the masts, to the effect that any woman who would be found in the ships after leaving Belém would be flogged publicly, even though she were married, [and in that case] her husband would be sent back to Portugal in chains, and if she were a captive or a slave she would be sold for the ransom of a captive.[4]

Subsequently he had three women thus discovered publicly flogged in Goa, but unauthorised women on ships continue to crop up here and there for a further 300 years.

By this time the Pope had divided the newly discovered routes and territories between the Spaniards and the Portuguese, but this division was not accepted by other western countries. Their sailors, too, were looking for profit in new places, and the first known report of a crossing-the-line ceremony is made by French seafarers Jean and Raoul Parmentier of Dieppe, in the record of a voyage to Sumatra in 1529.

On Tuesday, 11th May, in the morning, about fifty of our people were made knights and received the accolade on crossing the equator, and the mass *Salve sancta parens* was sung from music to mark the solemnity of the day, and a great fish called an albacore and some bonitos were caught and supper prepared from them to celebrate the crossing ceremony.[5]

In 1530–32 William Hawkins made his first voyage to Africa and Brazil, and in the year following his return an inventory is found of the goods which John Aborough, master of the *Michael of Barnstaple*, carried to sea with him to assist in navigation.

He had two compasses worth 10d, a cross staff, a quadrant, a lodestone and a [half-hour or] running glass worth 26s 8d; a rutter in English which took him one-and-a-half years to compile and a Castilian rutter and a 'reportery' [seamen's manual?] in Portuguese, for which he wanted at least 40s; a map in glass which cost 6s. 8d. He also carried a lute, a gospel and a card for the Levant.[6]

Several voyages had been made from England to Newfoundland waters in the early years of the sixteenth century. In 1536 Captain Robert Hore was in command of an expedition that sailed from Gravesend to Newfoundland, but food gave out and for a time those concerned subsisted 'on such roots and herbs as they could gather, and by the ingenious expedient of stealing the fresh fish from an osprey's nest that the hard working fishhawk brought to its unfortunate young'.[7] They were going to draw lots and eat each other but instead captured a French vessel and thus returned home.

A poem published in 1540 indicates that the Tudor seaman's baggy breeches were already proverbial.

Although a shipman's hose will serve all sorts of legs,
Christ's holy scripture will serve no rotten dregs.[8]

It was a year notable for the religious persecution of English mariners in Spain, and the government of King

Henry VIII was already bemoaning the decay of British shipping and aiming to do something about it.

> ... where the Navy of multitude of ships of this Realm in times past hath been and yet is very profitable, requisite, necessary and commodious, as well for the intercourse and concourse of merchants transporting and conveying their wares and merchandise, as is above said, and a great defence and surety of this Realm in time of war, as well for offense as defence, and also the maintenance of many masters, mariners and seamen, making them expert and cunning in the art and science of shipmen and sailing, and they, their wives and children have had their living of and by the same, and it also hath been the chief maintenance and support of the cities, towns, villages, havens and creeks near adjoining unto the sea coast, and the King's subjects, bakers, brewers, butchers, smiths, ropemakers, shipwrights, tailors, shoemakers, and other victuallers and handicraftsmen inhabiting and dwelling near unto the said coasts, have also had by the same a great part of their livings; and the same Navy and multitude of ships is now of late marvellously impaired and decayed, and by occasion thereof not only a great multitude of the King's liege people which thereby had their living, be now diminished and impoverished, but also the towns, villages and inhabitations near adjoining unto the sea coasts are utterly fallen into ruin and decay ...9

Twelve years later Thomas Barnaby contrasted the maritime energy of the French with the slackness of the English, instancing the trade in coal from Newcastle to France, which appeared to him to be largely in French hands: 'And as for them, ye shall see in place three or four score ships of Norman and Bretons at once, as soon as their fishing is done, and as they departed cometh as many more'.10 Nevertheless, an English voyage to the Levant had just been completed and in the following year, 1553, Sebastian Cabot drafted orders for Sir Hugh Willoughby's expedition in search of a northeast passage to 'Cathay' or China. Here are three of them.

Item, that no blaspheming of God, or detestable swearing be used in any ship, nor communication of ribaldry, filthy tales, or ungodly talk to be suffered in the company of any ship, neither dicing, carding, tabling, nor other devilish games to be frequented, whereby ensueth not only poverty to the players, but also strife, variance, brawling, fighting, and oftentimes murder to the utter destruction of the parties, and provoking of God's most just wrath, and sword of vengeance. These and all such like pestilences, and contagions of vices, and sins to be eschewed and the offenders once admonished, and not reforming, to be punished at the discretion of the captain and master, as appertaineth.

Item, that morning and evening prayer, with other common services appointed by the King's Majesty, and laws of this Realm to be read and said in every ship daily by the minister in the Admiral, and the merchant or some other person learned in other ships, and the Bible or paraphrases to be read devoutly and Christianly to God's honour, and for his grace to be obtained, and had by humble and hearty prayer of the Navigants accordingly.

Item, when any mariner or any other passenger shall have need of any accessory furniture or apparel for his body, and conservation of his health, the same shall be delivered him by the Merchant, at the assignment of the captain and master of that ship, wherein such needy person shall be, at such reasonable price as the same cost, without any gain to be exacted by the merchants, the value thereof to be entered by the merchant in his book, and the same to be discounted off the party's wages, that so shall receive, and wear the same.[11]

The slop-chest, familiar subsequently to generations of sailors, was thus established.

Separated by a storm off the Lofoten islands from Richard Chancellor in the *Edward Bonaventure,*

Willoughby and his sixty-two companions aboard the *Bona Esperanza* all perished in harbour in Russian Lapland in the winter of 1553–54. Chancellor was lost in the wreck of his ship on returning from a second voyage in 1556.

In 1555, before their fate was known, Richard Eden wrote,

> ... the merchants of London ... also divers noblemen and gentlemen as well as the [Privy] council as other ... have furnished and sent forth certain ships for the discovery of ... lands and regions ... unknown, [and] have herein deserved immortal fame, for, ... they have showed no small liberality upon uncertain hope of gain ... and ... the two chief captains of the same ... Sir Hugh Willoughby and the excellent pilot Richard Chancellor who have therein adventured their lives for the commodity of their country are men doubtless worthy for their noble attempts to be made Knights of the Ocean or otherwise preferred if ever God send them home again ... For as such have obtained absolute glory that have brought great things to pass so have they deserved immortal fame which have only attempted the same ...[12]

The English had not opened up a new route to the Far East but they had established a trading route to Russia. In 1556 Stephen Borough sailed north, in the pinnace *Searchthrift.*

> On St James's day, bolting to the windward, we had the latitude at noon in seventy degrees twenty minutes. The same day at a southwest sun, there was a monstrous whale aboard of us, so near to our side that we might have thrust a sword or any other weapon in him, which we durst not do for fear he should have overthrown our ship: and then I called my company together, and all of us shouted, and with the cry that we made he departed from us: there was as much above water of his back as the breadth of our pinnace, and at his falling down,

he made such a terrible noise in the water, that a man would greatly have marvelled, except he had known the cause of it: but God be thanked, we were quietly delivered of him. And a little after we spied certain islands, with which we bear, and found good harbour in 15 or 18 fathoms, and black ooze: we came to an anchor at a northeast sun, and named the island St James's Island where we found fresh water.[13]

In the next year, 1557, new rules were drawn up to govern Anthony Jenkinson's fleet. One of them attempted to moderate the stink of the bilge-water.

Also that no beer nor broth, or other liquor be spilt upon the ballast, or other place of the ship, whereby any annoyance, stink, or other unsavouriness shall grow in the ship to the infection or hurt of the persons in the same.[14]

Describing this voyage, Jenkinson wrote,

Thus proceeding forward and sailing along the coast of the said land of Lappia, winding southeast, the fourth day through great mists and darkness we lost the company of the other three ships, and met not with them again, until the seventh day, when we fell with a cape or headland called Swetinoz, which is the entering into the Bay of St Nicholas. At this cape lieth a great stone, to which the barks that passed thereby, were wont to make offerings of butter, meal, and other victuals, thinking that unless they did so, their barks or vessels should there perish, as it hath been oftentimes seen: and there it is very dark and misty.

The Russia Company's station was established at St Nicholas on the White Sea, but there were not profits enough for the Elizabethans in Russian trade and they often supplemented these profits by fishing and hunting walrus.

In 1560 the Portuguese carrack *Sao Paulo* left Portugal for India. On 19th June one lookout on the maintop fell to his death on a sudden roll.

Three days later another similar accident occurred, this time to the look-out man on the foretop. But he was luckier, for though the ship was wallowing in the high seas in which she pitched and rolled heavily, he fell from the top into the sea, grazing one of the flukes of an anchor, and he had such presence of mind that he grasped a cord and they dragged him aboard all covered with blood. For the anchor had taken all the skin off the top of his head and it hung like a friar's hood from his occiput. It was a miracle that such a blow did not harm any part of his body and left him white as snow. He was examined very carefully and cured still better, and so he recovered completely from this very serious mishap.

However, on this same voyage, on 21st January 1561, the ship was wrecked on an island off the coast of Sumatra.

The captain stood by the side with a drawn sword in his hand, preventing anyone from getting into the skiff until all the women (who totalled thirty-three, including some slaves) and the children had been safely disembarked ... And after they had all gone, the remainder of the people were disembarked before nightfall, it being high tide, with the weapons that each person could carry. We camped beneath a grove of trees, assembling round the banner of the holy relics, where we spent the night together in a body.

It is certainly a most miserable thing to recount the behaviour of human nature, and still more so to weep for its covetousness and wretchedness. For the ship was still drifting towards the inlet and had hardly struck before the seamen were pillaging chests, robbing cabins, and tying up bundles, bales, fardles and packages. And these were all taken ashore as if we were in our native land or in one of friends and neighbours, and as if there were safe and sure roads and pathways to traverse. And if the seamen were thus occupied, neither were the landsmen idle, for they were breaking open barrels, chests, and boxes, which the sea washed ashore, while others were disciplining themselves and receiving absolution from the Father for their sins, and others were occupied in working for the common good.

After hair-raising adventures the survivors reached Malacca, whereupon the narrator, an apothecary-passenger, quotes the 107th Psalm ('They that go down to the sea in ships'), and concludes, 'Wherefore experience teaches us that whoever can avoid a maritime life lives in greater tranquillity of spirit and avoids such strife. It is better to live ashore less desirous of riches than to traverse the sea in quest of such transitory and fleeting things.'[15]

CHAPTER 6

The First Elizabethans

1561–1581

Where William Hawkins had led, when he made his first voyage to Brazil in 1530-32, his son John followed. At the time when English sailors first voyaged to Russia, other Englishmen were venturing again to Guinea in West Africa, though for political reasons such voyages were officially prohibited. However, the slave trade seemed increasingly enticing and, after the accession of the Protestant Queen Elizabeth I in 1558, less heed was paid to Roman Catholic Spain and Portugal, and between 1562 and 1568 Sir John Hawkins made his three famous slave-trading voyages to the West Indies. Here is the provision made for the second voyage in 1564.

The estimated crews necessary for these ships were small; for the *Jesus*, 80 men; the *Solomon*, 35; the *Tiger*, 20; and the *Swallow*, 15 – in all 150 – subsequently increased to 170 by the gentlemen adventurers and their servants. Some details of the victualling are of interest, for such particulars have not commonly been preserved. Biscuit formed the staple food, of which 25 thousand-weight were provided. There were also 120 barrels of meal and 20 quarters of beans and peas. For flesh there were 40 hogsheads of beef, 80 flitches of bacon, 6 lasts of stock-fish, and 12 cwt of ling; for drink, 40 tuns of beer, 35 tuns of cider, and 40 butts of malmsey (the latter, at £6 per butt, evidently for the good cheer of the cabin). Among miscellaneous items occur a tun of oil, a pipe of vinegar, a hogshead of honey, and a quarter of aniseed. Provision for 500 negroes consisted of 120 quarters of beans and peas, no other victual being mentioned. There were also estimates for 'cotts' (perhaps partitions or bunks in the hold) and, curiously enough, for shirts and shoes for the blacks. The total cost of the expedition, not including the capital value of the ships, amounted according to these calculations to £4,990; but this sum includes nothing for cargo, of which some was carried on the outward passage, although not perhaps to as great value as that taken by the gold-traders; and the usual routine of the voyage entailed also some disembursements to various parties.[1]

At Ferrol, Hawkins issued his sailing orders: 'Serve God daily, love one another, preserve your victuals, beware of fire, and keep good company' [ie stay near other ships of the fleet].[2]

From the Spaniards we learn that Hawkins was as religious as they were.

In the flagship of the said John Hawkins ... every morning and evening the boatswain took a book in English, like those which the clergy had in England, and went to the mainmast, where all the sailors, soldiers [and the] captain knelt on the deck, and all attended under pain of twenty-four hours in irons. And all being on their knees, the said boatswain ... recited the Lord's prayer and the creed, word for word, and then made the same prayers which ... are made in England. Also [the witness] said that in the same manner the said boatswain read the epistle of St Paul and a gospel ... and that was done in all ships of the said fleet of John Hawkins, and in others.[3]

By 1567, however, the Spanish ambassador was complaining to Queen Elizabeth of the behaviour of Hawkins and other English sailors.

Your mariners rob my master's ships on the sea, and trade where they are forbidden to go; they plunder our people in the

streets of your towns; they attack our vessels in your very harbours, and take our prisoners from them; your preachers
insult my master from their pulpits, and when we apply for
justice we are answered with threats.[4]

However religious it might be, the mariner's life was a
tough one. In 1568 a ship's carpenter described how a
French vessel seized an English one off Belle Isle, the strait
between Newfoundland and Labrador, and used a method
of obtaining information which is also mentioned in other
places. '[The French] with great torture and pain wound a
rope about this "juratts" and the residue of his company's
heads and wrested the same to make them confess where
more money remained, [so that he thought] they would
have rung his eyes out of his head.'[5]

In this same year the fateful sea battle of San Juan de
Ulua, off the Mexican coast, which could be said to have
turned Drake into a privateer anxious to recoup the losses
he had suffered, marked the end of Hawkins' third slave-
trading voyage. Hawkins escaped in his ship the *Minion.*

The weather waxed reasonable, and the Saturday we set sail,
and having a great number of men and little victuals, our hope
of life waxed less and less. Some desired to yield to the
Spaniards, some rather desired to obtain a place where they
might give themselves to the infidels; and some had rather abide
with a little pittance the mercy of God at sea. So thus, with
many sorrowful hearts, we wandered in an unknown sea by the
space of 14 days, till hunger enforced us to seek the land; for
hides they thought very good meat, rats, cats, mice, and dogs,
none escaped that might be gotten, parrots and monkeys, that
were had in great price, were thought there very profitable if
they served the turn one dinner. Thus in the end, the 8th day of
October, we came to the land in the bottom of the same bay of
Mexico in 23 degrees and a half, where we hoped to have found
inhabitants of the Spaniards, relief of victuals, and place for
repair of our ship, which was so sore beaten with shot from our

enemies and bruised with shooting off our own ordnance, that our weary and weak arms were scarce able to defend and keep out water. But all things happened to the contrary; for we found neither people, victual, nor haven of relief, but a place where having fair weather with some peril we might land a boat. Our people, being forced with hunger, desired to be set on land; whereunto I consented. And such as were willing to land, I put them apart; and such as were desirous to go homewards, I put apart; so that they were indifferently parted a hundred to one side and a hundred to the other side. These hundred men we set a-land with all diligence, in this little place beforesaid; which being landed, we determined there to take in fresh water, and so with our little remain of victuals to take the sea.[6]

From the beginning of the slave trade there were people who objected to it on moral grounds. From the beginning of oceanic voyages there were sailors who recognised that lemon juice was good for scurvy. Henry Hawks, a merchant who traded for five years to Vera Cruz in Mexico, is unique, however, in implying as early as 1572 that the mosquito, which was a scourge of Europeans in America, was connected with malaria and yellow fever. This report, published by Hakluyt, aroused no interest in the medical profession either then or subsequently. Mosquito-borne diseases continued unchecked among sailors for another 300 years.

This town is inclined to many kind of diseases, by reason of the great heat, and a certain gnat or fly which they call a mosquito, which biteth both men and women in their sleep; and as soon as they are bitten, incontinently the flesh swelleth as though they had been bitten with some venimous worm. And this mosquito or gnat doth most follow such as are newly come into the country. Many there are that die of this annoyance.[7]

In 1572 Francis Drake returned with a small fleet to Central American waters – having married a seaman's daughter shortly after returning home from San Juan de Ulua – and decided, once there, to destroy the *Swan,* a vessel commanded by his brother, to ensure the better manning of his pinnaces.

But knowing the affection of his company, how loth they were to leave either of their ships, being both so good sailors and so well furnished, he purposed himself by some policy to make them most willing to effect that he intended. And therefore sent for one Thomas Moone (who was carpenter in the *Swan*) and taking him into his cabin, chargeth him to conceal for a time a piece of service which he must in any case consent to do aboard his own ship; that was, in the middle of the second watch, to go down secretly into the well of the ship and with a great spike-gimlet to bore three holes, as near the keel as he could, and lay something against it, that the force of the water entering might make no great noise, nor be discovered by boiling up ...

Our Captain, perceiving the feat wrought, ... demanded of them why their bark was so deep, as making no account of it. But by occasion of this demand his brother sent one down to the steward, to know whether there were any water in the ship, or what other cause might be.

The steward, hastily stepping down at his usual scuttle, was wet up to his waist, and shifting with more haste to come up again as if the water had followed him cried out that the ship was full of water. There was no need to hasten the company, some to pump, others to search for the leak ... [and] they ceased not, but to the utmost of their strength laboured all that they might till three in the afternoon. By which time, the company perceiving that (though they had been relieved by our Captain himself and many of his company) yet they were not able to free above a foot and half of water, and could have no likelihood of finding the leak, had now a less liking of her than before and a greater content to hear some means of remedy.

Whereupon our Captain, consulting with them what they thought best to be done, found that they had more desire to have all as he thought fit ...[8]

Subsequently Drake laid his ships up for a few weeks to lull the Spaniards into believing he had gone home.

But in the meantime we were not idle, for beside such ordinary works as our Captain every month did usually inure us to, about the trimming and fitting of his pinnaces for their better sailing and rowing, he caused us to rid a large plot of ground both of trees and brakes, and to build us houses sufficient for all our lodging, and one especially for all our public meetings, wherein the negro which fled to us before did us a great service, as being well acquainted with the country and their means of building. Our archers made themselves butts to shoot at, because we had many that delighted in that exercise and wanted not a fletcher to keep our bows and arrows in order. The rest of the company, everyone as he liked best, made his disport at bowls, quoits, keiles, etc. For our Captain allowed one half of the company to pass their time thus, every other day interchangeably the other half being enjoined to the necessary works about our ship and pinnaces, and the providing of fresh victuals, fish, fowl, hogs, deer, conies, etc., whereof there is great plenty. Here our smiths set up their forge as they used, being furnished out of England with anvil, iron, coals and all manner of necessaries, which stood us in great stead.[9]

Of those seamen whom Hawkins had been forced to leave behind in 1568 many fell into the hands of the Spanish Inquisition, and the fate of the men recorded below is by no means the end of the tale of horror.

The result was that at the first *auto da fe* held by the new Inquisition in February 1574 the following sentences were pronounced:

William Collins, of Oxford, age 40, seaman, ten years in the galleys; John Farenton [?Faringdon], of Windsor, 49, gunner, six years in the galleys; John Burton, of Bar Abbey, 22, seaman, 200 lashes and six years in the galleys; Paul de Leon, of Rotterdam, 22, seaman, 200 lashes and six years in the galleys; William Griffin, of Bristol, 24, seaman, 200 lashes and eight years in the galleys; George Ribley or Riveley, of Gravesend, 30, seaman, burnt at the stake, but first strangled; John Moon, of Looe, 26, seaman, 200 lashes and six years in the galleys; John Lee, of 'Sebria' in England, 20, seaman or gunner, 200 lashes and eight years in the galleys; William Brown, of London, 25 steward, 200 lashes and eight years in the galleys; Thomas Goodal, of London, 30, soldier, 300 lashes and ten years in the galleys; John Gilbert, of London, 29 seaman, 300 lashes and ten years in the galleys; Roger Armar, of Gueldres (Netherlands), 24, armourer, 200 lashes and six years in the galleys; Michael Morgan (alias Morgan Tillert), of Cardiff, 40, seaman, 200 lashes and eight years in the galleys; John Brown, of Ireland, 28, seaman, 200 lashes and eight years in the galleys; John Williams, of Cornwall, 28, 200 lashes and eight years in the galleys; Robert Plinton, of Plymouth, 30, 200 lashes and eight years in the galleys; John Grey, Englishman, 22, gunner, 200 lashes and eight years in the galleys; George Dee or Day, Englishman, 30, seaman, 300 lashes and eight years in the galleys.[10]

In the year in which these sentences were passed, William Bourne, a Gravesend innkeeper, printed the first practical manual of navigation, *A Regiment for the Sea,* a book in which he regrets that many shipmasters do not use bearing and distance tables and charts themselves, and mock those who do.

As touching those persons that are meet to take charge, that is to say, to be as master of ships in navigation, he ought to be sober and wise, and not to be light or rash headed, nor to be too fumish or hasty, but such a one as can well govern himself, for else it is not possible for him to govern his company well: he ought not to be too simple, but he must be such a one as must keep his company in awe of him (by discretion) doing his company no injury or wrong, but to let them have that which men ought to have, and then to see unto them that they do their labour as men ought to do in all points. And the principal point in government is, to cause himself both to be feared and loved, and that groweth principally by this means, to cherish men in well doing, and those men that be honestly addicted, to let them have reasonable pre-eminence, so that it be not hurtful unto the merchant nor himself, and to punish those that be malefactors and disturbers of their company, and for small faults, to give them gentle admonition to amend them: and principally these two points art to be foreseen by the masters, that is, to serve God himself, and to see that all the whole company do so in like manner, at such convenient time as it is meet to be done: the second point is, that the master use no play at the dice or cards, neither (as near as he can) to suffer any, for the sufferance thereof may do very much hurt in divers respects.[11]

By this time English, French, Spaniards, Basques and Portuguese were all fishing on the Grand Banks of Newfoundland but, according to Hakluyt,

the English had the best ships, and therefore gave the law to the rest, being in the bays the protectors of others, for which it was then, and had been of old, a custom to make them some sort of acknowledgement as Admirals, such as a boatload of salt, for guarding them from pirates and other violent intruders, who often drive them from good harbours.[12]

Having failed to find a northeast passage to China by way of Russia, the English conjectured that there might be a northwest passage to the north of Canada. To test this hypothesis Martin Frobisher, between 1576 and 1578, made three voyages to seek one but failed to do so. Regretfully, Frobisher did not take William Bourne's injunctions entirely to heart. He was, we are told, 'a very strict observer of discipline, even to a degree of severity which hindered his being beloved'.[13]

People with money provided him with three cockleshells of ships, two vessels each of 20 tons burden and a pinnace of only 10 tons, and this little fleet sailed in the summer of 1576. The pinnace was soon lost in a storm and never heard of again, and not long afterwards the other vessel deserted. However, Frobisher pushed on and, after sighting Greenland, nearly lost his own ship in a storm which pushed her over on her beam ends. Still he was not deterred. At the end of July he sighted Resolution Island, and in the middle of August he landed on an island in Frobisher Bay – or Strait, as he believed it to be – where he and his men met some apparently friendly Eskimoes. One of the Eskimoes agreed by means of signs to pilot them into those western seas which Frobisher believed to be so readily accessible, but he wished to go ashore to prepare himself. Frobisher sent him off in one of his boats with a crew of five men, but these men disobeyed instructions to land the Eskimo within sight of the ship and they were never seen again. Frobisher made repeated attempts to recover his men and even managed to capture another Eskimo as hostage but all in vain. A week or so after landing, he and his thirteen remaining men decided to return to England.[14]

Frobisher brought back with him what was probably iron pyrites or 'fool's gold'. Briefly, even Queen Elizabeth was taken in. But after his profitable Panamanian venture of 1572, Drake was a sounder bet. In 1577 Drake set out again after real gold and, in hunting for it, he too encompassed the world. His ships were the *Pelican* (later the *Golden Hind*), 100 tons; the *Elizabeth*, 80 tons; the *Marigold*, 30 tons; the *Swan*, 50 tons; and the *Christopher*, 15 tons. The captain of the *Christopher* was a Thomas Moone, no doubt the amenable ship's carpenter in his brother's ship five years earlier.

These ships he manned with 164 able and sufficient men, and furnished them also with such plentiful provision of all things necessary, as so long and dangerous a voyage did seem to require; and amongst the rest, with certain pinnaces ready framed, but carried aboard in pieces, to be new set up in smoother water, when occasion served. Neither had he omitted to make provision also for ornament and delight, carrying to this purpose with him expert musicians, rich furniture (all the vessels for his table, yea, many belonging even to the cook-room of pure silver), and divers shows of all sorts of curious workmanship, whereby the civility and magnificence of his native country might, amongst all nations whithersoever he should come, be the more admired.[15]

In the Strait of Magellan in 1578, Preacher Francis Fletcher, who accompanied Drake, tells us,

The winds were such as if the bowels of the earth had set all at liberty ... The ... were rolled up from the depths, ... so that the violent storm without intermission; the impossibility to come to anchor; the want of opportunity to spread any sail; the most mad seas; the lee shores; the dangerous rocks; the contrary and most intolerable winds; the impossible passage out; the desperate tarrying there; and inevitable perils on every side, did lay before us so small a likelihood to escape present destruction, that if the special providence of God Himself had not supported us, we could never have endured that woeful state; as being environed with most terrible and meet fearful judgments round about. For truly, it was more likely that the mountains should have been rent in sunder from top to bottom, and cast headlong into the sea, by these unnatural winds, than that we, by any help or cunning of man, should free the life of any one amongst us.[16]

A few weeks later fourteen men were landed on the South American coast to seek out the local facilities, but thirteen of them withdrew rapidly when a large party of Spaniards and Indians – Fletcher says 300 – appeared on the scene.

Only one Richard Minivy, being over-bold and careless of his own safety, would not be entreated by his friends, nor feared by the multitude of his enemies, to take the present benefit of his own delivery; but chose either to make 300 men, by outbraving of them, to become afraid, or else himself to die in the place; the latter of which he did, whose dead body being

69

drawn by the Indians from the rock to the shore, was there manfully by the Spaniards beheaded, the right hand cut off, the heart plucked out; all which they carried away in our sight, and for the rest of his carcase they caused the Indians to shoot it full of arrows, made but the same day of green wood, and so left it to be devoured of the beasts and fowls, but that we went ashore and buried it.[17]

After obtaining a considerable treasure on the Pacific coast of the Americas and exploring as far north as British Columbia, Drake returned, in 1579, to the neighbourhood of San Francisco, where he and his men were worshipped as gods.

When [the Indians] came to the top of the hill, at the bottom whereof we had built our fort, they made a stand; where one (appointed as their chief speaker) wearied both us, his hearers, and himself too, with a long and tedious oration; delivered with strange and violent gestures, his voice being extended to the uttermost strength of nature, and his words falling so thick one in the neck of another, that he could hardly fetch breath again. As soon as he had concluded, all the rest, with a reverend bowing of their bodies (in a dreaming manner, and long producing of the same), cried 'Oh': thereby giving their consents that all was very true which he had spoken, and that they had uttered their mind by his mouth unto us: which done, the men laying down their bows upon the hill, and leaving their women and children behind them, came down with their presents; in such sort as if they had appeared before a god indeed, thinking themselves happy that they might have access unto our general; but much more happy when they saw that he would receive at their hands those things which they so willingly had presented: and no doubt they thought themselves nearest unto God when they sat or stood next to him. In the meantime the women, as if they had been desperate, used unnatural violence against themselves, crying and shrieking piteously, tearing their flesh with their nails from their cheeks in a monstrous manner, the blood streaming down along their breasts, besides spoiling the upper parts of their bodies of those single coverings they formerly had, and holding their breasts from harm, they would with fury cast themselves upon the ground, never respecting whether it were clean or soft, but dashed themselves in this manner on hard stones, knobbly hillocks, stocks of wood and pricking bushes, or whatever else lay in their way, iterating the same course again and again. Yea, women great with child, some nine or ten times each, and others holding out till 15 or 16 times (till their strength failed them), exercised this cruelty against themselves. A thing more grievous for us to see or suffer, could we have holp it, than trouble to them (as it seemed) to do it. This bloody sacrifice (against our wills) being thus performed, our general with his company in the presence of those strangers fell to prayers; and by signs lifting up our eyes and hands to heaven, signified unto them that that God whom we did serve, and whom they ought to worship, was above: beseeching God, if it were His good pleasure, to open by some means their blinded eyes, that they might in due time be called to the knowledge of Him, the true and ever-living God, and of Jesus Christ whom He hath sent, the salvation of the Gentiles. In the time of which prayers, singing of Psalms, and reading of certain chapters of the Bible, they sat very attentively: and observing the end of every pause, with one voice still cried, 'Oh', greatly rejoiced in our exercises. Yea, they took such pleasure in our singing of Psalms, that whensoever they resorted to us, their first request was commonly this, 'Gnaah', by which they entreated that we would sing.

Our general having now bestowed upon them divers things at their departure they restored them again, none carrying with him anything of whatsoever he had received, thinking themselves sufficiently enriched and happy that they had found so free access to see us.[18]

In January 1580, homeward bound from the Celebes, the *Golden Hind* – by this time on her own – ran aground on a shoal.

As touching the ship, this was the comfort she could give us, that she herself was lying there confined already upon the hard and pinching rocks, did tell us plain that she continually expected her speedy dispatch ...

It was therefore presently motioned, and by general voice determined, to commend our case to God alone, leaving ourselves wholly in His hand to spill or save us, as seemed best by His gracious wisdom. And that our faith might be the better strengthened, and the comfortable apprehension of God's mercy in Christ be more clearly felt, we had a sermon, and the Sacrament of the body and blood of our Saviour celebrated.

After this sweet repast was thus received, and other holy exercises adjoined were ended, lest we should seem guilty in any respect for not using all lawful means we could invent, we fell to one other practice yet unassayed, to wit, to unloading of our ship by casting some of her goods into the sea: which thing, as it was attempted most willingly, so it was dispatched in a very short time: so that even those things which we before this time, nor any other in our case could be without, did now seem as things only worthy to be despised, yea we were herein so forward, that neither our munition for defence, nor the very meal for sustenation of our lives could find favour with us, but everything as it first came to hand went overboard; ...

The manner of our delivery (for the relation of it will especially be expected) was only this. The place whereon we sat so fast was a firm rock in a cleft, whereof it was stuck on the larboard side. At low water there was not above six foot depth in all on the starboard, within little distance as you have heard no bottom be found; the breeze during the whole time that we thus were stayed, blew somewhat stiff against our broadside, and so perforce kept the ship upright. It pleased God in the beginning of the tide, while the water was yet almost at lowest, to slack the stiffness of the wind; and now our ship, who required thirteen foot water to make her float, and had not at that time on the one side above seven at most, wanting her prop on the other side, which had too long already kept her up, fell a-heeling towards the deep water, and by that means freed her keel and made us glad men.[19]

On 4th April 1581, at Deptford, Drake entertained Queen Elizabeth I to a magnificent banquet on board the *Golden Hind.* After the banquet she knighted him. Such an act was in open defiance of Spain and made inevitable the eventual dispatch of the Spanish Armada against England.

CHAPTER 7

Momentous Years

1581–1589

Privateering was a consequence of political conflict between nations. Since navies in the modern sense had not been sufficiently developed by the end of the sixteenth century, some privately-owned vessels were authorised by governments to make war on enemy ships and allowed to keep the 'profits'. In these years ordinary trade was severely disrupted by conflict, and the English, ever more provocative of Spain, developed privateering into a weapon of considerable economic significance, as significant in Queen Elizabeth I's economy as car production in Queen Elizabeth II's. Although the royal ships grew in number as the years went by, and became differently organised and armed, merchant seamen, and many of their ships, have always been required to serve governments where necessary in time of war. But mercantile marine practice always differed from that of the royal ships, sometimes amusingly. In the year of Drake's return from his circumnavigation of the world, Captain Stephen Hare made a trading voyage to Portuguese territory in South America, on behalf of a group of London merchants. At Bahia in Brazil he quarrelled with Richard Earswick, one of the factors or merchants aboard. He thereupon displaced Earswick, 'and for his punishment, according to the order of the sea, he was bound to the mainmast with a base chamber about his neck for the space of half a quarter of an hour'.[1]

Two years later, in 1582, Captain Edward Fenton set out with four ships on a privateering voyage which was intended to outdo Drake. It was a failure, but the ships and crewing for such an expedition are typical.

In the galleon *Leicester*, Edward Fenton (General), William Hawkins (lieutenant), Nicholas Parker (captain at land), Richard Madox (minister), Miles Evans and Matthew Tailboise (merchants), about four score sailors, 24 necessary men beside, and a dozen boys.

In the *Edward*: Luke Ward (Vice-admiral), John Walker (minister), Randol Shawe and Peter Jefrei (merchants), Thomas Pearsie (master), about 54 sailors, 16 necessary men beside, and 8 boys.

In the *Francis:* John Drake (Captain), Wylam Markham (master), 14 sailors, 2 boys.

In the *Elizabeth*: Thomas Skevington (Captain), Rafe Crane (master), 12 sailors, 3 boys.[2]

The minister to the expedition, Richard Madox, recorded in his diary,

Athwart the Burlings we had espied a sail which our men said was a French man-of-war, and all were willing to contend for his goods. Captain Parker, both because he had a mind to the booty and because he would please the people, would needs have Captain Ward to set him on, which he did, but the ship was a Flemish hulk, so they thereupon heard my words and Mr Walker's in the *Edward* [and] the man had no hurt at all.

I took occasion at service to speak against their attempt the day before, but they were all, without pity, set upon the spoil. After noon, Captain Ward and Mr Walker came to us and told how greedy they were, especially Mr Bannister the surgeon, who for all his creeping hypocrisy was more ravenously set upon the prey than any of the most beggarly felons in the ship, and those also which on shore did counterfeit most holiness were now furthest from reason, affirming that we could not do God better service than to [de]spoil the Spaniard of both life and goods. But, indeed, under colour of religion all their shot is at the men's money.[3]

On his return to England in 1583 the surgeon Bannister wrote to the Earl of Leicester from the galleon which bore his name.

And now, my Lord, I will certify your honour of such persons as God had called to his mercy out of the galleon *Leicester*, and how diseased of every sickness. And first after we passed our own climate and drawing within four degrees of the tropic line of Cancer, which was about the 17th of June, at which time divers of our men fell suddenly sick, and such as had thin and dry bodies were infested with hot, burning and pestiferous fevers, but the other sort, which had gross and thick bodies, were molested with the scurvy. Of the first infection died eight and of the scurvy two, and three of a surfeit. All the rest, through God's providence, letting blood and purging were all recovered for that time. But when we came to the coast of Brasil, about the 20th of November, to a harbour which our General called the Bay of Good Comfort, which place standeth in 28 degrees of the southward of the Line, near unto the Tropic of Capricorn, the same day that we departed from that harbour, almost all our men fell sick with great pain in their heads, stomachs, backs, shortness of breath and heaviness of their whole bodies, which sickness I gather came partly by the changing of the climate and partly through their own disorder of insatiable feeding on fresh fish, much drinking of cold water, and lying in the air on the hatches in the night season. But, God be thanked, after purging and letting of blood, not one that perished of that sickness. Yet when we came to St Vincent's in the same coast about the 20th of January, 1583, which place standeth in 24 degrees the southwards of the Line, near under the tropic line of Capricorn, there did our men fall sick of a great looseness of their bodies, and by reason of discharge and biting humour there were made excoriations of the bowels, causing torments in their bellies and flux of blood still flowing with excrement. Of which sickness there died five.[4]

Thereafter, the text of this letter grows corrupt, but of the *Leicester*'s complement of 122, forty-five seem to have died. Bannister proposed to set down his remedies 'for the relief and succour of the many thousands that shall perform these watery pilgrimages', but Madox had no high opinion of his abilities.

> Divers of our men were sick and Mr Bannister had neither skill nor medicine, so that I would advise such as shall here after appoint such a voyage to prepare good provision of wholesome comfort and ordinary salves, and let them lie in the hands of some honest merchant, and let the surgeon be prepared to use the salve when need is, and some good clean cook to minister the other cherishings, and so £10 [will] go further and do more good than £100 in such wise as our money is bestowed. All this while I was seasick, and – no marvel, having changed at once air, exercise and diet – rheumatic I was, and exceedingly costive and troubled with heartburn, which be appendices of the sea, wherefore I could advise him that is to appoint such a voyage that he have of violet flowers, borage flowers, rosemary flowers and suchlike, which he may gather in England, conserves made, to comfort him, and barberry seed and rosemary and thyme to make a little broth in an earthen pipkin. These things are less costly but far more wholesome than all the suckets and paltry confections.[5]

To a book written by Sir George Peckham in 1583, to report the discoveries made in North America, Sir Francis Drake contributed a commendatory sonnet which sums up much of the spirit of the age.

> Who seeks, by worthy deeds, to gain renown for hire:
> Whose heart, whose hand, whose purse is pressed to
> purchase his desire:
> If any such there be that thirsteth after fame,

Lo, here a means to win himself an everlasting name.
Who seeks by gain and wealth to advance his house and
blood:
Whose care is great, whose toil no less, whose hope is all for
good:
If any one there be that covets such a trade,
Lo, here the plot for commonwealth and private gain is
made.
He that for virtue's sake will venture far and near,
Whose zeal is strong, whose practice truth, whose faith is
void of fear:
If any such there be, inflamed with holy care,
Here may he find a ready means his purpose to declare.
So that for each degree this treatise doth unfold
The path to fame, the proof of zeal, and way to purchase
gold.[6]

In this same year, 1583, Sir Humphrey Gilbert took possession of Newfoundland for himself under the Crown,
and sailed thence to the mainland. After losing all his fleet
except the 40-ton *Golden Hind* and the 10-ton pinnace or
'frigate' *Squirrel*, he decided to return home.

> ... the vehement persuasion and entreaties of his friends could
> nothing avail to divert him from a wilful resolution of going
> through in his frigate, which was overcharged upon their
> decks, ... too cumbersome for so small a boat that was to pass
> through the ocean sea at that season of the year, when by
> course we might expect much storm of foul weather. [For]
> when he was entreated by the Captain, Master and other of
> his well willers not to venture in the frigate, this was his
> answer: 'I will not forsake my little company going
> homeward' ...
>
> By that time we had brought the Islands of Azores south of
> us, yet we then keeping much to the north, until we had got
> into the height and elevation of England, we met with very
> foul weather and terrible seas breaking short and high

pyramid-wise, the reason whereof seemed to proceed ... of diversity of winds, shifting often in sundry points ... Howsoever it cometh to pass, men which all their lifetime had occupied the sea, never saw more outrageous seas. We had also upon our mainyard an apparition of a little fire by night, which seamen do call Castor and Pollux [also called St Elmo's fire, an electrical discharge caused by storm conditions] ... which they take an evil sign of more tempest ...

Monday the 9th September, in the afternoon, the frigate was near cast away, oppressed by waves, yet at that time recovered and, giving forth signs of joy, the General, sitting abaft with a book in his hand, cried out unto us in the *Hind* (so oft as we did approach within hearing), 'We are as near to heaven by sea as by land'.

The same Monday night, about twelve of the clock, or not long after, the frigate being ahead of us in the *Golden Hind* suddenly her lights went out, whereof as it were in a moment, we lost the sight, and withal our watch cried the General was cast away, which was true. For on that moment the frigate was devoured and swallowed up of the sea ... [7]

As the poet Henry Wadsworth Longfellow wrote nearly 300 years later,

> He sat upon the deck,
> The Book was in his hand;
> 'Do not fear! Heaven is as near,'
> He said, 'by water as by land'.

Gilbert's work of trying to establish a colony in North America was carried on by his half-brother Sir Walter Raleigh, who once commented that 'there are stranger things to be seen in the world than are between London and Staines'. Among the others involved was Sir Richard Grenville who wrote to Sir Francis Walsingham, principal secretary to Queen Elizabeth, two years later.

In my way homewards I was encountered by a Spanish ship whom assaulting me and offering me violence, God be thanked, with defence and safety of myself and all my company after some fight I overcame and brought into England with me her lading of ginger and sugar.[8]

Grenville would have had his own good reasons for trying to minimise his receipts from this capture but the profits of this particular privateering expedition may well have been of the order of £20,000 on an investment of half that sum. But the outcome could never be foretold. In 1585–86 – years in which John Davis, friend and neighbour of Gilbert, was exploring, without much profit, for a north-west passage – a large expedition by Drake lost money, as well as 750 men out of a total of about 3000. Between 1586 and 1588 Sir Thomas Cavendish completed the third circumnavigation of the world.

That the outcome of such voyages could never be foreseen was shown in the case of Thomas Cavendish, who had set out from Plymouth one week before Drake's return. The provision for this venture, which was to achieve the third circumnavigation, was modest. Cavendish's own ship, the *Desire* was of 120 tons, her two consorts of sixty and forty. The total complement was 123 men. They carried surgeons, and were victualled for two years. It was Cavendish's first voyage, but he must have learned much from other travellers. In West Africa they collected lemons off the trees, and although they did not reach Magellan until December, no scurvy had appeared. The only death had occurred on 3rd September, off Sierra Leone, the day after some men had landed to wash their shirts. They had been attacked, one man had been shot in the thigh with an arrow, and he had removed the shaft only. But 'he told the Chirurgions that he plucked out all the arrow, because he would not have them lance his thigh'. The arrow-head was poisoned, and the surgeons might not have been able to save his life, but the incident shows their lack of authority and the little esteem in which they were held.

After entering the Pacific there were two deaths from scurvy, but in Java, in March, 1588, they got eggs, hens, fresh fish, oranges and limes. Before this refreshment was obtained, however, a strange, new malady overtook them. Between the Philippines and Java, 'divers' of the sixteen men in the little 40-ton bark, *Hugh Gallant* 'fell marveilously sicke' for three weeks or a month, with 'great pains' and fever. The captain died after seven or eight days, but possibly from some other cause, for the prevailing fever appears to have created little alarm and may have been dengue. With the exceptions mentioned, all those who had left Plymouth returned again when Cavendish led his two remaining ships into port on 9th September, 1588. What happy chance produced this result can only be surmised: Cavendish knew the value of fresh water which had been filtered through sand, but his relative freedom from diseases carried by mosquitoes and other insects must have been due to his ships, with one exception, happening on healthy anchorages, or to the prevailing winds.[9]

Cavendish had missed the battle against the Armada. The conflict between Spain and England had been brought to a head while he was still on his way round the world by Drake's expedition to Cadiz in 1587, an expedition on which Drake recouped his losses of the previous year, making £17,000 personally, £40,000 for his Queen, and £140,000 overall, while at the same time destroying more than two dozen Spanish ships. However, the crew of the *Golden Lion*, a ship in Drake's fleet, wrote to their captain in the course of this expedition as follows.

Captain Marchaunt, Captain of the *Golden Lion* appointed by Sir Francis Drake, General of this fleet: We, the Queen's and yours, at this time desire that, as you are a man and bear the name of captain over us, so to weigh of us like men, and let us not be spoiled for want of food, for our allowance is so small we are not able to live any longer of it; for when as three or

81

four were wont to take a charge in hand, now ten at the least, by reason of our weak victualling and filthy drink, is scarce able to discharge it, and yet grow weaker and weaker; ... for what is a piece of beef of half-a-pound among four men to dinner or half a dry stockfish for four days in the week, and nothing else to help withal – yea, we have help, a little beverage worse than the pump water. We were pressed by Her Majesty's press to have her allowance, and not to be thus dealt withal, you make no men of us, but beasts ... [10]

That these mutineers, as they declared themselves to be, were never punished indicates that justice was overwhelmingly on their side. But these sailors had more to put up with than a shortage of food during the battle against the Armada, as we learn from Lord Howard of Effingham, commander of England's fleet, immediately after the action.

Sickness and mortality begin wonderfully to grow amongst us: and it is a pitiful sight to see here at Margate, how the men, having no place to receive them here, die in the streets. I am driven myself, of force, to come-a-land, to see them bestowed in some lodging; and the best I can get is barns and outhouses; and the relief is small that I can provide for them here. It would grieve any man's heart to see them that have served so valiantly to die so miserably.

The *Elizabeth Jonas,* which hath done us well as ever any ship did in any service, hath had a great affection in her from the beginning so as of the 500 men which carried out, by the time she had been in Plymouth three weeks or a month, there were dead of them 200 and above, so as I was driven to set all the rest of her men ashore, to take out the ballast and to make fires in her of wet broom three or four days together, and so hoped thereby to have cleansed her of her infection, and thereupon got new men, very tall and able as ever I saw, and put them into her; now the infection is broken out in greater extremity than ever it did before, and they die and sicken faster than ever they did, so as I am driven of force to send her to Chatham. We all think and judge that the infection remaineth in the pitch. Sir Roger Townsend of all the men he brought out with him hath but one left alive; and my son Southwell likewise hath many dead.

It is like enough that the infection will grow throughout the most part of the fleet, for they have been so long at sea and have so little shift of apparel, and so few places to provide them of such wants, and no money wherewith to buy it, for some have been – yea, the most part – these eight months at sea. My Lord [Burghley, principal adviser to Queen Elizabeth], I would think it a marvellous good way that there were a thousand pounds worth or two thousand marks worth of hose, doublets, shirts, shoes, and suchlike sent down; and I think your Lordship might use therein the Comptroller of the Navy and Waker, Mr Hawkins' man, who would use all expedition for the providing and sending away of such things; for else, in very short time, I look to see most of the mariners go naked. Good my Lord, let mariners be pressed and sent down as soon as may be, and money to discharge those that be sick here; and so in haste I bid your Lordship farewell.[11]

These were the men of whom Drake had written to the Queen shortly before the battle.

I have not in my lifetime known better men, and possessed with gallanter minds, than your Majesty's people are for the most part, which are gathered together, voluntarily to put their hands to the finishing of this great piece of work, wherein we are persuaded that God, the Giver of all victories, will in mercy look upon your most excellent Majesty, and us your poor subjects, who for the defence of your Majesty, our religion and native country, have resolutely vowed the hazard of our lives.[12]

Both Drake and the Earl of Cumberland were supposed, in 1589, to find profitable targets in the Azores. Homeward bound, the Earl, in the royal ship *Victory*, was driven so far to leeward, that we could fetch no part of Ireland, so as with heavy hearts and sad cheer, we were allowed every man three or four spoons full of vinegar to drink at a meal, for other drink we had none, saving only two or three meals, when we had instead hereof as much wine, which was wringed out of wine-lees that remained.

With this hard fare (for by reason of our great want of drink, we durst eat but very little), we continued for the space of a fortnight or thereabouts: saving that now and then we feasted for it in the mean time: and that was when there fell any hail or rain: the hailstones we gathered up, and did eat them more pleasantly than if they had been the sweetest comfits in the world. The raindrops were so carefully saved that, so near as we could, not one was lost in all our ship. Some hanged up sheets tied with cords by the four corners, and a weight in the midst that the water might run thither, and so be received into some vessel set or hanged underneath. Some that wanted sheets, hanged up napkins and clouts and watched them till they were thorough wet, then wringing and sucking out the water.

And that water which fell down and washed away the filth and soiling of the ship, trod under foot, as bad as running down the kennel many times when it raineth, was not lost, I warrant you, but watched and attended carefully (yea, sometimes with strife and contention) at every scupper-hole, and other place where it ran down, with dishes, pots, cans and jars, whereof some drunk hearty draughts even as it was, mud and all, without tarrying to cleanse or settle it. Others cleansed it first, but not often, for it was so thick and went so slowly through, that they might ill endure to tarry so long, and were loth to lose too much of the precious stuff. Some licked with their tongues (like dogs) the boards under feet, the sides, rails and masts of the ship. Others that were more ingenious, fastened girdles or ropes about the masts, daubing tallow betwixt them and the mast (that the rain might not run down between), in such sort that those ropes or girdles hanging lower on the one side than the other, a spout of leather was fastened to the lowest part of them, that all the rain drops that came running down the mast might meet together at that place and there be received.[13]

CHAPTER 8

Privateers

1589–1596

Prevented by the war with Spain from carrying on their normal employment, merchantman fought merchantman in the years following the battle of the Armada. Between 1589 and 1591 at least 235 English vessels acted as such 'ships of reprisal'. The ship featured below, however, failed in her enterprise through the stupidity of her officers and the treachery of the Spanish.

Being on the coast of Campeche [on the Gulf of Mexico in 1589] they escried a ship of great burthen taking in her lading in a road which they attempted to take and fought with her one whole day, and not being able to take her, wanting men and provisions, they came to parley with the Spaniards and demanded five thousand ducats to depart and suffer them load without doing them harm: and the Captain of the Spanish ship requested respect until next day to confer with his partners and merchants on land, and came on board the [*Black*] *Dog* and had speeches with the pilot and company of the *Dog* which was put in writing. And hereupon the pilot made the said Spanish Captain and his company with him good cheer, and at his departure the pilot Roger Kingson, William Mace the Master, the surgeon and three or four more could needs go in the ship's boat to bring the Captain on board his ship, and coming to the ship's side by sugar speeches were enticed to go on board the Spanish ship to be feasted by the Spaniards in like sort. And so went on board, and being in the Captain's cabin altogether the Captain made them good cheer, and in the meantime concluded with his company to arm themselves and come to the cabin door, and when he gave his token, to dispatch them: and thereupon the Captain came to the pilot and embracing him with many thanks, drew his dagger and stabbed the said pilot to the heart and presently a number more were ready at the cabin door with rapiers and stabbed him likewise, together with John Hughes the surgeon and Edmund Bense the corporal: and William Mace the Master and two others did leap overboard and were taken up by the boat and saved, although all wounded by the said Spaniards. By which treason they were bereft of their said enterprise and forced to be gone with the Dog and her said prize before taken.[1]

In the same year the 120-ton vessel *Delight* was supplied by William Walton, one of the most prominent privateering merchants of Bristol, to an ill-fated expedition led by John Chidley. Only six of the ninety-one crew survived the voyage.

We sailed toward the Strait of Magellan, and entered the same about the first of January [1590]. And coming to Penguin Island within the Strait we took and salted certain hogsheads of penguins, which must be eaten with speed for we found them to be of no long continuance; we also furnished ourselves with fresh water. And here at the last sending off our boat to the island for the rest of our provision, we lost her and 15 men in her by force of foul weather; but what became of them we could not tell. Here also in this storm we lost two anchors. From hence we passed into the Strait, and by Port Famine we spake with a Spaniard who told us that he had lived in those parts six years, and that he was one of the 400 men that were sent thither by the King of Spain in the year 1582 to fortify and inhabit there to hinder the passage of all strangers that way into the South Sea. But that and the other Spanish colony being both destroyed by famine, he said he

87

had lived in a house by himself for a long time, and relieved himself with his caleever [light musket] until our coming thither. Here we made a boat of the boards of our chests, which being finished we sent seven armed men in the same on land on the north shore, being wafted on land by the savages with certain white skins; who as soon as they came on shore were presently killed by an hundred of the wild people in the sight of two of our men, which rowed them on shore, which two only escaped back again to us with the boat. After this traitorous slaughter of our men, we fell back again with our ship to the north-east ward of Port Famine to a certain road where we refreshed ourselves with mussels and took in water and wood. At this time we took in the Spaniard aforesaid, and so sailed forward again in to the Strait. We passed seven or eight times ten leagues westward beyond Cape Froward, being still encountered with mighty northwest winds. These winds and the current were so vehement against us that they forced us back as much in two hours as we were getting up in eight hours. Thus after we had spent six weeks in the Strait striving against the fury of the elements and having sundry times, partly by casualty and partly by sickness, lost 38 or our best men, and three anchors, and now having but one anchor left us, and a small store of victuals, and, which was not the least mischief, divers of our company raising dangerous mutinies, we consulted, though somewhat with the latest [the would-be mutineers], for the safeguard of our lives to return while there was some small hope remaining.[2]

At Flores in the Azores Sir Richard Grenville lay, ... and immortalised himself in 1591, when commanding the *Revenge*, by fighting fifty-three Spanish ships alone. Grenville had sailed as second-in-command of a squadron of vessels sent to the Azores to intercept a Spanish treasure fleet. When the Spanish vessels approached in overwhelming numbers, the English retreated but Grenville was cut off.

'I have fought for Queen and Faith like a valiant man and true;
I have only done my duty as a man is bound to do:
With a joyful spirit I Sir Richard Grenville die!'

Thus wrote Tennyson, interpreting the Elizabethan spirit correctly even if a considered judgement might be that Grenville was insatiably ambitious, obstinate, tyrannical and perversely disobedient. A contemporary view by a foreigner depicts him thus:

He was of so hard a complexion, that as he continued among the Spanish Captains while they were at dinner or supper with him [apparently on his death bed], he would carouse three or four glasses of wine, and in a bravery take the glasses between his teeth and crush them to pieces and swallow them down, so that often times the blood ran out of his mouth without any harm to him at all.[3]

There were, of course, gains as well as losses in the business of privateering. A prize ship taken at sea which was worth £2000 would probably yield between £8 and £12 to an ordinary seaman, and this was better than ten shillings a month in the Queen's ships. It was also in 1591 that Sir Walter Raleigh, who was deeply involved in privateering as well as in colonising, wrote of a clear profit of over £12,000 made by one syndicate in which he was a shareholder as 'a small return; we might have gotten more to have sent them a-fishing'.[4] Raleigh's fall from grace came in the following year.

Five days before Grenville's last fight, on 26th August 1591, Thomas Cavendish set sail once more for the South Seas, this time in the galleon *Leicester,* with John Davis as his second-in-command aboard the *Desire,* the vessel in which Cavendish had circumnavigated the world. With them were also the *Roebuck,* a pinnace and a bark. In this venture Cavendish was among the many who lost their lives.

89

During contrary winds and calms on the equator lasting twenty-seven days, Antonia Knivet records that 'most of our men fell sicke of the Scurvie by reason of the extreme heat of the Sunne, and the vapours of the night'. They were still within the Strait of Magellan in April, 1592, and many were dying of cold and hunger. Scurvy was general, but in the *Desire*, Captain John Davis, this was finally checked by scurvy grass, gathered at Port Desire in Patagonia. They fried it with birds' eggs, 'using traine [whale] oil instead of butter. This herbe did so purge ye blood, that it tooke away all kind of swellings, of which many died, and restored us to perfect health of body, so that we were in as good case as when we came first out of England'. They also killed thirty-four thousand penguins and cured them with salt, which they dried in pans of sea water ashore. After December, 1592, each man received a measured ration: one and a quarter penguins and one and a half quarts of water daily; three spoonsful of oil on three days a week; one quarter pint of 'peason' [dried peas] on two days a week, and five ounces of meal a week. By then, however, only twenty-seven of the *Desire*'s original seventy-six men were alive, and they had parted company with the other ships, which disappeared without trace. The *Desire* turned back, but by the time she left the Brazilian coast for home her remaining men were suffering from shortness of breath and an oedematous condition, which may have been wet beri-beri, superimposed on scurvy. They attributed their condition to eating the dried penguin flesh, which had been so badly cured that it was putrid and infested with 'worms'. Only the captain and one boy were still healthy, and eleven of the twenty-seven survivors from Magellan died. As they neared England, the ship's company was so weak that only five could work her; there was no more food on board, and when they reached Bantry Bay on 11th of June, 1593, she had to be run ashore.[5]

While the men who had sailed with Cavendish were either dying or being 'so eaten with lice, as that in their flesh did lie clusters of lice as big as peason, yea and some as big as beans', others, sailing with Sir John Burrough, who commanded another force fitted out by Raleigh, had captured the marvellously rich East India carrack *Madre de Dios*. Besides jewels, which never came to light officially, she was stuffed with 900 tons of

> spices, drugs, silks, calicos, quilts, carpets, and colours, etc., The spices were peppers, cloves, maces, nutmegs, cinnamon, green ginger: the drugs were benjamin, frankincense, galingale, mirabolans, aloes, Zocotrina, camphor: the silks, damasks, taffeta, sarcenets, altobarsos, that is counterfeit cloth of gold, unwrought China silk, sheared silk, white-twisted silk, curled cypress. The calicos were book-calico, calico-lawns, broad white calicos, fine starched calicos, coarse white calicos, brown broad calicos, brown coarse calicos. There were also canopies, and coarse diaper-towels, quilts of coarse sarcenet and of calico, carpets like those of Turkey; whereunto are to be added the pearl, musk, civet and ambergris. The rest of the wares were ... elephants' teeth, porcelain vessels of China, coconuts, hides, ebony wood as black as jet, bedsteads of the same cloth of the rinds of trees very strange for the matter, and artificial in workmanship ... [6]

Having invested £3000 in two royal ships which sailed with Burrough's fleet, Queen Elizabeth recouped £90,000. In spite of this enormous profit she proposed that each seaman be allowed only twenty shillings for his share of the prize money, which no doubt explains why one crew member is said to have pillaged 'half a peck of pearls' and another sold '1800 diamonds and 200 or 300 rubies for 130 poundes'.[7]

The year 1591 is rich in records of maritime activity. The ships *Penelope, Marchant Royal* and *Edward Bonaventure* sailed for the East Indies by way of the Cape of Good Hope under the command of James Lancaster, and by the summer of 1592 they were between Malacca and Pegu.

> Here we continued until the end of August. Our refreshing in the place was very small, only of oysters growing on rock, great whelks, and some few fish which we took with our hooks. Here we landed our sick men on these uninhabited islands for their health, nevertheless 26 of them died in this place, whereof, John Hall, our master, was one, and M Rainold Golding another, a merchant of great honesty and much discretion. In these islands are abundance of trees of white wood, so right and tall that a man may make masts of them, being an hundred foot long. The winter passed and having watered our ship and fitted her to go to sea we had left us but 33 men and one boy, of which not past 22 were found fit for labour and help, and of them not past a third part sailors.[8]

In April 1593,

> We came to anchor at the island of St Helena, whereat we found an Englishman, a tailor, which had been there 14 months before we came thither: so we sending our boat on shore with some ten men, they found this Englishman in the chapel, who by reason of the heat of the climate was enforced to keep himself out of the sun. Our company hearing one sing in the chapel, supposing it had been some Portuguese, thrust open the door and went in unto him: but the poor man, seeing so many come in upon him on the sudden, and thinking them to be Portuguese, was first in such a fear, not having seen any man in 14 months before, and afterwards knowing them to be Englishmen, and some of them his acquaintance, in such joy, that, what between excessive sudden fear and joy, he became distracted of his wits, to our great sorrow.[9]

This voyage of Lancaster's was yet another which ended in disaster. But Christopher Newport's expedition of 1592 must have made a profit because two of his ships, the *Golden Dragon* and the *Prudence*, also had a hand in the

capture of the treasure-ship *Madre de Dios* whose cargo
has been itemised above. Here Captain Robert Thread of
the third ship *Margaret* tells his story.

... the *Dragon*, the *Prudence*, the *Margaret* and the *Virgin*
being set to sea by Master Cobb and other merchants with letters of reprisal did first at Dominica in the West Indies take a
prize laden with negroes and they set the negroes ashore at
Puerto Rico and burnt the ship, and out of the same they had
some rice and a small provision of victuals and nothing else.
Afterwards under the isle of Hispaniola they took three or
four empty frigates and made pinnaces of them and took them
along with them, and at Ocoa they landed with the said pin
naces and took an 'ingenio' of sugars [sugar-mill] and brought
from these aboard about two or three hundred sugar-loaves
for their provision and composition with the Spaniards for 20
oxen not to burn their sugar mills, which oxen they received
and so departed. From thence they sailed to La Yaguana upon
the same island of Hispaniola, and went in with their frigates,
and there took a frigate of 30 or 40 tons laden with bread of
that country, called cassava, dry beef and tallow and thereof
they took some part for their provision and burned the rest,
and then countered with about two hundred horsemen and
repulsed back and some others in fight, and thereupon they
rowed to a place called 'Aguanovo' not far off and burned the
town, being a poor place inhabited by Moors and Spaniards
where they had nothing but hens and victuals to his knowledge. From thence they rowed to their ships at Goave and by
consent brought them about to La Yaguana where they landed
before and had the repulse, and landed again all their force
being about 150 men, and marched up to the town and were
encountered with, and at last came to a parley with the
Spaniards to have them ransome the town, which they would
not for that they said they were sworn to the King, and thereupon this 'examinate' and his company entered the town and
found the Spaniards had carried all that ever they had into the
woods, and so burned the town not getting any pillage there

to his knowledge, and then marched back to their ships and sailed away and directed their course into the Bay of Honduras where under a town of garrison called Trujillo they chased a ship under the walls of the town and took the same being laden with hides and two or three chests of indigo, seven jars of balsam, four bolts of velvet and two or three bolts of damask and a piece of red cloth, which ship with their lading they carried off into the sea and 'fett' of two empty frigates from the shore which they carried along with them, and entered further into the bay to a place called Puerto de Caballos, where they took a frigate laden with a thousand hides, as it was said, and also two or three empty frigates, and forthwith went ashore and took the town, the people being fled with most of their substance as it appeared. Notwithstanding, they got there about 28 jars of quicksilver half full or thereabouts, six or seven tons of iron and some pillage which was put into the prize of hides taken before. Also this examinate got in ready money £12, and Captain Newport and Captain Kedgell got a small quantity of plate there, and all the company had pillage of apparel amongst them, how much he knoweth not. From thence they sailed away and overtook a great ship of 200 tons which came from the port of Caballos, being laden with hides, the company whereof fired themselves and shifted themselves ashore. Notwithstanding this, examinate and his company adventured to quench the fire and with much travail and adventure slaked the fire and recovered out of the same about 12 or 13 hundred hides and eight fardels of indigo wherewith they filled up the other two prizes taken before and sailed away, and being bound to water, this examinate in a storm lost the prizes, and by appointment of Captain Newport went to seek them and found them in the bay, and so this examinate in the *Margaret* and Captain Kedgell in the *Virgin* came away for England.[10]

In March 1593, homeward bound from India, the Portuguese carrack *Santo Alberto* was wrecked on the coast of Natal.

94

Such was the loss of this great ship *Santo Alberto* and such were the circumstances of its shipwreck, caused, not by the storms of the Cape of Good Hope (for she was lost before reaching it, in favourable weather), but by careening and over-loading, through which this great ship and many others lie buried in the depths of the sea. Both these defects are due to the covetousness of the contractors and navigators. The contractors, because it costs much less to careen a ship than to lay her aground, are delighted with the Italian invention [heaving the ship down on one side by strong purchase to her masts from a hulk or pontoon in the water], which though it is all right in the Levant, where galleys can ride out storms and tempests, and where one can put into port every eight days, in this our ocean its use is one of the causes of the loss of these great ships.

For besides the rotting of the timber caused by being so long in the sea (even though cut at the proper season), it is unduly strained when the hull is heeled over for careening, with the great weight of such huge carracks. When they are caulked in this way they do not take the oakum properly, being damp and badly dried ... This evil is increased by the artificers who undertake the work, or who do it under contract (which is a prejudicial system in any case). These, to save time when they cannot save on materials, never finish any-thing properly ...

The navigators are no less blameworthy for this loss, although it affects them still more closely, since they adventure their lives in the ship. They lade her without properly distributing the cargo, putting lighter merchandise in the lower part of the hold and the heavier on top, whereas it should be the other way around. To enrich themselves quickly, they overload the ship in such a way that they exceed her limited cargo capacity, which necessarily makes it impossible to steer her properly; and if any of the aforesaid mishaps occur, she opens at the seams and goes down.[11]

In this same year Richard Hawkins, son of Sir John, made a voyage to the South Sea in his ship the *Dainty*, only to finish a prisoner of Spain. To rustle up his crew he had to search all the lodging-houses and taverns.

> For some would be ever taking their leave and never depart. Some drink themselves so drunk that, except they were carried aboard, they of themselves were not able to go one step. Others, knowing the necessity of the time, feigned themselves sick; others to be indebted to their hosts, and forced me to ransome them – one his chest, another his sword, another his shirts, another his card and instruments for sea. And others, to benefit themselves of the imprest given them, absented themselves, making a lewd living in deceiving all whose money they could lay hold of, which is a scandal too rife amongst our seamen.[12]

Once at sea, he aimed at different behaviour.

> So with a general consent of all our company, it was ordained that in every ship there should be a 'palmer of ferula' [cane] which should be in the keeping of him who was taken with an oath; and that he who had the palmer should give to every other that he took swearing, in the palm of his hand, a palmada with it, and the ferula. And whosoever at the time of evening or morning prayer was found to have the palmer should have three blows given him by the captain or master; and that he should be still bound to free himself by taking another or else to run in danger of continuing the penalty: which executed, few days reformed the vice; so that in three days together was not one oath heard to be sworn. This brought both ferulas and swearing out of use.[13]

That he was more than ordinarily enlightened, Hawkins makes abundantly clear.

> Being betwixt three or four degrees of the equinoctial line, my company within a few days began to fall sick of a disease which seamen are wont to call the scurvy, and seemeth to be a kind of dropsy ... It bringeth with it a great desire to drink , and causeth a general swelling of all parts of the body,

especially the legs and gums, and many times the teeth fall out of the jaws without pain ... in twenty years, since that I have used the sea, I dare take upon me to give account of ten thousand men consumed with this disease ... That which I have seen most fruitful for this sickness, is sour oranges and lemons, and a water which amongst others (for my particular provision) I carried to the sea, called Dr Stevens his water, of which, for that his virtue was not then well known unto me, I carried but little, and it took end quickly, but gave health to those that used it ... Our fresh water failed us many days before we saw the shore, by reason of our long navigation without touching land and the excessive drinking of the sick and diseased, which could not be excused. Yet with an invention I had in my ship, I easily drew out of the water of the sea sufficient quantity of fresh water to sustain my people, with little expense of fuel, for with four billets I stilled a hogshead of water, and therewith dressed the meat for the sick and whole. The water so distilled we found to be wholesome and nourishing. [In the neighbourhood of St Anna Island] we found great store of the herb purslane, which boiled and made into salad, with oil and vinegar, refreshed the sick stomachs and gave appetites.[14]

There were other hazards on such a voyage.

Misplaced ridicule has at times been directed against Elizabethan and later sea-captains because of the instructions which some of them gave regarding urine tubs. In addition to a 'necessary seat' in the beak-head for the men and the galley aft for the officers, these tubs were placed between the decks, and the orders were that they must be left filled for use in the event of fire. Critics have suggested that these orders imply a belief that it was more reasonable to retain this liquid where it might put out a fire than to carry it to the upper deck, lower the bucket over the side, refill it with sea-water, and take it to a place where it could now no longer serve its primary purpose.[15]

In view of the remarks made by others about the poor quality of food at sea it is worth recalling that after entering the Pacific Ocean Hawkins noted,

> Here our beef began to take end, and was then as good as the day we departed from England; it was preserved in pickle, which, though it be more chargeable, yet the profit payeth the charge, in that it is made more durable, contrary to the opinion of many, which hold it impossible that beef should be kept good passing the equinoctial line.[16]

Drink, rather than food, was his enemy.

> ... the enemy I feared not so much as the wine, which, notwithstanding all the diligence and prevention I could use day and night, overthrew many of my people. A foul fault, because too common amongst seamen, and deserveth some rigorous punishment, with severity to be executed, for it hath been, and is daily, the destruction of many good enterprises amidst their best hopes.[17]

In 1594–95 Robert Dudley, 'afterward styled Earl of Warwick and Leicester and Duke of Northumberland', made the earliest recorded English attempt to occupy Trinidad. Looking for gold, he admitted that 'all is not gold that glistereth', and Captain Wyatt, who was with him, provides another description of bad weather.

> That night the wind began to show his force on us, driving us back again to Palma, where I think we were haunted with some devilish witches, or at least with some sea devils; for being there we were brought into such a labyrinth of surpassing troubles that to show the horrors thereof I shall rather want words of efficacy than matters defective. Such they were that those which had been seamen some 30, some 40 years, did never see the like. Such they were that those islanders which were fourscore years of age did never hear the like. And such they were that I beseech Christ we never endure the like.

Neither do I think that ever any suffered the like without either detriment of goods, spoil of tacklings, loss of men or overwhelming of all, sometimes having such dreadful flashes of fire that, although we might account it midnight by the computation of time, yet might we compare it to midday for the brightness of the air by the lightning which seemed to fire the very seas round about us, sometimes terrible thunders, other times both dark and dirty fogs, stinking and noisome mists, continuing thus some eight days together, that numberless were the storms we suffered, innumerable were the dangers we feared, but most infinite were the calamities we were subject unto.[18]

In 1595, the year in which Raleigh discovered Guyana, Drake and Hawkins sailed on their last expedition.

Provided by the queen with six ships, and having collected twenty-one other vessels, Sir Francis Drake and Sir John Hawkins sailed for the West Indies from Plymouth on August 28, 1595. They had manned them with two thousand five hundred mariners, and the Barber-Surgeons Company had provided them with a chief surgeon, James Wood, and assistant surgeons. Their plans had been carefully made and nothing that could be foreseen had been left to chance: they had paid out money to 'chirurgions in her majestys ships ... above their wages for the supplyinge of the severall chests before their goinge to sea'; they had provided 'two other spare chests of chirurgery carried for the relief of the whole fleet,' and had then furnished two more chests with 'provitions for phisicke and chirurgery' at the immense cost of £33 16s 2d each, as well as 'sundry other drugs'; they laid in a stock of spare apparel for the soldiers and sailors, including shoes and stockings, and they consulted Mr Hugh Platt (1552–1608) on the subject of their water supply and stores, recognising as they did that success or failure might be decided by these often neglected items. Long afterwards, when Platt had been knighted by King James, Sir Hugh used

the names of Drake and Hawkins to lend weight to advertise-
ments. In the broadsheet which he had printed he offered
'Certaine Philosophical Preparation of Foode and Beverage
for Seamen, in their long voyages.'

However much this may savour of quackery, Platt made
some sensible suggestions to Drake and Hawkins, furnishing
them with a 'cheape, fresh and lasting victuall, called by the
name of Macaroni amongst the Italians', which would be useful when fresh food ran out. He also advised them to carry
their essences of spices and flowers, used for flavouring
syrups, juleps and conserves, not in the form of essential oils,
which might grow mouldy, but as powders. All this was a
great advance on the normal victualling of a ship. The very
detailed accounts 'for the setting forth of a ship in the service
of the queens majesty ... ' in January 1590 show only fish,
dried and fresh; bacon; cheese; butter; peas; beer; vinegar; oil;
hops; bread; and biscuit in large quantities: the seaman's opinion of the dried fish is conveyed in the name 'Poore John', by
which it was commonly known among them.

But in spite of all precautions, of all Platt's claims, Sir John
Hawkins fell sick at the Virgin Islands on November 6, and,
after an illness of six days, died at San Juan de Puerto Rico.
The raiders sailed off Curacao, attacking where they could.
When they landed they took surgeons with them, but once
again it was not wounds that they had to fear. Sickness
increased in the fleet, and many officers and men were dying.
Two days after Christmas they reached the Nombre de Dios
river, and on December 31 they attacked and burned the port.
It was here, on January 15, 1596, that Drake first began to
keep to his cabin in the flagship *Garland*. He lingered for a
fortnight, but the dysentery slowly gained on him, and on
January 28 they wrote: 'at 4 of the clocke in the morning our
Generall sir Francis Drake departed this life, having bene
extremely sicke of the fluxe, which began the night before to
stop on him'. That day they attacked Puerto Bello and buried
Drake at sea. The expedition had now not only lost its two

leaders but its chief surgeon, for James Wood had died in the *Garland* not many hours before the admiral. At a muster on February 6, five hundred men were found to have died, and of the two thousand survivors, a great many were sick. Ships were being sunk, and their crews removed to man others. In May they sailed for home, but the account was not yet closed: when Thomas Midleton, one of the Treasurers for the Navy, made a final estimate of the cost of the expedition, one of the items was a bill for 'Diet & physick of sundry sick persons with the burial of divers of them at Plymouth' after the voyage ended.[19]

Dr Layfield, the Earl of Cumberland's chaplain, left an account of the disease which killed Drake and which brought the Earl's expedition of eleven ships in the same year to a disastrous end.

It was an extreme looseness of the body, which within a few days would grow into a flux of blood, sometimes in the beginning with a hot ague, but always in the end by an extreme debility and waste of spirits: so that some two days before death, the arms and legs of the sick would be wonderful cold. And that was held for a certain sign of near departure. This sickness usually within few days (for it was very extreme to the number of sixty, eighty and an hundred stools in an artificial day) brought a languishing weakness over all the body, so that one man's sickness (if he were of any note) commonly kept two from doing duties. And this was it, which rather than the number already dead, made his Lordship first think of quitting the place. For though towards the beginning of July there were not much above two hundred dead, yet was there twice as many sick, and there was no great hope to recover most of them. The ships were left weakly manned, for when we landed we landed about a thousand men, of which the greater part was dead or made unserviceable for the present. There were above four hundred reported dead when his Lordship left the Town [of Puerto Rico], and surely as many so sick, that most of them would not bring themselves aboard, before his Lordship left the place.[20]

Drake himself, in true Elizabethan fashion, is said to have been philosophic on his deathbed, remarking, 'It matters not man! God hath many things in store for us'.[21]

CHAPTER 9

The Gorgeous East

1596–1617

By the beginning of the seventeenth century the world's oceans, Australian waters apart, were fairly well charted, and Dutch, English and French seafarers were encroaching seriously upon all that had once been the preserve of the Spanish and Portuguese. Oceanic trade by this time was largely organised by 'chartered companies', groups of merchants who were given monopolistic privileges so that they might have the resources better to protect their commerce. The Dutch and English East India Companies were the most powerful of these. However, it was with the Spanish and Portuguese that Francesco Carletti, a Florentine trader, went round the world between 1594 and 1602. Here he describes the famous Spanish trading route on that pacific ocean from Acapulco to Manila.

Under license that the viceroy gave us ... we went back with our silver [from the city of Mexico] to the port of Acapulco, where two ships were being readied for the voyage. As soon as we arrived there, we embarked. And on the twenty-fifth of the month of March, 1596, we unfurled our sails to the wind and set our route to the west. We furrowed that immensity of sea, which is more than six thousand miles of open water, proceeding always along the same latitude of from fourteen to fifteen degrees in a direct line north from the equinoctial line – so that if our ship had left a mark where it had passed and made its way, it would be possible to see a spherical semicircle over the fourth part and more of the entire world. And in prosperous and very happy navigation we made it without ever moving the sails or slackening the yards, and always with a following wind. This is always the same wind, which smoothly and continuously blows through all the Torrid Zone from the east towards the west, so that it would not be possible to return along that same parallel. And therefore it is necessary to move out of the tropics in order to find southerly or austral winds that will propel you toward the east. That return journey is made in six months, the outward one in a little more than two, as we made it.[1]

In Nagasaki, Carletti describes 'sailortown'.

And it often happens that a girl's father or mother will discuss her price before she is married, this with no shame on anyone's part, selling her easily for money, but driven by great poverty, which indeed is very great throughout all that area, and which explains why they enter into every sort of venereal dishonour in such a manner and in such diverse and unheard-of ways that it seems impossible.

The Portuguese are good witnesses of this, especially those who come from China – that is, from the island of Macao – each year with one of their ships laden with silk either woven or to be woven, with pepper and cloves, which are used in dyestuffs, and with other sorts of merchandise to be sold in the region, for which they take silver in exchange, making their bargains in the city and port of Nagasaki, where they stay eight or nine months, it taking that long to dispose of the aforementioned goods. To these Portuguese, as soon as they have arrived, come the agents of the women, looking them up in houses in which they are lodging for that length of time. And they ask them if they want to buy a virgin girl or have her in some other way that would please them more, and this for the time that they will be there, or just to have her some nights or days or months or hours. And they make arrangements with them.

Or, sometimes, the agreement is made with the parents, they being paid the price. And if the men want them they bring the girls to their houses to be seen for the first time; or, sometimes, the men go to their houses to see the girls. Many of the Portuguese find this Land of Cockaigne much to their liking – and, what is better, it costs them but little ... Nor do [the girls] for having thus been used lose the occasion of marrying. But many of them would never be able to marry if they did not acquire a dowry in this way, ... [2]

From Macao, Carletti embarked for Goa.

In that season of the year 1559 two Portuguese ships were being loaded which had reached Macao from Goa, as takes place each year. They were commanded by a Portuguese captain, pilot, coxswain, mate, and other officers, but were manned by Arab, Indian, Turkish, and Bengali sailors, who gladly serve for so much per month, taking care of their own expenses under the rule of their head man, who commands them and whom they call their *saranghi*, and who also belongs to one of the aforementioned nations. They make their understandings with him, recognise and obey him, so that even the Portuguese captain, the master and pilot of the ship, is commanded by the *saranghi*.

And they all embark with their wives or concubines, which is a sight no less indecent than filthy and unseemly, and which causes such confusions as it is impossible to make clear. This in addition to the discomfort of the whole ship, and particularly of the passengers, to whom this evil example causes no little scandal, and especially to new Christians, who see this offense done to God while they are navigating at such peril through those seas and who so recently have learned that one should behave otherwise. But the need in that region for men ready for that activity forces the owners of those ships to make use of these men and to permit them these disgraceful things, they being unable to do anything else.[3]

The English East India Company was formed in 1600 and in that year Sir James Lancaster – the James Lancaster whose 1592-93 expedition had proved unprofitable – sailed to the Indies in command of the *Dragon* (or *Red Dragon*, 600 tons), *Hector* (300 tons), *Ascension* (260 tons), *Susan* (240 tons) and *Guest* (130 tons).

> Thus following on our course, the first of August we came into the height of thirty degrees south of the line, at which time we met the south-west wind, to the great comfort of all our people. For, by this time, very many of our men were fallen sick of the scurvy in all our ships, and unless it were in the general's ship only, the other three were so weak of men that they could hardly handle the sails. This wind held fair till we came within two hundred and fifty leagues of the Cape of Good Hope, then came clean contrary against us to the east, and so held some fifteen or sixteen days, to the great discomfort of our men. For now the few whole men we had began to fall sick, so that our weakness of men was so great that in some of the ships the merchants took their turns at the helm, and went into the top to take in the topsails, as the common mariners did ... And the reason why the general's men stood better in health than the men of other ships was this: he brought to sea with him certain bottles of the juice of lemons, which he gave to each one as long as it would last, three spoonfuls every morning fasting not suffering them to eat anything after it till noon. This juice worketh much better if the party keep on a short diet, and wholly refrain salt meat, which salt meat and long being at sea is the only cause of the breeding of this disease. By this means the general cured many of his men, and preserved the rest, so that in his ship (having double of men that was in the rest of the ships) he had not so many sick, nor lost so many as they did, which was the mercy of God to us all.[4]

Lancaster was wiser than Jean Mocquet, who voyaged to Africa and the East and West Indies in 1601.

I had that troublesome and dangerous malady 'lovende', which the Portuguese call 'berber' and the Dutch 'scorbut'. It rotted all my gums, which gave out a black and putrid blood. My knee joints were so swollen that I could not extend my muscles. My thighs and lower legs were black and gangrenous, and I was forced to use my knife each day to cut the flesh in order to release this black and foul blood. I also used my knife on my gums, which were livid and growing over my teeth. I went on deck each day, and over the bulwarks, clinging to the ropes, and holding a little mirror before me in my hand to see where it was necessary to cut. Then, when I had cut away this dead flesh and caused much black blood to flow, I rinsed my mouth and teeth with my urine, rubbing them very hard. But even with such treatment there was as much [swelling] again each day, and sometimes even more. And the unfortunate thing was that I could not eat, desiring more to swallow than to chew, because of my great suffering in this trying malady. Many of our people died of it every day, and we saw bodies being thrown into the sea constantly, three or four at a time. For the most part they died with no aid given them, expiring behind some case or chest, their eyes and the soles of their feet gnawed away by rats. Others were found dead in their bunks after having been bled. Moving their arms [in pain] they thus caused the vein to open again, and, their blood flowing out again, they passed into an intensely feverish stupor, dying with no one to help them. All that could be heard were cries of intense thirst and dryness. For very often, after having received their ration of water, which might be about a half-pint to a quart, they would place it close at hand to drink when thirst seized them, whereupon their companions, either those close at hand or those farther away, would come and snatch the poor dole of water from the miserable sick wretches when they were asleep or had their backs turned. And also, in the 'tween decks and in other dark places they struck at each other and fought without seeing their opponents, when they caught them stealing. And so, very often, thus deprived of water, they died miserably for the lack of a few drops. There was no one willing to give a little water to save life, no, not a father his son nor a brother his brother, so great did the desire to cling to life by drinking drive each to think of himself alone. Often did I find myself thus cheated and deprived of my ration, but I consoled myself with many another in the same evil case as myself. This was also why I dared not sleep too soundly, and why I put my ration of water in a place where none could seize it easily without touching me. Among us was the greatest confusion and chaos imaginable, because of the great number of men of every class who were there, vomiting, some here, some there, relieving themselves on each other. On every side were heard only the cries of those assailed by thirst, hunger and pain cursing the hour when they had come aboard, and calling down maledictions even on their fathers and mothers, so that they appeared bereft of reason.⁵

It is related of King James I that when, by a speedy voyage, a pineapple was brought from America in great perfection and he tasted it, he observed that 'it was a fruit too delicious for a subject to taste of'. His accession to the throne did the British seafarer no good.

The Chatham Chest [the fund for the relief of sick and aged mariners set up by Drake, Hawkins and others in 1590], which had begun to derive no trivial income from the sixpences of sailors whose numbers had greatly increased, became [Sir Robert] Mansel's own petty-cash box. He was in the happy position, when he himself went sailing, of having to approve his own lavish expense claim.⁶

Mansel had been appointed Treasurer of the Navy in 1604, a year or two before the redoubtable Captain John Smith arrived in Chesapeake Bay and had his life saved by the eleven-year old Pocahontas. Out exploring beyond the Potomac river in 1608,

... the eight newcomers of Smith's twelve men were sick. Only the seasoned [Jamestown] colonists (Nathaniel Powell, gentleman, soldiers Anas Todkill and Edward Pising, and Jonas Profit, sailor and fisherman) were able to help Smith with the barge. Small wonder it therefore is that they explored two of the rivers only superficially – without running across any Indians – and that they proceeded carefully, as anyone without a chart must do even today.

Crossing the bay somewhere above Bush River, the expedition unexpectedly 'encountered 7 or 8 canoes-full of Massawomekes', the redoubtable savages they had pretended to conquer before, who were prepared to assault the intruding barge.

Retreat being impossible, on account of the sick, Smith took the offensive and sailed right at them. Covering the deck with a tarpaulin to hide as well as to protect the incapacitated, Smith had the men's hats stuck up on sticks by the side of the barge, and stationed one man with two muskets between each pair of hats. The glint of the musket barrels, the mystery of the dark barge with perhaps no one but Smith himself (undoubtedly in full, shiny armour) visible aboveboard, and the inexorable advance of the strange white-sailed apparition unattended by human figures, was too much for the Massawomekes, brave as they were. They paddled for the shore But Smith pursued them until he anchored in shallow water 'right against them'. Then he beckoned for them to come on board ... two of the bravest braves paddled over, unarmed, to investigate. All the rest hovered in the background, waiting to see what would happen.

Somewhere on the barge, Smith received the daring emissaries (apparently without uncovering his sick bay), and presented them with a ball each. The gift being as unexpected as it was unusual, the rest of the Indians flocked up in a body. Trade ensued, and soon the English had acquired bear meat, venison, bearskins, fish, bows, arrows, clubs, and shields – the last-mentioned apparently of basketwork.[7]

Some sailors (including Smith) survived to die ashore. In 1609 James Beare, seafaring stepson of William Bourne, author for *A Regiment of the Sea*, died aged about sixty and his monument in Gravesend Church carried this epitaph:

> After much weary sailing, worthy Beare
> Arrived this quiet port and harbours here.
> As skilfully in honesty he brought
> His human vessel home, as he was thought
> Equal with any that by card or star
> Took out and brought again his bark from far.
> So let him rest in quiet ...[8]

Had Beare lived a year longer he could have read Sylvester Jourdain's *The Discovery of the Bermudas*, a sailor's book of memoirs which may have inspired Shakespeare to write *The Tempest*.

> ... a fantasy of the New World ... too full of the ether of poetry, and too many sided to be called a satire, yet Shakespeare, almost alone, saw the problem of American settlement in a detached light; and a spirit of humorous criticism runs riot in the lighter scenes. The drunken butler, accepting the worship and allegiance of Caliban, and swearing him in by making him kiss the bottle, is a fair representative of the idle dissolute men who were shipped to the Virginian colony. The situation of Miranda was perhaps suggested by the story of Virginia Dare, granddaughter of Captain John White, the first child born in America of English parents.[9]

It has been ably argued that Shakespeare may have gone to sea. Unlike any other song in his plays is the sailor's 'chanty' given to Stephano in *The Tempest*, which subsequently inspired W H Auden.

> The Master, the swabber, the boatswain, and I,
> The gunner and his mate,
> Loved Moll, Meg, and Marian, and Margery,

But none of us cared for Kate.
For she had a tongue with a tang,
Would cry to a sailor, Go hang!

She loved not the savour of tar nor of pitch,
Then to sea, boys, and let her go hang!

Hamlet and *Richard II* were both performed aboard Captain William Keeling's ship *Dragon* (or *Red Dragon*) around this time, and from the pages of his journal of a voyage to the East Indies in the years 1615–17 the crew come to life even more vividly than they do in the opening scene of *The Tempest*.

March 8, 1615 I ordered 30 stripes whipping to Luke a sailor for stealing a piece of fresh beef, the first I punished.

April 7 I sent my skiff [in mid-ocean to another ship] for Mr Boughton who intendeth to communicate with us upon Easter Day. I began to allow each mess a pottle [half a gallon] of water to drink by night ordering also the due expense of our lemon water to prevent the scurvy.

April 9 112 persons communicants feasting all our cheese in the *Dragon*, Mr Boughton also; I also allowed my company 2lb meal, 1lb currants and beer each mess extraordinary.

May 9 I made the variation 16.2 north-easting. Captain Harris came aboard me [still in mid-ocean] to let me know his beer was done. I fear some disorder of ill husbandry, I having yet spent but little.

June 5 About one this morning we spied the land; stood off 7 glasses [hours], then in again and anchored in the road of Soldania [Table Bay] about 10 this morning.

June 17 I dined with my Lord Ambassador aboard the *Lyon* who complained that the Surgeon had contemptuously answered one of my Lord's followers, who threatened to complain to his Lordship, that he cared not a fart for my Lord. I displaced the Surgeon though he denied it (yet answered touching my Lord peremptorily even to me) and took away his keys leaving them with my Lord, to be restored to him when he should submit to his Lordship.

July 2 The *Expedition's* fish being spent, I spared her 300 couple backalew [codfish]. I appointed our beverage at the mast, all jacks first taken away and a dish fastened thereto, whereat all men to drink to prevent waste.

July 22 I soon went ashore [in the Comoro Islands] where we saw cattle but could buy none; bought 300 lemons for two penny knives, nor find we yet any water.

October 11 I ducked White for striking Gravell ashore [in Surat]: one piece ordinance. We missed 7,000 small shot and 400lbs lead stolen and sold for toddy [palm wine]; whereupon I published in each ship that whosoever in such sort made away one more bullet should suffer 40 stripes with a whip upon the bare back.

April 30, 1616 I took Captain Harris and the best merchants and went to Court [in Achin], finding him [the King] sat within his 3rd Court well attended, begged the hulls of both our prizes when they were empty, and remitted all our customs here for these two ships now in harbour; only his exceeding welcome constrained us all to exceed the bounds of temperance in drinking, and the better to show how he favoured our nation he appointed two elephants to attend me at my house all the time of my stay there, gave me drink with his own hand, not usual, presented me with a kris or dagger, and for my more honour styled me Oran Caya Chuckee Hattee: which is the honourable man with the clear heart, ...

July 26 Will Bantack died of a 4 days calentura [a disease marked by delirium in which the victim imagined the sea to be green fields, into which he was impelled to leap; Bantack's was the thirty-sixth death on board].

October 9 I answered a Dutch ship come from the east side of Sumatra with 7 pieces, and Mr Coppindall's farewell 3 pieces.

We got an anchor aboard intending to set sail before day. The *Hozeander* came this day into the road who having lately shot 3 guns to John Davis [of Limehouse, master of the *Swan*] and by them by the gunner's negligence fired a budgebarrel of powder, hurt therewith many of her men, whereof 3 within 2 days died, 10 or 12 more being much burnt; the ship fired [caught fire] dangerously, her men in fear forsook her, Mr Munden her Master seeks to stay her base company from vainly fearful flight, but not prevailing, labours himself to quench the fired oakum of the seams. Mr John Skinner come happily aboard, who yet could not stay their cowardly flight till all her powder was gotten out of the ship at her gunroom port, then all returning soon quenched the fire without any manner of harm to the ship. Thus Mr Skinner reporteth and hereby the honourable Company take just occasion to prevent the like hazard and indeed too excessive expense of powder in their customary lavishness by prohibiting on their Commission (and that effectually by penalties) their such hazard and expense will not be amended, custom having there branded its omission with disgrace. Weak spirits have not the power of distinction twixt good and bad customs, wherein myself even against my wish was drawn to be very faulty. I shot 3 parting pieces to Mr Ball, 5 to the town, and 3 to Mr Skinner.

Keeling records sixty-two deaths among the *Dragon*'s company, but only one is attributed to scurvy. Homeward, the *Dragon* sailed in company with the *Expedition*. Both ships were crazed and leaky and short of provisions and sailcloth in the last weeks of the voyage. Of the shortage of sailcloth the master of the *Expedition* wrote,

> ... the original cause whereof proceedeth from the innumerable many rats which we have had in our ships all this voyage, for by them both sails and other provisions of the ships (besides private men's particulars) have been excessively spoiled ... It is almost incredible the noisomeness of that

vermin, who have been ready to eat us living (for they have bitten us in our sleeps), but some men that died this voyage in the nights, before morning have had their toes eaten quite off, and other parts of their bodies gnawed ... [10]

It was in this year, 1616, that Cape Horn was first rounded – by Willem Schouten, a Dutch navigator, who named it after Hoorn, his birthplace.

CHAPTER 10

A Larger Prison

1617–1642

'The world is itself but a larger prison, out of which some are daily selected for execution.' Thus commented Sir Walter Raleigh a few hours before his execution in 1618. Ships were small prisons, but with additional disadvantages. Raleigh had been a prime mover in establishing the first British settlements in North America. In 1620 William Bradford led the Pilgrims to New England in the *Mayflower*, and he made the following record of his voyage.

... according to the usual manner, many were afflicted with sea-sickness.

And I may not omit here a special work of God's Providence. There was a proud and very profane young man, one of the seamen, of a lusty able body, which made him the more haughty. He would always be condemning the poor people in their sickness, and cursing them daily with grievous execrations, and did not let to tell them that he hoped to help to cast half of them overboard before they came to their journey's end and to make merry with what they had. And, if he were by any gently reproved, he would curse and swear most bitterly.

But it pleased God before they came half seas over, to smite this young man with a grievous disease, of which he died in a desperate manner and so was himself the first that was thrown overboard. Thus his curses light on his own head; and it was an astonishment to all his fellows; for they noted it to be the just hand of God upon him.[1]

A year later the Portuguese carrack *Sao Joao Baptista* left Goa, where she had just been built, to have her rudder shot off by the Dutch in latitude 42°S. Here the Virgin Mary played her part.

While this [ie the making of a new rudder on deck] was being done, we expected hourly to go to the bottom, and had now no other hope than the salvation of our souls. The Religious who were passengers on board went about exhorting all the others to repent of their sins, making processions and scourging themselves nearly every day, nor was anyone else exempt therefrom, but rather they all joined in with many tears, both high and low alike. And in all these miseries we thought that it was a punishment from God that the enemy ships had separated from us, since it was an unprecedented thing that a dismasted and rudderless ship in such remote and stormy latitudes should be able to make any port at all. In which a miracle of the Virgin was manifestly displayed.[2]

In 1623 a British proclamation, not for the first, nor for the last time, made it clear that difficulties were encountered in raising men for the Crown's service.

We do straightly charge and command that no mariner or seafaring man absent, hide or withdraw himself from our service or prests, and that all such persons having our prest money given or tendered unto them, do dutifully and reverently receive the same and repair on board our ships at the times to them assigned, and thenceforth continue in our service as to the good duty of subjects appertaineth, and do not withdraw themselves or depart therefrom without special licence upon pain to incur the uttermost severity of our laws ... And we do further charge and straightly command that no person or persons that shall be trusted or employed for the pressing of any mariners do at any time, for favour, reward or other similar respect, forbear to prest the ablest and fittest men for such our service, or having prest them to discharge them again, or change them for persons less able and sufficient.[3]

A need for men called forth a need for instruction, supplied in 1627 by *A Sea Grammar* (a new and enlarged edition of a book published the previous year), written by the same Captain John Smith who had known Pocahontas. Here are four short passages from this work.

The Liar is to hold his place but for a week, and he that is first taken with a lie, every Monday is so proclaimed at the main mast by a general cry, A Liar, a Liar, a Liar. He is under the Swabber, and only to keep clean the beak head and chains [the ship's latrines].

The next is, to mess them four to a mess, and then give every mess a quarter can of beer and a basket of bread to stay their stomachs till the kettle be boiled, that they may first go to prayer, then to supper; and at six o'clock sing a psalm, say a prayer, and the Master with his side begins the watch. Then all the rest may do that what they will till midnight; and then his Mate with his larboard men, with a psalm and a prayer, relieves them till four in the morning. And so from eight to twelve each other, except some flaw of wind come – some storm or gust – or some accident that requires the help of all hands, which commonly, after such good cheer, in most voyages doth happen.

A consultation and direction in a sea fight, or how they bury their dead. 'Well, Master, the day is spent, the night draws on, let us consult. Surgeon, look to the wounded and wind up the slain, with each a weight or bullet at their heads and feet to make them sink, and give them three guns for their funerals. Swabber, make clean the ship. Purser, record their names. Watch, be vigilant to keep your berth to windward that we lose him not in the night. Gunners, sponge our ordnance. Soldiers, scour your pieces. Carpenters, about your leaks. Boatswain and the rest, repair the sails and shrouds, and

Cook, see you observe your directions against the morning watch. Boy!'

'Hullo, Master, hullo!'

'Is the kettle boiled?'

'Yeah, yeah.'

'Boatswain, call up the men to prayer and breakfast.'

'Boy, fetch my cellar of bottles. A health to you all, fore and aft, courage, my hearts, for a fresh charge!' *A preparation for a fresh charge.* 'Gunners, beat open the ports and out with your lower tier, and bring me from the weather side to the lee so many pieces as we have ports to bear upon him. Master, lay him aboard loufe for loufe. Midships men, see the tops and yards well manned, with stones, fire pots and brass balls to throw amongst them before we enter, or if we be put off, charge them with all your great and small shot. In the smoke let us enter them in the shrouds, and every squadron at his best advantage. So sound the drums and trumpets, and Saint George for England!'

The petty tally. Fine wheat flour, close and well packed; rice, currants, sugar, prunes, cinnamon, ginger, pepper, cloves, green ginger; oil, butter, Holland cheese or old cheese; wine vinegar, Canary sack, *aqua vitae*, the best wines, the best waters, the juice of lemons for the scurvy; white biscuits, oatmeal, gammons of bacon, dried neats' tongues, beef packed up in vinegar; legs of mutton, minced and stewed and close packed up with boiled suet or butter in earthen pots. To entertain strangers, marmalade, suckets [fruit preserves], almonds, comfits [sugar-preserved fruits or roots] and such like.

Some it may be will say I would have men rather to feast than fight; but I say, the want of those necessaries occasions the loss of more men than in any English fleet hath been slain since [15]88. For a man is ill or at the point of death, I would know whether a dish of buttered rice with a little cinnamon, ginger and sugar, a little minced meat or roast beef, a few stewed prunes, a root of green ginger, a flapjack, a can of fresh water brewed with a little cinnamon, ginger and sugar – be not better than a little poor John [hard dried cod], or salt fish with oil and mustard; or biscuit, butter, cheese or oatmeal pottage on fish days; or on flesh days, salt beef, pork and peas with six shillings beer.[4]

But Captain Smith's counsel was a counsel of perfection, honoured in the breach rather than in the performance, and rascally contractors and corrupt officials were not always combated as successfully as was the enemy. The following complaint, in one form or another, was heard for a further 300 years.

There were several parcels of ox, such as houghs, shins, shin-bones, marrow-bones, etc, thrown by and sold as not fit to be given to the seamen for meat, being most on end bones. These were, very providently, for the greater part cut and cast among the seamen's victuals. Thus in the case of pork, the cheeks, ears, feet, and other offal of the hog, that heretofore were saved and sold to the State's use, were by these good husbands thrown in, not over and above, but as part of the men's allowance, and such was their influence, not only upon the commissioners of the Navy but also upon the committee of the Navy and the then commission of the Admiralty, that they had countenance in this pretended thrift: and hogs' cheeks and bones with little flesh on them were reported, nay justified by some to be good victualling ... , which among other things caused the frequent running away of seamen from the service, rather than to live upon bones and drag-ends, souse and hogs's feet, when they knew the State allowed them better meat, especially having no power to complain or if they had, no redress upon complaint of these and much worse than these grievances.[5]

It was little wonder that Captain Sir Ferdinando Gorges summarised the grievances of mariners in 1628 as follows.

1st   They say they are used like dogs, forced to keep aboard without being suffered to come ashore to refresh themselves.

2nd   That they have not the means to put clothes on their backs to defend themselves from cold or keep them in health, much less to relieve their poor wives and children.

3rd   That when they happen to fall sick they have not any allowance of fresh victuals to comfort them, or medicine to help recover them.

4th   That some of their sick fellows being put ashore in houses erected for them are suffered to perish for want of being looked unto, their toes and feet rotting from their bodies, and so smelling that none are able to come in the room where they are.

5th   That some provisions put aboard them is neither fit nor wholesome for men to live on.

6th   That therefore they had as lief be hanged as dealt with as they are.[6]

Three years later, Richard Braithwaite, who was born in the year of the Armada and had a son killed by pirates, provided a character sketch of the mariner of his time.

The breadth of an inch-board is betwixt him and drowning, yet he swears and drinks as deeply as if he were a fathom from it ...

He makes small or no choice of his pallet, he can sleep as well on a sack of pumice as on a pillow of down. He was never acquainted with much civility; the sea hath taught him other rhetoric. Compassion himself he could never much, and much less another. He has conditioned with the sea not to make him sick; and it is the best of his conceits to jeer at a queasy stomach. He is more active than contemplative, unless he turn astronomer, and that is only in cases of extremity. He is most constant to his shirt, and other his seldom washed linen. He has been so long acquainted with surge of the sea, as too long a calm disturbs him. He cannot speak low, the sea talks so loud. His advice is seldom taken in naval affairs, though his hand is strong, his headpiece is stupid. He is used therefore as a necessary instrument of action; for he can spin up a rope like a spider and down again like lightning ... His visage is unchangeable varnish; neither can wind pierce it, nor sun parch it ...[7]

In this same year, 1631, Captain Luke Fox gave his name to Fox Channel in Hudson Bay. Of this voyage he wrote,

The ship of His Majesty's was of my own choosing and the best for condition and quality, especially for this voyage, that the world could afford – of burden eighty tons, the number of men twenty, and two boys, and by all our cares was sheathed, cordaged, built and repaired, all things being made exactly ready against an appointed time. My greatest care was to have my men of godly conversation and such as their years – of time not exceeding thirty-five – had gained good experience, that I might thereby be the better assisted, especially by such as had been upon those frost-biting voyages, by which they were hardened for endurance, and could not so soon be dismayed by the sight of ice. For beardless younkers, I knew as many as could man the boat enough; and for all our dependence was upon God alone, for I had neither private ambition nor vain glory.

And all these things I had contractedly done by the Master, wardens and assistants of the Trinity House. For a lieutenant I had no use; but it grieved me much that I could not get one man that had been on the same voyage by whose counsel or discourse I might better have shunned the ice. I was victualled completely for eighteen months; but whether the baker, butcher, and other, were master of their arts, or professors or no, I know not, but this I am sure of, I had excellent fat beef, strong beer, good wheaten bread, good Iceland ling, butter and cheese of the best, admirable sack and *aqua-vitae*, peas, oatmeal, wheatmeal, oil, spice, sugar, fruit and rice; with 'chyrugerie' [medicines], as syrups, juleps, condites [preserves], 'trechisses', antidotes, balsams, gums, unguents, plasters, oils, potions, suppositories, and purging pills; and if I wanted instruments, my surgeon had enough. My carpenter was fitted from the thickest bolt to pump nail or tack. The gunner, from the 'sacor' to the pistol. The boatswain, from the cable to the sail twine. The steward and cook, from the cauldron to the spoon.

And for books, if I wanted any I was to blame, being bountifully furnished from the treasurer with money to provide me; especially for those of study there would be no leisure – nor was there, for I found work enough.[8]

Fox had little time for 'mathematical' seamen, and many of his contemporaries were like-minded, and also ruled their crews by the rod or worse. The disciplinary methods described below were written down in about 1635.

As for the punishment at the capstan, it is when a capstan bar being thrust through the hole of that called the barrel or burrell of it, the delinquent's arms are extended to the full length and so made fast unto the bar crosswise; having sometimes a basket with some great shot in it or some other weight hanging about his neck. In which posture he is to continue until he be made either to confess some plot or crime whereof he is pregnantly suspected, or that he have suffered such condign punishment as he is sentenced to undergo by the Captain or Martial Court.

The punishment at the bilboes is when a delinquent is put in irons, or in a kind of stocks made for that purpose, the which are more or less heavy and pinching, as the quality of the offence is found to be, upon good proof.

The ducking at the main yard-arm is when a malefactor, by having a rope fastened under his arms and about his middle and under his breech, is thus hoisted up to the end of the yard and from thence is violently let fall into the sea, sometimes twice, sometimes three several times one after the other; and if the offence be very foul, he is also drawn under the very keel of the ship, which is called keel-raking. And whilst he is thus under water a great gun is given fire unto, right over his head, the which is done as well to astonish him the more with the thunder thereof, which much troubles him, as to give warning unto all others to look out and to beware of his harms.

And these are the most common and ordinary ways of inflicting punishments upon delinquents at sea, and are practised, even in merchant ships, by the Masters who command there in chief ...

As for all petty pilferings and commissions of that kind, they are generally punished with the whip (the offender being to that purpose bound fast to the capstan): the waggery and idleness of the ship's boys is paid by the Boatswain with the rod. And commonly this execution is done upon the Monday mornings, and is so frequently in use that some mere seamen and sailors believe in good earnest that they shall not have a fair wind until the poor boys be duly brought to the chest; that is, be whipped every Monday morning.[9]

However, it has been pointed out that, although keelhauling was practised in the French, Dutch and Egyptian navies, no instance is cited in the British navy.[10]

To some extent – or so it was suggested by Captain Boteler who recorded the various punishments suffered by sailors – the British sailor brought troubles upon himself by the food he ate.

Our much, and indeed excessive feeding upon these salt meats at sea cannot but procure much unhealthiness and infection, and is questionless one main cause that our English are so subject to calentures, scarbots, and the like contagious diseases above all other nations; so that it were to be wished that we did more conform ourselves, if not to the Spanish and Italian nations, who live most upon rice-meal, oatmeal, 'biscake', figs, olives, oil, and the like, yet at the least to our neighbours the

Dutch, who content themselves with a far less proportion of flesh and fish than we do, and instead thereof do make it up with peas, beans, wheat, flour, butter, cheese and those white meats (as they are called).[11]

But to another mariner the cause of poor Jack's health problems was adulterated beer.

The brewers have gotten the art to sophisticate beer with broom instead of hops, and ashes instead of malt, and (to make it look more lively) to pickle it with salt water, so that whilst it is new, it shall seemingly be worthy of praise, but in one month was worse than stinking water ...

They that know how hot the Southern countries are in the summer time, and the bare allowance of a sailor, would not wish him to drink of stinking puddle to quench his thirst, or if they should they were doghearted men. Let me but ask you why our men are more subject to the small-pox, to calentures, and to that terror of sailors, the scurvy, than other nations? Look unto the Hollanders, who drink water, and thou shalt find them healthy and as fat as Hebe. On the other side, but cast an eye into our English ships, who drink beer, and they look as mortally as a death's head with a bone in's mouth: they swallow the cause in their drink.[12]

In 1636 Sir Henry Mervyn wrote to the Board of the Admiralty (much as Lord Howard had written some fifty years earlier),

May it please your Lordships. The miserable condition of our poor mariners, who in the extremity of this cold tempestuous weather for want of clothing fall down daily into desperate sickness, inasmuch as I am forced to discharge more men by reason of their weakness than we can again supply ourselves withal from ships passing by, make me presume in their behalfs to be an humble suitor to your Lordships that you will be pleased to order £400 or £500 to be sent down for their relief, for on my credit the most part of them are barefooted, without stockings and scarcely rags to hide their skin. If your Lordships please have compassion on them in this way, I will, if your Lordships please, be accountant for the disbursement thereof ... Some clothes are here, but so unserviceable and deceitful, and the prices so unconscionable by reason of the fees paid to the clerks, pursers and others who send them and stop the moneys at the pay-days due for them little less than four shillings in the pound, which so raiseth the price of the clothes that the poor men had rather starve than buy them.[13]

CHAPTER 11

The Professionals

1642–1669

Between 1652 and 1674 the British fought three wars at sea against the Dutch and won them all. These wars greatly strengthened Britain's mercantile marine and enhanced her trade. Before and between these wars, however, it was not unknown for British seafarers to serve in Dutch ships; indeed sailors have ever been a cosmopolitan breed.

One such sailor was Edward Coxere, who eventually became a Quaker. A simple merchant seaman who made a living at sea as best he could, Coxere was born at Dover in 1633 and died at Scarborough in 1694. His adventures began round about 1650 when he came ashore in Deal from a Dutch vessel.

Though I was ashore, I was not safe because of the press, neither did I dare speak English. This kind Dutch skipper was so much my friend that he went with me to be my interpreter to hire a horse for me, lest in speaking English I might be discovered.

When done, I mounted and rode to Dover. I had a suit of clothes Dutch fashion, a cap buttoned up before, a pair of Spanish shoes, that when I came riding down James's Street I met with some soldiers who, I supposed, were pressing, that said, looking on me 'See to the Fleming a-horseback'. I kept forward to the Market, where I alighted. A boy took my horse and asked whether I would carry the horse back again. I was not willing to speak English. Old Robert Gallant, standing by, bid the boy take away the horse, for the Fleming had done with her. I went forward to old Michael Dehases, a Dutch merchant who lived by Leopoldus, to whom I had a letter from our skipper, he being something concerned in the ship; also I gave him an account of our misfortune. I spoke to him in Dutch, for I could express myself very readily in Dutch, for when I spoke English I was taken for a Dutchman. After I had given him an account of what I had to say, I took my leave of him in Dutch. He asked me where I was going. I told him 'Home'. With that he wondered, he looking on me to be a Dutchman. 'Home?' says he, 'Where is that?' I answered, 'At the Wheatsheaf.' 'Why!' says he, 'Are you the son there?' 'Yes', said I. 'Stay!' says he, 'I will take my cloak and go with you.'[1]

A couple of years later Coxere shipped out for the good wages of 43 shillings per month in the ship *Christopher*, laden with red herrings, and was caught in a storm in the Channel.

We were very badly fitted with an old vessel and materials, as sails and rigging, as also a drunken master, for in the night our mainsail blew to pieces, our blocks fell down about our ears, the ropes and strops being rotten, so that we were in a very great strait.

The master lay then drunk in his cabin and did not turn out. I bid the boy tell him the sail was blown away. He said he could not help it, but lay still when we were in a perishing condition in all appearance, the storm being then so violent. We through God's providence, without the help of our brandy-drinking master, kept from suffering shipwreck and being whelmed up in raging seas; this being in the night time, in the morning we were by the storm drove on the French coast near Guernsey. The master then turns out and, finding us in a strait without a mainsail, orders us to get the main topsail down. I and one more went up and got it down with no small difficulty, we being in such a tottered condition, our ropes so bad, and the tumbling of the vessel, that they below still looked when I should a been thrown over board, being out at the leeward arm. The meanwhile our master sat down at the cabin door with a stone bottle of brandy between his legs to give us a dram when we came down; but a fortunate sea, as I may call it, hove him and the bottle to leeward and broke it to pieces. So then for want of brandy our master was kept sober, so that then we had some help of him, for he was able enough when sober.[2]

Poor jack, however, had more to put up with than drunken shipmasters, the press-gang and enemies of the state.

At last a French man-of-war met with us and commanded us to put out our boat. That done, the master, myself, and one more went on board, where we were presently stripped of our clothes.

They took our boat and went aboard of our vessel, where they took our bed-sacks and filled them out of a dry vat of cloves we had on board and took such clothes we had and what they pleased, and then sent us on board of our vessel again. This they did though we were bound for France and had no wars neither. When we came aboard, we found our clothes gone, so that we had no more but what they left on our backs, a waistcoat and drawers or breeches, in the cold winter time. We were forced to take it as patiently as we could, to endure the weather and to pump or sink. Our master, having got some drink in his head, must needs fire a gun on parting, when they had robbed us, as if they had been our friends; which I did oppose. But that powder we had the Frenchman in rummaging had shattered, that when the gun was fired the powder took fire and blew away Edward Moor's beard and hair and burnt his hands, that his nails were like lantern-horns. I undertook to be his surgeon, to 'noint him with tallow candle, and tied his hands up in rags for about eight days' time, having no other salve.[3]

Worse still was to follow. Two years after his marriage in 1655, Coxere, aboard a vessel laden with currants and muscatel, was captured by Turks from Tunis.

We being not able to hold the dispute with him any longer, was forced to yield to those unreasonable barbarians, to whom we became their slaves, a heart-breaking sorrow. Considering my condition, knowing what I had before worked for I was deprived of, and what little I had was mostly with me, so that I knew I had not wherewithal to release myself, so that I knew not but that I might a ended my days a slave under the hands of merciless men; then the consideration of my poor wife at home, who had such an exercise with my troubles before, and now big with the second child, and this falling the heaviest blow at last: the reader may judge something how it might be with me at that time.

As for the entertainment I met with when we yielded to them I shall a little relate something of it. They came aboard with their boat and fetched us out of our ship and, being come to the Turks' ship side, I was first that went over, being on the deck. The Turks took me between several of them in their arms, I not knowing what they intended, and turned my heels upward and carried me to the main-hatch, the hold being open – this being on the upper deck – let me drop with with my head downwards. A parcel, being between decks, catched me there and let me fall into the hold, so that if I had slipped their hands I might a been killed ... The reason why they served me so, as afterwards I understood, was because it is their manner that the first slave that comes over into a ship which never took prize before, they serve them so, being a customary thing with them.[4]

Put to work in Tunis, Coxere was imprisoned in Portofarino Castle at night, a prey to bugs and lice.

I remember one passage as we were in this unpleasant hole. In the night Henry Hutsen and myself were both chained together. He having occasion to go to the tubs to ease himself, which stood in the middle of the room where we lay thick on the ground about them, we being chained together so that if one were asleep and had occasion to ease himself we were forced to go together, being chained fast together (for we had shackles about our legs like horses, with an iron bolt through, to which the chain was fastened), this my consort sitting on the tub and I standing by waiting on him, there being slaves over our heads, who laid on boards, the room being so thronged below, that through the weight of them and their chains the beams broke, and down come rattling the poor slaves with their chains amongst us below. Our removing from the place we lay to the tubs escaped danger, so that the provocation he had to go to stool at that time freed us from the danger of being hurt. But the poor men which fell were so tumbled together that it was a considerable time before they could clear themselves, they having so many turns about each other with their chains.[5]

Rescued at last by the English, Coxere's troubles were not over. He eventually arrived home again in 1658.

This voyage I had been from England a year and half, in which time I had been a slave with the Turks, a prisoner with the Spaniards, as being taken by them, and came home only my clothes to my back to my poor wife, but poor and penniless yet glad to see each other in health again after these troubles. My son Robert died whilst I was a slave, and Elizabeth was born. I was pitied by many, but counted fortunate. At this time my wife did begin to keep shop, there being a necessity for something to be done for a livelihood.[6]

But Coxere went back to sea the following spring – to load dried cod.

To perform this voyage to Newfoundland as chief mate, having lost all that I had before, I was forced to borrow fifteen pounds to fit myself with books, instruments, clothes, and a venture. I drove it so near that I made five pounds serve me for conveniences and ten pounds for a venture, which I laid out in

several sorts of commodities, which I thought would turn best to account, so that now I was fifteen pounds in debt. We had still wars with Spain, and we were bound for Newfoundland up into the Straits, that had we been taken by the Spaniards I had been undone again, and worse for my being in debt. We got well to Newfoundland, where that sort of goods I carried sold for good profit; hardly any goods exceeded it for the quantity as to profit. We sailed for the Straits when we [had] gotten our lading in of dried codfish, called poor Jack, which is the only commodity the land affords for merchandising, for they have a proverb sometimes used among them that –
If it were not for wood, water and fish,
Newfoundland would not be worth a rish [rush].

Having loaded with poor Jack, the ship sailed for the Mediterranean.

I sold my fish, which I bought in Newfoundland, well, and bought raisins cheap for eleven shillings a hundred, which in England sold for twenty-three shillings a hundred ...

We got well to London. We had been seven months or eight on the voyage. I had three pounds ten shillings per month, and with the returns of my venture this voyage proved very profitable to me, in which the Lord blessed my endeavours, though through much difficulty. I gained between fifty and sixty pounds. I soon paid my debts and had a stock against the next voyage of my own.[7]

It was in this year, 1659, that Edward Barlow – another professional sailor (and one who would have thoroughly understood the Anglo-Saxon sailor whose verses have been referred to in Chapter 3) – first went to sea. He was involved in the transport of Charles II back to England when the King was restored to his throne, Barlow's own cabin being 'much like to some gentleman's dog kennel', and the following year he made this typical but not unjustified comment:

Neither are ships and we poor seamen out of great danger of our lives in calms and fairest weather, for the least fire may set a ship on fire, many ships having been burnt by some careless man in smoking a pipe of tobacco; and in carelessness of the cook in not putting the fire well out at night, and of burning of a candle in a man's cabin, he falling asleep and forgetting to put it out; and by burning of brandy and other strong liquors; and in many other ways a ship is set alight, and when they are on fire, it is a hundred to one if that you put it out, everything being so pitchy and tarry that the least fire setteth it all in a flame; and also there is great danger of the powder, for the least spark with a hammer or anything else in the room where it is, or the snuff of a candle causeth all to be turned into a blast, and in a moment no hopes of any person's lives being saved from death in the twinkling of an eye.

And also many times a ship springeth a leak, so that all the pumps and inventions that they can make cannot keep her free from imminent danger. So that a man many times seeth death approaching on him as though one were going to suffer death for some foul act committed. So that I always said how happy were those men above us that lived at home in England and had the pleasures of the world to walk when and where they pleased, and all things at their wills, eating and drinking of the best, whilst we were suffering all manner of misery and extremities and only to keep them safe at home from foreign invasions and enemies. Yea, I always knew that the worst of prentices did live a far better life than I did, for they had Sundays and other holy days to rest upon and take their pleasure; but all days were alike to us, and many times it fell out that we had more work on a Sabbath day than we had on other days; and the hardships I endured made me think many times that I had better to have taken any other employment upon me than have come to sea; but I had always a mind to see strange countries and fashions, which made me bear these extremities with more patience.[8]

Describing his Christmas in Cadiz in that same year, he wrote,

So coming to 'Cales' the next day it was our Christmas Day and the first Christmas that I had ever had out of England, but not the last by a great many. We had but small Christmas cheer, not having Christmas pie or roast beef, or plum 'podich' and suchlike, I remembering that the poorest people in all England would have a bit of something that was good on such a day, and that many beggars would fare better than we did: for we had nothing but a little bit of Irish beef for four men, which had lain in pickle two or three years and was as rusty as the Devil, with a little stinking oil or butter, which was all colours of the rainbow, many men in England greasing their cartwheels with better and also we had not two or three days to play in and go where we would, as the worst of servants had in England, but as soon as we had ate our large dinner, which was done at three of four mouthfuls, we must work all the day afterward, and maybe a great part of the night, which made me many times to put in consideration what a hard task I had taken upon me for my lifetime.⁹

A different complaint was voiced in 1663.

... about four or five days afterward, having 'livered out all our goods, we were cleared from the ship, having been on our voyage one and twenty months, and we were paid about a week afterward, but when pay-day came, our commander and the owners of the ship would stop £3 from every man out of his wages for goods that had been damnified and spoilt in the ship, which they said the men in the ship were in fault of, for not stowing them better and not taking care enough of them.

And this is the comfort of your English seaman that they have many times when they come home of a voyage, after going with many a hungry belly and thirsty stomach, and many a stormy dark night with cold and wet coats, and hoping to receive what they have worked for with sweat and toil after venturing their lives amongst all manner of dangers, for to enrich others at home in all manner of pleasures and delights, wanting nothing that can please their senses; and in this manner are they recompensed, when the poor seamen are no more in the fault than the man that never saw a ship in all his life-time.[10]

In May 1666 the Dutch buccaneer Alexander Olivier Exquemelin, known in England as John Esquemeling, set sail from Le Havre in a French ship and, keeping close to the French coast to avoid the English, rounded the Pointe du Raz beyond Ushant.

Here, I shall not omit to mention the ceremony, which at this passage, and some other places, is used by the mariners, and by them called *Baptism*, although it may seem, either little to our purpose, or of no use. The master's mate clothed himself with a ridiculous sort of garment, that reached unto his feet, and on his head he put a suitable cap, which was made very burlesque. In his right hand he placed a naked wooden sword; and, in his left, a pot full of ink. His face horribly blacked with soot, and his neck adorned with a collar of many little pieces of wood. Being thus apparelled, he commanded to be called before him every one of them who had never passed that dangerous place before. And then causing them to kneel down in his presence, he made the sign of the Cross upon their foreheads with ink; and gave each one a stroke on the shoulders with his wooden sword. Meanwhile the standers-by did cast a bucket of water upon every man's head; and this was the conclusion of the ceremony. But, that being ended, every one of the baptised is obliged to give a bottle of brandy for his offering, placing it nigh the main mast, and without speaking a word; ... [11]

This was the year of the Great Fire of London, the English were at war with the Dutch, and Samuel Pepys was keeping his diary.

July 1 ... To the Tower several times, about the business of the pressed men, and late at it till twelve at night the shipping of them. But, Lord! how some poor women did cry; and in my life I never did see such natural expression of passion as I did here in some women's bewailing themselves, and running to every parcel of men that were brought, one after another, to look for their husbands, and wept over every vessel that went off, thinking that they might be there, and looking after the ship as far as ever they could by moonlight, that it grieved me to the heart to hear them.

July 10 Then to the office, the yard being very full of women (I believe about three hundred) coming to get money for their husbands and friends that are prisoners in Holland; and they lay clamouring and swearing and cursing us, that my wife and I were afeared to send a venison-pasty that we have for supper tonight to the cook's to be baked for fear of their offering violence to it ... I confess their cries were so sad for money, and laying down the condition of their families and their husbands, and what they have done and suffered for the King, and how ill they are used by us, and how well the Dutch [prisoners] are used here by the allowance of their masters, and what their husbands are offered to serve the Dutch abroad, that I do most heartily pity them, and was ready to cry to hear them.

October 31 ... And thus ends the month with an ill aspect, the business of the Navy standing wholly still. The seamen grow very rude, and everything out of order; commanders having no power over their seamen, but the seamen do what they please. Few stay on board, but all come running hither to town, and nobody can with justice blame them, we owing them so much money; and their families must starve if we do not give them money, or they procure it upon their tickets from some people that will trust them.

Of the press-gang – which often sought out merchant seamen before they had come ashore from a foreign voyage – Barlow has this to say in 1668.

It is a very bad thing for a poor seamen when he is pressed in this manner, for if he have wife and children he is not suffered to go to see them, nor to go and look after his wages, nor to take care of his venture but must leave it to the trust of one whom he knows not whether he will ever see it and to take up his wages for him. Many times the master of the ship payeth what he pleaseth when a man is pressed and not there to answer for himself; and some men having no friends or acquaintances to take care of them, then that poor man loseth all, which is a great loss and hindrance to a poor man who hath nothing but what he must get by hard fare and sore labour, His Majesty's ships taking pains to press poor men, but do not take care to see that they have their right which is due, or for which they have served, which maketh many poor men so unwilling to sail in His Majesty's ships, and many to abandon their country finding better entertainment in another.[12]

CHAPTER 12

Seaman and Surgeon

1669–1689

John Baltharpe has his unique place in maritime history as the only seaman to have published an account of a voyage in narrative verse, although John Masefield's *Dauber* comes near to being another, and Masefield, of course, was by far the better poet. Baltharpe's poem, though scarcely a work of art, describes with verve an expedition against Algiers when his ship, the *St David*, of about 685 tons, was part of the Mediterranean fleet. Ships of this size were found on only the longest sea routes, to India, the West Indies or the Levant, or, in time of war, in the service of the government, as the *St David* is here. The time is 1669–71 and, when Baltharpe goes a-pressing, he is on the side of authority, even though the naval rating is indistinguishable from the merchant seaman for another 200 years and more, except in the sense that he is a naval rating when the state is responsible for the payment of his wages.

> A seaman when he gets ashore
> In one day's time he spendeth more
> Than three months' short-allowance money.
> Perhaps he gets a Spanish coney;
> It may be not only in wine
> He drinks till he is almost blind –
> And then the Spaniard picks his pocket,
> If naught be there, he takes his jacket.[1]

It was January the third day
When towards Leghorn we sailed away.
Great talk there's now of Leghorn ladies –
Some swore that they would get them babies.
But 'stead of babies they did get
What they have hardly clawed off yet.[2]

Some at Leghorn they turned sick
Because clapt with French faggot stick,
Their greatest pain lay in their prick;
This all makes for the doctor's gains;
He with these men will not take pains
Except a bill under their hand
He hath some money to command.
In private to his cabin door
They come, and curse that pocky whore
And vow that they'll do so no more.
They sour faces make and cringe,
As you may see through the door hinge:
'Good Doctor oh I would not have
You give me more of that green salve;
It doth me torment very sore,
Therefore I pray give me no more'.[3]

Sir John he did appoint the Fleet
Him at Messina for to meet.
Three weeks we here at least did stay.
A market was on board each day,
Except on Sundays; then Sir John
Would cause them all for to begone.
All sorts of trade they brought aboard:
Silk stockings, brandy, wine they afford;
Some cabbages, some nuts, some figs,
Some Syracuse wine, some eggs.
When money's gone, they'll truck for bread;
No more needs now for to be said –

Old a drawers, old a waistcoat;
And so about the ship they trot;
Nay some, they'll truck even for old shoes –
There's naught so bad as they'll refuse.⁴

Though we belong unto the David, Saint,
For want of victuals we are now grown faint.
Our beef and pork is very scant –
I'm sure of weight one half it want.
Our bread is black and maggots in it crawl
That's all the fresh meat we are fed withal.⁵

To Naples that name famous city
We got the sixteenth day completely;
On seventeenth we practique get –
'Twas the best place we came to yet.
This place with plenty it is stored,
Bumboats on board when we were moored:
All things they brought what you could name,
And very cheap they sold the same.
Here each man did a dollar get,
But we did buy no lands with it;
Old trade it did proceed apace –
Some were half drunk for three days space.
The wine was cheap and very good,
It cheered our hearts and warmed our blood;
A quarter of a sheep a shilling
You might buy if you are willing.⁶

Such storm this voyage we never had,
Indeed 'twas weather very sad;
Two men were ducked at main-yard arm,
Bending new mainsail; yet no harm
They got that time as God would have it.
But they got in again, and both were saved!
Drank each a pint of wine, kept inside warm,
By means whereof the outside took no harm.⁷

And on April the second day
Into the Downs we got, I say;
Not one day's victuals was on board
When we came in, upon my word!
Our bread and cheese we had made even,
But we got more, thank unto Heaven –
For here provision we shan't want,
The same in England is not scant.
Pray God we may receive our pay,
When we get up, without delay.[8]

In 1672, shortly after Baltharpe's strictures on ship's doctors were written down, we find Edward Barlow, serving in merchant ships, writing on the same subject.

And the surgeons and doctors of physic in ships many times are very careless of a poor man in his sickness, their common phrase being to come to him and take him by the hand when they hear that he hath been sick two or three days thinking that is soon enough, and feeling his pulses when he his half dead, asking him when he was at stool, and how he feels himself and how he has slept and then giving him some of their medicines upon the point of a knife, which doeth as much good to him as a blow upon the pate with a stick.

And when he is dead they did not think that he had been so bad as he was nor so near his end. And when he is dead, he is quickly buried, saving his friends and acquaintance that trouble to go to the church and have his passing bell rung, nor to be at the charges of making his grave and his coffin, or to bid his friends and acquaintance to his burial or to buy wine or bread for them to drink or eat before they go to the church, and none of all this trouble but when he is dead to sew him up in an old blanket or piece of old canvas, and tie to his feet two or three cannon bullets, and so to heave him overboard, wishing his poor soul at rest, not having a minister to read over his grave, nor any other ceremonies but praying to God for the forgiveness of his sins, and there he hath a grave many times wide and long enough, being made meat for the fishes of the sea as well as for the worms on land.[9]

By this time in Holland the crimps had already established their trade of supplying crews to the Dutch East India Company, as the steward, Christopher Schweitzer, tells us in 1676.

These buyers and sellers of men are people that entice strangers to their houses, if they see that have but little money, or are in perfect want, or if they come of themselves through necessity, receive them, and provide them with meat, drink, and clothes plentifully, till the ships are ready to go, and the people embark; then each kidnapper brings his men, sometimes ten, twenty, thirty, to the East India House, and there gets them listed. Some days after this, he receives for each man, for his pains and charge, a note of 150 guldens, and two months ready pay, which the soldier or mariner, whatever he be, must earn out ...

These men, to entice strangers to go, make them believe strange stories of the Indies, promise them vast things, and are not ashamed to go so far as to put a hammer into their hands to knock diamonds out of the rocks they shall meet with.[10]

Schweitzer joined one of a fleet of five ships, the *Asia*.

There was in ours, the chief merchant, the master, the chaplain of the reformed religion, with his wife and four children, four steersmen, one book-keeper, five barbers and 'chirurgions', two mates, two stewards, two cooks, two gunners, four carpenters, three coopers, two sail-makers, two quartermasters, one sergeant, two corporals, two under-corporals, 150 soldiers, and 93 foremast-men, nine boys to swab the ship every day, and one boatswain; the whole number was 297 men.[11]

Some ten weeks later the ship was suffering bad weather near the equator.

While the tempestuous weather still lasted, the mate and his boy were catched together acting the abominable sin of sodomy. A council was held upon it, and sentence was given that they should be tied back to back (which was done by the boatswain) and tied in a sack and thrown alive into the sea. As the minister was doing his duty towards these malefactors, representing to them the heinousness of their crime and directing them to prepare for death, the boy, about 14 years of age, wept bitterly; but the mate, being an Italian about 40 years old, showed himself right ready to die, saying 'twas better he should be punished alone for his horrid sin than that the whole ship should suffer for his sake.[12]

However, the ship did suffer, losing sixty-three of those on board during the next ten days through sickness, including the chaplain and all four of his children. On 5th April 1676,

We had still a great many sick men, and not enough in health to be able to brace our main-sail, though the mortality ceased; so we were forced to make shift with our small sails. That day we caught with a hook one of the great fishes called sharks, that rowled and tossed about our ship. We designed to dress him, and refresh ourselves with it; but when we cut it open, we found in the belly of it our sergeant that we had thrown overboard, not yet digested. The sight of this so turned our stomachs that none could find in their heart to eat of the fish, so that we threw man and fish into the sea again ...

But I must not omit what happened to myself. As I fell ill and was in a swoon, he that looked after the sick took me for dead and fetched a new shirt out of my chest and was putting it on me; the sail-maker too was going to sew me up, and he handling me a little roughly, after all his pushing and tossing of me, I opened my eyes. Those that were about me were not a little startled; and said it was high time for me to open them for if I had winked a little longer, over I had gone. Our chief merchant gave me a glass of sack, which refreshed me very much.[13]

In 1678 a minister of the Church of England, the Reverend Henry Teonge, was rather luckier than the minister of the Dutch Reformed Church.

> Good Christmas Day. We got to prayers at 10, and the wind rose of such a sudden that I was forced (by the Captain's command) to conclude abruptly at the end of the Litany and we had no sermon. And soon after, by the carelessness of some, our barge at stern was almost sunk but recovered. We had not so great a dinner as was intended, for the whole fleet being in this harbour beef could not be got. Yet we had to dinner an excellent rice pudding in a great charger, a special piece of Martinmas English beef, and a neat's tongue, and good cabbage, a charger full of excellent fresh fish fried, a dozen of woodcocks in a pie, which cost 15d, a couple of good hens roasted, three sorts of cheese; and last of all, a great charger full of blue figs, almonds and raisins; and wine and punch galore, and a dozen English pippins.
>
> The wind so was so high all this night that we ever expected when it would have broke our cable or anchor. But the greatest loss we yet sustained was this: about 11 or 12 o'clock our honest Lieutenant, Mr Will New, died, and left a mournful ship's company behind him. Yesterday our Captain bought three Spanish hogs; the roughness of the weather made them so seasick that no man could forbear laughing to see them go reeling and spewing about the decks.[14]

Christopher Fryke was a German surgeon who served the Dutch East India Company both at sea and ashore in the Far East for nine years, from 1680 to 1689, though he recommended the English as better employers and commented that 'to those who are altogether strangers to the sea, the affliction we went in is altogether inconceivable'.[15]

He survived shipwreck in False Bay (Cape Hangklip), South Africa, to reach the East Indies where

we wished heartily to be ashore, and the more for the sake of
our sick. But we wanted more than a hundred miles sail to
the place we were to go to. But by God's assistance we
reached it, beyond our expectation, for by sun-setting a
sailor cried out, 'Land!' which caused a sudden joy amongst
us all; and the master straight presented him a ducat, or two
ricksdollars, two cheeses and a bottle of Canary, according to
custom.[16]

Off Bantam, in Java, half the Dutch fleet were given a little
'Dutch courage' and then, under the command of a member of the De Ruyter family, attacked over a hundred
native 'prawen'.

> Our Admiral de Ruyter judged himself strong enough to
> engage them; so having called a council, it was resolved to fall
> upon them. Upon this a gill of brandy (the best thing in the
> world to inspire courage into a Dutchman) was given to every
> one of them ... Those that were still coming up, and those that
> were in the prawen, we swept down like a swarm of bees, with
> our fire-pikes and other fire-arms, and hand grenades, into the
> sea; all that remained began then to provide for running off.
> But our prawen and light vessels followed them so close that
> they killed infinite numbers of them, and took up some that
> were fallen into the sea and made them prisoners, who were
> immediately hanged up altogether upon the said island. The
> sea all about us was pure blood, and we were all in a cloud of
> smoke though we had not fired one great gun. There were no
> less than two hundred and sixty of the enemy lay dead aboard
> my ship the *Europa*. The dead and wounded we threw one
> with another overboard, which caused a bitter outcry among
> those who were yet sensible or but slightly wounded. After
> this great victory our ships came all together again, and upon
> a review we found our loss to be two masters of ships, seven
> steersmen, eight officers, and about three hundred and eighty
> private soldiers, and seven hundred of our blacks. We lost two
> ships, the *Victor* and the *Ameland*, besides eighteen prawen,

three galliots and seven fire-ships; all which were burnt. But of
the enemy's ships, which were a hundred and twenty in number, there did not one single one escape; their men were com-
puted to have been 24,000.[17]

Fryke was no more immune than his patients from the ills
that an equatorial life brought to European seafarers.

As soon as we were come into the road of Banda, our master
went ashore. My legs which had been swelled for three or four
days were now so sore that I could not stir, else I would have
gone with him with all my heart; but my indisposition aug-
menting, I was forced to be carried ashore. There my swelling
increased, all upward, and my belly was now swelled to the
highest degree that I could be ready to break. And in this condition I continued the space of three weeks (so that I was left
here very comfortless, for the *Phoenix* was obliged to be
gone), and after that the distemper seized me so in all my
limbs that I wholly lost the use of them. And during a quarter
of a year I could not bring my finger to my mouth, so that I
truly despaired of ever recovering the use of my limbs
(although I was not sick inwardly) and therefore I often
prayed to God to take me to himself. I was carried every day
to the bagnio, where several other patients with me were set
upon seats, all in a ring, with blankets wrapt round us so close
that nothing but our heads stuck out. There was a great fire on
each side of us which made the heat intolerable, and then we
were laid over the steam of some medicinal herbs which were
boiled for the purpose; into which infusion they threw thirty
or forty red hot cannon bullets which raised such a steam and
made such a smother that not one in a hundred was able to
bear it, but they were forced to be taken out and carried away
upon quilts made for that purpose. I was taken out thus in the
beginning, but when I came to be used to it a little more I bore
it out bravely and found it very helpful. So keeping to this for
some weeks, I recovered apace, and then they began to anoint
my feet with *Oleum Terrae*, and prescribed me to drink

frequently a small glass of bitter brandy or arrack infused in bitter herbs; by which method, with the help of God, I perfectly recovered.[18]

Twice in Fryke's experience arrack was the cause of ships' fires, in this case destroying the ship.

> Our butler, according to custom [after a safe voyage from Ceylon to Batavia], and by the skipper's order, went down to fetch some arrack for the seamen, and as he was drawing it out of the bunghole with a sort of small pump which they had for that purpose, either by a snuff of the candle or by the candle itself, the arrack took fire; and that, spreading like lightning, set the whole on fire, for the European brandy doth not burn near so violently as arrack doth. All our men were immediately at work to put it out, but all in vain. It got a head after so furious a manner that it set fire in the ship itself and it was not long ere that was all in a flame. We had then nothing more to do but to look after ourselves and to endeavour to save our own lives; and it was a great mercy we could do that, for we could not save the least parcel of our goods, nor one of our chests, much less of the Company's goods. This was a mighty loss to the Company, who had an abundance of cinnamon and rich cinnamon oil on board, all which helped to its own destruction and increased the fire. For no sooner had we left the ship ourselves but the fire took in the powder-room where there was some tons of powder which blew up the ship and tore it all to pieces, and threw some if its cannon above a quarter of a mile up into the air.[19]

In Bali, Fryke, a sincere Lutheran,

> bought a young girl of a merchant for 18 rixdollars and took her with me to Batavia where I could make her earn me two shillings or eighteen pence a day.[20]

But relative values were different in the East. One hundred leagues off Malacca his ship was becalmed.

> During this calm we suffered more than ever we could have done in the most terrible tempest, for we were under the Line

146

and the excessive heat caused several to fall sick, and what was worse still was that we had no great provision of water by reason it was looked upon to be but a short voyage, so that with heat and thirst we were all in danger of being suffocated. Our water was now so far spent that a draught of it could not be had under a couple of rixdollars. At last it came to that pass that there was a necessity of setting two sentinels to guard the water cask, out of which they used to distribute every man his portion, and to set four locks upon it. And when the portions were given out in the morning, it was not above one quarter of the measure that it used to be.

In this miserable condition I have been forced to give a dozen of my silver buttons off my waistcoat for one draught of water, and to gnaw bits of wood, hoping I might suck some of the moisture out of it. In short, it put us all upon trying all the ways we could imagine to allay our excessive drought. We had now but six barrels of water left, and we saw no prospect of relief, so that many of us often wished that our ship would sink down right with us. We neglected not to call upon God, and to send up our prayers to him constantly thrice a day that he would have compassion on us; and as this was more becoming Christians than the rash wishes which our desolate condition forced from some, if not the greater part of us, so it was that undoubtedly which was most effectual, for our merciful God sent us a seasonable relief, and surely because we cried unto him in our trouble, he delivered us out of our distress.

The moon, which shined very bright, was all of sudden a little overcast and at length a black cloud came which deprived us wholly of the sight of it, and gave us mighty hopes that we were going to have some rain. This gave us all new life, and set us all at work to spread out our sails ready, fastening them by the four corners with a bullet in the middle to receive the water. Thus we stayed between hope and fear for about three hours. At last the weather grew very cool, and the clouds gathering together, the sky was all darkened, and suddenly the rain came pouring down upon us. But never were men so heartily glad to be wet to the skin. The first water that came through the sails was very bitter, so we threw that away. And then we fell to filling our vessels, which done, we hoisted up our wet sails and ran briskly before the wind.[21]

Ordeals were not always so great, though earlier in his experience a young member of the crew had lost his life in the way described below.

As we were come back, it was my fortune to fall once more into the sea. For as I went to ease nature on the outside of the ship, according to the usual way, I held fast by the rope, which broke, so I dropped. The ship's crew was more ready to laugh at me than to lend me their hand, and I was doubly put to it to swim with my breeches down. But at last my comrade threw me out a rope by which I got up, and praised God for my safety. This made me more careful for ever after; and that the boatswain might be more diligent to see for the future that such things were firm and strong, the master gave him a severe reprimand and laid a fine on him.[22]

Pirates caught by the Company were given short shrift. Some thousands, mostly Javanese, and no doubt mostly innocent, were rounded up in the neighbourhood of Blue Pepper Mountain.

Of the whole, one part was broke upon the wheel, some were quartered, some were whipped, some had their ears and noses cut off, and some were burned in the forehead. The three Hollanders were hanged, the two Danes beheaded, and a great number of others were sent to several islands, to burn lime, hew stone, etc., and there remain slaves all their lives. Their wives and children were served after the same manner, that it might more effectually prove a terror to others.[23]

Where there is fear and the danger of violent death, Thomas Hobbes had suggested in his *Leviathan* a generation earlier, the life of man is likely to be nasty, brutish and short, but there could be exceptions, as Fryke indicates in a passage where he prepares to return home.

Then was there again a day appointed to implore the blessing of the Almighty, which was duly observed both at land and on board our ships. Then the masters of the ships and the factors were invited ashore to take their farewell dinner with the General, and to receive his order for sailing, and to take their oaths of fidelity. After which they repaired every one to their several ships, with orders to set sail with the first fair wind. But the wind was so changeable for three or four days that it made us weigh our anchors and drop them again four or five times. Some of our more debauched seamen, and others, did so fret and fume at these frequent disappointments, and grew so very impatient that they could not forbear venting their rage in very undecent and profane expressions; for which the master, a good old man of near 90 years of age, reproved them very sharply and threatened them severely if they did not refrain from such words, telling them that this was not the way to obtain their desires, but that they ought rather to pray to God to send us a favourable wind and patiently wait His will and pleasure.[24]

CHAPTER 13

The Manila Ship

1689–1709

The development of shipping and trade in the seventeenth and eighteenth centuries was not wholly beneficent. The transfer of horses from Europe to America contributed greatly to the near annihilation of the native inhabitants, as did the transfer of the plague, smallpox and measles. The great new trades were largely unnecessary – drugs and spices from the East did not cure any illnesses nor preserve any foods; rum and sack turned some into alcoholics; sugar rotted their teeth; and tobacco was and remains a killer of powerful proportions. To gain these useless products many thousands of seafarers met a premature death. And on top of all this was imposed the horror of the slave trade, in which the English became increasingly engaged from this time on, and the legacy of which is still very much with us.

> Beware and take care of the Bight of Benin,
> Few come out, though many go in.

Thus said the seventeenth-century slavers of fever-ridden West Africa where they went to pick up their slaves. One such, Captain Thomas Phillips, wrote in his journal in 1693 of the deadly 'middle passage' that they then took to the Americas across the Atlantic Ocean.

> We spent in our passage from St Thomas to Barbados two months eleven days in which time there happened much sickness and mortality among my poor men and negroes, that of

the first we buried 14, and of the last 320 whereby the loss in all amounted to near 6560 pounds sterling. The distemper which my men as well as the blacks mostly die of was the white flux, which was so violent and inveterate that no medicine would in the least check it, so that when any of our men were seized with it we esteemed him a dead man, as he generally proved.[1]

Captain Nathaniel Uring, who spent a quarter of a century at sea, was also familiar with the growing slave trade. On his second voyage to sea in 1697, shortly after he had been taught the 'rudiments of navigation' in London, his ship was captured in the English Channel by a French privateer.

> The colours being struck, the privateer sent his boat on board, and took possession of the ship. Captain Read would have ransomed her, but the French captain would not sell her for the price offered. I began again to repent my choosing a seafaring life, subject to so many accidents; and thought it very hard to be plundered of all my new clothes and other necessaries, and the loss of an adventure which I had entertained great hopes of making a considerable profit by. After being stripped of most of my wearing apparel, I was sent on board the privateer, where I was again plundered of what little things I had left. The privateer standing off and on the English shore, I looked with many a wishful eye on my native country; and thought with myself I should be extremely happy if I could get thither again, ...[2]

which he does, only to ship out again to experience in the following year fire on board his ship in Virginia.

> I being left on board alone, ... went to sleep in the gun-room, where I chose a close cabin to lie in for warmness, it being in winter and very cold weather, especially when the north-west winds blow. How long I had been in bed I cannot tell, but was

waked in the night almost suffocated: I did not imagine the
cause of it, but thought I was seized with some violent distemper that the country is subject too; and in this struggle for
breath, when I was in a very little of being choked, I opened my
cabin door for relief, but found I was still in the same condition,
not apprehending the cause. I made haste to get upon deck, but
almost choked before I found the scuttle into the steerage;
when I recovered my breath, and looking upon deck, to my
great surprise, saw the forecastle all in a blaze. I searched for the
bucket in order to draw water, and to have used my endeavour
to put out the fire, but could not find it; then remembering it
had been left upon the forecastle. The fire grew so fierce in an
instant, there was no coming near it: the wind blowing fresh, it
increased prodigious fast, and in a few moments the upper deck
and gunwales, as far as the chesstrees, were all in a blaze. I
thought it high time to save myself from being consumed in the
flames; but being afraid to go down between decks for my
clothes, naked as I was, I went into the boat, ...[3]

He suspected arson at the hands of the mate, who should
also have been on board. Having lost this ship, he sailed
aboard a sloop where several of the crew were sick with
small-pox and, believing 'that those who were not afraid of
that distemper would not be infected with it',[4] he soon
contracted small-pox himself.

At this same time a charming and companionable Roman
Catholic priest, Father Labat, was serving in the French
West Indian colonies, and in 1700 he provides a record of a
very different, perhaps specifically Gallic, seafaring.

We set sail from Esterre on Friday, 18th February. Our barque
had two cannons but only one cannon ball, and this round
could not be fired, as it was used to crush the mustard we used
with our *cochon boucanné*. There were seventeen of us on
board, including the cabin boy and my slave, who was sixteen
to seventeen years old. The following day we had contrary
winds and did not make the Caymites till the 25th. The waves

Going to Sea, by William McTaggart, 1858 (Kirkcaldy Art Gallery).

Tenth-century
depiction of a Viking
ship (University
Library, Cambridge).

A medieval cog
(Bodleian Library).

Elizabethan seaman
(Peter Knox).

The River Thames in
the late seventeenth
century (Greater
London archives).

Top: The press-gang in action, a James Gillray cartoon. Although the cartoon dates from the end of the eighteenth century, the press-gangs were active from the sixteenth century onwards (National Maritime Museum). Above: The merchantman *Beatty* off Gravesend, by L J Pearce. Built in Liverpool in 1786, she was established by the Marine Society as the first training ship for seamen.

A boy taken off the streets by the Marine Society and kitted out before being sent to sea. Jonas Hanway founded the society in 1756.

Thomas Rowlandson's Portsmouth at the end of the eighteenth century (National Maritime Museum).

Jeanette by Leslie Wilcox – the sailor's dream. Jeanette stowed away to be with her husband and is said to have been precipitated naked into the water when the French warship *Achille* was sunk at the Battle of Trafalgar. The painting can be seen in Fortnum & Mason's tea-room.

The East Indiaman *Buckinghamshire* arriving home off Gravesend in 1823. The illustration is taken from the unpublished journal of Edward Coverly by permission of Captain Jack de Coverly.

...towing the mainsail on a windjammer, drawn by Stan Hugill who served in sail.

Samuel Plimsoll photographed with a ship's crew towards the end of the nineteenth century.

Early twentieth-century ship's captain sampling food brought to the bridge by a steward.

Sick seamen at the Seamen's Hospital Dispensary in London Docks.

Coaling ship.

"Do you HAVE to bring that filthy pipe into MY room?"

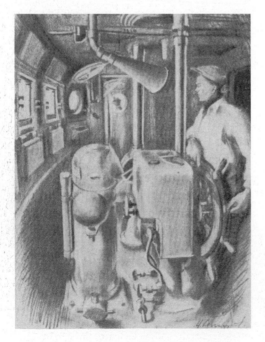

Above: Norman Mansbridge's cartoon of a fourth engineer's cabin, between the two world wars.

Left: A quartermaster at the wheel in the Second World War, drawn from life by Chief Officer Michael Lester (afterwards a professional artist).

The armed merchant cruiser *Jervis Bay* steaming into action against the German pocket battleship *Admiral Scheer*.

The Masterpiece by Jan Sanders. In the 1960s the author arranged, through the Seafarers Education Service, for an artist to be sent to sea with the object of interesting seafarers in drawing and painting. The idea was greeted with derision in some quarters but it proved successful and the practice was continued for thirty years.

'First trippers' aboard the *Esso Pembrokeshire*, a sketch by Grenville Cottingham, the first artist to be sent to sea.

appeared to be trying to see which could jump the highest and sweep us from stem to stern, and one of them was so clumsy that it carried away our galley, a terrible misfortune for men with good appetites.[5]

Cochon boucanné, or smoked ham, was produced and sold in the West Indies by *boucaniers,* who caught the feral pigs for this purpose. The boucaniers were transmogrified into buccaneers and, in 1701, one the most colourful of them, Captain William Kidd, was hanged at Wapping. He was drunk at the time and therefore, to the chagrin of the chaplain, not fit to meet his Maker.

Of course, all sailors liked their stomachs and commonly fished at sea whenever this was possible. Uring, this time on a slaving voyage, bemoans the loss of his trident off the coast of Guinea.

I saw a large broad fish, at least four foot over, and a proportionable length, much like a skate, but a longer tail, with some little difference; they are commonly called amongst the seamen 'devil fish'. I struck it with the fish-gigg in the middle of the back from the round-house; and the line of the fish-gigg being made fast to the deep-sea line, I was in the hopes to have caught it, but the fish being very large and strong, swam away very swiftly, with the gigg standing upright in his back; and the line hitching about my foot had like to have pulled me overboard, and had not the knot luckily slipped where the line was fastened, I should have been in great danger, but I came off only with the loss of my slipper. The loss of our fish-gigg was a very great misfortune to us, having no more on board, and therefore could strike no more fish, by which means we lost many a good meal during the voyage.[6]

Uring, although a survivor, appears to have been accident-prone. Having 'buried' twenty slaves on the middle passage and loaded sugar for England, he sailed for England as mate in 1702 and, at the onset of a gale,

I ... ordered the people up to furl the topsails, and myself and
another man went to furl the spritsail; but going to the leeward
arm, and having passed one turn with the gasket, which is the
line we fasten it with, and stepping further in upon the
footrope, it broke, and I fell below the yard; but having the gasket in my hand, I held it fast, and endeavoured to get upon the
yard again; but before I could reach it, the ship pitching, dipped
me in the sea; which additional weight forced the gasket a
fathom through my hands, and I plunged into the sea over my
head, but keeping my hold, the head of the ship rising with the
sea, raised me out of the water, and immediately dipped me
again; and finding the gasket slack when I was in the water, I
turned it several times round my wrist, and called out lustily for
a rope, being apprehensive of the gasket's breaking; which if it
had, I must have gone to the other world, for the sea ran so
high, there was no possibility of hoisting out the boat. I lay
bobbing on the water, like a bait for a 'Shirk', for more than a
quarter of an hour, before they could find means to get me into
the ship, having lost all my strength in that time; but through
Providence I was wonderfully preserved when I least expected
it, and was several days before I recovered my strength.[7]

He survived this voyage only to be taken by the press-gang
on his return home, for the War of the Spanish Succession
had broken out.

I was impressed into the *Eagle*, and in four or five days turned
over on board the *St George*, under Sir Stafford Fairbourn,
who was Rear-Admiral of the White. He examined me, and
having informed him that I had been first mate of a merchant
ship to the coast of Africa and the West Indies, and that I had
been impressed out of her but a few days before, he bid me not
be concerned, and ordered I should act as a midshipman. I
returned my thanks to the Admiral; but thought it very hard
to be carried abroad again after so long a voyage, before I had
opportunity of setting foot upon the shore of my native
country.[8]

Coming back to Europe in 1705, Father Labat, the amiable Catholic priest, escaped the English and

> as all the crew were Provencaux you may be sure that they had not forgotten the fife and the tambourine. You know that one man plays both instruments at the same time. The tambourine is fastened to his left side and is beaten with the right hand, while the fife is held and played with the left hand. One does not have to ask Provencaux to dance, so as soon as the fife and tambourine were heard everyone came on deck, and I believe that this music would have cured any invalid among our crew had there been one. While some danced, others leaped about, and we had apprentices and young sailors aboard who could make the most celebrated rope-walkers look to their laurels.9

Uring, on the other hand, did not escape the French. In December 1707, about 50 miles westward of the Scillies, he was chased by two ships when in command of a packet-boat which carried government mail. 'I caused great part of the seamen's chests to be hove overboard, beginning with my own, that nothing might be in the way of the guns.'10 But despite further lightening of the ship to help her outsail the enemy, the French ships gained ground and Uring was

> preparing to engage, when the seamen came to me in a body and told me they would not fight, by reason they said they did not understand there was any provision made for them in case they were wounded; that if they lost a leg or an arm, they must be beggars all their life after. I told them that they had a just title to the same benefit as any of the men in the Queen's ships; and to encourage them to fight, I told them that I would get up a cask of the merchant's money, and to every one that received any hurt by the enemy in the engagement, I would give a reasonable gratuity as 'smart-money', if we escaped.11

The men then agreed to fight but the gun-ports were too near the waterline and water came into the ship in great quantities.

Before the privateer came up with us, I had caused the ensign to be nailed to the staff, and that made so fast that none of my people should be able to strike it; and having all I was worth on board, was not willing to lose it easily.[12]

But the man at the helm was killed and both officers and crew went below. While Uring was in the cabin to throw the mail overboard, his lieutenant gave up the ship. Poor Uring became a prisoner of war and, on being exchanged for French prisoners nine months later, was arrested in England for giving his ship away; for packet-boats were supposed to flee from their enemies and not be caught.

While Uring was languishing in his French prison, Captain Woodes Rogers was planning to 'cruise for the Manila ship' – the dream of all contemporary sailors – and thus made his circumnavigation of the world, rescuing Alexander Selkirk, prototype of Robinson Crusoe, on the way. The 'Manila ship' was any Spanish vessel which carried silver from the mines in Mexico across the Pacific Ocean to the Philippines and brought back in its hold the Far Eastern treasures that the silver bought. In 1708 Woodes Rogers tells us:

> Our crew were continually marrying whilst we stayed at Cork, though they expected to sail immediately. Among others there was a Dane coupled by a Romish priest to an Irish woman, without understanding a word of each other's language, so that they were forced to use an interpreter; yet I perceived this pair seemed more afflicted at separation than any of the rest: the fellow continued melancholy for several days after we were at sea. The rest understanding each other, drank their cans of flip till the last minute, concluded with a health to our good voyage, and their happy meeting, and then parted unconcerned.[13]

Woodes Rogers explains his purpose, which eventually netted him and those with him a profit of at least £800,000 – well over £64 million at modern prices.

Most of us, the chief officers, embraced this trip of privateering round the world, to retrieve the losses we had sustained by the enemy. Our complement of sailors in both ships was 333, of which above one-third were foreigners from most nations; several of Her Majesty's subjects on board were tinkers, tailors, hay-makers, pedlars, fiddlers, etc., one negro, and about ten boys. With this mixed gang we hoped to be well manned, as soon as they had learned the use of arms, and got their sea-legs, which we doubted not too soon to teach 'em, and bring them to discipline.[14]

It was not long, however, before he had a mutiny on his hands.

While I was on board the Swede [a neutral ship they had stopped to search for contraband] yesterday, our men mutinied, the ringleaders being our boatswain and three other inferior officers. This morning the chief officers having kept with me in the after-part of the ship, we confined the authors of this disorder, in which there was not one foreigner concerned. We put ten of the mutineers in irons, a sailor being first soundly whipped for exciting the rest to join him. Others less guilty I punished and discharged, but kept the chief officers all armed, fearing what might happen; the ship's company seeming too much inclined to favour the mutineers made me the easier to forgive. Some begged pardon, and others I was forced to wink at; however, they began to find their design frustrated, which was to make a prize of the Swede, who they alleged had much contraband goods aboard, though we could see none; yet they obstinately insisted that we apparently gave away their interest by letting her go without plundering her.[15]

The trouble did not end there, but a fortnight later.

This day, according to custom, we ducked those that had never passed the Tropic [of Cancer] before. The manner of doing it was by a rope through a block from the main-yard, to hoist 'em above half way up to the yard and let 'em fall at once into the water, having a stick cross through their legs, and well fastened to the rope, that they might not be surprised and let go their hold. This proved of great use to our fresh-water sailors, to recover the colour of their skins which were grown very black and nasty. Those that we ducked after this manner three times were about 60, and others that would not undergo it chose to pay half-a-crown fine, the money to be levied and spent at a public meeting of all the ships' companies when we return to England.[16]

Woodes Rogers ruled largely by committee, and all his officers and men signed the following agreement in October 1708:

1. That all plunder on board each prize we take by either ship shall be equally divided between the Company of both ships, according to each man's respective whole share, as shipped by the owners or their orders.
2. That what is plunder shall be adjudged by the superior officers and agents in each ship.
3. That if any person on board either ship do conceal any plunder exceeding one piece of eight in value 24 hours after the capture of any prize, he shall be severely punished and lose his shares of the plunder. The same penalty to be inflicted for being drunk in time of action, or disobeying his superior officer's commands, or concealing himself, or deserting his post in sea or land-service; except when any prize is taken by storm boarding, then whatsoever is taken shall be his own, as followeth: A sailor or landman £10. Any officer below the carpenter £20. A mate, gunner, boatswain and carpenter £40. A lieutenant or master £70. And the captains £100 over and above the gratuity promised by the owners to such as shall signalise themselves.
4. That public books of plunder are to be kept in each ship attested by the officers, and the plunder to be appraised by officers chosen, and divided as soon as possible after the capture. Also every person to be sworn and searched as

soon as they shall come aboard by such persons as shall be appointed for that purpose: the person or persons refusing shall forfeit their shares of the plunder as above.

5. In consideration that Captain Rogers and Captain Court-ney, to make both ships' companies easy, have given the whole cabin-plunder (which in all probability is the major part) to be divided as aforesaid, we do voluntarily agree that they shall have 5 per cent, each of 'em, over and above their respective shares as a consideration for what is their due of the plunder aforesaid.

6. That a reward of twenty pieces of eight shall be given to him that first sees a prize of good value, or exceeding 50 tuns in burden.

7. That such of us that have not signed already to the articles of agreement indented with the owners, do hereby oblige ourselves to the same terms as the rest of the ship's com-pany have done; half shares and half wages etc.,[17]

Approaching Cape Horn, Woodes Rogers and his men prepared for cold weather.

Clothes and liquor were now in excellent commodity amongst our ship's company, who are but meanly stored: we had six tailors at work for several weeks to make them clothing, and pretty well supplied their wants by the spare blankets and red clothes belonging to the owners; and what every officer could spare was altered for the men's use.[18]

In February 1709, at what was thought to be the uninhab-ited island of Juan Fernandez, off the Chile coast,

our pinnace returned from the shore, and brought abundance of crawfish, with a man clothed in goatskins who looked wilder than the first owners of them. He had been on the island four years and four months, being left there by Captain Stradling in the *Cinque-Ports;* his name was Alexander Selkirk, a Scots man who had been master of the *Cinque-Ports,* a ship that came here last with Captain Dampier who told me that this was the best man in her; so I immediately agreed with him to be a mate on board our ship ... The reason of his being left here was a difference betwixt him and his Captain ...

He had with him his clothes and bedding, with a firelock, some powder, bullets, and tobacco, a hatchet, a knife, a kettle, a Bible, some practical pieces, and his mathematical instruments and books ... [He] employed himself in reading, singing psalms, and praying; so that he said that he was a better Christian while in this solitude than ever he was before, or than, he was afraid, he should ever be again ...

When his powder failed, he took [goats] by speed of foot; for his way of living and continual exercise of walking and running, cleared him of all gross humours, so that he ran with wonderful swiftness through the woods and up the rocks and hills, as we perceived when we employed him to catch goats for us ... He came at last to relish his meat well enough without salt or bread, and in the season had plenty of good turnips, which had been sowed there by Captain Dampier's men, and have now overspread some acres of ground. He had enough of good cabbage from the cabbage-trees, and seasoned his meat with the fruit of the piemento trees, which is the same as the Jamaica pepper, and smells deliciously. He found there also a black pepper called malagita, which was very good to expel wind, and against griping of the guts.

He soon wore out his shoes and clothes by running through the woods; and at last being forced to shift without them, his feet became so hard that he run everywhere without annoyance, and it was some time before he could wear shoes after we found him ...

He was at first much pestered with cats and rats, that had bred in great numbers from some of each species which had got ashore from ships that put in there to wood and water. The rats gnawed his feet and clothes while asleep, which obliged him to cherish the cats with his goats-flesh, by which many of them became so tame that they would lie about him in hundreds and soon delivered him from the rats ... Having some linen cloth by him, he sewed himself shirts with a nail, and stitched 'em with the worsted of his old stockings, which he pulled out on purpose. He had his last shirt on when we found him on the island.

At his first coming aboard us, he had so much forgotten his language for want of use that we could scarce understand him, for he seemed to speak his words by halves.[19]

Subsequently, on the proposed sacking of Guayaquil, further rules on the subject of plunder and behaviour ashore were laid down, and in the event the sailors behaved like gentlemen.

The houses up the river were full of women, and particularly at one place there were above a dozen handsome genteel young women well dressed, where our men got several gold chains and ear-rings, but were otherwise so civil to them that the ladies offered to dress 'em victuals and brought 'em a cask of good liquor. Some of their largest gold chains were concealed, and wound about their middles, legs and thighs, etc., but the gentlewomen in these hot countries being very thin clad with silk and fine linen, and their hair dressed with ribbons very neatly, our men felt the chains, etc, with their hands on the outside of the lady's apparel, and by the linguist modestly desired the gentlewomen to take 'em off and surrender 'em.[20]

To the prisoners and hostages he took, Woodes Rogers allowed liberty of conscience and they went to mass. In one of his prizes, the *Harve de Grace*, renamed the *Marquiss*, he found

near 500 bales of Pope's bulls, 16 reams in a bale. This took up abundance of room in the ship; we throwed most of them overboard ... These bulls are imposed upon the people and sold here by the clergy from 3 ryals to 50 pieces of eight apiece, according to the ability of the purchaser. Once in two years they are rated, and all the people obliged to buy them against Lent; they cannot be read, the print looking worse than any of our old ballads, yet the vulgar are made believe it's a mortal sin to eat flesh in Lent without being licensed by one of these bulls, the negro slaves not being exempted. This is one of the greatest branches of income the King of Spain has in this country, being a free gift from the Pope to him, as the Spaniards and natives told us.[21]

Also found aboard a prize were

a great quantity of bones in small boxes, ticketed with the names of Romish saints, some of which had been dead 7 or 800 years; with an infinite number of brass medals, crosses, beads and crucifixes, religious toys in wax, images of saints made of all sorts of wood, stone and other materials, I believe in all near 30 tun, with 150 boxes of books in Spanish, Latin, etc, which would take up much more stowage than 50 tuns of other goods: All this came from Italy, and most from Rome, designed for the Jesuits of Peru; but being of small value to us, we contented ourselves to take only a sample of most sorts to shew to our friends in England, and left the rest.[22]

On 29th August 1709,

Captain Cooke buried one John Edwards, a youth who died of a complication of scurvy and the pox, which he got from a loathsome negro whom we afterwards gave to the prisoners that she might do no further mischief on board.[23]

The following day,

We put our young [Roman Catholic] padre ashore and gave him, as he desired, the prettiest young female negro we had in the prize, with some baize, linen and other things, for his good services in helping to promote our trade for provisions here. ... The young padre parted with us extremely pleased, and leering under his hood upon his black female angel. No doubt he will crack a Commandment with her, and wipe off the sin with the Church's indulgence.[24]

After raiding the coast of South America, Woodes Rogers decided that the time had come to 'cruise for the Manila ship' off Cape St Lucas, the southernmost cape of California, and, after further committee meetings which laid down the rules relating to the division of spoils and which banned all forms of gambling, Woodes Rogers' dream was realised on 22nd December 1709, but not without cost to himself.

At daybreak we saw the chase upon our weather bow, about a league from us, the *Dutchess* ahead of her to leeward near about half as far. Towards 6 our boat came aboard, having kept very near the chase all night and received no damage, but told us the *Dutchess* passed by her in the night and she fired 2 shots at them, but they returned none. We had no wind, but got out 8 of our ship's oars and rowed above an hour; then there sprung up a small breeze. I ordered a large kettle of chocolate to be made for our ship's company (having no spiritous liquor to give them); then we went to prayers, and before we had concluded were disturbed by the enemy's firing at us. They had barrels hanging at each yard-arm that looked like powder barrels, to deter us from boarding 'em. About 8 o'clock we began to engage her by ourselves, for the *Dutchess* being to leeward, and having little wind, did not come up. The enemy fired her stern chase upon us first, which we returned with our fore chase several times till we came nearer and, when close aboard each other, we gave her several broadsides, plying our small arms very briskly, which they returned as thick a while, but did not ply their great guns half so fast as we. After some time we shot a little a-head of them, lay thwart her hawse close aboard, and plied them so warmly that she soon struck her colours two thirds down. By this time the *Dutchess* came up and fired about five guns, with a volley of small shot, but the enemy, having submitted, made no return. We sent our pinnace aboard and brought the captain with the officers away and having examined 'em, found there was another ship out of

Manila with them of a bigger burthen, having about 40 brass guns mounted and as many patererocs, but they told us they lost her company three months ago and reckoned she was got to Acapulco before this time, she sailing better than this ship. This prize was called by the long name of *Nostra Seniora de la Incarnacion Disenganio,* Sir John Pichberty Commander. She had 20 guns, 20 patereroes and 193 men aboard, whereof 9 were killed, 10 wounded and several blown up and burnt with powder. We engaged 'em about three glasses, in which time we had only myself and another man wounded. I was shot through the left cheek, the bullet struck away great part of my upper jaw and several of my teeth, part of which dropped down upon the deck where I fell. The other, Will Powell, an Irish landman, was slightly wounded in the buttock.[25]

CHAPTER 14

A Cruise on the Spaniards

1710–1735

By 1710 it seemed that the easy money was to be made in the South Seas, that is, in Spanish America. With the war of the Spanish Succession drawing to its close, the British expected to make large profits from a slave trade extended in that direction and it was this prospect that inspired the establishment, in 1711, of the South Sea Company. South America was more accessible than India, and less civilised. Instead of being a drain on Britain's precious metals, like India, the 'South Seas' would take British cloth and ironmongery and pay in bullion and such precious commodities as dyestuffs, logwood and cochineal.

Insider dealing and gross ministerial corruption drove up the price of South Sea stock and when, in 1720, the directors proposed taking over responsibility for a large part of the national debt, the stock rose eightfold in as many months. The Poet Laureate, a forgotten parson named Laurence Eusden, wrote in the summer an ode celebrating the King's birthday. It prophesied that generations still unborn would tell of the monarch who gave them silver and gold mines, 'all the commerce of the Main' – that is, of the Caribbean region – 'and made South Seas send home the wealth of Spain'.

Later in the year, the South Sea bubble burst with the first great stock exchange crash. The year before, when enthusiasm for the South Seas was nearing its height and Britain was once more at war with Spain, Captain George Shelvocke, accompanied by his son, set off 'to cruise on the Spaniards'. He had hoped to lead the two privateers *Success* and *Speedwell*, of 350 and 200 tons respectively, with Captain John Clipperton as his second-in-command. In the event, the owners decided otherwise and it was Shelvocke who was appointed second-in-command aboard the *Speedwell*. With a second captain named Hatley, who had been third mate to Woodes Rogers, and a copy of Woodes Rogers' book about his voyage round the world and his capture of the Manila ship, Shelvocke soon separated from the *Success* and proceeded independently. From the first, his crew, 'four fifths of which were landsmen', appeared mutinous. Following the practice of other commanders, after crossing the Atlantic he put in at the island of St Catherine's, off the coast of Brazil. Before sailing from St Catherine's he tells us,

I ... added very considerably to our stock of provisions, and did not make the least expenditure or our European stores (liquors excepted), for my people did eat nothing but fresh provisions during our stay on the island. I purchased twenty-one head of black cattle, some at four dollars, and others at eight; several hogs, at four dollars each; and two hundred large salted drum-fish, at ten dollars per hundred; together with one hundred and fifty bushels of *Farina de Pao*, which is the flower (sic) of the Cassader (cassava) root, as fine as our oatmeal. It is very healthy eating, and prepared without any further trouble than boiling the water and soaking a quantity of this Farina in it, which makes a burgoo immediately. I likewise bought one hundred and sixty baskets of Calavances [a sort of pulse or bean], some of which I purchased with money, at the rate of a dollar per bushel, and some with salt, exchanging one bushel with another, and added to all this a very necessary article, viz. a good stock of tobacco.[1]

Despite such extra provision, appetites were scarcely satisfied as the ship neared Cape Horn and the weather grew
colder, and he had further trouble with the crew. On 1st
October:

> At seven in the evening, as we were furling the mainsail, one
> William Camell cried out that his hands were so benumbed
> that he could not hold himself; but before those who were
> next to him could come to his assistance he fell down and was
> drowned.
>
> The cold is certainly more insupportable in these than in
> the same latitudes to the Northward; for though we were
> pretty much advanced in the summer season and had the
> days very long, we were nevertheless subject to continued
> squalls of sleet, snow and rain, and the heavens were perpet-
> ually hidden from us by gloomy, dismal clouds. In short, one
> would think it impossible that anything living could subsist
> in so rigid a climate, and indeed we all observed that we had
> not had the sight of one fish of any kind since we were come
> to the Southward of the Straits of Le Mair; nor one sea-bird
> excepting a disconsolate black albatross, who accompanied
> us for several days, hovering about us as if he had lost him-
> self, till Hatley (my second Captain) observing in one of his
> melancholy fits, that this bird was always hovering near us,
> imagined from his colour, that it might be some ill omen.
> That which, I suppose, induced him the more to encourage
> his superstition, was the continued series of contrary tem-
> pestuous winds, which had oppressed us ever since we had
> got into this sea. But be that as it would, he, after some fruit-
> less attempts, at length shot the albatross, not doubting (per-
> haps) that we should have a fair wind after that.[2]

A century or so later, Wordsworth was to claim that he
presented Coleridge with the notion that his ancient
mariner should shoot the albatross, Wordsworth being in
the process of reading Shelvocke's account of his voyage at
the time the poem was written. The death of the albatross

did not bring luck to the *Speedwell*, as Captain Hatley hoped, for those on board did not sight the coast of Chile until some six weeks later. Nor did it bring luck to Hatley himself, who went coasting for prizes in a small vessel called the *Mercury* which Shelvocke and his crew captured at the Chilean port of Conception.

The very next day after they [Captain Hatley and William Betagh] departed from us they took a small bark laden with rice, chocolate, wheat flour etc., and the day following took another. On the fourth day of their absence they became masters of a ship of near two hundred tons, worth one hundred and fifty thousand pieces of eight. Flushed with this success, it seems, Betagh prevailed on Hatley and the greatest part of the people with them not to join with me again, telling them that there was sufficient for themselves to appear like gentlemen as long as they lived; but that it would be nothing when the owners' part were taken out, and the remainder divided into five hundred shares. 'And what is more', continued he, 'we expect to meet with the *Success* every day, [Shelvocke's instructions included various places at which he might rendezvous with Clipperton if they were separated from one another] and then it is ten to one but they will take all from us'; and therefore he thought, since fortune had been so kind to them, that they would be highly to blame if they did not lay hold of this opportunity of going to India. However, shortly afterwards they were captured by a Spanish man-of-war which put paid to any independent piratical venture. [3]

Deserted by Hatley and Betagh, Shelvocke went plundering to the north, saw action against the Spaniards, and decided to withdraw to Juan Fernandez for refreshment. But there his ship was wrecked on an uninhabited island:

It was happy for us that our masts fell all over the off side, which gave us room to make a raft, by which means (and having hands ashore, who had been there before the wind came on, and who came down on the beach to assist us) we were all saved except one man. I myself made a very narrow escape. In this surprise, the first thing I took care of was my commission [as a privateer]; and remembering the powder to be uppermost in the bread-room, I got most of it up, with about seven or eight bags of bread. These were secured to windward and saved, the ship not coming to pieces immediately. In a few minutes after she first struck, she was full of water; so that the surgeon's chest being stowed below there was little or nothing preserved out of that. We saved two or three compasses, and some of our mathematical instruments and books. Before it was quite dark we were all ashore, but in a very wet uncomfortable condition; no place to have recourse to for shelter from the bitter cold wind and rain, except the trees, nothing to cheer our spirits after the fatigue and hazard in getting from the wreck to the rocks; and no other prospect but that, after having suffered much in this uninhabited place, we might, in process of time, be taken away by some ship or other. Our ears were now saluted by the melancholy howlings of innumerable seals on the beach, who lay so thick that we were obliged to clear our way of them as we went along, and nothing presented itself to our sight but rocky precipices, inhospitable woods, dropping with rain, lofty mountains, whose tops were hid by thick clouds, and a tempestuous sea, which had reduced us to the low state we were now in. Thus we were without any one thing necessary in life; not so much as a seat whereon to rest our limbs, except the cold wet ground, which so far as we could see, was also like to be our bed and pillow, and proved to be so.[4]

Nevertheless, Shelvocke and his men managed to live off the land – eating seals, cats, goats, fish, wild sorrel and the central bud of the palm trees, which was known as 'palm-cabbage' – and on certain foodstuffs salvaged from the wrecked *Speedwell.* Some of them – the mutinous sailors did little or nothing to help – also began to build a new vessel from the remains of the *Speedwell.* This 20-ton two-masted bark was 30 feet long, 16 feet wide and 7 feet deep and Shelvocke christened her *Recovery*. Of his island home Shelvocke wrote,

> It enjoys a fine wholesome air, insomuch that out of seventy of us that were on it for the space of five months and eleven days, not one had an hour's sickness, notwithstanding that we fed on such foul diet without bread and salt, so that we had no complaints among us, except an incessant craving appetite, and the want of our former strength and vigour. For my own part, I must acknowledge the bounty of Providence that gave me strength to cope with such vexations as I met with; for although I lost much of my flesh, I became one of the strongest and most active men on the island, from being very corpulent and almost crippled with gout. I walked much, and worked hard every day, without being in the least afflicted with that distemper, ... [5]

He sailed on the *Recovery* with only forty men, the rest having elected to remain behind. His provisions consisted of a cask of beef, six bushels of cassava flour, 60 gallons of seals' oil to be used for frying, five live hogs which had been reared on putrefied seal carcasses, and 2300 conger eels which they had dried and smoked. The men lay on bundles of eels.

> Being in no method of keeping ourselves clean, all our senses were as much offended as possible. There was not a drop of water to be had without sucking it out of the cask with the barrel of a musquet, which was made use of by everybody promiscuously, and the little unsavoury morsels we daily ate, created perpetual quarrels, every one contending for the frying-pan. All the conveniency we had for a fire was only an half tub filled with earth, which made it so tedious that we had a continual noise of frying from morning till night! [6]

Shelvocke's audacious plan was to capture a better vessel on the Chilean coast and, having failed twice, and after a raid or two ashore, he took the 200-ton *Jesus Maria,* laden with pitch, tar, copper and plank, and renamed her *Happy Return.* In the *Happy Return* he provisioned himself on the west coast of Mexico and here at last he met Captain Clipperton in the *Success* but, by his account, Clipperton deserted him and they missed the Manila ship. At Sonsonnate in Mexico (latitude 13°N) he took the 300-ton *Sacra Familia* and decided to use this vessel henceforward, translating her name into English. But in this *Holy Family*, now with a crew of forty-three, including acquired negroes, he became desperately short of water.

> We constantly drank our urine, which, though it moistened our mouths for a time, excited our thirst the more. Some attempted to drink large quantities of the sea water, which was like to have killed them. An universal fever and languid decay of spirits now reigned amongst us, and there was not one of us at that time that was not fitter to be carried to a sick bed than to be obliged to labour at the hard work which is requisite to manage a large ship in a place subject to sudden and violent squalls of wind; ...7

He eventually managed to obtain some water, after which he captured a bark and another 200-ton Spanish ship, *de Conception de Recova.* By this time he had eighty prisoners, several of note, and only twenty-six of his own crew. Four of his men were then murdered by the Spanish crew on the bark, so he took what he wanted from the 200-ton vessel and let his prisoners sail her to Panama. He now decided that he had cruised on the Spaniards enough and sailed west from Southern California on 18th August 1721, keeping to a track which ran 13° North of the equator.

> A fortnight after we had left California, my people, who had hitherto enjoyed an uninterrupted state of health, began to be afflicted with a sickness which particularly affected their

stomachs, which was undoubtedly in the greatest measure owing to the quantities of sweetmeats they were continually devouring, and also to our common food, which was puddings made of coarse flour and sweetmeats, and salt water instead of fresh to moisten them, and dried beef, which was partly destroyed by ants, cockroaches and other vermin. We could not afford fresh water to boil the kettle once in the whole passage, so that this way of living brought the scurvy and other distempers upon us, which was a melancholy condition for us to be in who had no medicines to apply to those who were already sick, nor to prevent those who were well, from falling into the same state.[8]

There were several deaths. Shelvocke himself was seriously ill 'and had no expectation of living much longer, till the gout, seizing upon me, gave me some painful hopes of the continuance of my life'. This, by his account, in spite of having no liquor on board. The whole beakhead of the ship now became loose, the bowsprit fetched away, and for some time the mainmast was without shrouds on the larboard or port side. Only six or seven of the crew were fit for work, but even so he did not put in at Guam for fear of the inhabitants. On 11th November, after picking up a Chinese pilot, he reached Macao, and another pilot took him up to Whampoa, the anchorage for Canton, where he sold his ship for £650 but had to pay, he said, over £2000 port dues, grossly more than bigger and better ships paid. He then arranged a passage home in the East Indiaman *Cadogan* which sailed in December 1721. The voyage proved a pleasant one, though he was still unwell, and he arrived in London on 1st August 1722, having been away three years, seven months and eleven days.

In the course of his voyage eighty-three of his companions had died, been captured or killed. He shared his booty with thirty-two others and may have netted as much as

£7000 himself. He was sent to prison for a supposed act of piracy involving a Portuguese ship, but he escaped. He probably cheated his owners, and William Betagh, who eventually arrived back in London, accused him of inciting the mutinies on his ship. But Shelvocke survived another twenty years, dying at last in the Lombard Street home of the son who had accompanied him round the world. By this time his son was secretary of the General Post Office.

CHAPTER 15

A Golden Time

1735–1750

When, in 1740, Commodore George Anson's squadron set off 'to distress the Spaniards' and, if possible, to capture the Manila ship, the time was a golden one for privateering. However, it did not appear so to those on board Anson's store-ship *Wager*. Crewed by surly pressed men, the *Wager* had never been a happy ship. After rounding Cape Horn she struck a sunken rock off the coast of Chile and for months afterwards the survivors lived meagrely off the harsh land and from stores salvaged from the ship. The *Wager*'s captain, Captain Cheap, thought it proper – and more likely of success – that, with the ship's boats, they should seek to capture a Spanish vessel and look for Commodore Anson in the Pacific Ocean. Seventy-two of his crew thought otherwise and decided to return to the east coast of South America through the Magellan Straits. These took the ship's long-boat, which had been cut in half and lengthened by 12 feet, and a cutter, leaving Captain Cheap and the rest with a barge and a yawl. With Cheap was the Hon John Byron, grandfather of the poet, aged sixteen.

The barge and the yawl were both lost soon afterwards but, in March 1742, Cheap, Byron and three more officers embarked in canoes with some native Indians to go north to Chiloe Island, where they might meet with some Spaniards. Their Indian guide brought them to a place where he picked up a very large canoe. This canoe, wrote Byron,

> would have required at least six men to the oar to have made any kind of expedition: instead of that, there was only Campbell and myself, besides the Indian, his companion, or servant to row, the cacique (chief) himself never touching an oar, but sitting with his wife all the time much at his ease ... This was dreadful hard work to such poor starved creatures as we were, to be slaving at the oar all day long in such a heavy boat; and this inhuman fellow would never give us a scrap to eat, excepting when he took so much seal that he could not contrive to carry it all away with him, which happened very seldom. After working like galley-slaves all day, towards night, when we landed, instead of taking any rest, Mr Campbell and I were sometimes obliged to go miles along shore to get a few shellfish; and just as we have made a little fire in order to dress them, he has commanded us into the boat again, and kept us rowing the whole night without ever landing. It is impossible for me to describe the miserable state we were reduced to: our bodies were so emaciated, that we hardly appeared the figures of men. It has often happened to me in the coldest night, both in hail and snow, where we had nothing but an open beach to lay down upon, in order to procure a little rest, that I have been obliged to pull off the few rags I had on, as it was impossible to get a moment's sleep with them on for the vermin that swarmed about them; though I used, as often as I had time, to take my clothes off, and putting them on a large stone, beat them with another, in hopes of killing hundreds at once, for it was endless work to pick them off. What we suffered from this was ten times worse even than hunger. But we were clean in comparison to Captain Cheap; for I could compare his body to nothing but an ant-hill, with thousands of those insects crawling over it; for he was now past attempting to rid himself in the least from this torment, as he had quite lost himself, not recollecting our names that were about him, or even his own. His beard was as long as a hermit's: that and his face

being covered with train (seal) oil and dirt, from having long accustomed himself to sleep upon a bag, by way of pillow, in which he kept the pieces of stinking seal. This prudent method he took to prevent our getting at it whilst he slept. His legs were as big as mill-posts, though his body appeared to be nothing but skin and bone.

The story of the seventy-two men who embarked for the Magellan Straits is told by John Bulkeley, the gunner, together with John Cummins, the carpenter, who length-ened the long-boat. The accompanying cutter, vital for easy access to the shore, was soon lost. 'The loss of the cut-ter gives the few thinking people aboard a great deal of uneasiness; we have seventy-two men in the vessel, and not above six of that number that give themselves the least con-cern for the preservation of their lives, but rather the reverse, being ripe for mutiny and destruction; ... '.²

Before the boat reached the Straits, eleven of the men, together with their share of the provisions, were put ashore at their own request. At the opening of the Straits the gunner wrote,

I never in my life, in any part of the world, have seen such a sea as runs here; we expected every wave to swallow us, and the boat to founder. This shore is full of small islands, rocks, and breakers; so that we can't haul further to the southward, for fear of endangering the boat; we are obliged to keep her right before the sea. At five broach'd to, at which we all believ'd she would never rise again.³

She did rise again, but then the deaths from starvation began. The second to die was Thomas Caple.

This night departed this life Mr Thomas Caple, son of the late Lieutenant Caple, aged twelve years, who perish'd for want of food. There was a person on board who had some of the youth's money, upwards of twenty guineas, with a watch and silver cup. Those last the boy was willing to sell for flower [flour, ie part of someone else's share]; but his guardian told him, he would buy cloaths for him in the Brazil. The miserable youth cry'd, sir, I shall never live to see the Brazil; I am starving now, almost starv'd to death; therefore for G-d's sake, give me my silver cup to get me some victuals, or buy some for me yourself. All his prayers and intreaties to him were vain; but heaven sent death to his relief, and put a period to his miseries in an instant. Persons who have not experienc'd the hardships we have met with, will wonder how people can be so inhuman to see their fellow-creatures starving before their faces and afford 'em no relief: but hunger is void of all compassion, every person was so intent on the preservation of his own life, that he was regardless of another's and the bowels of commiseration were shut up.[4]

A further death was that of Thomas Harvey, the purser, of whom the diarist wrote, 'he died a skeleton for want of food: this gentleman probably was the first purser, belonging to his majesty's service, that ever perish'd with hunger'.[5] By 10th January 1742, three months after they had left Captain Cheap, Bulkeley wrote,

We have nothing to eat but some stinking seal, and not above twenty out of the forty-three which are now alive have even that; and such hath been our condition for this week past; nor are we better off in regard to water, there not being above eighty gallons aboard.[6]

A few days later, at Freshwater Bay, there were plenty of seals on the beach but because of the dangerous surf they could not get close to the shore. A few swam ashore and had later to be left behind. The rest watched.

We think ourselves now worse off than ever, for we are actually starving in the sight of plenty. We have but two people on board that can swim; to give them all the assistance we can, the lieutenant and myself, with the rest of the people, proposed to haul the vessel nearer in, and make a raft for one of the two to swim ashore on, and to carry a line to haul some of the seal aboard: with much entreaty these two swimmers were prevailed upon to cast lots; the lot falling on the weakest of 'em, who was a young lad about fifteen years of age, and scarce able to stand, we would not suffer him to go. While our brethren were regaling in the fulness of plenty ashore, we aboard were oblig'd to strip the hatches of a seal-skin, which had been for some time nail'd on, and made use of for a tarpawlin; we burnt the hair off the skin, and for want of anything else fell to chewing the seal skin.[7]

Two days after eighty-two-year old Thomas Maclean, the ship's cook, died, the thirty survivors reached the Rio Grande, where the Portuguese governor took them in charge, and eventually the gunner and the carpenter returned to Lisbon from Rio de Janeiro aboard the Brazil ship *St Tubas*. It was not, however, the end of their troubles.

On Monday the 23rd November, in the latitude 39 : 17 north, and longitude 6 : 00 w. that day at noon the rock of Lisbon bearing S by W sixteen leagues; we steer'd ESE to make the rock before night. At four o'clock it blew a very hard gale, and right on the shore; the ship lay to under a foresail with her head to the southward; at six it blew a storm, the foresail splitting, oblig'd us to keep her before the wind, which was running her right on the shore. The ship was now given over for lost, the people all fell to prayers, and cry'd out to their saints for deliverance, offering all they had in the world for their lives; and yet at the same time neglected all means to save themselves; they left off pumping the ship, though she was exceeding leaky. This sort of proceeding in time of extremity is a thing unknown to our English seamen; in those emergencies all hands are employ'd for the preservation of the ship and people, and if any of them fall upon their knees, 'tis after the danger is over. The carpenter and myself could by no means relish this behaviour, we begg'd the people for God's sake to go to the pumps, telling them we had a chance to save our lives, while we kept the ship above water, that we ought not to suffer the ship to sink, while we could keep her free. The captain and officers hearing us pressing them so earnestly, left off prayers, and entreated the men to keep the pumps going, accordingly we went to pumping, and preserv'd ourselves and the ship. In half an hour afterwards the wind shifted to the WNW then the ship lay south, which would clear the course along the shore; had the wind not shifted, we must in an hour's time have run the ship ashore. This deliverance, as well as [that on a] former [occasion], was owing to the Intercession of Nuestra Senhora Boa Mortua: on this occasion they collected fifty moydores more, and made this pious resolution, that, when the ship arriv'd safe at Lisbon, the foresail, which was split in the last gale of wind, should be carried in procession to the church of this grand saint, and the captain should there make an offering equal in value to the foresail, which was reckoned worth eighteen moydores.[8]

A sailor's pay ceased when he was shipwrecked and so Captain Cheap's people could not be charged with mutiny for having left him in Chile, a state of affairs the Admiralty soon sought to remedy. Incredibly, Cheap himself survived and was able to retire on the prize-money which he obtained in his next command, afterwards marrying a widow by whom he had several children. Bulkeley, the gunner, emigrated to Pennsylvania. Byron went on to become an admiral.

In rounding Cape Horn, Commodore Anson had lost more of his squadron than the *Wager*. The *Severn* and the *Pearl*, two of his most powerful ships, had turned back; and only his own Command the *Centurion*, the *Gloucester*, the tiny *Tryal*, and a 'victualler' called the *Anna Pink* limped into the old privateering base of Juan Fernandez. Two-thirds of their crews were dead, mostly from scurvy. The account of Anson's voyage round the world relates that

It is not easy to compleat the long roll of various concomitants of this disease; for it often produced putrid fevers, pleurisies, the jaundice, and violent rheumatick pains, and sometimes it occasioned an obstinate costiveness, which was generally attended by a difficulty of breathing; and this was esteemed the most deadly of all the scorbutick symptoms. At other times the whole body, but more especially the legs, were subject to ulcers of the worst kind, attended with rotten bones, and such a luxuriancy of funguous flesh, as yielded to no remedy. But a most extraordinary circumstance, and what would be scarcely credible upon single evidence, is, that the scars of wounds which had been for many years healed, were forced open again by this virulent distemper. Of this, there was a remarkable instance in one of the invalids on board the *Centurion,* who had been wounded above fifty years before at the battle of the Boyne; for though he was cured soon after, and had continued well for a great number of years past, yet on his being attacked by the scurvy, his wounds, in the progress of his disease, broke out afresh, and appeared as if they had never been healed: Nay, what is still more astonishing, the callous of a broken bone, which had been compleatly formed for a long time, was found to be hereby dissolved, and the fracture seemed as if it had never been consolidated. Indeed, the effects of this disease were in almost every instance wonderful; for many of our people, though confined to their hammocks, appeared to have no inconsiderable share of health, for they eat and drank heartily, were chearful, and talked with much seeming vigour, and with a loud strong tone of voice; and yet on their being the least moved, though it was only from one part of the ship to the other, and that in their hammocks, they have immediately expired; and others, who have confided in their seeming strength, and have resolved to get out of their hammocks, have died before they could well reach the deck; and it was no uncommon thing for those who were able to walk the deck, and to do some kind of duty, to drop down dead in an instant, on any endeavours to act with their utmost vigour, many of our people having perished in this manner during the course of this voyage.[9]

After having recovered their health on Juan Fernandez, Anson and the survivors proceeded to sea once more to harry the Spaniards in accordance with their instructions. By the time they cruised, in vain, for the Manila ship off Acapulco, Anson's remaining men were so few that only the *Centurion* and the *Gloucester* were manned and the Commodore decided to set off across the Pacific Ocean. The dreaded scurvy reappeared and the *Gloucester* was scuttled, so that only the *Centurion* reached the Ladrones Islands where Anson stopped for refreshment. He then proceeded to Macao and gave it out that he intended to proceed thence to Batavia and Europe. However, before doing so, he had resolved secretly to cruise off Cape Espíritu Santo, the Spanish landfall for the Philippine Islands, anticipating that the Manila ship might come that way. The *Nuestra Senora de Covadonga* answered his prayers.

Mr Anson in the meantime, had prepared all things for engagement on board the *Centurion*, and had taken all possible care, both for the most effectual exertion of his small strength, and for the avoiding the confusion and tumult, too frequent in action of this kind. He picked about thirty of his choicest hands and best marksmen, whom he distributed into his tops, and who fully answered his expectations, by the signal services they performed. As he had not hands enough remaining to quarter a sufficient number to each great gun, in the customary manner, he therefore, on his lower tier, fixed only two men to each gun, who were to be solely employed in loading it. Whilst the rest of his people were divided into different gangs of ten to twelve men each, which were constantly moving about the decks, to run out and fire such guns as were loaded. By this management he was enabled to make use of all his guns; and instead of firing broad-sides with intervals between them, he kept up a constant fire without intermission, whence he doubted not to procure very signal advantages; for it is common with the Spaniards to fall down upon the decks when they see a broadside preparing, and to continue in that posture till it is given; after which they rise again, and, presuming the danger to be for some time over, work their guns and fire with great briskness, till another broad-side is ready: But the firing gun by gun, in the manner directed by the Commodore rendered this practice of theirs impossible.

[By such stratagems] was the *Centurion* possessed of this rich prize, amounting in value to near a million and a half of dollars ... The galeon was larger than the *Centurion*, had five hundred and fifty men and thirty-six guns mounted for action, besides twenty-eight pidreroes [light swivel guns] in her gunwale, quarters and tops, each of which carried a four pound ball. She was very well furnished with small arms, and was particularly provided against boarding, both by her close quarters, and by a strong net-work of two inch rope, which was laced over her waist, and was defended by half pikes. She had sixty-seven killed in the action, and eighty-four wounded, whilst the *Centurion* had only two killed, and a Lieutenant and sixteen wounded, all of whom but one recovered. Of so little consequence are the most destructive arms in untutored and unpractised hands.[10]

It was a reasonable boast, even given that the *Centurion* was, in fact, bigger than the *Covadonga*. The booty was said to be the biggest ever returned to England in a single hull, and the 145 survivors – one in ten of the original number – all returned rich men.

In 1753, only nine years after Anson came home, Dr James Lind, who had been a ship's surgeon, published his *Treatise of the Scurvy*. Stimulated by Anson's experiences, he showed that scurvy was essentially a dietary disease: 'Every common sailor ought to lay in a stock of onions', he opined. (Robin Knox-Johnston – now Sir Robin – took this advice when he sailed round the world alone in 1968.) 'A cask of rich garden mould,' Lind continued, 'put occasionally in boxes on the poop and sown with the seeds of garden cresses would furnish these ['wholesome salads'] at any time'. In only a few isolated instances was any notice taken of Lind's writing in the years that followed.[11]

Commodore George Walker, one of the most successful privateers of his time, did not operate in the South Seas. He preferred Atlantic waters. He was a man of infinite resource and good humour, fond of music, popular with crews, and even with prisoners. The memoirs that covered his years at sea between 1739 and 1748 may well have been written by a gentleman friend who played either the violin or the horn on board his ship. At the outbreak of the War of Jenkins' Ear he obtained letters of marque, that is, government permission to act as a privateer, for the *William*, a ship of which he was a considerable owner, and he sailed her on a trading voyage to South Carolina by way of Gibraltar.

> ... he fitted her out with twenty guns; but did not incumber his trade with a greater expense than that of taking thirty-two men, his business being only to secure his voyage: for which purpose he also took with him a parcel of marine cloaths and other things, to make a shew of men answerable to the force of the ship; in case of meeting with an enemy.[12]

In command of the *Russia Merchant* in 1744, he wondered how to get home safely from Gothenburg in Sweden.

> He remembered his former scheme of adding a mockery of men to his ship the *Duke William* [actually *William*]: but then she was really a ship of force. Here he had no more than four guns, and nothing that looked military, whereupon, as casting cannon there might be expensive and tedious, he got a most compleat set of wooden guns, finely modelled, which he painted of a true metallic colour, and fixing nettings or

tarpolins upon the quarters, set her out in appearance, even to a near eye, a ship of war, being snow-rigged like a king's sloop.[13]

In other words she might well be supposed a 16-gun sloop of war carrying a crew of a hundred instead of the sparsely manned 130-ton merchantman that she was. Yet another ruse used by Walker two years later, when he commanded a fleet of four ships, is described as follows.

> But it now growing dark, the commodore called the carpenter to him, and making him fix a step in a large bathing tub he had for his own use, and set a pole upright in it like a mast, he put into it a quantity of ballast, and ordered him to nail a tarpaulin closely over it; then hanging a lantern and light to the top, he let it down over the stern into the sea. We then shut up all our lights and altered our course, as did the *Duke* [who kept close company] also. At day-break we saw nothing of the three French men-of-war, ... This finesse ... was certainly the cause of our preservation ...[14]

By this time seamen were again in short supply, as they often were in wartime, and in 1745 a Captain Tailor, in conjunction with a Mr Coats, tried to persuade some of Walker's men at Dartmouth, where Walker was fitting out the *Boscawen,* a captured French man-of-war, to desert him to join ships in Exeter which belonged to Tailor and Coats. John Cabel, the wit of the *Boscawen,* accepted a bribe from Tailor and then addressed others members of the crew.

> Gentlemen, you know my name is Cabel [pronounced cable], you'll say a good name for a sailor. Well, gentlemen, if you'll trust this *cabel* it shall be a *sheet cabel* of profit to you. There has been a *poor tailor* on board our noble captain's ship, endeavouring to *take measure* of our loyalty of the noble captain, that is, gentlemen, to *list* us in the service of one Mr *Coats*. Now, my boys, to *suit* him in his own *cut*, suppose we

patch up a kind of a scheme to be *paid for work* we shall never do, and then *sheer off*. I have got three guineas here, with which we will to-night make merry, and then think upon it tomorrow.[15]

Walker did not lose any men, although others beside Cabel accepted bribes from Coats' agents. On the contrary, Walker and his partners apparently gained some of Coats' best men who, as Cabel might have put it, turned turncoat.

After another profitable cruise, Walker and his fleet returned to Bristol, his prisoners including several French officers and an elderly French lady of distinction whom Walker provided with clothes and a hired coach while she was awaiting repatriation.

Being obliged to go to London, he [Walker] requested the favour of using her coach as far as Bath, and to have the honour of staying a week with her there, that he might shew the place to her, the [French] Commodore, and another of the captains. The rest of the French gentlemen had leave afterwards of going by themselves.

The morning Mr Walker and his company set out, they were most divertingly and unexpectedly overtaken on the road by a new kind of cavalcade of the honest tars, who having heard that their captain was going to Bath with the French lady, were determined every one to shew it to their ladies also, as everyone who had not a lady of his own, had bought or borrowed one for the time; and thinking it a compliment to him to set out on the same day, they were resolved to make the genteeler figure on the occasion. The generous-hearted jacks, knowing that ribbands are a great part of the state shew of a lord mayor's day, in graceful knots and roses on the manes and tails of the horses, were led by the like desire of gentility to the purchase (for the expence was the least article considered) of all the variety of colours, tied up in streamers, that might have passed for the strings of so many rainbows, or in knotted roses to adorn their triumph. These, when brought home, most of their ladies fell in love with; so that the number was increased, and equally disposed of on the necks and rumps of the horses, and in the hats and on the breasts of the ladies. Besides these, all the men had similar cockades for themselves.

Never, sure, were horses, whores, and ribbands so dear in one day at Bristol! They who got coaches were, no doubt in their own thoughts, set out the most genteel, whereas they were most the caricatures of gentility; whilst those who flaunted in open chaises exhibited a more loose and easy picture, tho' they run the greatest risque of breaking their necks. The waggons and their horses, adorned with boughs, ribbands and bells, trotted on in the gayest dress of all, and seemed most happy in themselves. Some few appeared, like straggling attendants of the procession, on horseback; and he who would not be thought without a mistress, took her behind him. But they who could get neither coach, chaise, nor waggon, going in search of something with wheels, and finding some brewer's trundles (which thro' policy or good nature were not refused them, as otherwise they would perhaps have been piratically borrowed for the occasion) sawed a butt or large hogshead into two; and nailing it down to the trundle, with a board across for a seat, set out as much in pomp as their fellows, and more in character of a triumphal car; obliged to the ready invention and contrivance peculiar to their species for this their happy equipment. Besides having an equal ornament of parti-coloured streamers properly disposed, these machines, of which there were at least twenty, were decorated with an additional fancy of an ensign or jack, set on the head of the foremost horse, a pennant on a pole erected on the foremost part of the trundle, and colours, hung out by the like contrivance on a sloping one, at the stern; which made them of an amphibious kind, or a mixture of land and water carriage ... This new invention bore much the greatest applause, and made the most corresponding and gay figure of the whole triumph.

In this pomp and order, tho' with a little more swiftness than is usually agreed to, in the like processions of a lord mayor, or lord keeper on the first days of term, the several retinues ran by Mr Walker's company, to the great pleasure and delight particularly of the old lady, who was very sedulous in returning the compliments of salutation, as they huzzaed and passed.

'No wonder', says she to Mr Walker, 'your country, with this spirited liberty, beats the world at sea'.[16]

CHAPTER 16

The Transit of Venus

1750–1785

By the middle of the eighteenth century, after a century of development, Britain's colonies in America were prospering. One-third of a century later still, by 1783, the American War of Independence was over and the United States was born. In the meantime a new spirit of scientific enquiry had developed and further discoveries were being made in the South Seas.

The slave trade was now at its height and Captain John Newton, a born-again Christian who was in command of slave-ships at this time, thanked God for leading him into 'an easy and creditable way of life'.[1] IN 1751 he wrote to his wife,

I am as absolute in my small dominions (life and death excepted) as any potentate in Europe. If I say to one, Come, he comes; if to another, Go, he flies. If I order one person to do something, perhaps three of four will be ambitious of a share in the service. Not a man in the ship must eat his dinner till I please to give him leave; nay, nobody dares to say it is twelve or eight o'clock in my hearing, till I think proper to say so first. There is a mighty bustle of attendance when I leave the ship and a strict watch kept while I am absent, lest I should return unawares, and not be received in due form ... [These] are old-established customs and necessary to be kept up; for, without a strict discipline, the common sailors would be unmanageable.[2]

Seafarers 200 years later would have known such shipmasters. On 21st December 1753 Newton recorded in his journal:

> Corrected the carpenter with a catt for having behaved very mutinously in my abscence, daring the officers and refusing his duty; likewise for making a disturbance on shoar on Wednesday, when I sent for him to cut stantients [stanchions or posts], where he grossly abused Mr Billings and swore he would not proceed in the ship. The barricado [enclosed space] not being built I could not afford to put him irons. Mem: gave him 2 dozen stripes.

Two days later, a Sunday, a day on which Newton normally conducted a religious service and spent time 'in retirement and reflection', he wrote that the carpenter was at work building the barricado in which he should have been confined in irons.

The slaves carried were normally shackled together in pairs and, on learning of a planned rising among them, Newton did not hesitate to use neck yokes and thumb screws. He did not, however, tolerate abuse of the women if it were discovered: 'In the afternoon while we were off the deck, William Cooney seduced a woman slave down into the room and lay with her brutelike in view of the whole quarter deck, for which I put him in irons. I hope this has been the first affair of the kind onboard and I am determined to keep them quiet if possible.'[3] In 1754 Newton came ashore and subsequently took holy orders and wrote the hymn 'How sweet the name of Jesus sounds'. He had come to the conclusion that the slave trade was 'an unhappy and disgraceful branch of commerce' and was instrumental in persuading William Wilberforce to take up the abolitionists' cause. Twenty-four years after he left the sea, he wrote: 'I know of no method of getting money, not even that of robbing for it upon the highway, which has so direct a tendency to efface the moral sense, to rob the heart of every gentle and humane disposition, and to harden it, like steel, against all impressions of sensibility.'[4] On the crews of his slave-ships he commented:

> We are for the most part supplied with the refuse and dregs of the nation. The prisons and glass houses furnish us with large quotas and boys impatient of their parents or masters, or already ruined by some untimely vice and for the most part devoid of all principles ...[5]

The death rate among the sailors in slave-ships – perhaps 20 per cent per year – was higher than that among the slaves, for the latter were valuable merchandise. The sailor was subject to many different risks but the effects of sexual depravity were not the least of them.

> When I was in the trade I knew several commanders of African ships who were prudent, respectable men, and who maintained a proper discipline and regularity in their vessels; but there were too many of a different character. In some ships, perhaps in the most, the licence allowed in this particular [access to female slaves] was almost unlimited. Moral turpitude was seldom considered, but they who took care to do the ship's business, might, in other respects, do what they pleased. These excesses, if they do not induce fevers, at least render the constitution less able to support them; and lewdness, too frequently, terminates in death.[6]

Poor Jack's consolations were few. When Newton gave evidence to a committee of the House of Commons about the effects of the trade on seamen, he said, 'I suppose there is no trade in which seamen are treated with so little humanity ... I have myself seen them when sick beaten for being lazy till they have died under the blows'.[7]

The aims of many of those now sailing the Pacific Ocean were very different. Like his predecessors, Commodore Anson had sought the Manila ship there, but in 1764, twenty-three years after he suffered and survived in Chile as a young officer with Anson's fleet, the Hon John Byron, now an admiral, was sent there to look for a southern continent which was thought to exist as a counterweight to Eurasia. In this he failed, as did Captain Philip Carteret in HMS *Swallow* and Captain Samuel Wallis in HMS *Dolphin*, who followed him in 1766. Nevertheless, the time of the genuine explorers, the skilled navigators and the men of science had arrived.

The southern continent was definitively discovered by Captain James Cook on his first voyage to the South Seas in 1769–70, when he was sent to observe, among other things, the transit of the planet Venus in Tahiti. In the sights of his sailors, and many others of their generation, were exemplars of Venus of a more earthly kind, not slaves but as free as the wind that blew steadily past their homelands.

Wallis, in 1767, had rediscovered Tahiti – the Spaniard de Quiros was there in 1606 – but it was Louis Antoine de Bougainville, leader of a French expedition which visited Tahiti shortly after Wallis, who left the most graphic description of what he found.

> The crowd of dugouts was so thick around the ships that we had a great deal of trouble anchoring. All the inhabitants came toward us crying *tayo,* which means friend, and making gestures of friendship: they asked for nails and earrings. The dugouts were filled with women whose faces were as beautiful as most European women's, and whose bodies were more beautiful. Most of these nymphs were naked, since the men and old women who accompanied them had taken off the nymphs' robes. These women at first made signs to us from the dugouts, and in spite of their naiveté, one could make out in their gestures a slight embarrassment, either because nature has embellished women everywhere with a certain timidity, or because, even in countries where the openness of the Golden

Age still exists, women pretend not to want what they in fact most desire. The men, more simple or more free, expressed themselves more clearly: they urged us to choose a woman and to follow her to land, and their unequivocal gestures made it plain how we were to treat her. I ask you, how was one to keep four hundred young French sailors, who hadn't seen women in six months, at their work in the midst of such a spectacle? Despite all the precautions that we took, a young girl got on board and came onto the forecastle and stood by one of the hatchways which are over the capstan. The girl negligently let fall her robe and stood for all to see, as Venus stood forth before the Phrygian shepherd; and she had the celestial shape of Venus. The sailors and soldiers rushed to get at the hatchway, and never was a capstan turned with such eagerness.

We managed to restrain these bedeviled men, however, but it was no less difficult to control oneself.[8]

For the romantic French, Tahiti became the New Cythera (Kithera), island of love. To Sir Joseph Banks, who accompanied Cook, it was an Arcadia, inhabited by those noble savages who formed the ideal of Rousseau and other contemporary idealists. Wallis had been more pragmatic.

Chastity does not seem to be considered as a virtue among them, for they not only readily and openly trafficked with our people for personal favours, but were brought down by their fathers and brothers for that purpose: they were, however, conscious of the value of beauty, and the size of the nail that was demanded for the enjoyment of the lady, was always in proportion to her charms.[9]

Wallis and his officers had not immediately understood why their ship was falling to pieces: so many nails had been removed by the crew. But Cook discovered that by 1769 the serpent had entered the Garden of Eden.

... the Ships company, what from the constant hard duty they had had at this place and the too free use of women were in a worse state of hilth then they were on our first arrival, for by this time full half of them had got the Venereal disease ...[10]

On 28th June 1774, Cook, on his second voyage and in the neighbourhood of Australia, went ashore to look for fresh water. He was received by the natives with great courtesy and they conducted him to a pond.

I was no sooner return'd from the Pond the first time I landed than this woman and a man presented to me a young woman and gave me to understand she was at my service. Miss, who probably had received her instructions, I found wanted by way of Handsel [gift] a Shirt or a Nail, neither the one nor the other I had to give her without giving her the Shirt on my back which I was not in a humour to do. I soon made them sensible of my Poverty and thought by that means to have come off with flying Colours but I was misstaken, for I was made to understand that I might retire with her on credit, this not suteing me neither the old Lady began first to argue with me and when that fail'd she abused me. I understood very little of what she said, but her actions were expressive enough and she shew'd that her words were to this effect, sneering in my face and saying what sort of a man are you thus to refuse the embraces of so fine a young Woman.[11]

Cook could submit with apparent indifference to every kind of self-denial, and always set the highest standards of behaviour. On discovering Hawaii in 1778, on his third and fatal voyage, he wrote in his journal:

As there were some venereal complaints on board both the Ships, in order to prevent its being communicated to these people, I gave orders that no Women, on any account whatever were to be admitted on board the Ships, I also forbid all manner of connection with them, and ordered that none who had the venereal upon them should go out of the ships. But

193

whether these regulations had the desired effect or no time can only discover. It is no more than what I did when I first visited the Friendly Islands [Tonga] yet I afterwards found it did not succeed, ... [12]

By this time good officers had a very fair idea of how to care for their men. In the Magellan Straits in 1767 teams were sent ashore from the *Dolphin* to collect wild celery, cranberries and mussels. George Robertson, master under Wallis, wrote,

That the Ship's Company may be well supplyed with the above articles, we send a Man of each Mess every Day to gather the whole, we still continue giving the men Ground White [wheat] with Cellery and Portable Soop boild in it for Breakfast, which makes the best Meal I ever saw for Seamen onb'd His Majesty's Ships, we likeways Boil Cellery and Portable Soop amongst the Pese, the Mussels they Rost or Stew as they please, and they catch small fish with hook and Line allongside. Every man has his full allowance over and above this refreshments, besides the Men thats Employed in any Extra Duty such as fishing with the Sean [seine], cutting fire wood or Sounding and Surveying, has Double Allowance of Good old Rum or Brandy Grog – and if any Man gets weet he is ordered to Shift and put on dray cloas the instant he comes onb'd, nor is sufferd to put the least ragg of weet cloas below, to prevent the vile nasty sour unhealthy smell, which is too frequent onb'd of all ships. We keep the fire in from four in the Morning untill Nine at Night, which gives the people an Opportunity of Draying there weet Cloaths in Rainy Bade weather, and the ship is cleand both above and Below every Day, and every Slugish nasty fellow is punished the instant that he is found out, but to do our Ships Company Justice there is but few slugish Dirty fellows in her, and those who was is now cured by the care of the Officers, all this precautions and Indulgences has contrabute greatly to preserve the healths of all our men. At this Instant we have not one sick man in the ship nor the least complaint to be heard amongst them except a few slight colds.[13]

Crossing the Pacific Ocean, Robertson observed,

It may not be Amiss to take notice of the Quantity of provisions we had onb'd at this time, which we have since found all Good of their kind – Beef, Pork & Sewet about fifteen Months full allowance – Peas, Flower [flour], Wheat and Oatmeal near the same. Bread about ten months, Brandy and Rum about Nine Months Besides Mustard Vinegar and pickeld Cabag – the Mustard and Vinegar was Generally served out every fortnight, but the Pickeld Cabag was only served when the Surgeon thought it proper that Article was mostly preserved for those who Complaind of the Scurvey which was now beginning to Make its Appearance, but its Progress was greatly checked by using the three last Articles we also had twenty half hh^ds of Malt Onboard but did not begin to use it untill we got a great way to the Westward, and found our Men falling down very fast, it was then made into wort, and was of great use to the sick.[14]

Captain Carteret's crew in HMS *Swallow*, a month or so behind the *Dolphin*'s, also suffered scurvy, but were lucky in their water supply.

Many of the people began now to be affected with the Scurvy, As in all this traverce, we had much hard rain, & wet weather; but happily we caught a good deal of water, by a little Awning, I had caused to be made with some wood, I had got while we were in the Streights Magellan, it was cover'd over with a clean painted Canvass, which had been allowed for a floor cloth in my Cabbin, but thus put to much more usefull service, so that all the water that fell on this little Awning, was always saved without trouble or attendance; as there was Casks ready to receive it, & by the means of this Supply, I was enabled to give my people plenty of water without the Necessity of putting them at a stated allowance; every time the cask out of which the people drank their water was filled, the Surgeon put into it, a certain quantity of Spirit of Vitriol, and the grog was like-wise made with this water. I attribute the good health, the People enjoyed so long, to have been greatly owing to the use this little Awning was of, both in the procuring us so great plenty of water, and in sheltering the people from the inclemency of the weather.[15]

Cook above all was at pains to care for his men, taking with him what he could to keep scurvy at bay, giving his crews every possible chance to refresh themselves ashore, and providing warm clothing in cold climates. On 20th December 1772 he writes in his journal: 'Set all the Taylors to Work to lengthen the sleves of the Seamens Jackets and to make Caps to shelter them from the Severity of the weather, having order'd a quantity of Red Baize to be converted for that purpose. Also began to make Wort from the Malt and give to such People as had symptoms of the Scurvy; ...'[16] A fortnight later he notes: 'First and middle parts strong gales attended with a thick Fogg Sleet and Snow, all the Rigging covered with Ice and the air excessive cold, the Crew how-ever stand it tolerable well, each being cloathed with a fearnought jacket, a pair of Trowsers of the same and a large cap made of Canvas and Baize, these together with an addi-tional glass of Brandy every Morning enables them to bear the Cold without Flinshing.'[17] Earlier, he records: 'Got by the Still 14 gallons of Fresh Water from one Copper the time the Pease was boiling (viz) from half past 7 o'clock in the Morning till Noon.'[18] The results of such care, after rigor-ous months in antarctic seas, proved as follows.

We had been a long time without refreshments, our Provisions were in a state of decay and little more nourishment remained in them than just to keep life and soul together. My people were yet healthy and would cheerfully have gone where ever I thought proper to lead them, but I dreaded the Scurvy lay-ing hold of them at a time when we had nothing left to remove it. Besides it would have been cruel in me to have continued the Fatigues and hardships they were continually exposed to longer than absolutely necessary, their behaviour throughout the whole voyage merited every indulgence which was in my power to give them.[19]

The seamen, as throughout history, were often their own worst enemies, even when well led. 'Every innovation whatever [Cook observes] tho ever so much to their advantage is sure to meet with the highest disapprobation from Seamen. Portable soup and Sour Krout [two of Cook's specifics against scurvy] were at first both condemned by them as stuff not fit for human being[s] to eat '[20]

It was not only in government vessels that humane commanders were to be found. The lawyer William Hickey provides a graphic picture of some officers who served the East India Company at this time.

Captain Waddell [in command of the East Indiaman *Plassey* in 1769–70], then about forty years of age, naturally grave, with an appearance of shyness or reserve, possessed one of the mildest and most equal tempers that ever man was blessed with; nor did I, during a voyage out and home which I made in his ship, ever once see him angry, or hear him utter a single oath or hasty expression. He loved to set young people at some gambol or other, and was constantly promoting it. He was himself wonderfully active and strong, amongst various proofs of which, he did one feat that amazed the whole ship's company, and which I never knew any other person come at all near. It was this – standing upon the quarter-deck under the main shroud, he laid hold of the first ratline with his right hand, then sprang to the second, with his left, and so on alternately right and left up to the last, close to the futtock shrouds. The exertion in accomplishing this must have been prodigious, nor was there another man in the ship – and we had many fine, active fellows on board – that could get beyond the third ratline, and only two that reached the third.[21]

Captain Arthur Gore of the East Indiaman *Nassau,* on the other hand, was a man of a highly suspicious nature who became 'terrified beyond measure' when in 1779 thirty-three of his crew succumbed to scurvy.[22]

Captain Gore's chief mate was a drunken sot,[23] but Captain Waddell's, known as 'Black Sam' or 'Blackguard Sam' and an American by birth, was different again. 'He never uttered a sentence without embellishing it with oaths, "Damn your eyes" always uppermost, and he chewed tobacco in large quantities; yet ... there never existed a better-hearted man, or a more zealous friend. In his profession he could not be surpassed.'[24]

In the *Nassau* the second officer, Chisholme, was a proud and handsome Scot of good education, 'upwards of six feet high, and a perfect seaman',[25] while the dressy third mate of the *Plassey,* although careful of his money, was known in the service as 'Count Douglas'. He apologised for the dirty state of the ship when Hickey joined at Gravesend – a state unavoidable when receiving cargo.

> The ship certainly was in a sad dirty plight [writes Hickey]; but Mr Douglas's cabin was an exception to the general filth, being neatness itself, and most elegantly fitted up. It was painted a light pea green, with gold beadings, the bed and curtains of the richest Madras chintz, one of the most complete dressing tables I ever saw, having every useful article in it; a beautiful bureau and book-case, stored with the best books, and three neat mahogany chairs, formed the furniture. In all my subsequent voyages I never saw so handsome an apartment in a ship.[26]

From Whampoa in China, Hickey travelled the 18 miles to Canton in company with a 'guinea-pig', or trainee-officer, from the East Indiaman *Cruttenden,* who was named Bob Pott and who was not quite fourteen years of age. Pott's family were shipowners in the East India Company.

We were shown, when nearly half way, a small inlet or creek called 'Lob Lob Creek', from whence in *sampans* (the name of the country boats) came forth certain prostitutes, who, if required so to do, board the boats passing up and down, and thus satisfy the carnal appetites of the people belonging to the ships, this being the only spot where opportunities of that nature offer; for the magistrates of China are very rigid on that point, making it extremely difficult, indeed almost impossible, to procure a woman within the city or environs of Canton, or even on board the ships.

The females who ply at Lob Lob Creek are supposed so to do by stealth. I say 'supposed', because the fact is that they pay a proportion of their earnings to the mandarin upon duty, who thereupon, like an upright administrator of justice, shuts his eyes and his ears to the breach of the law, those public officers being invariably corrupt ...

When we were off Lob Lob Creek [on the way back to Whampoa] one of the boatmen, opening the cabin door, peeped in and said 'Master, Caree Lob Lob?' to which Bob directly answered, 'Yes', holding up two of his fingers. In five minutes a little open boat came paddling towards us, and two very pretty girls jumped in at our window. Bob retired with one to the after cabin, leaving me with the other. We had been a very short time together when the same man opened the door again, quickly crying out 'Chop Chop Lob Lob, mandarin dee come'. Regardless of him or his words, which I did not understand, I continued the business I was engaged upon; which when finished I called to Bob, who desired me to come in, and I found him and his companion sitting very quietly together. Having dismissed our Lob Lob ladies, we continued our voyage to Whampoa, ... Early the following morning [after spending the night on the *Cruttenden*] we went to the *Plassey*, where Rogers insisted upon our spending the day. Mentioning to him the circumstances that had occurred on our passage down and my astonishment at such a stripling as Bob thinking of a woman, he observed that in all probability we should both have cause to remember Lob Lob Creek for some time to come, there being no more than six women to satisfy the lusts of a fleet of five-and-twenty ships, the consequence of which had already shown itself, a number of their junior officers being diseased.[27]

Pott had, in fact, been wise enough to leave his girl alone.

On the voyage back to England the *Plassey* struck soundings in 70 fathoms, and the following morning an English cutter of 150 tons burden was sighted less than a quarter of a mile away. A small boat was despatched from the cutter and a man came aboard the *Plassey*.

He was of a Herculean form, with a healthy ruby face. From his dress and appearance I should not have supposed he possessed ten pounds in the world. Captain Waddell conducted him into the round house, where the following short dialogue ensued.

Stranger: 'Well, Captain, how is tea?'
Captain: 'Twenty pounds.'
Stranger: 'No, that won't do; eighteen – a great number of Chino ships this season.'
Captain: 'Very well, you know best.'
Stranger: 'How many chests?'
Captain: 'Sixty odd.'
Stranger: 'Come, bear a hand then and get them in the cutter.'

By this I found our new visitor was a smuggler. The foregoing was all that passed in completing the sale and purchase of so large a quantity of tea. In the same laconic manner he bought the stock of the different officers ...

The tea being all removed to the cutter, pen, ink, and paper was produced; the smuggler, sitting down at a table in the round house, calculated the amount due for his purchase; which Captain Waddell admitting correct, he took from his pocket-book a cheque, which filled up for twelve hundred and twenty-four pounds he signed and delivered it to the captain. I observed it was drawn upon Walpole and Company, Bankers in Lombard Street, and was astonished to see Captain Waddell with the utmost composure deposit it in his escritoire.[28]

Hickey, although only at sea for, perhaps, five years, experienced at least two hurricanes. One was in eastern waters, and thirteen members of the crew lost their lives, most of these washed overboard.[29] The other was in home waters, where Hickey had come ashore at Deal from the West Indiaman *New Shoreham*, to await better weather.

There were upwards of a hundred ships of the fleet that had sailed with us at anchor in the Downs, and by noon upwards of seventy more came in, most of them having sustained damages, some materially, by loss of topmasts or lower yards ... Before five it blew an absolute hurricane; the ships in every direction were seen driving from their anchors, although the masts and yards were lowered, as well as every other possible precaution taken ...

[The following morning] a sad scene of desolation and ruin presented itself to my view. Of the numerous fleet that but twenty-four hours before had been proudly riding at anchor in the Downs, no more than eight now remained; and three of those were totally dismantled ...

Having breakfasted, I walked toward Sandwich. The beach was covered with pieces of wreck, dead bodies of the unfortunate persons that had perished, and hundreds of sheep and hogs from the Government transports.[30]

In 1775 Thomas Curtis made a voyage to the Gulf of St Lawrence and experienced bad weather.

I think it was the third Sunday we lost one of our pigs and knew not how, on the fourth another and on the fifth another on the Sixth we lost the sow. It being in the After noon several saw her fall overboard. There was a great Swel and but little wind the Vessel rold very mutch and her feet Slipping could not save her self. Our Captn being informd of the misfortune came on deck when we could see her Swim remarkable well at a considerable distance from the Vessel. I believe half a mile. The mate whose name was Johnson an Excelent Swimer said if the Captn would order the Ship about he would fix a rope to him and Swim after her. This being done we soon came near her and the mate swam to her and made a rope fast round her and we hauld her in again. John Compton went a loft to see this performd and had the misfortune to fall overboard. Though he was a good Swimer was so mutch frighted that he had not power to Strike one Stroke but lay on the Water like a log of Wood. When the mate had made the rope fast on the Sow we then haul'd her up. She seemd not the Worst for it & continued very well afterward.

The Mate then Swam to Compton & making a rope fast to him we hauld him in.[31]

The American War of Independence had begun and John Paul Jones, the Scottish-born seafaring hero of the Americans in that war, wrote to Congress giving details of what he considered desirable in an officer at sea.

It is by no means enough that an Officer of the Navy should be a capable mariner; ... He should be as well a gentleman of liberal education; refined manners, punctilious courtesy, and nicest sense of personal honour. Coming now to view the Naval Officer aboard ship, and in relation to those under his command, he should be the soul of tact, patience, justice, firmness and charity.[32]

Captain Cook and Captain Waddell were not alone in measuring up to such high specifications.

CHAPTER 17

God Help Sailors!

1785–1815

The American War of Independence was over, the Dutch were no longer a menace to the British at sea, and the French had lost the Seven Years War which had ended in 1763. However, war at sea continued to dominate mercantile trade and was more or less continuous from 1793 to 1815, when the British at last defeated the French and established their supremacy upon the oceans, a supremacy which then lasted for more than 150 years.

John Nicol, who was born near Edinburgh in 1755, went to sea as a cooper (known in the navy as 'Bungs'), and was serving aboard the *Surprise,* a 28-gun frigate, during the American War of Independence. At St John's, Newfoundland,

One of our men was whipped through the fleet for stealing some dollars from a merchant ship he was assisting to bring into port. It was a dreadful sight; the unfortunate sufferer tied down on the boat, and rowed from ship to ship, getting an equal number of lashes at the side of each vessel from a fresh man. The poor wretch, to deaden his sufferings, had drunk a whole bottle of rum a little before the time of punishment. When he had only two portions to get of his punishment, the captain of the ship perceived he was tipsy, and immediately ordered the rest of the punishment to be delayed until he was sober. He was rowed back to the *Surprise,* his back swelled like a pillow, black and blue; some sheets of thick blue paper were steeped in vinegar and laid on his back. Before he seemed insensible, now his shrieks rent the air. When better he was sent to the ship, where his tortures stopped, and again renewed.[1]

Aboard the *King George,* with Captain Portlock, who had sailed with Captain Cook, Nicol was with the first sailors after Cook to visit Hawaii. As a very good brewer of spruce beer, he would have commended himself to Cook, who valued it as a specific against the scurvy. Once again nearly every man on board took a mistress from among the native women.

In 1789, as steward aboard an early convict ship to New South Wales, Nicol also took a mistress from among the 245 female convicts aboard the transport *Lady Julian,* most of them prostitutes and few of them vicious.

> When we were fairly out to sea, every man on board took a wife from among the convicts, they nothing loath. The girl with whom I lived, for I was as bad in this point as the others, was named Sarah Whitelam. She was a native of Lincoln, a girl of a modest reserved turn, as kind and true a creature as ever lived. I courted her for a week and upwards, and would have married her upon the spot, had there been a clergyman on board. She had been banished for a mantle she had borrowed from an acquaintance. Her friend prosecuted her for stealing it, and she was transported for seven years. I had fixed my fancy upon her from the moment I knocked the rivet out of her irons upon my anvil, and as firmly resolved to bring her back to England, when her time was out, my lawful wife, as ever I did intend anything in my life. She bore me a son in our voyage out.[2]

By Nicol's account it was a true love match but, although he tried, he never afterwards found trace of Sarah or their son. He heard that Sarah had left Australia for Bombay before her term had expired.

His experience of Portuguese sailors in bad Atlantic weather echoed exactly that of John Bulkeley, gunner of the *Wager*, half a century earlier. After being three years away he arrived home from Lisbon in a merchantman in 1792.

When we arrived at Gravesend a man-of-war's boat came on board to press any Englishmen there might be on board so we stowed ourselves away among some bags of cotton, where we were almost smothered, but could hear every word that was said. The captain told the lieutenant he had no more hands than he saw, and they were all Portuguese. The lieutenant was not very particular, and he left the brig without making much search When the boat left the vessel we crept from our hiding hole, and not long after a custom-house-officer came on board ... [I] gave the custom-house-officer half-a-guinea for the loan of his cocked hat and powdered wig; the long gilt-headed cane was included in the bargain. I got a waterman to put me on shore ... I enquired of the waterman the way to the inn, where the coach set out from for London; I at the same time knew as well as him. I passed for a passenger. At the inn I called for a pint of wine, pens and ink, and was busy writing any nonsense that came into my head until the coach set off. All these precautions were necessary. Had the waterman suspected me to be a sailor, he would have informed the press-gang in one minute. The waiter at the inn would have done the same.

By these precautions I arrived safe in London, but did not go down to Wapping until next day, where I took up my old lodgings, still in my disguise.[3]

But a few months later he arranged for his landlord to betray him to the press-gang, pocketing the six guineas with which his landlord was rewarded. His hope was that he might get to Bombay and look for Sarah Whitelam but, instead, aboard the *Nottingham,* he sailed direct for China.

I witnessed off the Cape of Good Hope ... a dreadful example
of what man will dare, and the perils he will encounter, to free
himself from a situation he dislikes. A man-of-war had been
washing her gratings, when the India fleet hove in sight. They
are washed by being lowered overboard, and allowed to float
astern. Four or five men had slipped down upon them, cut
them adrift, and were thus voluntarily committed to the vast
Atlantic, without a bit of biscuit, or a drop of water, or any
means of guiding the gratings they were floating upon, in the
hope of being picked up by some vessel. They held out their
arms to us, and supplicated in the wildest manner, to be taken
on board. The captain would not. The *Nottingham* was a fast
sailing ship, and the first in the fleet. He said, 'I will not; some
of the stern ships will pick them up'. While he spoke, these
unfortunate and desponding fellow-creatures lessened to our
view, while their cries rung in our ears.[4]

On his return he was seized once again by the press-gang
and thus, in 1798, saw service with Nelson at the Battle of
the Nile. Nicol was aboard the *Goliath*.

I saw as little of this action as I did of the one on the 14th
February off Cape St Vincent. My station was in the powder
magazine with the gunner ... Any information we got was
from the boys and women who carried the powder. The
women behaved as well as the men, and got a present for their
bravery from the Grand Signior ... In the heat of the action, a
shot came right into the magazine, but did no harm, as the
carpenters plugged it up, and stopped the water that was rushing in. I was much indebted to the gunner's wife, who gave her
husband and me a drink of wine every now and then, which
lessened our fatigue much. There were some of the women
wounded, and one woman belonging to Leith died of
her wounds, and was buried on a small island in the bay.
One woman bore a son in the heat of the action; she
belonged to Edinburgh. When we ceased firing, I went on
deck to view the state of the fleets, and an awful sight it was.

The whole bay was covered with dead bodies, mangled, wounded and scorched, not a bit of clothes on them except their trowsers ...

One lad who was stationed by a salt-box, on which he sat to give out cartridges, and keep the lid close, – it is a trying berth, – when asked for a cartridge, he gave none, yet he sat upright; his eyes were open. One of the men gave him a push; he fell all his length on the deck. There was not a blemish on his body, yet he was quite dead, and was thrown overboard. The other, a lad who had the match in his hand to fire his gun. In the act of applying it a shot took off his arm; it hung by a small piece of skin. The match fell to the deck. He looked to his arm, and seeing what had happened, seized the match in his left hand, and fired off the gun before he went to the cockpit to have it dressed.⁵

Paid off in 1802, Nicol returned to Edinburgh and married a cousin. 'I was once more my own master, and felt so happy, I was like one bewildered. Did those on shore only experience half of the sensations of a sailor at perfect liberty, after being seven years on board a ship without a will of his own, they would not blame his eccentricities, but wonder he was not more foolish.'⁶ He dictated his memoirs at the age of sixty-seven, by which time, unable to obtain any pension, he had been in want for some years.

As Nicol sailed to Australia in his convict ship, after having tasted the delights of the South Seas in Hawaii, Captain William Bligh was having trouble with his men in the *Bounty*. After nearly six months of *la dolce vita* in Tahiti, whither they had gone to load breadfruit plants for the West Indies, Fletcher Christian, one of two master's mates, and other seamen mutinied because they had left this earthly paradise. On 28th April 1789 Bligh and eighteen crew members who were loyal to him were dumped at sea in the *Bounty*'s 23-foot launch. Christian supplied them with twine, canvas, sails, cordage, fishing lines, a 28-gallon cask of water, sixteen two-pound pieces of pork, 150 pounds of bread, six quarts of rum, six bottles of wine, a quadrant and a compass. The carpenter was allowed to take his tool chest, and four cutlasses were thrown into the boat after it was launched. By this time the boat was in deep water.

Thus began an epic voyage of nearly 4000 miles, which took forty-five days. Bligh kept a journal[7] from which the following extracts are taken.

[After 5 days] I served a tea-spoonful of rum to each person, (for we were very wet and cold) with a quarter of a bread-fruit, which was scarce eatable, for dinner: our engagement [Bligh's plan to reach Timor in the Malay Archipelago] was now strictly to be carried into execution, and I was fully determined to make our provisions last eight weeks, let the daily provision be ever so small.

[After 12 days] The weather continued extremely bad, and the wind increased; we spent a very miserable night, without sleep, except such as could be got in the midst of rain. The day brought no relief but its light. The sea broke over us so much, that two men were constantly baling; and we had no choice how to steer, being obliged to keep before the waves for fear of the boat filling.

The allowance now regularly served to each person was one 25th of a pound of bread, and a quarter of a pint of water, at eight in the morning, at noon, and at sunset. Today I gave about half an ounce of pork for dinner, which, though any moderate person would have considered only a mouthful, was divided into three or four.

[After 22 days] At dawn of day, some of my people seemed half dead; our appearances were horrible; and I could look no way, but I caught the eye of someone in distress. Extreme hunger was now too evident, but no one suffered from thirst, nor had we much inclination to drink, that desire, perhaps, being satisfied through the skin. The little sleep we got was in the midst of water, and we constantly awoke with severe cramps and pains in our bones. This morning I served about two tea-spoonfuls of rum to each person, and the allowance of bread and water as usual. At noon the sun broke out and revived everyone.

At the beginning of this voyage Bligh had picked up bread-fruit in the Friendly Islands. Now, after thirty days at sea, he sighted Australia and made his way northward, stop-ping from time to time to collect clams and berries. Then he struck out once more into the open sea to reach Timor eleven days ahead of schedule.

It is not possible for me to describe the pleasure which the blessing of the sight of this land diffused among us. It appeared scarce credible to ourselves, that in an open boat, and so poorly provided, we should have been able to reach the coast of Timor in forty-one days after leaving Tofoo [the Friendly Islands], having in that time run, by our log, a dis-tance of 3618 miles; and that, notwithstanding our extreme distress, no one should have perished in the voyage.

Sailing via the Dutch settlements of Coupang and Sourabaya, he reached Batavia [Jakarta] on 1st October where, though he fell seriously ill, he was hospitably entertained.

My illness (fever) prevented me from gaining much knowl-edge of Batavia. Of their public buildings, I saw nothing that gave me so much satisfaction as their country hospital for sea-men. It is a large commodious and airy building, about four miles from the town, close to the side of the river, or rather in the river; for the ground on which it stands has, by labour, been made an island of, and the sick are carried there in a boat: each ward of a separate dwelling, and the different diseases are properly classed. They have sometimes 1400 patients in it: at this time there were 800, but more than half of them were recovered and fit for service, of whom 300 were destined for the fleet that was to sail to Europe. I went through most of the wards, and there appeared great care and attention. The sheets, bedding, and linen, of the sick were perfectly neat and clean. The house of the physician Mr Spurling, who has the management of the hospital, is at one extremity of the building: and here it was that I resided. To the attention and care of this gentleman, for which he would receive no payment, I am probably indebted for my life.[8]

This dedicated and dauntless officer was not as obnoxious as he has sometimes been depicted. He flogged only one man, who received two dozen lashes for insolence, on the way to Tahiti. His crew suffered little sickness, and the mutiny took him by surprise. Five years afterwards he went back for more breadfruit, and this time he made the delivery to the West Indies.

Between these two voyages made by Captain Bligh, William Richardson joined a slave-ship, *The Spy*, as fourth mate. Off the Guinea Coast in 1790 water was short.

In order to make our water last long (and none taken from the scuttle butt), it was headed up with a hole at the top to admit a musket barrel with its breech off, and through this we had to suck up a drink (captain and mate excepted). We found it very difficult at first, but practice soon made it easy, and in my opinion it is better than being on an allowance, for when that is gone you have to suffer till next serving, but the gun-barrel you can always have recourse to; some ships being stricter, a man after his suck had to take the barrel to the mast-head, and when another wanted a suck he had to go there for it, so no man would do that except he was thirsty.[9]

As we were coming in from our ship [in the ship's pinnace] the chief mate [who had escaped from a Liverpool prison after throwing the ship's cook into the boiling coppers] intimated that we were now going to Bonny, and that some of us who had not been seasoned to the climate would most likely leave our bones on Bonny Point, the place where they bury

European seamen; but, poor man, he little thought then that he would be the first on board to leave his bones there.[10]

The mate succumbed to what Richardson called 'the blind fever' a few weeks later.

During the first two months the slaves were brought to us pretty regularly and I suppose we must have got about two hundred of both sexes, but after that they came slowly. Poor creatures! it was pitiful to see the distress they were in on coming on board, for some of them think that we live on the ocean and wanted them for food. Some of the females fainted, and one of them went out of her mind; we did all we could to comfort them, and by degrees they got more composed.[11]

When he could, Richardson passed a little extra water to the slaves.

I was obliged to be very cautious in this business, for our captain began to show himself in his proper colours and would flog a man as soon as look at him, and assumed as much consequence as if he had been captain of a line-of-battleship: all we four mates had to attend him with hats off at the gangway in going out or coming in to the ship; he flogged a good seaman for only losing an oar out of the boat, and the poor fellow soon after died.[12]

The 450 slaves were sold in Jamaica for £44 each. On his return the press-gang took Richardson off Beachy Head but in 1791 he joined the 800-ton *Prince of Kaunitz* at Ostend as a quartermaster. Built of teak at Bombay, and owned by a Scotsman and a Frenchman, she sailed, with a mixed crew, under Genoa colours. He left this ship (with twelve others) in Calcutta – they all sacrificed their wages in consequence – and joined a 'country' ship to trade opium. When the harvest failed, he joined the brig *Active*, which swarmed with rats, ants, cockroaches and scorpions. 'One of our people (a Yorkshireman)', he comments, 'used to skin, grill and eat [the rats], and they tasted as well as rabbits.'[13] In Madras,

An English transport with troops on board anchored ahead of us, and we soon after saw a great many pieces of salt pork thrown overboard, and come floating towards us. We soon jumped into our boat and picked them up: some were rusty and some not, and wondering why they threw such good meat overboard we thought an infection might be among it, therefore threw the worst overboard, but could not bear to part with the best, so took our chance and ate them; had we known that the pork was thrown overboard because the pickle had leaked out of the cask when surveyed on board the transport, we should have kept the whole and been glad of it. Had those troops been living on rice, doll [dhali] and ghee, as we were, they would have jumped mast-high for such good meat![14]

In 1797, during the Napoleonic Wars, Richardson married and his wife was with him when sickness broke out aboard his ship when she was in Martinique in the West Indies. Many on board died though his wife, who fell seriously ill, recovered after taking no food for a while and drinking only tisane.[15]

In 1805 Richardson was appointed gunner of the *Caesar* at three shillings a day, and was still on board her in 1810 when Samuel Morgan was sentenced for desertion.

Sent Samuel Morgan, a prisoner for desertion, on board the *Barfleur* to await his trial, and next day he and two men belonging to the *Kent* (likewise for desertion) were tried by a court-martial and each sentenced to three hundred lashes. Poor Morgan was much pitied, being a good and mild creature, and almost fainted when the sentence was pronounced. By the kind interference of the humane Lady Hardy poor Morgan afterwards got reprieved, but the other two poor fellows were punished round the fleet; but did not receive their number of lashes because they could not bear it, so they were sent on board the flagship until they recovered to receive the remainder. Horrid work, could anyone bear to see a beast used so, let alone a fellow creature? People may talk of negro slavery and the whip, but let them look nearer home, and see a poor sailor arrived from a long voyage, exulting in the pleasure of soon being among his dearest friends and relations. Behold him just entering the door, when a press gang seizes him like a felon, drags him away and puts him into the tender's hold, and from thence he is sent on board a man-of-war, perhaps ready to sail to some foreign station, without seeing either his wife, friends, or relations; if he complains he is likely to be seized up and flogged with a cat, much more severe than the negro driver's whip, and if he deserts he is flogged round the fleet nearly to death. Surely they had better shoot a man at once; it would be greater lenity.[16]

After thirty-nine years at sea, twenty-six of them in the Navy, Richardson was retired on a pension of £65 a year.

Robert Eastwick was thrown in at the deep end in 1784 when he started his apprenticeship, at the age of twelve, aboard a whaler. The mate was brutal, but a gruff old seaman of sixty-five, who had seen service in the King's ships, befriended the young Eastwick.

There is no justice or injustice on board a ship, my lad. There are only two things. Duty and Mutiny – mind that. All that you are ordered to do is duty. All that you refuse to do is mutiny.[17]

In 1792 Eastwick was fortunate enough to join the East India Company and became fifth mate of the *Barwell*, commanded by the appropriately named John Welladvice, 'a good seaman and a kind gentleman of whom I always retained the most friendly recollection'. All seven of the officers were 'gentlemen by education and family'.[18] Not long afterwards, Eastwick was given command of a vessel in country service in India, a ship which traded in opium to China. Eastwick commented that the ship was 'equal to at least £4000 a year'; in other words, this was the salary that he might expect. This, however, was after shipwreck in command of a rotten old American-built brig.

> About an hour afterwards another wave carried overboard the ship's steward, who was a Parsee and like a fish in the water. His greed of lucre had well-nigh done for him, for he tied round his neck a bundle of silver-plate, in a towel, worth a few paltry pounds at the outside, yet in his anxiety to save it, he had not hesitated to load himself ... he tried to swim towards the wreck, but he could not keep his face above water; so he began to fumble at the knot behind his neck to untie it, and his head kept slowly sinking lower and lower, until his feet were kicking in the air ... With convulsive efforts he kept coming to the surface ... At last he deliberately dived down head foremost, and I believed him gone for ever, when in about half a minute he came up again, having by this expedient slipped the noose over his head. Being now relieved from the weight, he struck out swimming and regained the wreck, where he immediately began blubbering at his ill-fortune in having lost his silver plate, as though it had been wantonly sacrificed at the value of his life.[19]

Eastwick himself won and lost three modest fortunes before he made £10,000 – enough to retire on – in thirteen months' active employment in the new trade in South America.

Captain Edmund Fanning, a native of Stonington, Connecticut, first sailed for the South Seas in 1792. From 1797 to 1799 he took the brig *Betsey* round the world to obtain fur seal skins for the market in Canton. Gathering penguin eggs along the way, he recorded:

> I have kept these penguins' eggs in a good state of preservation, on board ship, for a period of nine months, by first

immersing them in seal oil, though any will answer, then packing them in a cask with dry sand; a layer of sand, then a layer of eggs, and so on until the cask is filled, placing them all on their sides, with one end towards the bung, then heading the cask up, and stowing it bung up, in such a place as it can be got at on the third day, in order to be turned bung down, and so on, being turned every third day, until wanted for use, this method keeps the yolk from settling to the shell, and the sand mixing with the oil, forms a crust of sand and oil over it, by which the shell is kept perfectly air tight, and thus the egg is preserved from destruction.[20]

On the otherwise uninhabited island of Tinian in the Philippines, he came across the shipwrecked crew of the East India Company's annual supply from Canton to Sidney, New South Wales, whose life was reminiscent of that of the *Swiss Family Robinson*, a romance that was published fifteen years later.

It was now upward of thirteen months since this ship had been cast away; the crew, however, were so happy as to be thrown on one of the most fertile spots in the world; they had tamed a milk cow, a few young cattle, a number of swine, and domestic fowls; these all run wild. They had, moreover, a large supply of bread-fruit, cocoa-nuts, and many other excellent tropical fruits, besides which, their cargo, from its assorted character, furnished them with suitable clothing, as well as some of the most to be wished for articles for the table; so that they were only to be considered as suffering from the want of society.[21]

In the neighbourhood of Sumatra the *Betsey* was attacked by a fleet of piratical proas.

On a nearer approach, they commenced shouting most tumultuously, and opened their fire upon us; the centre division by this time was within musket shot distance, and discovered a set of the most hideous animals that ever the light of the sun shone upon; to add to this savage appearance, as well as with a view of intimidating our crew, they increased their yellings, to a rate that would have been creditable to the lungs of a war party of wild Indians. At this moment I clapped the helm a weather, hauled up the courses, and the ship, quickly wearing off, brought her broadside as handsomely as mortal could wish, to bear directly on the proas. We let them have it, in this the first discharge dismantling the centre vessel, and disabling two on each side of her; the effect produced was as expected; they instantly stopped their headway by means of their sweeps, and were apparently making up their minds as to, how next, we now wore ship again, and the better to assist their meditations, gave them another broadside with a suitable proportion of musketry.[22]

The proas then withdrew, leaving the dismantled one to its fate, but Fanning allowed it and the crew to depart in peace after he had destroyed all its armament.

Piracy in eastern waters was – and is – no new maritime activity. Nor was war between nations. As the eighteenth turned into the nineteenth century Britain and France, with one brief intermission, continued to wage war at sea. Its impact was felt in Cumbria by William Wordsworth and his sister Dorothy, who kept a journal.

Monday, 21st December 1801 As we came up the White Moss, we met an old man, who I saw was a beggar by his two bags hanging over his shoulder, but from a half laziness, half indifference, & a wanting to *try* him if he would speak I let him pass. He said nothing, & my heart smote me. I turned back & said You are begging? 'Ay' says he, – I gave him a halfpenny. William, judging from his appearance joined in I suppose you were a Sailor; 'Ay' he replied, 'I have been 57 years at sea, 12 of them on board a man-of-war under Sir Hugh Palmer'. Why have you not a pension? 'I have no pension, but I could have got into Greenwich hospital but all my officers are dead'. He was 75 years of age, had a freshish colour in his cheeks, grey

hair, a decent hat with a binding round the edge, the hat worn
brown & glossy, his shoes were small thin shoes low in the
quarters, pretty good they had belonged to a gentleman. His
coat was blue, frock shaped coming over his thighs, it had been
joined up at the seams behind with paler blue to let it out, &
there were three Bell-shaped patches of darker blue behind
where the Buttons had been. His breeches were either of fust-
ian or grey cloth, with strings hanging down, whole & tight &
he had a checked shirt on, & a small coloured handkerchief
tyed round his neck. His bags were hung over each shoulder &
lay on each side of him, below his breast. One was brownish &
of coarse stuff, the other was white with meal on the outside,
& his blue waistcoat was whitened with meal. In the coarse bag
I guess he put his scraps of meat &c. He walked with a slender
stick decently stout, but his legs bowed outwards.²³

Monday, 15th March 1802 Mr Luff came in at one o'clock,
he had a long talk with William – he went to Mr Olliff's after
dinner & returned to us to tea During his absence a sailor
who was travelling from Liverpool to Whitehaven called he
was faint & pale when he knocked at the door, a young Man
very well dressed. We sate by the kitchen fire talking with him
for 2 hours – he told us interesting stories of his life. His name
was Isaac Chapel – he had been at sea since he was 15 years
old. He was by trade a sail-maker. His last voyage was to the
Coast of Guinea. He had been on board a Slave Ship the Captain's name was Maxwell where one man had been killed a
Boy put to lodge with the pigs & was half eaten, one Boy set
to watch in the hot sun till he dropped down dead. He had
been cast away in North America & had travelled 30 days
among the Indians where he had been well treated – He had
twice swum from a King's ship in the Night & escaped, he
said he would rather be in hell than be pressed. He was now
going to wait in England to appeal against Captain Maxwell –
'O he's a Rascal, Sir, he ought to be put in the papers!' The
poor man had not been in bed since Friday Night – he left
Liverpool at 2 o'clock on Saturday morning, he had called at

a farm house to beg victuals & had been refused. The woman said she would give him nothing.[23]

Two days later yet another sailor, on his way to Glasgow, begged at the Wordsworths' door. He spoke 'chearfully in a sweet tone'.

The following year thirteen-year-old Robert Hay, who had been a weaver in Paisley since he was ten but who had also read *Robinson Crusoe*, ran away to sea. He was fortunate in meeting much kindness at sea and his mentor, not unlike Roderick Random's character Jack Rattlin, was Jack Gillies.

> 'Let us have the necessaries first, Robert', said he, 'and we will attend to other matters afterwards'. Accordingly the cutting out and making of jackets, shirts and trowsers, the washing of them when soiled, and the mending of them neatly when they began to fail, took precedence. The making of straw hats and canvas pumps came next in order. Then followed various operations in seamanship, according as opportunities occurred for displaying them, or according to the importance they bore in Jack's eye. Jack had been at sea ever since he was the height of a marlin spike, and a better practical sailor was not to be found from stem to stern.

Among Jack's many accomplishments were sailmaking, flute-playing and speaking French, the latter learned as a one-time prisoner-of-war.

> Jack, moreover, could play at all-fours, at whist, at loo, at cribbage, and at least a dozen of other games on the cards; he could play at fox and goose, at chequers, at backgammon, and I know not what all besides; but as he knew well that the Admiral's anticipated examination would not touch these topics, we agreed to postpone them sine die. What may seem strange, Jack, with all his acquirements, did not know the alphabet.

Hay could not persuade Gillies to learn to read, though he admired learning.

He was ashore on a cruise one day, and in his rambles fell in with a stand of second-hand books. Knowing my love of these articles, he thought he could not do less than buy me one. He lost no time with this matter, but the largest and handsomest on the stand was buttoned under his jacket in a twinkling.[24]

Unfortunately, Gillies' generous gift proved to be a dry law book called *Contingent Remainders*.

Gillies' failing was an ardent love of a 'dhrop of the cratur' and, in gratitude for his help, Hay made over to him his daily rum ration. However, the sad day came when this worthy sailor met a fellow Irishman, had a drop too much, and was found dead from a fall.

Hay, in lodgings in Plymouth in 1811, provides a picture of what he could see.

From the windows which faced the Harbour, hundreds of vessels were seen riding at anchor in Hamaoze, and great numbers occasionally floating past with the tide. Watermen's skifs, Merchantmen's yawls, Warships, Launches, Pinnaces, cutters, gigs, etc., were every moment landing. Porters were trudging along under their ponderous burdens. Women of pleasure flirting about in all directions watching for their prey, jews stalking about with hypocritical gravity hunting for dupes, and lastly the jolly tar himself was seen with his white demity trowsers fringed at the bottom, his fine scarlet waistcoat bound with black ribbon, his dark blue broadcloth jacket studded with pearl buttons, his black silk neckcloth thrown carelessly about his sunburnt neck. An elegant hat of straw, indicative of his recent return from a foreign station, cocked on one side: A head of hair reaching his waistband; a smart switch made from the backbone of a shark under one arm, his doxy under the other, a huge chew of tobacco in his cheek, and a good throat season of double stingo recently deposited within his belt by way of fending off care.[25]

Jack Gillies had learned French in a French prison before
the Peace of Amiens (1802). John Wetherell, shipwrecked
in HMS *Hussar* on the French coast in 1804, learned the language after that Peace. Unlike Robert Hay's, Wetherell's
experiences of naval officers were not happy ones. The
crew of the *Hussar* had written to the Admiral complaining of their treatment by Captain Wilkinson, who was in
command. Wetherell, by his own account, was accused
falsely of losing the studding sail boom. When he tried to
protest the captain bawled,

> 'Gag the rascal I say, gag him with a pump bolt and stop
> his damn'd lip'. Immediately a pump bolt was introduced
> into my jaws and tied back of my head. In this manner
> they gave me four dozen and punished me for a thing that
> was done three days after I was in irons for what they term'd
> a crime ...
>
> After cutting my flesh in a dreadful manner they cast me
> loose and poor Barney Appleby was called up and order'd to
> strip. 'For what sir?' says Barney. 'There is no occasion to
> stand spending my breath with this damn'd fellow. Gag him.'
> These orders were fulfilled and the poor fellow had six dozen
> then was cast loose and him and me both order'd to our duty.
> Beat to quarter; we were so cut and our backs so stiff and sore
> we sat still and did not go to our quarter. This was reported
> and a boatswain's Mate was sent to start us up with rope ends,
> and made us exercise guns nearly two hours in this mangled
> state. God help Sailors.[26]

Wilkinson's incompetence led to the wreck of the *Hussar*
and, despite the ravages of fever, Wetherell's eleven years in
a French prison were comparatively pleasant when compared with his early years at sea. In addition to learning
French and navigation there:

> My inclination led to drawing and music, to which I devoted
> the greatest part of my time all this winter, by the side of a

good stove, which we supported by keeping a canteen in our room, called the interpreters hotel; it being the room where we that were interpreters all lived together. We were six Mess-mates, and a young man named George Critchlow was bar keeper; we got our liquor at the lowest rate, had permission to have our beer from the brewer by the barrel, and we used fre-quently to share from four to five crowns each man, weekly clear of all our expences.[27]

Wetherell, the son of a whaling captain who sailed out of Whitby, survived to marry an American girl and to sail in command of his own ship out of New York. William Robinson, however, who was at sea and at the Battle of Trafalgar – while Wetherell was in prison, deserted from the Navy in 1811, never to return to sea. At Spithead, in the *Revenge*, after the blockading of Cadiz, he recalls,

After having moored our ship, swarms of boats came round us; some were what are generally termed bomb-boats, but are really nothing but floating chandler's shops; and a great many of them were freighted with cargoes of ladies, a sight that was truly gratifying, and a great treat: for our crew, consisting of six hundred and upwards, nearly all young men, had seen but one woman on board for eighteen months, and that was the daughter of one of the Spanish chiefs, who made no stay on board, but went on shore again immediately.

So soon as these boats were allowed to come alongside, the seamen flocked down pretty quick, one after the other, and brought their choice up, so that in the course of the afternoon, we had about four hundred and fifty on board ...

Of all the human race, these poor young creatures are the most pitiable; the ill-usage and the degradation they are dri-ven to submit to, are indescribable; but from habit they become callous, indifferent as to delicacy of speech and behaviour, and so totally lost to all sense of shame, that they seem to retain no quality which properly belongs to a woman, but the shape and name.[28]

In port the officers in naval vessels were not normally allowed to have women on board at this time, but could go ashore in their leisure hours. For fear of their desertion, the ordinary sailors, many of them press-ganged merchant seamen, were not allowed ashore in home ports.

CHAPTER 18

Lucky for Some

1815–1835

The twenty years following the Napoleonic Wars were a time of slump in shipping. Missionary societies were beginning to be established to help poor seamen and their orphans but, despite evidence that not all was well at sea, the government's attitude at this time was one of *laissez faire*. Sailing ships were being improved, especially by the Americans, and the steamship came into coastal waters, but losses at sea grew with the growth of trade consequent upon the beginning of the industrial revolution. For the deep-sea sailor little changed, except that he was no longer likely to be made a prisoner-of-war.

A year after the end of the Napoleonic Wars the American Captain Edmund Fanning was in command of the ship *Volunteer*, anchored off the island of St Mary's on the coast of Chile.

> While we lay here, our poor steward received a severe scald from a pot of boiling hot tea, which one of the men had just taken out of the galley kettle and was carrying below, this was at the dusk of evening, the steward not perceiving the seaman's approach, was coming up the gangway ladder, and striking his head against the pot turned it over, and being uncovered, the scalding contents were thrown on his head, down the neck, back, and shoulders, making so severe a burn that the back part of the scalp, with the skin, came off in the attempt to dress it, leaving a raw and deep wound. The boat very fortunately had

just before this misfortune, brought on board a quantity of greens which had been gathered on the island; among the lot was a parcel of very large leaves of the dock herb, very similar to that growing in our fields about the barns; having heard that this was a healing herb, I determined to apply the same to the steward's wound, which was forthwith done, after first causing a strong decoction to be made by pouring boiling water on the green leaves, and simmering them a short time over a slow fire, then after this preparation had cooled, washing the wound with it; after bruising the fibres of the same leaves to make them soft, and dipping them in the concoction, they were spread over the wound two or three thicknesses. It was astonishing how soon this application healed the wound, for not only was immediate relief from the pain and smarting obtained, but a new skin began to grow over without leaving scarcely the appearance of a scar; what added to the surprise was, that the hair grew on immediately the same as before: the dressings and washings were repeated every few hours, or as often as the leaves lost their moisture and became somewhat dry.[1]

The purpose of the *Volunteer*'s voyage was to secure seal-skins. Later, on this same voyage, some grass huts were built ashore in the Falklands and these huts caught alight. To escape death, a young sailor had to pass through a sheet of flame.

... this he proceeded to effect but having over his other garments a frock highly charged with oil from the fat or blubber of the seal skins which he had worked in, he had not more than entered the flames before it took fire, so that by the time he had crossed the burning grass, all his clothes were burnt to a cinder, and his body and limbs completely roasted, so much so, that after he had been plunged in the water and taken out, the skin cracked and came off with flesh attached to the remaining portions of the dress; ...

Mr Pendleton having heard that oil and fresh skins of animals was a good application in giving relief from burns, directed several of the penguins then near by to be killed, and their skins to be taken off with about half an inch thickness of the fat and flesh attached; binding them in this state around the roasted body of the young man, an immediate relief from pain resulted from it; ...

Fresh skins were applied twice a day for ten days. 'No other application was made use of, and the rapidity of his recovery was truly astonishing, for a new skin like as of an infant grew over his person, and in one month's time he could move alone about the deck, and shortly after attend to his duty again.'[2]

Two years later, in 1818, Captain Fanning was in command of the ship *Sea Fox* which went through a violent storm in April in latitude 38° 8' N, longitude 68° 25' W.

Somewhere about 11.P.M. the lightning struck the main-mast, and followed it down to the fair leader; here two of our choicest men were hauling in the fore-braces, who in an instant were hurled into the lee waist. At this moment, the dreary darkness gave way to the bright glare of a flash, yet this, if it were possible, left all things darker as it vanished; the ship was filled, both on deck and below, with a most disagreeable sulphurous smell, somewhat like that caused by burning damaged gun powder, rendering it difficult to breathe for some minutes, though the smell remained for hours after. The two men who were wounded, were immediately taken into the cabin, and attended to by our first officer, Mr D. Mackay, who possessed, of all others on board, the greatest knowledge in physic and surgery; they were found to be differently wounded; the eldest, who came to his senses first, had received two injuries, one on the arm near to the shoulder, which was burnt a little, and a hole perforated nearly through the thick or fleshy part of the thigh, in size like that caused by the ball of a rifle, while on the opposite side of the limb, or at the termination of the progress of the fluid, the flesh was seared quite hard, and about the size of half a dollar, resembling in look a piece of horn; the nails of the hand were also seared, and though there was scarcely any bleeding, the wound, however, was very painful. The other man was, as it were, complete roasted, from his neck down to his knees; by putting any pressure on the skin, it would snap or rather crack, similar to that of a roasted pig; – poor fellow! it was a sad sight. His outer garments had remained untouched by the lightning, those underneath being slightly scorched, while the waistcoat was a little burned but the guernsey robbin nearest his person, was burned black and to a tinder. Even philosophy was put to a stand, to account for so different an effect upon two persons clinging to the same rope, ... [3]

Both men recovered.

The fate of the whaleship *Essex,* sunk in 1820 by a whale in the middle of the Pacific Ocean – the *Essex* was cruising on the equator, some 119 degrees west of Greenwich – inspired the writing of *Moby Dick,* but the true story is perhaps even more graphic. Three of the ships' boats got away, with twenty crew between them, and managed to keep together for nearly nine weeks. The first mate, Owen Chase, took five other men in an old, frail and patched-up whale-boat.

In my chest, which I was fortunate enough to preserve, I had several small articles, which we found of great service to us; among the rest, some eight or ten sheets of writing paper, a lead pencil, a suit of clothes, three small fish hooks, a jack-knife, a whetstone, and a cake of soap.[4]

Three and half weeks later, by which time their water was exhausted, Chase and his crew were in dire straits.

In vain was every expedient tried to relieve the raging fever by drinking salt water, and holding small quantities of it in the mouth until, by that means, the thirst was increased to such a degree, as even to drive us to despairing, and vain relief from our own urine. Our sufferings during these calm days almost exceeded human belief. The hot rays of the sun beat down upon us to such a degree, as to oblige us to hang over the gunwale of the boat, into the sea, to cool our weak and fainting bodies. This expedient afforded us, however, a grateful relief, and was productive of a discovery of infinite importance to us. No sooner had one of us got on the outside of the gunwale than we immediately observed the bottom of the boat to be covered with a species of small clam, which, upon being tasted, proved a most delicious and agreeable food.[5]

The clams did not last long but, a few days later, all three boats landed on an uninhabited island which supplied water but only a week's food. They had left the wreckage of the *Essex* on 21st November. On 12th January, sixteen days after sailing from the uninhabited island, the three boats were dispersed by a storm and never came together again. By 8th February, in Chase's boat:

Isaac Cole, one of our crew, ... lay in the greatest pain and apparent misery, groaning piteously until four o'clock, when he died, in the most horrid and frightful convulsions I ever witnessed. We kept his corpse all night, and in the morning my two companions [two others in Chase's boat were already dead] began as of course to make preparations to dispose of it in the sea, when after reflecting on the subject all night, I addressed them on the painful subject of keeping the body for food. Our provisions could not possibly last us beyond three days ... It was without any objection agreed to, and we set to work as fast as we were able to prepare it so as to prevent its spoiling. We separated his limbs from his body, and cut all the flesh from the bones; after which, we opened the body, took out the heart, and then closed it again – sewed it up as decently as we could, and committed it to the sea. We now first commenced to satisfy the immediate cravings of nature from the heart, which we eagerly devoured, and then eat [ate] sparingly of a few pieces of the flesh; after which, we hung up the remainder, cut in thin strips about the boat, to dry in the sun:

we made a fire and roasted some of it to serve us during the next day. In this manner did we dispose of our fellow-sufferer; the painful recollection of which, brings to mind at this moment, some of the most disagreeable and revolting ideas that it is capable of conceiving ... I have no language to paint the anguish of our souls in this dreadful dilemma.[6]

After being separated from Chase, Captain George Pollard and his companions soon found that such provisions as they had were consumed.

Two men died; we had no other alternative than to live upon their remains. These we roasted to dryness by means of fires kindled on the ballast-sand at the bottom of the boat. When this supply was spent, what could we do? We looked at each other with horrid thoughts in our minds, but we held our tongues. I am sure that we loved one another as brothers all the time; and yet our looks told plainly what must be done. We cast lots, and the fatal one fell upon my poor cabin-boy. I started forward instantly, and cried out, 'My lad, my lad, *if you don't like your lot,* I'll shoot the first man that touches you.' The poor emaciated boy hesitated a moment or two; then, quietly laying his head down upon the gunnel of the boat, he said, '*I like it as well as any other.*' He was soon dispatched, and nothing of him left. I think, then, another man died of himself, and him, too, we ate. But I can tell you no more – my head is on fire at the recollection; I hardly know what to say.[7]

Pollard was picked up at sea some days later, and Chase reached the coast of South America. Altogether there were five survivors and their boat journey had exceeded 3000 miles. After a further shipwreck, Captain Pollard decided that no one would employ him again because, 'I am an *unlucky* man.'

Edward Coverly, on the other hand, had little to complain about as poulterer aboard the East Indiamen *Canning* and *Buckinghamshire* from 1820 to 1824, though he

did not approve of everything he witnessed. At Whampoa
in China,

> On the 20th December the Captain gave us our three days lib-
> erty allowed by the Company, at which time the men are suf-
> fered to do as they please [on board], no complaints whatever
> are listened to. The liberty commenced with three hearty
> cheers, after which a dram was served, then eggs and bread, as
> much as each man could eat, at eleven a pint of grog per man,
> after which roast geese in abundance. At 2 o'clock another
> pint of grog, with six oranges per man. For tea, eggs and
> bread, and a pint of grog at seven p.m. But this was not
> enough for some of the drunken beasts. They demanded
> another pint of grog from the commanding officer, who told
> them that three pints of grog and a dram was all the Captain
> allowed. The men answered that they would go to work next
> morning and wait until the Captain came down [from Can-
> ton] before they had the other two days. Thus the liberty
> stopped until the 24th, when the Captain came down and
> acceded to the wishes of the crew. Accordingly next morning
> the sucking pigs came on board by dozens and everything
> went on peaceably. In the afternoon Neptune and his wife
> made their appearance walking into the Cuddy to shake hands
> with the commanding officer. Among other amusements a
> public office was erected, the Magistrate and clerk taking their
> seats to hear cases and, after swearing in constables, a number
> of warrants was issued. After apprehending offenders, a
> prison was necessary. The pigs therefore were quickly dis-
> lodged and the styes filled with prisoners, some of which got
> so dead drunk by their friends bringing them grog that they
> remained in the pig styes the whole of the night. In this man-
> ner lasted and ended the three days of liberty.[8]

Coverly disapproved equally of the *Buckinghamshire*
crew's behaviour at the outset of the second voyage in 1823.

> After mooring the ship to the Company's buoy [at North
> Fleet in the Thames], the Boatswain pip'd to dinner. Here a

scene presented itself which beggars description. In the ship's galley were more than a dozen men, swearing and fighting for the frying pans to cook their beef steaks, while others, who had their wives or companions on board, were devouring their steaks which their wives had cook'd while the ship was going down [river]. At one end of the deck might be seen clusters of lumpers, drinking down the table beer by gallons, and devouring the beef as though they had not had a dinner for a month. The scene was grotesque in the extreme, and might well have employ'd the pencil of an Hogarth.[9]

Having loaded cargo the ship sailed to an anchorage in the Lower Hope, where it was usual to pay the ship's company two months' wages.

After paying the ship's company two months' advance, two hours were allow'd to lay out their money with the boat alongside, and to take leave of their wives and companions. And here a scene revolting to human nature commenced. The crimps, and other plunderers, had provided a good supply of liquor, which they freely gave to those whom they intended to plunder, and then, when nearly dead drunk, made out a bill for certain articles, which no doubt the poor fellow never had. But Jack is an easy fellow, and easy parts with his money, which he sets little value on, and satisfies himself that money will be no use at sea, and when the voyage is over he will have plenty more, therefore, what is the use of grumbling.

The two hours allow'd as stated was spent in the most disgusting manner, men and women, inflamed with liquor, pouring the most abusive language on one another, some fighting, others lamenting the period of parting. Indeed such a scene can be compar'd to nothing but a floating Hell.[10]

Opportunities for redemption came at sea.

Sunday 10 August lower'd the jolly boat into the Hole, this being the first Sunday we had spent at sea, the men were order'd to be clean'd by 10 o'clock, ready for muster. At ½ past 10 the Bell toll'd for church, this was rather a novel sight for some, the quarter deck from the gang way to abaft the capsan was regularly set out with capsan bars (resting on buckets) which were fill'd with the seamen. From the capsan to the cuddy, there was a half circle of chairs and stools, which was occupy'd with the officers; the union jack being thrown over the capsan, prayer books was serv'd out to those who chose to have them, everything now being as still as death, with the exception of a quack from a duck, or a squeak from a pig, or now and then a heel over of the ship which nearly capsized the whole of us. The Captain now came out of the cuddy as stately as a priest, and commenced to read the church prayers, standing at the capsan, everything wore a solemn aspect, and however it savour'd more of the form than the power of religion, yet it was an acknowledgment of a Supreme Being, even in the Atlantic Ocean.[11]

About 35°S, after several days of bad weather,

... the ship now roll'd so tremendous heavy that it was necessary to have life lines along the deck as it was almost impossible to keep our feet. It was found necessary to batten the hatches down, yet, amidst all the awful contention of the elements, the second mate on Friday morning, had the Humanity to make the watch on deck Holy stone the upper deck. When the ship roll'd heavy, the men had to pick themselves up in the lea scuppers, wet to the skin, by the heavy seas that were continually breaking over the ship. To add to the pleasure, three spare anchor stocks got adrift and roll'd from side to side, clearing everything before them. After much difficulty they were secured and about 7 o'clock the sun broke through the clouds, the violence of the gale somewhat abateing. At 8, pip'd to breakfast, and it may be supposed that after such a tempestuous night, we all had sharp appetites; but we had nothing but a pint of tea and some hard biscuit full of maggots to satisfy our hunger.[12]

Coverly came near to death in the Indian Ocean.

> About 3 o'clock this afternoon, Monday Oct 27 1823, I nearly
> lost my life by my own imprudence, for having got out on the
> gigs davit to catch sharks, I incautiously coil'd the line across
> my thighs, which got intangled with my legs, while a shark
> which I had caught was plunging most violently; I was on the
> point of being pulled overboard, and can truly say, that there
> was but a step between me and death, for at that moment there
> were six large sharks under the stern, which would have
> devoured me before any assistance could have been rendered;
> but thanks, eternal thanks to that God, whose eye was upon
> me, and whose power was display'd at this critical moment, in
> causing the monster to about ship, and thus slacking the line,
> which enabled me to disentangle it from my legs.[13]

While Coverly was carrying tea to Europe from China, the
great exodus of men and women from Europe to North
America had begun. The emigrant ships did not always
enjoy a good name, but the *Diana* of Dumfries and her
crew earned this encomium from one passenger:

> ... Our beds were dry and comfortable in all weather, and we
> were able always to keep the hatches open, Our water was
> good, being put up in clean new casks, and the supply abun-
> dant. The ship was free from all vermin whatever. Our Captain
> was cheerful and accommodating in the highest degree; and to
> any of the passengers who had need of cordials, the best his
> cabin afforded were offered in the most obliging manner pos-
> sible. The sailors were friendly, and willing to help us at all
> times, in any thing we were unable to do for ourselves, for
> which we gave them in return nearly the whole stock of spirits
> we had laid in; for few of us could swallow any thing stronger
> than water or beer, our taste was so much altered by the sea air.
> Every kind of cooking was performed upon the deck, except
> during four or five days, when it was rather inconvenient from
> the roughness of the sea; and except two or three married
> women who were unwell with colds, and who suffered from

want of dry clothes, we were all rather improved in health than otherwise; and, as there was neither dishonesty nor distrust amongst us, I may say with truth that a more comfortable passage was never made across the Atlantic. Should any of my countrymen, therefore, wish to take the same course, I could not recommend to them a more clean, healthy and comfortable ship, than the *Diana* of Dumfries, nor a more kind and obliging Captain than Captain Martin.[14]

When Richard Dana, a law student, sailed as a sailor from Boston in the brig *Pilgrim* in 1834, he did not find life as agreeable as it seems to have been under Captain Martin. Rounding Cape Horn,

The only time we could be said to take any pleasure was at night and morning, when we were allowed a tin pot full of hot tea (or, as we sailors significantly call it, 'water bewitched,') sweetened with molasses. This, bad as it was, was still warm and comforting, and, together with our sea biscuit and cold salt beef, made quite a meal. Yet even this meal was attended with some uncertainty. We had to go ourselves to the galley and take our kid of beef and tin pots of tea, and run the risk of losing them before we could get below. Many a kid of beef have I seen rolling in the scuppers, and the bearer lying at his length on the decks. I remember an English lad who was always the life of the crew, but whom we afterwards lost overboard, standing for nearly ten minutes at the galley, with his pot of tea in his hand, waiting for a chance to get down the forecastle; and seeing what he thought was a 'smooth spell', started to go forward. He had just got to the end of the windlass, when a great sea broke over the bows, and for a moment I saw nothing of him but his head and shoulders; and at the next instant, being taken off his legs, he was carried aft with the sea, until her stern lifting up and sending the water forward, he was left high and dry at the side of the long-boat, still holding on to his tin pot, which had now nothing in it but salt water.[15]

Off Point Conception in California, the captain was show-
ing off his vessel to other shipmasters by carrying as much
sail as possible when the *Pilgrim* was struck by a squall.

Then it was 'haul down', and 'clew up' royals, flying-jib, and
studding sails, all at once. There was what the sailors call a
'mess' – everything let go, nothing hauled in, and everything
flying ... The mate and some men forward were trying to haul
in the lower studding-sail, which had blown over the sprit-sail
yard-arm and round the guys while the topmast-studding-sail
boom, after buckling up and springing out again like a piece of
whalebone, broke off at the boom-iron. I sprang aloft to take
in the main top-gallant studding-sail, but before I got into the
top, the tack parted, and away went the sail, swinging forward
of the top-gallant sail, and tearing and slatting itself to pieces.
The halyards were at this moment let go by the run; and such
a piece of work I never had before, in taking in a sail. After
great exertions I got it, or the remains of it, into the top, and
was making it fast,when the captain, looking up, called out to
me, 'Lay aloft there, Dana, and furl that main-royal.' Leaving
the studding sail, I went up to the cross-trees; and here it
looked rather squally. The foot of the top-gallant-mast was
working between the cross and trussel trees, and the royal-
mast lay over at a fearful angle with the mast below, while
everything was working, and cracking, strained to the utmost.

There's nothing for Jack to do but to obey orders, and I
went up upon the yard; and there was a worse 'mess', if possible, than I had left below. The braces had been let go, and the
yard was swinging about like a turnpike-gate, and the whole
sail having blown over to leeward, the lee leach was over the
yard-arm, and the skysail was all adrift and flying over my
head. I looked down, but it was in vain to attempt to make
myself heard, for every one was busy below, and the wind
roared, and the sails were flapping in every direction. Fortunately, it was noon and broad daylight, and the man at the
wheel, who had his eyes aloft, soon saw my difficulty, and
after numberless signs and gestures, got some one to haul the

necessary ropes taut. During this interval I took a look below. Everything was in confusion on deck; the little vessel was tearing through the water as if she were mad, the seas flying over her, and the masts leaning over at a wide angle of forty-five degrees from the vertical. At the other royal-mast-head was Stimson, working away at the sail, which was blowing from him as fast as he could gather it in. The top-gallant-sail below me was soon clewed up, which relieved the mast, and in a short time I got my sail furled, and went below; but I lost overboard a new tarpaulin hat, which troubled me more than anything else. We worked for about half an hour with might and main; and in an hour from the time the squall struck us, from having all our flying kites abroad, we came down to double-reefed topsails and the storm-sails.[16]

At Monterey, Dana met Bill Jackson off the *Loriette,* which had a Sandwich Island crew.

In addition to these Islanders, the vessel had two English sailors, who acted as boatswains over the Islanders, and took care of the rigging. One of them I shall always remember as the best specimen of the thoroughbred English sailor that I ever saw. He had been to sea from a boy, having served a regular apprenticeship of seven years, as all English sailors [who aspire to be officers] are obliged to do, and was then about four or five and twenty. He was tall, but you only perceived it when he was standing by the side of others, for the great breadth of his shoulders and chest made him appear but little above the middle height. His chest was as deep as it was wide; his arm like that of Hercules and his hand 'the fist of a tar – every hair a rope-yarn'. With all this he had one of the pleasantest smiles I ever saw. His cheeks were of a handsome brown; his teeth brilliantly white; and his hair, of a raven black, waved in loose curls all over his head, and fine, open forehead; ... Take him with his well-varnished black tarpaulin stuck upon the back of his head; his long locks coming down almost into his eyes; his white duck trowsers and shirt;

blue jacket; and black kerchief, tied loosely round his neck; and he was a fine specimen of manly beauty. On his broad chest he had stamped with India ink 'Parting moments'. – a ship ready to sail; a boat on the beach; and a girl and her sailor lover taking their farewell ... On one of his broad arms he had the crucifixion, and the other the sign of the 'foul anchor'.

He was very fond of reading ... He had a good deal of information, and his captain said he was a perfect seaman, and worth his weight in gold aboard a vessel, in fair weather and in foul.[17]

The *Pilgrim* loaded hides on the California coast, and the captain was a tyrant. He had flogged one sailor whom he disliked, and immediately afterwards he flogged one of this sailor's companions, John the Swede, because John had asked, 'What are you going to flog that man for, sir?'

When he [John] was made fast, he turned to the captain, who stood turning up his sleeves and getting ready for the blow, and asked him what he was to be flogged for. 'Have I ever refused my duty, sir? Have you ever known me to hang back, or to be insolent, or not to know my work?'

'No', said the captain, 'it is not that that I flog you for, I flog you for your interference – and for asking questions.'

'Can't a man ask a question here without being flogged?'

'No', shouted the captain; 'nobody shall open his mouth aboard this vessel, but myself'; and he began laying the blows upon his back, swinging half round between each blow, to give it full effect. As he went on, his passion increased, and he danced about the deck, calling out, as he swung the rope, 'If you want to know what I flog you for, I'll tell you. It's because I like to do it! Because I like to do it! It suits me! That's what I do it for!'

The man writhed under the pain until he could endure it no longer, when he called out, with an exclamation more common among foreigners than with us: 'O Jesus Christ! O Jesus Christ!'

'Don't call on Jesus Christ,' shouted the captain; '*He can't help you. Call on Captain Thompson!* He's the man! He can help you! Jesus Christ can't help you now!'[18]

Dana writes movingly of the joy of receiving mail from home after a long absence, of the pleasure of finding a good book on board ship, and of those 'sweets of liberty' enjoyed on a rare day ashore, in this case San Diego. The latter, however, could be marred by nautical protocol.

It is the universal custom with sailors for each one, in his turn, to treat the whole, calling for a glass all round, and obliging every one who is present, even the keeper of the shop, to take a glass with him. When we first came in, there was some dispute between our crew and the others, whether the new comers or the old California rangers should treat first; but it being settled in favor of the latter, each of the crews of the other vessels treated all round in their turn, and as there were a good many present (including some 'loafers' who dropped in, knowing what was going on, to take advantage of Jack's hospitality), and the liquor was a *real* (12½ cents) a glass, it made somewhat of a hole in their lockers. It was now our ship's turn, and Stimson and I, anxious to get away, stepped up to call for glasses, but we soon found out that we must go in order – the oldest first, for the old sailors did not choose to be preceeded by a couple of youngsters, and *bon gré, mal gre*, we had to wait our turn, with the twofold apprehension of being too late for our horses, and of getting *corned*; for drink you must, every time; and if you drink with one and not with another, it is always taken as an insult.[19]

Eventually, Dana is able to effect a transfer to the *Alert,* a happier ship than the *Pilgrim*, and enjoys the prospect of voyaging home again.

As we had been about a year on the coast, it was time to think of the voyage home; and knowing that the last two or three months of our stay would be very busy ones, and that we

should never have so good an opportunity to work for ourselves as the present, we all employed our evenings in making
clothes for the passage home, and more especially for Cape
Horn. As soon as supper was over and the kids cleared away,
and each one had taken his smoke, we seated ourselves on our
chests round the lamp, which swung from a beam, and each
one went to work in his own way, some making hats, others
trowsers, others jackets, etc., and no one was idle. The boys
who could not sew well enough to make their own clothes,
laid up grass into sinnet, for the men, who sewed for them in
return. Several of us clubbed together and bought a large piece
of twilled cotton, which we made into trowsers and jackets,
and giving them several coats of linseed oil, laid them by for
Cape Horn. I also sewed and covered a tarpaulin hat, thick
and strong enough to sit down upon, and made myself a complete suit of flannel under-clothing, for bad weather.[20]

In Monterey he has one last liberty day, the first for three
months.

On Sunday morning, as soon as the decks were washed, and
we had breakfast, those who had obtained liberty began to
clean themselves, as it is called, to go ashore. A bucket of fresh
water apiece, a cake of soap, a large coarse towel, and we went
to work scrubbing one another, on the forecastle. Having
gone through this, the next thing was to get into the head, –
one on each side, – with a bucket apiece, and duck one
another, by drawing up water and heaving over each over,
while we were stripped to a pair of trowsers. Then came the
rigging-up. The usual outfit of pumps, white stockings, loose
duck trowsers, blue jackets, clean checked shirts, black
kerchief, hats well varnished, with a fathom of black ribbon
over the left eye, a silk handkerchief flying from the outside
jacket pocket, and four or five dollars tied up in the back of
the neckerchief, and we were 'all right'.[21]

The following morning the 'hands' turn to, as usual,
despite the intemperance of most and little or no sleep at

238

night for all. To free it from pests, the ship is sealed and 'smoked' for thirty-six hours, before sailing for home, by 'a slow fire of charcoal, birchbark, brimstone, and other matters, on the ballast in the bottom of the hold'.

When a pig is killed, the sailors get one meal from it, the rest going to the officers. When bad weather washes a complete meal away, the crew take consolation in the thought that it has taken the officers' chicken pie and pancakes, whereas they have lost only 'old horse' – the hard, dry pieces of salt beef. At Cape Horn, Dana's face swells 'nearly as large as two' with toothache and he can scarcely open his mouth, but the captain, asked by the steward for rice on his behalf, replies, 'No! damn you! Tell him to eat salt junk and bread, like the rest of them!'

He recovers before the *Alert* reaches the tropics and there, perhaps, inspires one of Eugene O'Neill's most lyrical passages.

One night, while we were in these tropics, I went out to the end of the flying-jib boom, upon some duty, and, having finished it, turned round, and lay over the boom for a long time, admiring the beauty of the sight before me. Being so far out from the deck, I could look at the ship, as at a separate vessel; – and there, rose up from the water, supported only by the small black hull, a pyramid of canvas, spreading out far beyond the hull, and towering up almost, as it seemed in the indistinct night air, to the clouds. The sea was as still as an inland lake; the light trade-wind was gently and steadily breathing from astern; the dark blue sky was studded with the tropical stars; there was no sound but the rippling of the water under the stern; and the sails were spread out, wide and high; – the two lower studding-sails stretching, on each side, far beyond the deck; the top-mast studding-sails, like wings to the topsails; the top-gallant studding-sails spreading fearlessly out above them; still higher, the two royal studding-sails, looking like two kites flying from the same string; and, highest of all, the little skysail, the apex of the pyramid, seeming actually to touch the stars, and to be out of reach of human hand. So quiet, too, was the sea, and so steady, the breeze, that if these sails had been sculptured marble, they could not have been more motionless.[22]

CHAPTER 19

Sail and Steam

1835–1860

By the middle of the nineteenth century Britain possessed a mercantile sailing fleet of 3.6 million net tons,
perhaps seven times the tonnage of a century before, and
thirty-six times that of the Elizabethan fleet. In addition,
and measurable for the first time, the fleet included 275,000
gross tons of steamships, one ton of steam being equivalent
in carrying capacity to about three tons of sail. No other
country could rival the extent and size of Britain's trade.

But not all was well with British ships. In just three days
in January 1843, 240 British ships were wrecked with the
loss of 500 lives. This inspired Parliament to establish a
select committee to enquire into shipwrecks and all British
consuls were asked to report on the quality of British shipmasters. 'Some shipmasters are shamefully illiterate', replied the consul in Odessa. From Pernambuco the consul
commented that hardly a British ship arrived without the
seamen complaining of brutality and starvation, and of
their ship being shorthanded, and that in nine cases out of
ten he was obliged to decide in favour of the men. The consul in Danzig wrote bluntly, 'Taken as a whole, there is not
– and I say it with regret – a more troublesome and
thoughtless set of men, to use the mildest term, to be met
with than British merchant seamen'.

In 1850 the Board of Trade established a marine department which was given responsibility for seamen's welfare.

For the first time, examinations were made compulsory for masters and mates, and a scale of accommodation, food and medical supplies was laid down for ships. Four years later shipmasters were compelled to specify the kinds and amounts of food they would provide on a voyage and weigh-scales were to be at hand for the crew to check their 'whack'. Soon, topsail yards were being hoisted to a sea shanty which began,

> You'll do no good by grumbling,
> You know how well you're whacked
> With lime juice and vinegar,
> According to the Act.

and ended:

> You'll do no good by grumbling,
> I'll tell you for a fact,
> They can sew you up and dump you
> According to the Act.[1]

Although steamships had arrived, and were seen increasingly along the coast, sail remained pre-eminent. One old seafarer recalled that from the coast of Northumberland he would see over 200 sailing vessels pass by day, and as many more would pass at night.

I have seen them running for Holy Island and the Forth when they were smothered with seas, so that little of the hull was visible. I have seen them passing here plunging bows under, and their sails blown away when they were driven along with a heavy gale; at intervals furious squalls from the west sometimes blew the sails out of the bolt ropes and sent the ribbons flying over the feather-white sea. I have seen them jumping half out of the water and plunging bows under when carrying a press of canvas against a choppy head sea, when racing with each other or struggling to make a harbour of refuge during gales that blew from the east, north or south ... never a winter passed without wrecks being scattered here and there along the coastline.[2]

Walter Runciman, a Geordie shipmaster who made a fortune out of steam, sailed in a collier down this east coast of England.

I made a voyage in one of these old hookers, which in stormy weather shivered and shook as though she were falling to pieces. Her forecastle deck used to open and shut like bellows, and every plunge or roll she took gave the impression that she was splitting in two. The oiled tent-covers that were stretched from head to foot of our canvas hammocks could not prevent some of the water getting on to the pillow, blankets and 'donkey' breakfast. It availed nothing to growl about having to take what sleep we could on wet bedding, or about having to pump or sink. We had to go through with it. Nor was it affection that led me to take service in this money-making swill, but hard necessity.[3]

Of his further experiences, Runciman wrote,

Neither coasters nor southern-going ships had any sanitary arrangements until the end of the 'sixties and beginning of the 'seventies. In the larger vessels the windlass and crew's quarters were under the topgallant forecastle, which was perfectly open at the after part, and there they were frozen to death sometimes in cold winter climates. Many of them contracted a lingering consumption, and others were galloped by the same disease into eternity ...

There was little to choose between the forecastle furnishings of the large cotton and timber carriers and that graciously bestowed on the crews of the collier brigs. The difference was that their forecastles were under-deck, and the space, proportionately smaller, was bulkheaded off from the hold. The men and boys slept in hammocks that thumped against each other at sea when there was any motion. The bulkhead was littered with lumber, and the cable-stage was piled high with ropes,

243

blocks, tar barrels, water casks, and all sorts of spare gear. The chain locker was placed near the forepart of the foremast at the after part of the forecastle. It was the job of the youngest apprentice to stow the cable-chain away as it was hove in when weighing anchor. It was a dirty, smelly job, as much of the mud and filth of the Thames and other anchorages not only destroyed the boy's clothing, but was allowed to gather and remain in the locker. The smell from this and other ingredients was intolerable until one became seasoned.[4]

In these respects little had changed a hundred years later in the corvettes which hunted U-boats in the Second World War. The hammocks in the forecastle still thumped against each other. The chain locker was still at hand, and stowing cable was just as filthy and smelly.

It was, of course, dangerous to fall asleep when on watch.

One of the most embarrassing and risky methods of breaking the habit of sleeping when on watch in nearly every case cured the culprit, but it often destroyed his nerve. An opportunity was taken to reeve a rope through the lee scupper-hole, bend it on to a coal-basket, ship a running bowline over the sleeper's shoulders and throw the basket into the sea, and, if the vessel was going at a good speed, he was quickly pulled right up to the scupper-hole, sprawling and shouting for someone to help him out of his difficulties.[5]

But this was a minor hazard compared to some associated with the seaman's job.

The jibboom of a collier and short-sea trader had innumerable guys and methods of securing it as substantially as the bowsprit, which had less gear, and it was always a tough task to take in, as was the rule then when entering a port and putting to sea again. Sometimes the vessels were plunging bows under when this unwieldy but very essential spar was being rigged out. This job enlisted the whole crew except the man at the wheel and the captain, even in fine weather. But on dark, stormy nights everybody had to hang on by the eyelids to avoid being washed over the bows, and in spite of all precautions this sometimes occurred. I was shipmates once with three men of whom one had his leg broken and the other two an arm each at this work, and, instead of receiving sympathy, they were spoken of by some of those who completed their job unscathed as being 'clumsy fatheads who had no gumption'.[6]

Charles Abbey, who was born in Brooklyn in 1841, kept a diary during his first four years at sea, from 1856 to 1860. After his first voyage he nearly left the sea, but subsequently he enjoyed his seatime and made a distinguished career in the American Revenue Marine or Coast Guard. His first voyage, from New York to Whampoa, was made aboard the 1261 ton clipper *Surprise*. Four days after sailing he wrote,

This morning we shook the reef out of the maintopsail & having only the watch on deck took the topsail halyards to the capstan to hoist the yard[,] got the turns around & the bars in in their holes but still the word to heave did not come so we leaned up against our bars & waited. bye & bye the last man came down from the yard & the 2nd mate met him as soon as his feet touched the deck with a 'thumper' right in the mouth & nose & then asked him what he meant by leaving the earings flying[.] the man maddened by the unexpected blow, growled out some unintelligible words at which the mate got mad & ran 'aft', to get a belaying pin with which he struck the man and ordered him to the capstan. He did so but words were constantly passing between them & at last the man spoke out loud enough to be heard by all around & said, That, 'If he struck him again he was as able as the next man to strike him back & would do so', at which the mate made a spring for a belaying pin again & the man ran forward, aft the foremast & soon came walking or rather running back with a capstan bar[.] the mate met him & ordered him to put it down[.] he

245

would not do it & the mate then struck him a quick blow on the knuckles which made him drop his weapon & run with the mate after him striking him in the back and head[.] he got to the capstan & we 'mast headed' the yard & then he went aloft & made fast the – troublesome earings.[7]

Abbey relates further that on the *Surprise* both the first and third mates were prone to fall asleep in the night watches but that if they observed one of the boys doing likewise he would be aroused with a capstan bar end and made to shoulder it and pace up and down like a sentry.

Two months out from New York he wrote,

It is blowing 40 horse Power today & the ship is ploughing through the water at the rate of 14 knots I am so hungry I would eat anything I could get hold of & so are all the rest of the crew. Being an allowance of water we cannot have our Rice beans or codfish in fact all we have is '*Duff*' 3 times a week & all the other times 5 seabiscuits & a piece of Salt Junk. All this time they live like princes in the cabin, I only hope I may have a chance some time of serving out old '*Bully Ranletts*' rations, I would starve him as sure as I live. He finds the ship in provisions under a contract & he starves the crew.[8]

Captain Ranletts died aged 101.

A week after complaining about the food, young Abbey was given a specific job.

I have been appointed Mizzen Skysail boy & have to loose furl, & bend the sail, send the yard up or down as the case may be & in fact have the entire charge of the yard during my watch on deck one of the boys in the other watch tends to it the rest of the time. It is an awful job when the ship is pitching to go up & loose or furl it for being so high up & the foot ropes too short the halyards loose on deck & the mast in the same state as the British left the old flag staff on the battery N.Y. upon evacuating it [i.e.greased], you can get nothing but your finger nails and eyelids to hold on to. Many a time I been *'almost'* gone when another lurch would bring me back only to have the operation repeated. When one gets up there he is well tired with the exertion of climbing so high & then to have to balance himself upon his stomach on the yard & 'pick up' 44 yard of canvas stow it & pass his gaskets make them fast and get down on deck in about 5 minutes & then perhaps be told he must do it quicker, it is hard. But all this is comprised in 'going to Sea' & any one who is fool enough to go must take his share of it.⁹

In Whampoa, Abbey transferred, for the homeward voyage, to the 1055-ton *Charmer* (Captain Lucas), where one of his shipmates was flung into the sea by a flapping sail.

Man overboard we all sung out at once & ran aft the man at the wheel stood ready with the grating (on which the helmsman stands) & as he passed the stern he hove it to him, but he had his head down in the water & was paddling dog fashion to all appearances. I saw him for the last time about ½ a mile astern as his red shirt came up on the top of a wave. Just then the Captain came up from the cabin & asked in his usual tone *'Who's overboard?'* *'Peter sir'* was the answer he didn't say anything then till the man was out of sight when he observed *'Well he's gone, the best man in the ship'*.⁹

Captain Lucas met his own fate by falling overboard and drowning in mid-ocean.

Arriving home in 1857, Abbey shipped out once more in the 1078-ton *Henry Brigham*, which he found much more to his taste.

Every one is called by his right name & all are treated like men and gentlemen at that ... Capt Dow is a man of about 40 or 50 years of age (to judge from appearance) & is my very beau ideal of a Sea Captain. In warm weather he may be seen lounging about under the quarter awning open shirt collar, loose baggy trowsers broad brimmed sombrero on his head, & his only companion an immense Grass cloth hdkf, which he constantly uses, & as he moves about like a Polar bear on the line, every once in a while saying 'Whew aint it hot' he would provoke a smile from any one. But now in cold & freezing latitudes he is appareled in, first, a pair of very heavy cloth pants, an immense though fine fitting pilot cloth overcoat, reaching down to the calfs of his legs, a large pair of high topped sea boots. (french by the way) a round red cap which he obtained up the Persian gulf, & all the beard & mustaches he has been able to raise since he left New York, & as he moves about the poop with his spy glass under his arm ever & anon taking a view of the coast of Staten land & Terra del Fuego he is as I before observed my Beau Ideal of a Sea Captain.[10]

And Captain Dow ran a happy ship.

Any night at sea a stranger would be surprised at the change in the aspect of affairs between 5 minutes of 8 & 5 minutes after. At the former he might hear, laughing, joking, singing, playing, dancing, almost any thing, but at the moment 8 oclock comes everyone stops & 5 moments after nothing would be heard but the tread of the officer on the poop & the man at the lookout. There are a great many who write of the monotony of sea life, the horrors of being confined as though in jail. As for monotony I never found any as there is always enough to do, & to keep your thoughts on something else. And I never felt confined unless I knew there was some land within 100 miles of me, then indeed I have often thought 'we have hardly room enough just now'.[11]

Aboard his next ship, the 1836-ton *Intrepid*, the crew were mostly free of work on Saturday as well as Sunday. Bound for Shanghai, he wrote,

We lead a very pleasant life on the whole, not having a great deal to do. If I have the forenoon watch on deck I am not as a general thing set to work before one bell [8.30am] & the time

(4 hours) slips along quite pleasantly in yarning & listening to Yarns spun by veteran 'Yarners' then I have the Aftn below until 4 oclock when I again come on deck but only to put away the tools & work which may have been under way, which occupies us until 2 bells (5 o'clock) & then the other watch are all sitting about eating their suppers & talking & Yarning again with us. Then 4 bells strikes & I get my supper after which I take a hand of whist, Euchre or 7 up. Or else join the singers on the forecastle.[12]

Of his fellow sailors Abbey concludes that they

are for the most part generous to a fault, never *going back* on a shipmate. All ways help one another, especially if they get into any sort of scrape. Crews often (nowadays) knock off duty & refuse to work until some shipmate who has been put in irons is free'd, & let a poor fellow board a ship in a foreign port & tell the men he is a sailor & has neither money, friends, or ship, if the captain wont ship him he is sure to turn up 'on board' the day after sailing.[13]

Of course, the sailor without money, friends and a ship was not always so lucky. He was more likely to be shipped out by a crimp or boarding-house keeper, like the infamous Paddy West of Liverpool who 'professed to make a greenhorn ... into a fully fledged Able Seaman in a matter of days'.

Then the potential seaman was handed the papers of some real sailor – one who had been knifed or clubbed, probably, in some earlier drunken brawl. Paddy would give him a sea-chest full of second-hand gear – if there were two candidates, he would furnish one suit of oilskins between the two of them, 'I'll see to it that the mate puts y'z in different watches'. Paddy wouldn't tell them what might happen in a case of 'All hands on deck!' ... Of course, Paddy didn't go to all this trouble for nothing; he always received the 'Paddy Wester's' advance note, a month or two's wages.[14]

To counter the activities of such crimps, 'do-gooders' were establishing 'sailors' homes' and bethels in the ports, and Charles Dickens visited the pioneer one in London's Dock Street in 1851.

> Even as certain carved floating pieces of wood informed Columbus that he must be drawing near land, so changing aspects informed me that I was arriving at nautical regions. Marine stores tempted, instead of shawls. The Eastward Jews, happily adapting themselves as ever, sold pea-jackets and straw hats, as those of the West sell flash waistcoats ... And along the narrowing street, tumbling round corners with a peculiar jerk – half suggestive of the shooting of The Irishman's gun – and walking along (one foot on the pavement, one on the street) came seamen of every age and clime. A merchant seaman in a red shirt; a sailor boy 'done brown' while still 'tender'; being, as it were, spitted on top-gallant yards, and cooked before tropical suns; a black negro cook, greasy and grinning, with little ear-rings as ornamental as a ring in a pig's snout. These were the most notable specimens.[15]

As they walked towards the Sailors' Home along Ratcliffe Highway, some sailors might sing the song of that title which was also used at sea as a capstan shanty and pumping song.

> As I wuz a-rollin' down the Highway one morn,
> I spied a flash packet from ol' Wapping town,
> As soon as I seed her I slacked me main brace,
> An' I hoisted me stuns'ls an' to her gave chase.
>
> Her flag wuz three colours, her masthead wuz low,
> She wuz round at the counter an' bluff at the bow;
> From larboard to starboard an' so rolled she,
> She wuz sailin' at large, she wuz running free.
> I fired me bow-chaser, the signal she knew,
> She backed her main tops'l an' for me hove to;

I lowered down me jolly-boat an' rowed alongside,
An' I found madam's gangway wuz open an' wide.

I hailed her in English, she answered me clear,
I'm from the Black Arrow bound to the Shakespeare';
So I wore ship wid a what d'yer know,
An' I passed her me hawser an' took her in tow.

I tipped her me flipper, me towrope an' all,
She then let her hand on me reef-tackle fall;
She then took me up to her lily-white room,
An' in her main riggin' I fouled me jibboom.

In the verses that follow the lady is reported as giving poor Jack the pox – acquired, no doubt, from one of his fellows – but Jack is stoical about it and concludes, 'If I meet that flash packet I'll board her again'.[16]

Back at sea Jack had to 'flog the dead horse' for a month or two – that is, work for nothing – to pay back Paddy West and his like. Then, from old canvas and rope and a couple of holystones (sandstones used for scrubbing the decks), the sailmaker would fashion a 'horse' which was dragged along the deck to the poop where, with luck, the Old Man would give each sailor a tot of rum.

Then, the horse would be attached to a gantline, the gantline being rove through a block on the main yard-arm. Up aloft, the youngest member of the crew would be sitting athwart the yard with a knife in his hand. On the word of command, the men would grasp the gantline, running through a head-block on the deck, and the shantyman would start the shanty dedicated to this job:

Oh, I say ol' man yer horse will die

and the crowd would yell:

An' we *say* so, an' we *hope* so!

pulling aloft the horse on the words 'say' and 'hope'. There were many verses to this song, in order to make it last until the horse reached the yard-arm. Then, with much cheering, the lad aloft would cut the gantline and the horse would drop into the 'drink'.[17]

Earning money once more, the sailor would then look forward to the next 'sailortown', and of these the most sought after was San Francisco's Barbary Coast.

> No Sailortown, before or since, had ever equalled the Barbary Coast, and, although the crimps spoiled the fun somewhat, every sailor once in his life tried to get on a ship bound through the Golden Gate, even if he knew he would leave this wonderful port without a stitch to his back, a straw palliasse, no sea-boots, and a Cape Horn winter rounding ahead of him ...
>
> In the famous year of forty-nine [the year of the Californian gold rush], ships came to San Francisco in their hundreds, many of them never to leave again. Crews deserted to a man – even the captains and the mates skinning out – leaving the ships and their cargoes to the mercy of looters or the weather. Crews would commandeer ships' lifeboats and row and sail up the Sacramento River to the diggings.[18]

The gold rush was a short term phenomenon, but the Barbary Coast brothels were not; shades of them were still to be found in Panama City in the Second World War.

> The three main types of Barbary Coast bordels were the cowyards, parlour-houses, and cribs. The cribs were the smallest, filthiest and most dangerous of the red-light houses, where venereal diseases were rampant, and the cow-yards nothing more than dozens of cribs in a big building. The parlour-houses were the most elite of these brothels, their girls being somewhat cleaner and charging from five to twenty dollars for 'all night', and two to ten dollars for a 'short time', whereas the crib-girls only charged twenty-five cents to a dollar for a 'short time'. Some of the cow-yards contained as many as three hundred girls. After being thrown out of a parlour-

house, thanks to disease or old age, the 'girls' would naturally enter the cow-yards or cribs.[19]

But danger of a new kind was met at sea in 1852 – the loss by fire, not of a sailing vessel, which happened often enough, but of the paddle-steamer *Amazon* on her first and last voyage. She bore the reputation of being the largest timber-built steamship in the world – 300 feet long and of 2256 tons burden. Built for the Royal Mail Steam-Packet Company for the West Indian Trade, she carried 110 crew and about fifty passengers. When she set out it was observed that her engines became greatly heated by their own working and the ship had to keep stopping to let them cool. As she steamed into the Bay of Biscay against a violent headwind flames spread amidships, cutting communication between the officers aft and the crew in the forecastle. The crew could not now stop the ship, which was doing 13 knots, and the forward life-boats caught fire.

The boats in the *Amazon* were not only suspended from the davits as usual, but had the keels grasped in projecting iron cradles to prevent them from swinging. It does not seem that any on board were aware of this new device; and in the darkness on one side, and the fire-glare on the other, it was not recognised until, through the ignorance of those who handled the tackling several boat-loads of poor wretches had been capsized into the raging sea, and had perished.[20]

Five boats eventually got away safely and fifty-eight were saved out of 162 on board. The captain went down with his ship.

But there were some happy endings, and even a few provident sailors.

At the end of a voyage in 1860, John had been paid-off – in sovereigns. Twenty he'd got. He put them in his money-belt: Reckoned he'd catch the train to Maryport in the morning. Left his dunnage-bag in the Seamen's Mission and went to the boozer.

He woke up next morning remembering nothing except that he had to get back to his wife in Maryport. But he had a terrible thirst, and his coppers were hot [ie his money was burning a hole in his pocket]. So, he shoulders his bag and goes to the boozer for a glass of rum before catching his train.

The rum cost 4d. John feels in his belt and gives the barman what he thinks is a sovereign.

The barman gives him 8d change.

John seizes the barman's wrist. 'I gave you a sovereign. You owe me nineteen shillings!'

'If you can find a sovereign in this bar you can have it,' says the barman. 'You gave me a shilling'.

John examines the contents of his money-belt. Only a few shilling pieces. Someone, it seems, has robbed him while he slept, substituting shillings for sovereigns to allay suspicion. John was done for. Twenty sovereigns was a fortune in those days. He couldn't go back home with no money. Nothing for it but to get another ship and go back to sea.

John takes up his bag and goes down to the dock. A ship is just leaving. He signs on.

The voyage was a long one. Two years later, John Benn returns to Liverpool and gets paid-off.

This time he takes no chances. It's the first train to Maryport.

'Where have *you* been to?' asks Mrs Benn.

'Back to sea' says John. 'I was robbed the voyage before. I had to get another ship.'

'You great fool!' says his wife. 'You weren't robbed. It was the Minister at the Mission. He found you drunk. Took your money for safe keeping. Left you with some shillings for drink. He was waiting for you in the morning to get you some breakfast, but you never turned up. In the end he sent me the money'.[21]

CHAPTER 20

Fiddler's Green

1860–1885

Although by 1860 steamships were going regularly round Cape Horn, the most dramatic consequence of the gold rush in California, and the subsequent discovery of gold in Australia, was the stunning development of the clipper. In the 'golden' days before steam could compete economically in distant trades, sailing ships of over 2000 tons were built to make record passages to San Francisco, China, Australia and New Zealand. This was an era when shipowners could not but make money, whether they were in steam or in sail. But the young were not held in high regard by many masters in the sailing clippers.

... a boy's life was not regarded as of much value aboard ship. They were sent to accomplish tasks that men would refuse to do. My father served his time in West Indiamen during the mid-sixties when they flew studding-sails. When stuns'l tacks carried away, boys were sent out on the booms to reeve them off again. They wouldn't risk a man on the job, but a boy's life was of small account!

Boys have fallen overboard when the ship was running with square yards. When the captain was told it was one of the boys gone over the side, he said: 'What! only a boy? Keep her as she goes.' To risk spars for the purpose of picking up a boy was not to be thought of.

The loftiest sails in the ship were the boys' charge. They were sent aloft in squalls to muzzle skysails and royals when able seamen refused to go.[1]

To indicate what going aloft in a sailing ship might involve, this seafarer offered the following description.

Assume that a stout pole is thrust out of a fourteenth-floor window for a length of 30 feet. The pole has an iron rod running along the top of it and a loose wire rope suspended below it. From the street level, without using the elevator, a man climbs the stairs to the fourteenth floor and creeps out on the spar, his feet on the loose wire rope, his hands on the iron rod. This, in a crude way, gives an idea of what it means to climb aloft and lay out on the upper topgallant yard of a ship like the *Grand Duchess.*

But instead of the solid security of flights of stairs, the climbing is done up a series of iron rods or ropes stretched across wire ropes in the form of a ladder. The higher up one travels, the ladder narrows and becomes almost perpendicular. Envision the conditions on a dark night, the wind blowing, the rain driving. And when one finally reaches the yard one finds a great sail thrashing and ballooning over the spar, threatening to knock you off.

The ship may be rolling and plunging. The yard is swaying too and swinging across from side to side. The sail has to be caught by the fingers and rolled up into a compact mass and ropes tied several times around it and the yard. This job cannot be done with one hand clutching the iron rod, or jackstay, and the other free to furl the canvas. It requires *both* hands, and one must work standing upon a wire rope which has an alarming fashion of swinging before and behind one as well as giving to the weight of other men standing upon it.[2]

L A Woollard records the death at the hands of the captain of a fellow apprentice who was kept aloft for three hours in the vicinity of Cape Horn. The captain had caught an albatross which he then secured to the deck and encouraged his pet terrier to attack it.

The albatross, a fairly large one, had one of its legs tied to a rope which was in turn made fast to one of the rail stanchions on the poop, so that it lacked space to manoeuvre from the dog's attack. Whilst these birds have a powerful beak which can make a good impression when attacked, it was not only a cruel and vicious sport that was being enacted, but an unfair and unequal combat. From aloft came a shout from Frank Aplin, one of my brother apprentices, who was putting twine stoppings on the main royal buntlines, to request the captain to stop his dog mauling the albatross to pieces. This peremptory demand appeared to have infuriated our captain who, in reply, ordered Aplin to remain aloft on the royal yard for the rest of the [forenoon] watch as punishment for his impertinent behaviour ...

In the early afternoon of that day, the wind had veered and increased again and at 4 p.m. all hands were ordered to 'wear ship'. It was whilst carrying out this task that young Aplin went overboard. He was standing close to me at the time, and as he stepped across the foresail sheet, which was lying slack on the deck, the sail gave a mighty flap, the sheet tautened like a bar and, catching him between the legs, shot him overboard like a stone from a catapult and it all happened so swiftly that nothing could be done to save him from reaching the sea. He fell on the crest of a large receding wave and, although a good swimmer, did not appear to make an effort to strike out and keep afloat, either because he had been injured or perhaps had not sufficiently recovered from his three hours punishment aloft, for when he eventually came down at noon, he had the greatest difficulty in reaching the deck again, for he was almost frozen to the bone ... He quickly disappeared astern and was never seen again.[3]

J W Holmes had been at sea a year when, at the age of fifteen, he joined the 443-ton wooden barque *Blair Atholl*, a Black Sea trader. She sailed to Berdianski in the Sea of Azov.

> Every day we rowed or sailed the Old Man ashore seventeen miles through icy spray. We would wait for him in the boat till midnight by which time he had drunk himself blind and would send word to us to fetch him in the morning! Then seventeen miles back in the freezing darkness and by the time we had made the ship it was, 'Stand by for anchor watch', and after that, 'Begin loading', till we took the boat ashore again, to repeat the same proceedings over again.[4]

But the first time was almost the last because the boatswain, who rowed the boat with Holmes, 'chummed up with an Italian boat's crew nearby' and they supplied him with vodka.

> About midnight a Russian came down to the shore and said, 'Cap'n say go aboard now and come for him tomorrow'.
> But by that time the happy bo'sun lay in the bottom of the boat, dead to the world, so the unhappy boy had to hoist the sails single-handed, sail out seventeen miles, and find the ship in darkness. When I did find her I could awaken no response from her, despite my frantic yelling and screaming. I was blown away several miles astern. Then I had to beat up again and once more my wildest yells failed to provoke any attention. I was going away to the leeward yet again when I brought her up with the anchor. Lowering the sails I rolled myself up in the mainsail to thaw my numbed body. After this brief respite from the buffeting of the icy wind and spray I hove up the anchor, hoisted sails and again beat up to the ship. This time the mate threw me a rope over the stern and I made fast. After bending the rope round the unconscious bo'sun and seeing him hoisted aboard, I climbed the rope myself. As I touched the deck, dripping wet and dropping with fatigue, the mate said briefly, 'Get out of your wet duds, and turn to at once at shifting ballast'.[5]

That was in 1870. A few years later Holmes was serving as second mate in the 845-ton barque *Loch Fergus.*

> On leaving London we were kept continuously and strenu-
> ously on the move from 5 a.m. till 8 p.m. The climax came on
> the third Sunday out when the Old Man ordered all sails to be
> brought up from the bottom of the sail locker and overhauled
> and dried. This meant working all day Sunday on a job that
> was merely invented to keep them working, and the men nat-
> urally objected. My watch was called aft and ordered to go
> down into the lockers. There was much grumbling down
> below, and then the men came up and refused to touch the
> nails on Sunday. The mate's watch was then summoned, and
> likewise refused. Then [the captain] came on to the main deck
> with his official log, and asked each man in turn if he refused
> duty, and entered his name in the book, after which he had the
> whole of both watches put in irons down in the sail locker,
> while the mate, the second mate and two apprentices worked
> the ship for over a week.[6]

On arrival at Wellington, New Zealand, the entire crew deserted. Meanwhile, the full-rigged ship *Kingsport* was
being built of wood on the Bay of Fundy, Nova Scotia.
Mick Mulligan joined her there as boatswain.

> ... she was as fine a looking craft as ever I set eyes on, but she
> had a weakness. She didn't have enough iron bolts and tree
> nails to hold her hull together.
>   The builders had run short o' bolts, but the owners
> wouldn't wait. They said she was good enough and decided to
> have her sent under sail to England to be finished. They had a
> cargo of lumber lying on shore out in the open for months ...

The timber was full of frost, but the ship was filled with it
'from keelson to deckhead, packed so tight there wasn't
room for a matchstick in the hold'. In the warm Gulf
Stream,

The frozen timber in the hold started to thaw, and, as it thawed, it swelled! Well, mates, as the hull was not properly fastened, the pressure from the inside opened her seams, and she begun to leak like a basket.

Pumping ship proved ineffective, so the captain called the crew together.

He mustered us at the break o' the poop. 'Now, men' he says, 'the ship's waterlogged, and pumpin' won't do any more good. Ye can see for y'rselves she can't sink, on account o' the cargo o' lumber, but if it keeps swelling she'll bust her sides and fall to pieces under our feet. There's only one thing to do, and that's to lash her together. We'll put the anchor chains round her, and there'll be no watch below till the job's done, so, if ye want to save y'r hides, turn to with a will, and look lively.'

... We put one length round her by the foremast, another by the main and a third by the mizzen. That was nine hours work for all hands, and good work at that, though I say it myself, as by this time she was both rails under and wallowing like a turtle ...

The galley was washed out, and the fo'csle was belly-deep in water, but we carried on, making about two knots, and in thirty-two days we made Holyhead, sixty miles from Liverpool, the port we were bound for. By this time the position was desperate.

We were forty days out from the Bay o' Fundy, and living on dog biscuits, as the harness cask was empty. Every man had salt-water boils, and we were weak as kittens.[7]

Like the captain of the *Loch Fergus*, Captain Absalom of the brig *Pioneer* thought nothing of putting seamen in irons.

August 23rd [1882] The brig *Pioneer*, of Blyth, Captain Absalom, which arrived at Leith from Oran, had three of the crew in irons. The men were chained to the winch amidships, and attracted a good deal of attention. It is stated that the men, who had a worn-out and emaciated appearance, had been kept chained to the winch during the voyage, extending over 35 days, and that their only food was a pound of hard biscuits and a pint of water per day. [The minimum for good health is reckoned to be two pints per day.] On being taken to the police station, a medical gentleman ordered their removal to hospital. They were very weak, one especially trembling from head to foot and being hardly able to walk. Captain Absalom stated that the vessel sailed from Greenock about three months ago, bound for Algiers with a cargo of coal. On arriving there in July he alleged that three of the seamen, named James Noonan, Henry Bryant, and Wm. Hall, refused to do duty, and were taken before the Consul-General. As they still declined to work, he ordered them to prison. Two or three days later the captain went to the prison, but only one of the men, Noonan, agreed to pay expenses and return to duty. The captain stated that Noonan informed him that the other men asked the latter while in gaol to join in a conspiracy to take his life when they got on board, and, on Noonan refusing to do so, he was attacked by them, the officials of the gaol having to interfere and place Hall in solitary confinement in a dark cell. Another of the crew, who had been in hospital, declined to pay expenses. The men were, therefore, kept in gaol until the departure of the ship, when they were conveyed down in irons. After getting on board, the captain stated that they made a rush at him, and one of his thumbs was dislocated. They were overpowered and chained to the stanchion and the Consul ordered them to be taken to England for trial. At Oran they were chained to the winch, with a wooden platform to sleep on, and an awning overhead.[8]

There were those who knew well enough the root causes of much insubordination at sea.

Yes, Mr. D., there are two great causes out of which nine-tenths of the mutinous insubordination on the part of seamen arises: first, the supplying of bad provisions ...; those who have the care and working of the expedition [ie the crew] are left to be dealt with by owners, many of whom may bestow less anxiety for the seamen's supplies than they would for that of their dog ...

The second great cause of mutinous insubordination, Mr. D., has its origin in the conduct of captains and officers, but most frequently resulting in the overbearing arrogance of the former reflecting through the officers on the crew; ...

Why, do you know, Mr. D., that the marine department of the Board of Trade is, in my estimation, a grand maritime burlesque.[9]

These were, of course, the years in which Samuel Plimsoll was campaigning against coffin ships and Havelock Wilson was endeavouring to build a seamen's union. The latter, who was later to become a ship's cook, suffered less on his initiation at sea than many.

We were allowed three quarts of water a day for cooking and washing, and this was served out at four o'clock in the afternoon ... In tropical weather we could almost polish off our allowance in two drinks, then for the next twenty-four hours we had to wait patiently for the next issue. We could not afford any of this precious water for washing purposes, so we went week after week without having a wash, except on Saturday afternoons, when we received one bucket of water for washing purposes, between sixteen men. Those who felt inclined to wash the salt from their faces would wash in the bucket, but the time nine or ten had performed this operation the water was somewhat thick. Being fresh water, it was too precious to throw away, so some of them would wash cotton shirts, jackets or trousers in it, and rinse them out in salt water ...

On Monday we were entitled to one-and-a-quarter pounds of salt pork – sometimes it was very good, rather on the fat side. Pea-soup measured out according to Act of Parliament. An eighth-of-an-ounce of tea – and old cookie extracted the

best of this tea. He would put his pan on to boil at about three
o'clock, and at three-thirty he would put in the tea, when it
would stew well until five o'clock for the first watch. Then, at
six p.m., when the other watch came off duty, they got the
benefit of the stewing. No milk was allowed.

We were allowed one pound of sugar per week. The boys
would finish up the sugar about Wednesday, so that from then
until Saturday we had unsweetened tea. On Tuesday we had
one-and-a-half pounds of salt beef. Sometimes it was exceedingly salt, and, moreover, pretty tough if it was from a cask
that had been left over from the previous voyage ... I have
seen little models of ships carved out of salt junk ...

Sunday was a very important day as far as food was con
cerned. We only had half our allowance of salt junk, but in
lieu of the other half we received a tin of preserved beef. The
sailors used to call it 'Harriet Lane', a reference to a poor
unfortunate woman who had been murdered in the East End
of London ... The preserved meat was made into a sea-pie in
what was called a 'three-decker' – potatoes and preserved
meat at the bottom, then a layer of paste, a further supply of
meat and potatoes, and so on until the three decks were laid ...
we boys looked forward to Sunday and 'Harriet'.[10]

After he had become President of the National Union of
Seamen, Wilson, surrounded by union officials who acted
as assistant cooks, still cooked a sea-pie from time to time
at the Union headquarters. Many shipowners, and their
jackal journalists, opposed seamen's attempts to form
unions. A quasi-sympathetic observer wrote:

Jack is proverbially a heedless man. People who do not care so
long as the passing hour is comfortable and cheerful are not
likely to exhibit much of a front when they call themselves a
union. The despair of Jack's friends has always been that he
will not give himself any trouble.

We must take human nature as we find it. The gravest of
City merchants might forget his special kind of gravity and

might find his perception of the exact value of the sovereign
dulled were he to pass a year of his life in a ship's forecastle
in the light of a lantern, fed with slush, with warm water and
peas instead of soup, pork of acrid taste and greenish hue
instead of venison and grouse, and a black liquor full of short
sticks called tea in place of his favourite brand of champagne.
We must take the sailor as he is, with his vices and virtues.
Seeing this, it is to be feared that Sunderland's excellent
project of a National Union for mariners must come
to nothing.[11]

Nor was Wilson encouraged by some of those evangelistic
parsons who had set out to save the souls of seamen in seamen's bethels.

I shall ever remember what occurred when I went on board to
see the Parson to arrange for holding the meeting. If I remember him aright, he had a stately though humble appearance,
and was rather fat. I introduced myself. He had never heard of
me before, which hurt my vanity, as I thought the whole
world had heard of Havelock Wilson, but it was not so as far
as this person was concerned. I told him the object of my visit
was to ask if he would be kind enough to allow me to have a
meeting on the ship for the purpose of organising and establishing a branch of the National Amalgamated Sailors and
Firemen's Union of Great Britain and Ireland. I thought the
very title of the union would be enough to impress him. He
was not at all alarmed either at the title or myself. I said that I
could get the use of any number of large rooms attached to
public houses – and there were many such places. In those
days most of the Trade Unions held their club meetings, as
they called them, in public houses – and I added that I thought
shipowners and others would prefer that the men of the sea
should transact the business in places other than public
houses. As soon as the parson had recovered from the shock,
he gave me a most anti-Trade Union sermon. 'How dare you
come on board my ship to ask me to allow you, a common
agitator, and the rest of your gang to hold a Trade Union

meeting?' he roared. 'Look here, my young man' (and I certainly must have looked youthful) 'I'll give you a bit of good advice – if I had my way I would have you and the likes of you stretched up to a triangle, and with the strongest cat-o-nine-tails that could be manufactured I would just like to deliver forty good lashes across your bare back'.[12]

Wilson and the mission padres were at one, however, in wanting to combat the infamous crimps.

... rowing boats [were] making for us, each boat containing three or four men; they were the crimp boarding-housemasters and their runners. Nearly all this gang were ex-seamen of the worst type. The runners were employed because of their pugilistic ability. Anyone with a pugilistic and thieving tendency was sure of employment with the boarding-house keepers. The bigger the thug the larger the wages.

It was not long before this fleet of boats were alongside our ship. They carried a pole twelve feet in length, with a big iron crook on the end of it. Attached to the pole was a rope, and after getting alongside the ship the hook would be put on the rail or rigging, or any place they could hook to. They would then slack away the rope and be towed whilst the ship was making headway through the water.

Once alongside, they were soon swarming on board. Some carried ladders in their boats, and others hooks to go over the rail of the ship. During this time the crew were aloft stowing sails and making them fast.

The runners swarmed up the rigging after the men, with bottles of whisky in their pockets, helping the crew to stow the sails, and making their acquaintance. They were wonderfully ingenious in this. They would go up to a man and greet him by name, Tom or Bill, and say, 'Do you remember the last time we were together?' Perhaps they had never met before, but that did not matter so long as an acquaintance was struck up. Two or three nips of whisky helped that along. They gave the crew business cards, which contained invitations to their boarding-houses.

Whilst this was going on the rest of the gang were in the forecastle packing the men's bags; they were not particular as to whose bag or which clothes they put in. Sometimes they would mix the clothes deliberately. The bags would then be passed out of the forecastle over the side to the boats, and the men would be invited to identify their particular bag at the boarding-house; so they would have to follow the runners ...

Our ship made a good haul for the crimps, for it had not taken them very long to find out just exactly what was due to each man in the way of cash – six months' wages at forty dollars a month. The rule among these sharks was never to allow a man to remain long on shore. They went in for quick returns and big profits, and most of them were signed on again in less than eight days, the crimps getting one hundred and fifty dollars blood-money from the Captain for each man, a bonus paid by the Owners for shipping the men, and sixty dollars in addition out of each man's wages.[13]

According to Havelock Wilson, 'Jimmy the Drummer', a notorious crimp, was one sailor short on one occasion, so he went to the mortuary and bribed the keeper to supply him with a corpse. The corpse was put on board with the rest of the crew as 'a good sailor, but dead drunk'. The mate tried to rouse him with a belaying pin after the ship had sailed.[14]

Ashore for his few days in Liverpool – or any other home port – Jack would hope to have a good time.

Canning Place was the centre of the South End Sailortown. Here stood the Customs House, with, close by, the Sailors' Home, and, not far away, Cleveland Square and Pitt Street, the Liverpool Chinatown. Around the statue of Mr Huskisson, in the centre of Canning Place, and outside the Home, groups of painted harlots would parade, a sailor having to fairly run the gauntlet to pass them.

When I steered into her, I hadn't got a care,
She wuz cruisin' up an' down ol' Canning Place,

> She wuz dressed in a gown so fine, like a frigate of the line,
> An' being a sailorman I gave chase.

So runs the old ditty of Maggie May. This state of affairs was to be found all down Paradise Street and St John's Street, along Castle Street, around St George's Church in Derby Square, and in Brunswick Street. An army of prostitutes infested these thoroughfares as far as the Exchange Flags and Rumford Street. The customers of these 'Liverpool Judies' were, in the main, sailormen. *The Liverpool Judies have got us in tow* was the chorus of a popular capstan song in the old days. They would accompany the drink-befuddled sailors down to the docks to say goodbye to them as they sailed, standing on the quayside yelling bawdily, as they lifted their many coloured and striped petticoats with obscene gestures: 'Take a good look, Johnny, it'll be along time afore yeez'll see annuder wan!'[15]

But there could be compensations in the South Atlantic.

In the tropics, when barely a rope would be touched, the hands would gather around the knightheads, under the cool down-draught of the fore-topmast-stays'l, with pipes going and chaws of baccy in their cheeks. Or maybe they would sit on the fore-bitts, close to the windlass or capstan, their bare feet dangling on the warm planking of the deck. Perhaps the ship would have a 'fufu' band, consisting of a squeeze box (concertina), a fiddle (very often home-made from a cigar box), triangle, 'Spoons' and pig-bladder drums (the bladders having been extracted from the stores, by bribing the sea-cook).[16]

And one might arrive, after a month or two, in Buenos Aires.

The infamous Fiddler's Green of B.A., La Boca, was the rendezvous of criminals and assassins of all kinds, and the police – the Marineros – turned a blind eye to waterfront happenings ...

By the eighties B.A. was a thriving port, its Boca and South docks chock-a block with windbags from every corner

of the globe. The newer British, French, and German iron
and steel four-masted barques would be moored side by side
with older Down-East wooden ships. And real old-timers,
mainly from Spain and Italy, with stern-galleries and fancy
figureheads, would be rubbing shoulders with Yankee bar-
quentines, Nova Scotian barques and West Indian schooners,
all lying stern-on to the quays. Scandinavian timber-ships
from the Gulf, hide and bone droghers, grain carriers and
general traders, aboard which powerful-looking, dark-
skinned *trabajaderos* with long thin knives stuck in their
black *facas*, sang lustily as they worked the cargoes, also
helped to fill the docks. Of an evening, all these craft spewed
ashore their rollickin', rantin' rovers, hell-bent for the dives
of the Boca.

The road, such as it was, running from the Boca up to the
more respectable part of the town – the Pasoe de Colon I
believe it was called – was traversed by horse-drawn trams,
with its one side resplendent with pubs, cafés, dance-halls and
brothels. Here stood the famous Liverpool Bar, renowned
among sailormen; the Liverpool House, equally famous, or
perhaps notorious is a better word; and the Flags of all
Nations.[17]

The Liverpool Judies and other sea shanties, like sailing
ships themselves, were on the way out, as steam super-
seded sail.

My father, who was a real windship sailor, declared that no
shantying worthy of the name was to be heard after 1880. He
served his time in West Indiamen with negro crews, back in
the 'sixties, and he dilated many times upon their wonderful
chorusing, their harmonious singing ...

A well-known *prima donna* came down to the pierhead [in
Liverpool] one Sunday, he told me once, while their ship was
hauling out, and she declared that the shantying of *Ladies
Fare-ye-Well!* by the negro crew was the most beautiful
singing she had ever heard from the throats of men.[18]

The Fiddler's Green of Buenos Aires was not the true Garden of Delights. That was to be found only after death.

When an old 'fifty years at sea' shellback dies he does not go to the orthodox heaven but to a place called Fiddler's Green. To get there, he turns into a gull or albatross and flies to the South Pole. Near the Pole there is an open hatch which spins around very quickly with the revolution of the earth. The reincarnated sailor must watch his chance to fly into it. Once inside, he resumes his natural form and finds himself in Fiddler's Green – a mythical Paradise said to lie 'seven miles to loo'ard of Hell, where the drinks and smokes are logged, but never paid' Sailors used to say that all the goodlooking women on this mundane sphere repair to Fiddler's Green for the sole purpose of filling the pot and pipe of poor Jack![19]

CHAPTER 21

The Last of the Windjammers

1885–1910

In 1887 Queen Victoria celebrated her Golden Jubilee – fifty years upon the British throne – and Prime Minister Benjamin Disraeli added the jewel of India to her Crown. British merchant shipping attained its peak, its unique position as a carrier of world trade, with half the world's tonnage in its ownership. Never before and never since had one country so dominated the world economy. Throughout the period covered by this chapter, maritime Britain was on the crest of its wave and, with great improvements in marine engines, the building of steamships of 15,000 and more tons became an economic proposition. It was an era when great fortunes were made for the families of shipping entrepreneurs, but little of the money made came the way of poor Jack. The great sailing ships, the windjammers, were on their way out, and life aboard became even harder than it had been before as they found it increasingly difficult to compete against steam.

> I saw those sailing seamen cotton clad,
> Housed in wet kennels, worm-fed, cheated, driven,
> Three pounds a month, and small delight they had,
> Save the bright water and the winds of heaven.

John Masefield, author of these lines and later Poet Laureate, made one voyage to sea as an apprentice in the early 1890s. Landed sick in Iquique, Chile, after rounding Cape

Horn, he never went to sea professionally again but, unlike his contemporary, Captain Jan de Hartog, he retained a romantic view of the sailor. 'In my memory,' wrote de Hartog, 'the stalwart salts with the hearts of oak were moronic bipeds dangling in the branches of artificial trees in constant peril of their lives.'[1] But de Hartog was essentially a steamship man and the truth was more complex. As Commodore Sir James Bisset, also of the age of Masefield and de Hartog, wrote,

> The lore of sail has become obsolete in our mechanised age, but part of its fascination was in the romantic and sometimes inexplicable names of every part of the sailing vessel and of all the gear and equipment. The nautical lingo made sailors of all nations a race apart from landlubbers. This Esperanto of the sea had evolved, during centuries of usage, from sources almost impossible to trace, passed on by word of mouth from generation to generation of seamen, most of whom were unable to read or write; but knew unerringly the meanings of hundreds of technical terms that had a power of enchantment. At times their very lives and the lives of all on board a vessel might depend on the correct and instantaneous response to an order given in that nautical jargon which was gibberish to a landsman but of vital reality to a sailor.[2]

A sailor might be drunk ashore but he was necessarily sober at sea.

> Life under sail appealed to men of a roving disposition, who sought, in the freedom of the wide oceans and in the constant movement of far voyaging, to get away from the restrictions of home life on shore or the monotony and sometimes sordid greed of shore jobs. Though they soon found that life at sea had many disadvantages, they became aware also that it had many moments of beauty, not only of scene but of action, which appeal to man's romantic or poetic instincts. This was the compensation for all the discomforts that had to be endured.[3]

Even the food was not always bad. James Learmont came up 'through the hawse pipe', that is, served as crew when he first went to sea, but by the 1890s he was second mate in the full-rigged ship *William Law,* 1664 tons net.

> The food was very good for every member of the crew. My first surprise in this matter was when I asked the boys at 5.30 a.m. if they had finished their coffee; back came the reply, 'No sir, we are waiting for the steward to give us our cakes.' The food was improved by the attention given to it by the cook. Instead of the meat for the crew being served out whole in mess kids it was sliced up by him and mixed, beef, pork, and corned meat on special plates with baked beans for everyone every day.[4]

However, the master of the *William Law* was of the common mould in other ways.

> It was almost unheard of for a mate to see the chart. In many cases the mate had to get in league with the steward to find the observed position, so that he could check up the Dead Reckoning that he kept and entered in his logbook. The second mate did no navigation of any sort or kind.[5]

Many officers hoarded their hard-won knowledge like gold and their responsibility towards the young was taken lightly.

> My earliest impression on going deep-water [wrote Learmont] was the utter disregard for their apprentices shown by the masters, with the notable exception of the master of the *Strathdon.* An indenture had been drawn up, and signed, between owners and apprentice; on their part he was to be taught seamanship and navigation, and on his, he had to behave in a certain manner, for instance he must not visit 'alehouses'. Almost without exception neither masters nor officers paid the slightest attention to the education of apprentices and when on shore they could go just where they liked. They

were left to acquire seamanship from the men in the fo'c'sle with whom they were put to work as helpers, whilst navigation was a closed book; even those who began training on *Conway* or *Worcester* forgot what they had learned during the subsequent years of neglect.[6]

It was at about this time that the 1862-ton ship *Acamas* was in Eureka, north of San Francisco, to load redwood for the United Kingdom. As was often the case, poor food, bad conditions and the unlikelihood of regular leave ashore had caused many of the crew to desert when the ship arrived on the west coast of America.

We had towed up from Frisco with a skeleton crew, and now the extra men required had arrived by coast boat from Frisco having been supplied by the Boarding House Masters at about fifty dollars per man. The bunch consisted of a Mulatto, a few Scandinavians, a Britisher and a Frenchman ...

The new hands came on board in a very doped condition with few if any clothes. They all had a few plugs of chewing tobacco, blocks of sulphur matches, some cheap soap and corn-cob pipes, and that was about the lot.[7]

A year later the *Acamas* was in Pisagua, Chile.

By this time we were rather short-handed as some of the sailors had cleared out and were supposed to be working at the saltpetre mines. One or two who had been given leave ashore were serving in gaol for getting drunk. It was the practice to give sailors a day's liberty on the West Coast, and this invariably meant a bad time for a few of them.

The first thing they did on getting ashore was to get in the nearest saloon and fill themselves with 'fire-water'. The police well knew their failing and would watch for them. A mounted gendarme, whenever he saw a drunken sailor, would lassoo his victim and drag him off to the Calaboose. There he was stripped of everything he had and put into the chain gang, and for several days this gang would be employed in cleaning the streets under guard. Other sailors would get into quarrels with the Chilanos and often end up by being severely stabbed, the Chilano being an expert with the knife which he always carried.[8]

James Learmont had learned by experience and by example. Promoted to the command of the *Brenhilda,* he found himself in Valparaiso.

Now that I was able to carry out what I thought was right, even if it was most unusual on board British ships, I allowed one watch to go ashore each Sunday. After breakfast they dressed ready, pulled the boat themselves to and from the Mole and had to be on board sober by 8 p.m. Through my allowing the crew this privilege they worked exceedingly well and returned on board and according to my conditions having evidently enjoyed their run ashore.[9]

Later in the year (1895) he commented,

We had been nearly five months on the coast, but we had not lost a man, there was never a complaint from the crew and they worked well. On my part I used every opportunity to get them fresh provisions. In this I was helped by my owner who always encouraged me to buy outside of the recognised practice of getting everything from a shipchandler.[10]

Learmont also tried to make life at sea agreeable both for himself and his crew.

As a sailor before the mast I hated to hear that call 'All Hands on Deck!' I had pictured it as Dana described it and found out that it was much the same in my fo'c'sle days. 'Watch and Watch', cold and miserable on deck you were glad to get below for rest and sleep. When this rest was disturbed and at times lost altogether, it had the effect of reducing the efficiency of the crew and tended to increase the sick list. This was something that I set out to reform in my own ships and during my years of command I do not remember ever having to call all hands on deck. Many a soaking came to me personally in helping the watch to shorten sail. I am not going to say that my actions in this direction were purely sentimental; I realized that a well-cared-for crew would help me to make good passages and this was my one and only ambition.[11]

In a lifetime at sea, even a shipmaster of Learmont's calibre could not avoid trouble. Two of his crew fell from the fore upper topsail yard in a gale north of the Falklands and died from their injuries. His ship was reported to have foundered on the Goodwin Sands as his wife was giving birth in his cabin to a daughter, though on that occasion the outcome for both ship and family was a happy one. On the new and well-found ship *Bengairn* the rats left in Newcastle, New South Wales, and the cargo of coal shifted and all the boats on the lee side were swept away when the ship sailed into very heavy seas. 'Working night and day at trimming the cargo and at the pumps we were gaining ground. I was at both jobs along with the crew, hungry, dirty and sleepy. The passing of days had not meant anything to me but about now I realized that it was five days since the cargo shifted.'[12] The ship survived and there were compensations, even where there were also added dangers.

The moon had now risen over one of those nights only experienced in Antarctica, a sky without a cloud, blazing with stars – visible only in these latitudes to advantage on account of the clarity of the atmosphere ...

From my position in the fo'c'sle head the scene, had one been free to admire it, was grand and yet awful. Ice that breaks away in the Antarctic is quite flat when it leaves the Barrier. After months, perhaps years, of drifting, in the process of melting the bergs or islands alter in shape. Some of them were reared towards the sky, while others were listing as if they were going to turn turtle. To get through a very narrow opening we had to go so close along the weather side of one of the bergs that we were in its backwash, which was coloured a deep brown by the melting ice. This was probably owing to the its having been near to a volcano in the Antarctic.

I drove the ship to her utmost capacity, for I was determined to make the most of my chance; difficult as it was, it was preferable to dodging along under easy canvas and prolonging the risk ...

On finding our position at noon I estimated that we had passed through 278 miles of the South Atlantic studded with ice-islands and bergs, from five in the morning of September 2nd to four a.m. on the 3rd.[13]

1905 was a particularly bad year round Cape Horn.

During the months of May, June, and July no fewer than 130 sailing vessels left European ports for Pacific coast ports of North, Central and South America. Of this number 62 were British, 34 French, 27 German, 4 Italian, 2 Norwegian, one Russian (*Fennia*) and one Dane. Out of this number 52 arrived at their destination, four were wrecked, 22 put into ports in distress after Cape Horn damage and 53 had not arrived or were unaccounted for by the end of July.[14]

Learmont attributed his safe passage to 'my consideration for a good crew'. Things were different aboard the steel built, full rigged ship *British Isles*, commanded by Captain James P Barker. The *British Isles* could carry 4000 tons, and in 1898 held the record for the fastest voyage – eighty days – from London to Sydney. It was a different story in 1905 when apprentice W H S Jones joined her.

The daily diet was monotonous in the extreme. At 7 a.m., one boy of the watch below, and one man, would each take a 'bread barge' – an oblong box – to the cabin door, where the steward would dole out the day's allowance of 'Liverpool pantiles', a hard-baked biscuit which was the substitute for bread throughout the whole voyage, and the sailors' staff of life.

At seven bells the same two would go to the galley, to receive a billy of tea – the billy being an empty 7-lb jam-tin. Only twice a week was a small ration of sugar, tinned milk and tinned butter doled out, which usually lasted only one day. On the other days we had black stewed tea, without milk and sugar.

Breakfast, for the watch below, at 7.30 a.m., consisted of pantiles soaked in tea to soften them, washed down with what remained of the tea.

Midday dinner consisted of a small piece of salt beef, with pantiles.

For the evening meal, the breakfast menu – pantiles and tea – was repeated.

On Sundays and Thursdays, there was salt pork instead of 'salt horse' for dinner, and one boiled potato per man – the only vegetables we ever saw. The 'spuds' were issued only as long as they lasted, which might be for three weeks in a three-months voyage ...

... If the salt beef or pork went rotten, and the biscuits became weevilly, as often happened, there was a real danger of starvation, or at least of serious malnutrition, among the crews of sailing ships.[15]

On the way to Cape Horn it was discovered that the un-insured cargo of coal was on fire. The crew were or-dered to dig down to the seat of the fire, hoisting the buckets of coal out by hand and building a heap of coal along the deck. The donkey-engine and winch were not used to hoist out the coal because the engine would require coal to fuel it and this would lose the owners money.

Progressive thermometer readings showed temperatures increasing steadily from 170 degrees F to 200 degrees F, as we dug further and further in. Coal-shovelling is hard enough work without being half-suffocated at the same time and hav-ing one's boots shrivelled by standing on a hot bed while working. The heat scorched the soles of our feet, as we frantically hopped from one foot to the other to obtain a moment's relief, and kept the hopping up for hours on end ...

On the fourth day, we reached the seat of the fire, where the coal was smouldering and smoking. Some of it burst into flame while being hoisted in the baskets. It was dumped overboard, presumably to the sorrow of the owners. To shovel these glowing embers was a task to break the stoutest hearts, and changes of the gangs below were made frequently. At midnight, scarcely able to stand from weariness, we had the satisfaction of knowing that the fire was beaten, and the last of the glowing embers thrown overboard.[16]

But the fire was not the worst of the troubles endured by the crew of the *British Isles* on this voyage. Week after week they tried to sail the ship round the Horn.

The floor of the half-deck was awash, with from 6 to 12 inches of water, and remained so night and day for more than a month. With every sea that broke on board some water squirted through the door-jamb and through the division between the upper and lower sections of the door. Our sea-chests were lashed to the lower bunks, but were soon soaked by the water splashing over them. Within a few days the contents were also more or less wet, even though we had wrapped everything in pieces of tarpaulin purloined from the sail-locker.

The pillows and blankets in our bunks were damp. The 'hash-kits' – tin pannikins and plates – played hide-and-seek on the floor as the water washed them about.

There was no stove on the half-deck. Hardy boys could be expected to do without such a luxury, even in 60 degrees South latitude in mid-winter ...

Coming off watch, each boy would stand on his sea-chest to take off his oilskins and outer garments, and hang these on the iron uprights supporting the bunks. Then, watching his chance with the roll of the ship, he would tumble over the lee-board into his bunk, in his damp underclothes, to wrap himself in his damp blankets, and, wearied to exhaustion-point, to fall into a deep sleep instantly ...

The constant chafing of the oilskin cuffs, on wrists wet and salt-grimed, caused every man in the ship, after a week or two, to develop painful boils on the wrists, for which there was no prevention or cure. Bandages were useless, as they were quickly saturated and dried hard with the salt deposited in them by the sea-water, this being more painful than to leave the boils exposed to further fraying from the sharp cuffs. The skin peeled off, leaving raw and lacerated flesh to be stung by the salt water, a severe physical irritation which soon became a mental obsession, making the sufferer short-tempered.17

To draw six or seven buckets of fresh water a day – the ration for thirty men – became a major task, for the pump was situated on deck where it was most exposed to the seas breaking over the ship.

As we drifted further and further to the southward, a heavy hoar frost settled on every part of the ship exposed to the open air. I dare say the temperature dropped to 20 degrees below freezing-point, although I have no record of the thermometer readings. In these circumstances, to touch any ironwork or wires with bare hands meant an instant and severe 'frost-burn' or frost bite, resulting in swollen and inflamed fingers, so painful as to incapacitate a man suffering from this injury, as he could no longer hold on aloft or to the lifelines on the deck, or use his fingers in any kind of work. In the same way, water freezing inside sea-boots could cause frost-bitten toes, which swelled up and made it impossible for the sufferer to put on his boots, or to work any more on deck or aloft.

... These men were in agony, as there was no known cure for severe frost-bite, except to wrap the injured parts in bandages smeared with vaseline, and hope for the best. In some cases gangrene set in, and fingers or toes festered and eventually dropped off, after a prolonged period of intense pain.18

Then came a gale of ferocious violence which shattered the main-topgallant mast and yards and shredded the fore and main topsails. The side of the port forecastle was stove in, the two lifeboats disappeared, and the whole ship was in chaos. One man was seriously injured and another was swept overboard on this day alone. Soon after, Captain Barker had to cut off a gangrenous leg.

> The ship was rolling and tumbling in the heavy sea, as the Greek, deeply unconscious, was lifted from his bunk, and lashed down to the forecastle table ...
>
> Overcoming nausea at the terrible stench of the gangrene, the Old Man, after binding and tightening ligatures on the thigh, cut through the living flesh, above the knee, and bared the bone.
>
> Blood spurted from the severed arteries. With the red-hot poker the Captain instantly cauterized the cut, and stopped the bleeding, as the stench of burning flesh filled the forecastle.
>
> Then, seizing the meat-saw, he quickly cut through the thigh-bones, and applied the red-hot poker again, and again.
>
> Gronberg, picking up the putrid severed leg, rushed out of the door and threw it overboard.[19]

It took seventy-two days for the ship to make 650 miles towards its destination. Captain Barker wrote his own account of this voyage and summed up this passage as follows.

> Ten weeks had elapsed since the British Isles had passed St John's Point [Staten Island], and in that interval of time the assaults of the elements had accounted for all our casualties which, summed up, were as follows:
>
> Four men ... permanently laid up with bad cases of frostbite.
>
> Nine men completely exhausted with rheumatism, severe colds, etc., ...
>
> One man, Jerry the Greek, leg amputated.

Three men dead: 'Santiago', the Chileno, swept away by the heavy sea; *Isaacson*, lost overboard from the foreyard; *Harry*, killed by heavy water on deck.

Those of the crew who had remained on duty throughout practically the entire period of bad weather were far from being in robust condition; ... [20]

Six worn-out seamen and four worn-out apprentices eventually sailed the ship to Pisagua, the nitrate port in Chile. 'Of the twenty seamen who had signed on for that tragic outward-bound voyage of the *British Isles*, three were lost overboard, three more died of injuries, two were permanently disabled, and three partially disabled – a heavy price to pay for delivering 3,600 tons of black diamonds [best Cardiff coal].'[21]

In Pisagua what remained of the crew had to unload the coal, each of them working an eleven-hour day. On top of that the apprentices had to man the gig to take the captain ashore or ship-visiting. When the ship was ready to sail again, the crimps delivered new crew.

Back in Newcastle, New South Wales, Captain Barker bought a second-hand motor launch which he intended to be the envy of other sailing-ship masters in Iquique, on the Chile coast, who had to have themselves rowed ashore. Jones, now a senior apprentice, was appointed 'engineer'.

When we had gone half a mile, and were still near the ships, the engine belched, and stopped dead.

'What's wrong with it?' asked the Captain, testily.

'It has stopped, sir', I said.

'Damnation, I know it has stopped! Get it started again!'

Like myself, the Old Man knew that the heap of iron amidships was an engine, but how it worked was a perfect mystery to us both. The indignity of a breakdown was most embarrassing, and would soon be perceived by onlookers who had hitherto been moved only by envy.

Never at a loss in an emergency, the Old Man rose to the occasion.

'Turn the fly-wheel, m'son!' he ordered.

I obeyed, and, as the engine was still in gear, the boat moved slightly forward.

'Turn it faster, m'son! Damn it, we are hardly moving!'

Realizing that the Captain's dignity must be upheld in all circumstances, but especially in the present unfortunate situation, I bent my back to the task with a will, and, stooping, turned the heavy fly-wheel round and round, round and round, without respite, at the maximum number of revolutions of which I was capable. The boat moved slowly forward as I puffed and panted, and we resumed our progress, though at greatly reduced speed.

There was half a mile to go, to reach the jetty, but we were slowly and surely drawing away from the near observation of spectators on the ships. When we met one or two boats coming off from the shore, manned by apprentices, with their captains sitting up in the sternsheets, my Captain, while gravely saluting his cronies, managed to rock the launch unobtrusively, to create a bow wave, which might appear to the observers to indicate that we were travelling at a speed of six or seven knots ...[22]

Captain Barker had gone to sea in 1894, serving in the *Lurlei* under Captain Simon Gunn.

'All I knows I learned m'self ... [proclaimed Gunn] No, mister there ain't no frills on Simon Gunn. I can work a latitude by meridian altitude of the sun, find a longitude by chronometer, and keep a good dead reckonin'. I've been master over thirty years, and I've never stranded or lost a ship or caused the underwriters any expense. Book learnin', mister', he rattled on, as I shuffled uneasily, 'may be all right to them that needs it, but I takes no stock in it. And I reckon Simon Gunn's as good if not better than the rest.'[23]

Arrogance was endemic among shipmasters of the period and Barker himself developed few saving graces.

While all hands had been struggling on the fore yard to furl a frozen fores'l, two men in the starboard and one in the port watch had become frost-bitten. In a short time their fingers and toes were red and shrunken. Despite my treatment, which was applied according to the instructions in the Board of Trade's *Ship Captain's Medical Guide*, the affected parts daily became worse; they changed in colour from red to white, from white to yellow, and finally to the bluish hue of a ripe plum - gangrene had set in! I expected that the victims would lose their toes and fingers, and this they did in a few days, becoming entirely unfit for duty.

* * *

For three long hours they struggled with the frozen canvas, and only after their gnarled and calloused hands were cut and bleeding was it finally captured. The second mate afterwards told me the story of what had occurred up there ... When the sail was up on the yard a man sat down on the footrope to pass the gasket to a waiting hand, the hand invisible in the darkness, but after much unsuccessful fumbling someone else began to curse impatiently: 'You – shopkeeper! get a move on – blast you!'

Thus roughly admonished the man on the footrope made another effort to flick the gasket; but at that moment his bleeding fingers slipped from the ice links of the lower tops'l sheet. He lashed out blindly with both arms in a vain effort to save himself, and a wild, agonising yell escaped his lips to rise above the roar of the wind and sea as he hurtled down into the blackness beneath.

The poor devil might just as well have fallen into a cauldron of molten steel for all the chance he had. No one wasted a breath by shouting, 'Man overboard!'

* * *

As there were no blankets carried in the slop-chest of the *British Isles,* I had no means of furnishing watch below coverings for the men, other than to hand out both new and used canvas which at least kept from their bodies the chilly salt water that persisted in seeping into their bunks.[24]

Captain J W Holmes was luckier than Barker and more of the Learmont mould.

During all the years I was in command I was very fortunate in having good weather and good crews, and it is a comforting reflection for a man who has spent fifty-four years of his life upon the world of waters to recall that he has never had a ship in trouble.[25]

He shipped only English, Scots, Scandinavians and Australians since 'they were good seamen and of good conduct, and got on well together'.[26]

Some of these men had made many voyages with me, Chips, Sails and Lamptrimmer coming with me from the *Lencadia*. The latter indeed followed me into the *Inverurie*, and, although a white-haired man when he first joined the *Lencadia* (being then over sixty-four years old), he sailed with me as lamptrimmer, steward and cabin-'boy' for over twenty years, and died in 1926 at the age of ninety-three without having lost a hair of his leonine white mane and beard, which, from the first voyage, gained him the name of 'Old Dad'. His head inside was as remarkable as its exterior, for his memory went back to his first voyage in a Geordie at the age of nine years, and even when over ninety he could converse fluently upon the ships he had sailed in, and even remember the name of every officer.[27]

Holmes' daughter, who sailed with him, recalled that life at sea was not all struggle, and there were blissful days in the tropics when, with every sail drawing, 'the ship glided like a swan', and her father commented,

The amount of amusement a good tempered crew can make for itself from very slight material is amazing ... It is noticeable that a ship which could muster a concertina, a banjo, and a mouth organ or two, usually had a good-tempered crew, just as a crew that could sing and haul at the ropes was always the best working.[28]

Reflecting on life in sail in 1898 James Bissett wrote,

In the *County of Pembroke* nineteen men and three youths were confined for three months within the deck space of a barque only 221 feet long from stem to stern, existing on unpalatable food, and 'with nothing to see but the sea', having no alcohol (except a rare occasional tot), no contacts with femininity, no news of the world, no organized recreations, sports or entertainments, no luxuries of any kind, no milk or eggs, no fresh fruit or vegetables, no holidays, and working an eighty-four-hour week ...

[But] They knew well that life at sea, though often uncomfortable and at times dangerous, was never tedious since no man knew what lay ahead of him, in the next week, the next day, the next watch, or the next hour or minute, in the ever-changing conditions of wind and weather and the vessel's geographical position ... In most of [his] tasks, a sailor had to use his brains as well as his muscle. He had to be constantly alert, not only for his own safety, but for the safety of the whole company on board.[29]

If time passed slowly in the doldrums, the new boy, like Bisset, might be sent to find the non-existent 'key of the keelson' or to fetch the 'green oil' for the starboard light. Released at last to go ashore, say, in Callao, he might get drunk, again like Bisset, and finish up on the treadmill in the local gaol – the treadmill raised water from wells to high tanks for the town supply. In the Chincha Islands in Chile he would be set to work to unload the pebble ballast and then to load guano.

As the work proceeded, after several days all the ballast was discharged and we were then sent down below to shovel the guano into the far corners of the hold, and to rake, trim and tamp it down, to get in as big a cargo as possible. This meant that we had to plod around in the powdery stuff for hours on end, sinking in it up to our knees and breathing in the dust and fumes ...

What with the heat, poor food, shortage of drinking water (our whack being strictly limited, in view of the long voyage ahead of us), the all-pervading stink of guano, and hard labour in the daytime and roaring of sea lions to keep us awake at night, we longed for the day when we would heave up the anchor and set sail from this place of torment.[30]

On the voyage home the water taken on board in Callao proved tainted and, due to the Captain's negligence, the coffee, tea and cocoa all ran out.

In the previous weeks, when the water had been boiled and tinctured, however slightly, with coffee, tea or cocoa we had been able to stomach it; but now, when we began drinking it unboiled, to quench our thirst, we suffered from severe 'guts ache' and 'vomiting'. The captain tried permanganate of potash 'to kill the germs' but eventually decided to boil it ... The bad food and water had caused most of us to break out in boils.[31]

On this voyage the crew were starving by the time they reached mid-Atlantic, trying to eat the fat and scum the cook skimmed off the pots in which salt beef and salt pork had been boiled and which was kept for greasing down the masts. Luckily, they received food from a passing steamer.

The first edition of the *Ships' Captains' Medical Guide*, which Captain Barker congratulated himself on using, had appeared in 1867. Captain Holmes commented:

It is a curious fact that a man untrained even in first-aid was presumed to acquire some miraculous life-saving power on taking command of a ship. As captain he was responsible for the lives of all on board in every circumstance, and he was equipped for the profession of physician and surgeon by the magic possession of the ship's medicine chest and a small paper-backed *Medical Guide.* With these alone, and without anaesthetics, in the complete isolation of a three to six months' voyage, he had to deal with all manner of accidents, diseases, epidemics and even insanity.[32]

Bisset, taken ill with dysentery on leaving Melbourne, had experience of his captain's expertise.

The Captain dosed me with chlorodyne twice a day for a week, with no good effect, until the chlorodyne bottle was empty. This bottle was Number 15 in the medicine chest, to correspond with the numbers in *The Ships' Captains' Medical Guide.* I had eaten nothing since leaving Melbourne and had grown thin, weak and pale. I thought my last days had come.

The Captain said to me, 'Well, m'son, I don't know what to do with you. According to the book, Number 15 should have cured you, but now the bottle is empty and you are no better. I think I'll give you some Number 10 and Number 5. That adds to fifteen'.

I was too sick to care what he gave me. It happened that Number 10 was a brown powder with a nasty taste. It was a diarrhoea mixture. Number 5 was a syrupy cough mixture. The Old Man mixed these two in a glass, diluted them with a little water, stirred vigorously, and I swallowed the dose. Almost immediately I felt better. After two more doses, I was cured.[33]

It was not such a happy outcome aboard the steamship *Bellastaire,* some of whose crew succumbed to el vomito or yellow fever in Santos. The mate tells the tale.

Men, women and children dropped in the stinking thorough-fares, and writhed in atrocious agony before they died, or were picked up casually as so much refuse and slung into trundling carts ...

Shore-leave was forbidden, as a necessary precaution against infection. Captain Serisen was so scared of the plague that he isolated himself in his stern cabin and held no communication with the outside world: carbolic sheets guarded his doors … Two of the crew, a seaman and a fireman, showed signs of liquor one morning; accused of having sneaked ashore, both strenuously, blasphemously, denied the impeachment.

We got no clean bill of health, naturally, leaving an infected port; but the agent, a Brazilian half-caste, hoped we'd have a healthy voyage and none too long a quarantine.

We dropped the pilot at the appointed place and headed full speed to open, invigorating sea. It was like Heaven-plus, to breathe untainted air, and lick salt from one's parched lips. Captain Serisen left his isolation and, reeking of carbolic, assumed command. He was a notoriously mean man, a Scandinavian, holding a Board of Trade master's ticket, and engaged, probably, because he would accept smaller pay than a Briton.

Three days out one of the suspects went down with ominous symptoms – yellow fever, sure enough, those symptoms answered all the questions in the medical guide. 'Have him isolated', directed Serisen. We had no ship's hospital, naturally, we carried no doctor. But a spare store-locker was hastily cleaned up and disinfected, a rough bunk erected by the carpenter; and carbolised sheets slung across the door.

'How about nursing him, sir?' I inquired. 'He'll need pretty regular attention'. The man who had spent most of the time in port on his knees in prayer, or staring haggardly through his cabin scuttle, said: 'I'll do that; you look after the ship'.

Three crew members, all nursed by the captain, fell ill of yellow fever, though two survived, but then the captain himself died of it. The mate was there.

I was with him when he died, – in the desperate paroxysms that afflict Yellow Jack patients when *in extremis*. He gripped my hand with his skeleton fingers and dragged me down to his mouth.

288

'You must tell my wife', he said. 'Write to her, don't cable her from New York – too expensive'.34

With the coming of the steamer the live carriage of cattle and sheep became possible on transatlantic routes. It was a cruel, insensitive trade.

With the beef-cattle embarked, fifteen hundred lowing sheep were led by a bell-wether into the pens on the matchwood upper deck. Tons of fattening alfalfa were stacked in the only vacant spaces – mostly around the funnel. Fires were frequent; and the hoses were regularly in use. If the sheep took a scare and scampered to one side or the other, the ship canted some-what alarmingly. Within a few hours the stench and filth were indescribable, for this was a southern midsummer; and flies beyond anything endured since the plagues of Egypt swarmed in clouds ... In the shoal water of the River Plate estuary, a high sea was kicked up as if by magic. The livestock took fright as the ship rolled her rails under with swift persistence. In ten minutes the decks were indescribable, sluicing with liq-uid manure; and foothold for the scared steers was almost impossible. A call to the cattlemen to bear a hand elicited no response. Their capatary, or foreman, was sicker than the rest of them put together; his underlings simply surrendered with the complete fatalism of the Latin-American when faced with disaster. A dozen prime steers slithered this way and that before they fell, breaking their legs. It was up to the crew to do what was possible – not much. The vicious rolling and pitching loosened the flimsy fittings, and they creaked and groaned portentously as the helpless sheep skidded from side to side, their sheer mass weight snapping the confining barriers. A cascade of be-fouled sea-water poured into the cattle pens, flooding them belly-deep, for the scuppers had plugged themselves almost at the outset. There was nothing for it but the aid of the ship's crew. For my own part, I shot the broken-legged animals to ease their obvious agonies; whilst one of the deckhands, with a rollicking bass voice, paced the alleyways singing loudly, as he'd sung, he explained, when functioning as a cowboy on a Mid-western ranch.[35]

Less than 30 per cent of the animals were unshipped at Deptford.

Trouble of a different kind faced the barque *Dee* (1115 tons) when, in the Roaring Forties, she sighted the dismasted barque *Cumbrian Chieftain*. The *Cumbrian Chieftain* was lying on her side, with her boats, midship bridge and everything movable swept away.

With great skill Captain Pope manoeuvred the *Dee* to windward, and with the gale blowing its hardest, the Second Mate and four members of the crew volunteered to attempt a rescue. They got their boat away and with superb seamanship made the lee side of the distressed barque. There they saw that the water was up to her hatch coamings. Her top-hamper of masts, yards, and tangled gear prevented them from getting alongside but they were stirred to action by the sight of the Captain's wife and her two small children on the almost vertical poop.

Quickly a method was evolved to get them off to safety. The peak signal halliards were unrove and the children were secured in the bight of the rope. One end of the halliard was thrown to the boat and the other kept clear on the poop for slacking away. Then the children were lowered into the sea and hauled over the bow of the boat. By this method the Captain's wife, the apprentices and as many of the crew as could be taken safely, fourteen in all, were rescued. The boat would hold no more so they made their way back to the *Dee*. Mountainous seas threatened to engulf them, and in spite of careful handling by the Second Mate, the boat was half full of water by the time the rescued were safely on board.

The crew of the boat were exhausted, so the second trip was made by the Second Mate with three different men of his own crew and one of the rescued sailors of the *Cumbrian Chieftain*. Their shipmates were anxiously watching them battling their way back when a terrific sea capsized the boat. Neither the boat nor the crew were seen again. It was impossible to launch another boat although there was no lack of volunteers. So the *Dee* was compelled to sail away with Mrs Thomas and her children mourning the loss of their husband and father.[36]

Miraculously, the *Cumbrian Chieftain* survived to reach Coquimbo in Chile and Captain Thomas was restored to his family.

Few descriptions of the power of the sea are better than that found in an account of the wool-clipper *Routenburn*'s rounding of Cape Horn in 1895.

She went into that comber deliberately and with a will, as if, tired of it all, she meant to commit suicide. She stuck the end of the jibboom into the base of it, and the roaring, foaming crest, many feet higher, curled over her forecastle head. It descended like an irresistible cataract, rolled along aft and turned the main-deck into the bed of a river in spate. It was so sudden that few of us escaped being knocked down and washed about. It wrecked the forecastle head. It washed away the skylight, two ventilators and the after rail. It lifted the spare anchor out of its place, and in doing so tore away a part of the deck. It wrenched the heavy iron capstan free and flung it on to the main-deck, where it emphasised the simile of the bed of a river in spate by rolling along it like a boulder. It brought up against the bulkhead at the break of the poop and stove it in after trundling aft well over two hundred feet. The rushing water burst both forecastle doors open and filled the forecastle up to the level of the top bunks. It tore a large teakwood hen-coop from its fastenings and, fortunately, threw it over the side instead of washing it along the deck to kill someone. For a matter of five minutes few of us knew where we were, or whether the *Routenburn* had sunk or was still afloat.[37]

With the decline of sail, professional seafarers 'went into steam' and, as Sir David Bone, Commodore of the Anchor

Line, put it, 'became converts to the new order'.

> There was no longer a need for our precious 'stand by', and
> we unrigged the wind tackle and accepted our new shipmate,
> the marine engineer, as a worthy brother seaman. It was not
> only the spars and the cordage and the sails we put ashore.
> With all the gallant litter we unloaded, condemned to the junk
> heap, went a part of our seamanship as closely woven to the
> canvas as the seams our hands had sewn.[38]

But for another seventy years the men remained much the
same.

> I marvelled then, I still do, at that strange mixture of great sea-
> manship, ruthless conservatism, blasphemy and strange inar-
> ticulate warmth that was the Atlantic Captain of those days ...
> Even in my early days his legend survived in the story of the
> White Star Captain of the 'nineties, who took a positively
> exhibitionist delight in every kind of [religious] service. There
> came the time during a funeral service when fog arose, which
> entailed his handing over to his Chief Officer and rushing to
> the bridge. Once the fog had lifted he lost no time in return-
> ing to his cabin and donning his old frock coat. He arrived
> back at the funeral to hear the Chief Officer intoning 'I am the
> resurrection and the life ... '. I like to think of the raised eye-
> brows amongst the burial party as the Captain then took over
> the Bible, reasserting his authority with a brisk 'No, no,
> Robinson. *I* am the resurrection and the life'.[39]

When the new, grand Atlantic liners arrived in down-
town New York in the early years of the twentieth century,
however, the old way of life was still very much in evidence
in South Street.

> This was a wonderful street, with all those sailing ships at the
> piers, sticking their jibbooms across the street, very near to the
> houses opposite. And those wonderful smells! And the street
> hawkers selling fresh oysters and clam chowder and buck-

wheat cakes! Makes my mouth water still, just thinking about those things. And freshly cooked clams, and a cob with butter, and a large cup of coffee with two doughnuts used to be 5 cents, and for 5 cents you could also get a schooner of beer and eat your fill of a free lunch besides. You know I think it was much nicer in those days. They used to load and discharge the ships with horses at the piers. Those horses just lifted a certain weight, and, if there was one pound more in the sling, that horse would not budge. In South Street you found nothing but ship chandlers and rigger- and sailmaker lofts, and of course a lot of pubs and boarding houses.[40]

CHAPTER 22

All Cargo and no Comfort

1910–1935

After the launching of the *Mauritania* in 1906, Atlantic liners continued to grow in size and to compete in speed and luxury. In 1911 the White Star *Olympic* of 45,324 gross tons became the biggest ship in the world. The *Queen Mary*, built a quarter of a century later, was 81,235 gross tons, a far cry from Chaucer's shipman's vessel of, perhaps, 60 tons, or even the 2000-ton 'giants' of the last days of sail. If the SS *Titanic*, which sank after hitting an iceberg in 1912, is excluded, life in the new great steamers was, of course, less hazardous than was life in sailing vessels, but the sailor's life remained an arduous and dangerous one. '... seafaring has a higher death-rate from all causes than any other occupation ... [and] that for violence is quite beyond the range of land experience ... the seamen's mortality from disease exceeds the average by 48.8 per cent, and his mortality from violence by 430 per cent.'[1]

Training was inadequate, indeed often non-existent.

The crew of the *Titanic* was a new one, of course, and had never been through a life boat drill, or any training in the rudiments of launching, manning and equipping the boats ... Had there been any sea running, instead of the glassy calm that prevailed, not a single passenger would have safely reached the surface of the water. The men did not know how to lower the boats; the boats were not provisioned; many of the sailors could not handle an oar with reasonable skill.[2]

The following description of the steward's life in a passenger vessel dates from 1912, the year of the *Titanic*'s demise.

The 'glory hole' [crew quarters] was a beauty. It was situated just over the rudder, accommodated forty men, and its berths were two high in long rows so that to get in them one had to climb over the foot of the bunk. The sloping bulkheads were also lined with what berths shipbuilding ingenuity had contrived to cram in. The general atmosphere was of suffocation and congestion.

My shipmates were beginning to join. They were of all nationalities and in as varied degrees of sobriety. Soon the room was filled with the din of ribald songs, drunken quarrels about berths, and coarse shouting. The stench of tobacco, foul breaths, stale liquor, the total lack of privacy and the utter vulgarity of my room-mates were revolting to me. Sleep being impossible I dressed and went on deck for fresh air and stayed there till it was time to start work again the following day.

Breakfast was a revelation to me. To my timid inquiries as to where the 'Refectory' was (all hotels have a Refectoire) I was tersely told 'This is a fucking ship, not a fucking monastery.' I meekly followed the rest and with my 'betters' stood up to my breakfast like a horse at the trough.[3]

Conditions for emigrants in the steerage accommodation were even worse, but they did not have to work as the sailor did.

Until 1914, the regular working hours for both the deck and the engineering forces were twelve hours a day, or four hours on, and four hours off. His tasks during part of the twelve hours may have been at times comparatively light; but for all the twelve hours on duty he was subject to the orders of his superior. His twelve hours below, however, were not completely his. The watch was always called a quarter of an hour before eight bells. He thus surrendered forty-five minutes below for waking and dressing. On his watch below he had also to attend to the mundane jobs of washing and repairing his clothes, eating, shaving (if fastidiously inclined), and other personal matters which absorbed time which otherwise might have been spent in rest or recreation. So his week's work extended beyond the eighty-four hours given to the ship. It must always be assumed that the ship remained in the same longitude. Going west there are some thirty or forty minutes to be placed at his leisure; but going east, they are taken from him as fast as the ship travels. But every hour of the week, Sunday included, was charged against his account. The old rhyme has it,

> Six days shalt thou labour and do all thou art able,
> On the seventh, holystone the decks and scrape the anchor
> cable.[4]

The character of the seaman changed little in the transition from sail to steam. As the sailor Frank Bullen wrote:

But one peculiarity I have often noticed among sailors is their preternatural suspicion allied to a blind trustfulness, two opposite qualities meeting. Only with the perversity of poor human nature, they exercise suspicion where they should be most trustful and confidence where they should be most cautious. Any scoundrel that lays himself out to cajole and cheat a sailor is almost certain to succeed, while a philanthropist aiming only at the seaman's highest welfare will find it a most difficult and disheartening task to gain his confidence or even attention.[5]

Occasionally, tragic events at sea had a happy ending. It was also in 1912 that the crew of the British barque *Inverness*, fully laden with 3500 tons of coal, discovered that fire had broken out in the main hold. After five days of fire-fighting in the Roaring Forties, they were forced to abandon their now blazing ship.

Our position at the time was latitude 38° south, longitude 149° west, the nearest land being seven hundred miles to the north – the island of Rapa, southernmost island in the Austral group of South Sea islands, a tiny island a mile and half wide. The nearest shipping lane was a thousand miles away, and the only chart we possessed to cover the area was a general chart of the South Pacific Ocean – a pin-point on it marked our objective. A chronometer, sextant, nautical tables and almanac were all our navigational equipment, not forgetting the boat's compass, the error of which was anybody's guess ...

The difficulty of navigating a small boat in mountainous seas is something that has to be experienced to be understood. The boat tossed about, with the horizon visible for no more than a second or two at a time as we staggered over the crests of the waves and the ocean swell. The second officer was lashed to the mast with his sextant for the noon sight, the Captain snatching his chance to take the chronometer reading. His navigation books were soaking wet and he had to take great care to separate the pages without tearing them.

On the seventh day the wind was fresh and favourable and the now familiar swell was still with us. Bailing still went on without stop, night and day, with all hands feeling thirsty, cold and wet, and every member of the crew now suffering from numerous salt water boils, mostly on the hands and feet. By this time our lips were brown and badly cracked but, strangely enough, our cuts and lacerations were healing well. There was very little talking now but everyone maintained an interest in the safety of the boat. This day's run was the best yet – one hundred and eleven miles – but during the evening we noticed that we were being followed by three very large sharks ...

The sharks were still with them when, shortly before dusk on the eighth day, the island of Rapa was sighted.

At four o'clock in the afternoon the boat touched the shore, coming to a standstill among the bracken in a tiny cove. We had arrived – a marvellous feat of navigation under the most difficult conditions. In nine days we had covered seven hundred miles.

While still stunned by our good fortune we were approached out of the bushes by dozens of fine-looking amber-skinned Kanakas, people like the natives of Tahiti, clad only in strips of goat skin, the women with fine long black hair and adorned with rows of beads made of small shells. They stared at us in amazement for a moment but then hurried forward to help us out of the boat. Half-walking and half-carried, we covered the few hundred yard to their village of mud huts, the only habitation on the island. The huts were surrounded with orange trees and banana palms, all in full fruit, and a grand feast celebrated our arrival. Wild pigs were roasted whole on hot stones and chickens were boiled in kerosene cans, while taro or bread fruit, oranges and bananas were handed round with cans of hot coffee. This was paradise indeed.[6]

Although on his way into history, the bucko mate still survived here and there in sail. Captain A G Course came across him aboard the barque *Lorton* in 1913. On the way to Britain from Iquique the barque suffered light winds and calms for weeks on end and food became short in supply. One night at 8pm a sullen Scandinavian seaman came aft and, within hearing distance of the watch, reported his relief to the mate without using the customary 'Sir'.

It was done deliberately and he knew quite well that such insubordination would not be tolerated on a British ship.

'Report properly!' the Mate snapped out.

Again the 'sir' was omitted.

The Mate jumped to the poop ladder, slid down it, and the Scandinavian found himself lying in the scuppers. It happened so quickly that the fo'c'sle crowd were quite unprepared for retaliation. They helped their shipmate forward.

We knew that this show of contempt for the officer of the watch was merely a feeler. It must have been well discussed in the fo'c'sle and, no doubt, was a preliminary to further action. The atmosphere on board grew worse and the after-guard got ready for trouble. Nothing happened until the middle watch (midnight to 4 a.m.). Then the biggest and fittest man in the fo'c'sle – a young Colonial able seaman – was due for the midnight to 2 a.m. look-out. He should prove a match for the Mate.

We waited to see what would happen. He omitted the 'sir'. No second chance was given this time. The fight only lasted five minutes, but the young Colonial had to be carried forward to his bunk where he remained several weeks. The Mate was hardly scratched. This was the end of the trouble. The men accepted defeat.[7]

It was 1914 and war was approaching rapidly. Captain Course's ship had been sold in Callao and the apprentices were staying in the Mission to Seamen awaiting repatriation.

One of our able seamen, Arthur Winter, a German who was known on board as Fritz, was also staying at the Mission. One morning he was missing, his body being found later on the foreshore. He had drowned while bathing, and we went to the morgue to identify his body. While he lay there the British and German Consuls argued as to who should make the arrangements for and meet the expenses of the burial. The British Consul said that Fritz was a German subject and was the responsibility of the German Consul, while the latter argued that as he had only just been paid off a British ship the British Consul should see to the burial. Meantime in the hot tropical climate of Callao, the position in the morgue deteriorated, and the Missions to Seamen, deciding that something must be done quickly, made arrangements for the burial at the British Cemetery.

This was half-way between Callao and Lima, and we boys took the electric tram in order to attend the graveside service. The hearse was drawn by two spirited mules and they made up their minds to keep pace with that tram, but at one point they took a bend too quickly. The hearse heeled over, and the coffin shot off with such force as to remove the lid and deposit Fritz on the ground. We got off the tram and returned to find the driver of the hearse standing at a respectful distance; nothing would induce him to replace Fritz in the coffin, so there was nothing left for it but to do the job ourselves. It was far from pleasant.

As we were unable to fasten the lid of the coffin, the service at the graveside was carried out with the mourners well windward and standing by for a shift of wind in case it should be necessary to 'go about'.[8]

Captain J W Holmes, who reported running before a gale in heavy seas for sixteen days en route for Adelaide from Montevideo, wrote,

> But perhaps the worst thing about this decidedly unpleasant period was the number of corposants which appeared every night – eerie, creeping things well called the 'souls of dead sailors'. There is something uncanny in the sight of these phosphorescent balls crawling out on the yardarms, down the backstays, up on the maintruck, as if impelled or propelled by some demoniacal power. Never before have I seen so many of the accursed things, nor ever in these latitudes.[9]

In the carnage of the war that followed, many a drama went unremarked.

> The sailing ships *Monkbarn* and *Archibald Russell* had successfully made their long voyages from the west coast of South America, but the latter ship had suffered considerably from lack of provisions. I remember when a sugar cargo was a godsend to us miserable little underfed boys, and a wheat cargo would have been salvation in this case, but unfortunately the *Archibald Russell* carried nitrate. She had been obliged to leave the West Coast understored, hoping to obtain provisions from a passing ship. But not a ship did she fall in with on her five months' voyage, and the sufferings from scurvy and starvation were appalling.
>
> The captain had his wife and child with him, and he had to watch his infant son slowly die of starvation and his starving wife demented with grief ...

It was one of the epics of the sea. It passed unnoticed in the general tragedy of war.[10]

Another wartime drama was being enacted in Antarctica where, in October 1915, Ernest Shackleton's ship *Endurance* was crushed by ice and abandoned.

The boats were lowered onto the ice and pulled away to a larger, more solid floe with the stores and other useful gear. The dogs, fighting madly, were then rushed onto the ice and tethered to the boats, and everyone grabbed what he could. Our position was 69° South Latitude and our home was very low in the water. We were hundreds of miles from the nearest known land, marooned under the most appalling conditions, and there were no hopes of saving the ship.

We rigged up our tents for shelter during our first night on the ice. Cold, hungry, and very depressed, it was the worst night any of us had ever spent and we were glad when dawn came. Those who had kept watch during the night had lit a fire with the aid of splintered wood and seal blubber. Our cook, with the help of volunteers, soon managed to get a hot drink for all hands, and later on a meal, which was much appreciated.

Snow Hill lay roughly four hundred miles to the northwest but it was hopeless to try and reach it under those conditions. There was nothing we could do but wait until the ice drifted far enough north and we could take to our small boats. With luck we might then get to one of the islands north and west of Graham Land.

Incredible as it may seem, things continued in this way until April, 1916, when we landed on Elephant Island, five months after we had abandoned ship. During that period we had drifted hundreds of miles on the ice. We had killed and eaten seals and penguins, and many of our dogs, too, had found their way into the large stewpot. At last, after seven days in the boats, we scrambled ashore, still alive. It was eighteen months since we had sailed from South Georgia.

We had landed on solid rock and we still had to find a way to return to civilisation. There was only one way, and Shackleton called for volunteers for the long boat journey. Captain F. Worsley, the Carpenter, Tom Crean, J. Vincent and McCarthy went with him and they sailed away under terrible conditions. As all the world knows, they landed seventeen days later, all badly frostbitten and weak from exposure.[11]

W E How, who wrote this account, returned to sea in the middle of the First World War, serving with the Orient Line. Shortly thereafter the coasting schooner *W.D. Potts* – a mere 88 tons – was in the Irish Sea.

We were about ten miles off from the Wigtownshire coast, in company with a big full rigged ship, when a German submarine surfaced about one hundred yards away and immediately opened fire on us without warning. We rushed to get out our boat and although it generally took two of us to lift her stern with the after tackle, in this instance I did it alone while the rest of the crew pulled up the bow. She was just clear of the rail when all the yards and mast head came tumbling down and although we got away unhurt a hole was knocked in the boat, and I kept bailing water until we landed at Portpatrick in the early hours of the next morning. It was a rather hectic time while it lasted and we have nothing to say in favour of our German enemies who kept firing regardless of our situation until our ship disappeared and only the quick and competent way in which our crew worked in getting the boat in the water saved our lives. It was in keeping with the Kaiser's policy of sink at sight. The ship in our company was also sunk by gunfire.[12]

The captain of the German raider *Moewe*, a 4500-ton steamer, was of a different kind. If possible his captured crews were taken on board before their ships were sunk, and they were all well treated.

Some of the captured British officers had met the *Moewe*'s officers, before the war, in Australian ports, and were invited to renew the acquaintance in the cabins where many hours were spent yarning of the happier days of the past and in drinking the toast: 'To the end of the war'.[13]

However, war was war, and prisoners were hurried down the iron ladder to the forepeak if action threatened.

On one occasion we thought it was the end. The deafening roar of the forward gun fired above our heads – the base of it was in the fore peak – was terrifying; the vibration and echoing of the explosion in our steel box sent cold shivers down our spines in spite of the unbearable heat; rust flying off the bulkheads blinded and choked us; we could scarcely breathe. If only we could see!

We came up again to meet the crew of the *Flamenco*, the British steamer that had just been sunk in action. Only two hours previously they had signalled H.M.S. *Glasgow*, and, in spite of the raider's warnings, continued to send wireless messages giving the *Moewe*'s position. The raider opened fire at close range and the first shot blew half the *Flamenco*'s wireless room away revealing the operator tapping away in the other half. He carried on. The crew did not abandon ship until she was ablaze fore and aft and was sinking; one lifeboat capsized flinging its occupants into the sea where sharks went into the attack immediately. The *Moewe*'s motor launches sped to the rescue and, beating the man-eaters off, the Germans hauled the British seamen to safety. Only one fireman was lost although several of the crew had been wounded during the shelling.[13]

Captain Syd Gorrell was an Appledore man. His grandfather, 'Cap'n John', had gone to sea as a cabin boy of nine in 1830. His father followed at the age of nine in his father's ship. In 1919 Gorrell himself started in sail, also as a cabin boy, but at the advanced age of fifteen.

My father's sea career was finished through ill-health, but there were other sail captains out of Appledore and I was put with the hardest of them all, a Viking of a man whose ginger beard matched his golden earrings and formed a suitable portal for the outpouring of profanity with which he expressed his contempt for work ill-done.

It was a hard life, for the term 'cabin boy' was really a euphemism. Being the youngest member, I was a target for the old adage 'you have to be cruel to be kind'. Treat 'em rough to start with for there is a hard life ahead, and the introduction must not mislead the weakling and waste good men's time. This was the measure of it in those old days of sail and looking back it seems a good measure, though a trifle full and overflowing at times. After two years I felt justified in looking ahead and decided that there were other aspects of training to digest in this rapidly evolving profession, so, as Cap'n John would have put it, I gave up the sea and went into steamboats. This was luxury indeed. Why, we only had to work twelve hours a day and, when one went below for a four-hour spell to match the four hours' duty completed, one felt almost guilty satisfaction that here were no tops'ls to be beaten into submission on a wildly swaying yard, up there in the darkness and the driving rain where a slip would mean certain death.[14]

Times were changing, and forty years later a greaser recalled that in 1919 a near-toothless cook spotted some apprentices joining his ship and these were his remarks: 'Oh, look at Lord Ginger! Hey, hey, Jack, come an' look at this. Marchin' up the gangway carryin' bloody suitcases! Ho, ho, ho! Where's yer brass buttons, me lords? Sailors with suitcases! Gawd.'[15] But poor Jack's life, while improved in many ways by the triumph of steam, could still prove dangerous and unpleasant:

Coal-burning ships recall for me the pitiful picture of blistered, fissured and often septic hands, or the image of a man with that agonising condition known as fireman's cramp. The latter is due to excessive intake of cold fluids after a long spell

of intense heat in the stokehold. The hands and feet are so
contracted that they look like claws. The jaw is set in fixed
rigidity and the stomach muscles like taut ropes. Imagine a
cramp in the calf of the leg and then think of the frightful pain
of such generalised cramp. The condition occurs when there
has been a severe loss of body salt through prolonged
sweating ...

I have seen 24 men in the fo'c'sle, 18 trimmers bunked
together, and 30 stewards in one 'glory hole'. A couple of
benches represented the seating. There was a deal table in the
larger quarters. Damp, dirty or drying gear was everywhere.
Light was poor and ventilation a joke. Smell varied according
to the department. The worst was that of the kitchen and the
butcher's staff, whose working gear was impregnated with the
odour of fish, rancid fat and stale vegetables.[16]

This writer was a ship's doctor in the mighty Cunard, serving the great transatlantic liners. The one below was a wireless operator, by this time transmogrified into a radio
officer, serving in trampships, which were the work-horses
of the mercantile marine. (Since 1922 the mercantile marine
had been graced by King George V with the title of
Merchant Navy.)

Coal-firing firemen were a race apart – long since extinct.
I suspect that many of them are still feeding furnaces below.
It used to be said that their sole gear on joining ship was a
pack of cards and a sweat rag, and this was not far from the
truth.

Often they had no more than the clothes they stood up in.
Our lot in that particular ship were no exception. They would
sally forth ashore in the same rig, regardless of whether the
temperature was 10 below or 110 in the shade. They were
quite impervious to cold or heat and scared of nobody.
Invariably our crowd were brought back by the local
gendarmes, battered and bruised but in no way mollified.
Come the night they would set off for a return bout.

Food had improved since the days of sail, and in tramp-ships even the stewards could sit down to it.

We had a fourteen-day ice-box situated on the lower bridge. The old hands could tell to the day when the ice would melt and the meat inside go rotten. After that it was salt-beef, salt-pork, and dried fish, none of it particularly appetising ... Our Old Man so enjoyed the cook's dried fish cakes that he was prone to ask for this in restaurants ashore, and appalled when told they did not serve rotting cod to their customers. Curry appeared every morning for breakfast. It varied a lot in contents and smell. When it was particularly obnoxious and nobody dare touch it, the Old Man would delight in having two helpings. Then he would leave the saloon and bring the lot up in his toilet. The message was that if he could eat it so could we. Thursdays and Sundays were gala days. On those occasions we had an egg for breakfast and duff for lunch. Duff was a dessert, and a cook's reputation was made (or lost) on the duff he made. Sometimes it was very good and filling, which was most important.

A tin of condensed milk was supposed to last each man three weeks. A well-known lady Member of Parliament denied in the House that this was insufficient, for she herself had experimented and found it adequate. Needless to say she was hardly the number one pin-up aboard ships. Much ingenuity was shown in preserving the precious tin from the ravages of cockroaches and other marauding insects. Usually this consisted of suspending the tin from the deckhead underneath another can containing water in the hope that the little beasts would meet a watery grave.

Water was still scarce much of the time, and oil-lamps still much in use, despite the coming of electric light.

In port the lighting went off at 5 p.m. This was an economy to save the donkeyman's overtime. After tea there would be a mad rush to get shaved, washed and dressed before the blackout and usually one was caught about halfway. We all had oil lamps with a single wick but the mate, being a man of some position, had two wicks. We [the officers] then queued up in his cabin to tie our ties and comb our hair before the exodus to the shore. The mate also possessed a small portable electric fan – the envy of everybody as it was the only one on board. He would solemnly take this into the saloon and position it to waft a cooling breeze on himself. One considered oneself very fortunate to sit even on the fringes of this sybaritic luxury.[17]

Descriptions of the life of a fireman aboard coal-burning ships come usually from others on board. The following reminiscence by one who was a fireman is unique. In 1926 he was serving aboard the SS *Crockelton*, a vessel which foundered with the loss of all hands ten years later. On this occasion the *Crockelton* was logging a steady 10 knots towards Shanghai.

Cleaning a fire is indescribable. It is a blur of fire, ashes, clinker, steel rakes, slices and shovels, with yelling, sobbing, oaths and profanity, in an atmosphere of steam, poisonous sulphur fumes and thick coal dust all richly combined. Brawn is not the most essential thing here, it's a big heart that's needed most – a big heart and a dogged spirit. Out it comes, red hot, white hot, ashes and clinker pitter-pattering on the stokehold plates, with me pleading loudly and desperately for water to douse the fierce flames and a faraway form whom I know to be old Liverpool, because he's the trimmer, yelling to wait a something stronger than a blinking minute. Then I'm madly shovelling coal into the jaws of a very giant who's eating it up so quickly as to leave me wondering hazily whether I'll stay to satisfy that fierce appetite or drop with an exhaustion that's steadily increasing for the want of good, clean, wholesome air. I'm lightheaded now and this must surely be Dante's Inferno. Devils are all around me, devils and pitchforks, flames and stifling heat complete. I'm going to collapse in a minute. I'm sure of that because one part of me seems to be at home, in an ice-cream shop of all places, while the other part is wobbling over a heap of steaming ashes. Down goes the furnace door with a bang and somewhere out of the dark beyond is a voice saying, 'Steady on there, mate. Steady on!' There's a pressure at my back and I feel myself slowly moving away from the heat. Must be old Satan himself, thinks I, playing about with poor little me like a cat playing about with a mouse. Couldn't be anyone but the devil, unless – as a stream of cool air strikes me – unless it's an angel.

When I come to I'm under the ventilator with my two mates. Five-foot-four is gasping like a fish out of water, while Liverpool is wiping the perspiration from his begrimed face. 'Thought the two of yer were out for the count this time', he grunted, then added, rather anxiously, 'How about a growler of tea?' It comes back to me that we are still at sea, and the twelve-to-four watch still have three heart-rending hours to put in.

Devil's Island holds no terrors for us, the French Foreign Legion is a leisure activity, and if we had to be hanged at, say, twenty minutes to three, then we'd die and thank you for it.[18]

To a lesser degree, everyone on a tramp ship suffered from coal.

Bunkering was always associated with flying dust which reached all parts of the ship, inside and out. In the United Kingdom the coal was tipped into the bunkers in ten-ton loads, often from a height, but elsewhere the chutes and grabs were equally dust-raising and dirty. Almost invariably the ship left the bunkering port with many tons of coal loose on deck, to be shifted down as space became available below in consequence of the efforts of hard-working firemen and trimmers.

Another cargo during the loading of which we could never feel clean was the copper pyrites which we sometimes loaded at Morphou Bay in Cyprus. This had a sulphur content which clogged the nose and irritated the throat. Day and night for about a week the loading went on, a week of noise, clattering winches, and of earthquake reverberations as the two-ton skips tipped the ore down our five holds. Only extreme tiredness allowed us to sleep.[19]

'All cargo and no comfort' was how one seafarer described the British tramp steamer, and salt beef and weevilly hard tack were still dietary mainstays.

There were many 'two-mate' ships in which the chief and second officers kept alternate watches. Sometimes they were expected to chip, scrape and paint holds, or sew canvas. When down the holds at sea, they left a whistle with the man at the wheel and, if a vessel hove in sight, the helmsman blew the whistle and the officer came to the bridge. When such ships reached port, although the officers were worn out by lack of sleep, they had to go on cargo watches.[20]

There were occasional compensations. Carrying kerosene to Banda in Indonesia, for example, the crew were invited to a wedding party. Banda had once been a prosperous port, a centre for the spice trade and a place in which rich Dutch traders had lived.

Leading the wedding party was a brass band, a collection of rugged individualists who insisted on blowing their own thing. 'Yes, we have no bananas' seemed to provide the underlying theme of the first piece. It was followed by another musical epic dimly recognised as having something in common with 'It's a long way to Tipperary'. The British had undoubtedly arrived. After the band came the happy couple, the policeman in his uniform, his bride in white.

It was a romantic place for a wedding reception, this decayed mansion of a merchant prince. We sailed the following day, but the memory is as brilliant and scented as was the reality when I was second mate.[21]

In 1922 Radio Officer Dorrington Graves was aboard the P & O liner *Egypt* when she was sunk in fog in the English Channel with over £1 million in gold and silver bars on board. When the lower bridge was almost level with the water he swam off and, when it appeared that he was clear of suction,

> I stopped to look about me. Nothing! There was no sign of life on the smooth, fog-bound sea.[22]

However, he was eventually picked up by the *Seine,* the French cargo vessel which had sunk the *Egypt.*

In 1933 Chief Engineer A D Blue's problem was of a different kind. He was captured in China from the ship *Nanchang* and held to ransom. Fortunately, he was ransomed six months later.[23]

Some adventures could even seem funny after the event. Apprentice John Aldiss was night watchman aboard his ship which was stranded in winter-time New York after having been on fire.

> It was a particularly cold and stormy night with the wind blowing from the frozen north when I awoke bursting for 'pump ship'. Befuddled by sleep I clawed from beneath a mountain of blankets clad only in pyjamas. By the light of the oil lamp I rushed from the cabin just in time to release the pent up stream into the scuppers.
>
> Immediately the intensity of the cold struck me like a physical blow, wrapping itself about my scantily clad body and exhausting its heat at an alarming rate. The one thought on my mind was to regain the warmth of the cocoon of blankets from which I had emerged.
>
> A sudden crash told me that the cabin door, which I had flung open in such haste, had blown shut. I was locked out. In the urgency of the moment I had forgotten to sneak up the tongue of the Yale lock and the door stood implacably shut

before me. The horror of the situation engulfed me. I knew I must succumb to the cold before I could get even half-way to the all-night café. I panicked. I seized the brass door handle in both hands and tugged at it with all my strength. The door was solid, built to withstand waves breaking over the ship. My efforts at forcing an entry with bare hands were as futile as farting against thunder.

With enormous effort I regained a degree of self-control. I realised that my chances of survival outside, measured in time, were but a matter of minutes. My only hope of access to the cabin lay in forcibly removing the brass ventilator that covered a six-inch diameter hole at the top of the door. If I could do that then I might push my arm into the hole and grasp the milled knob of the lock and turn it to withdraw the sneck. For security the ventilator was screwed to the door from the inside. I tried pushing it in the hope that the screws might yield but my efforts were in vain.

In spite of the cold I took off my pyjama jacket and wrapped it round my clenched fist and punched that stubborn piece of brass with all the force I could muster, but to no avail. The physical agony I suffered from the cold is beyond the scope of descriptive writing. I recall the hopeless feeling of life being sucked from me when, suddenly, like St Paul on the road to Damascus, I had a blinding flash. I remembered having seen a small metal tool on the hatch at the foot of the well deck that the Glaswegian carpenter called a 'spoogel bar'. It was an implement about two feet in length with a pair of claws at one end and a curved chisel at the other. Would it still be there?

In my pyjama trousers I climbed down into the well deck and groped around on the hatch with hands that could only feel pain. They closed round the divinely revealed spoogel bar and the metal froze to my skin as though coated with glue. The ascent of the steel ladder to the bridge deck was like trying to scale the Matterhorn. Even the normally simple act of breathing became intolerable exertion, but somehow I regained the cabin door.

With every ounce of strength remaining in my body I jabbed at the brass ventilator. Suddenly the screws were torn from the wood and the ventilator disappeared into the cabin followed by the spoogel bar as it flew from my nerveless hands.

Now I could get my arm through the hole in the door and with the tips of my fingers touch the top of the lock. But stretch and strain as I would, I could not reach the milled knob to unlatch the door. Terrifying symptoms of approaching death manifested themselves like patches of light and darkness as consciousness came and went from my brain. A forlorn human heap, I slumped at the foot of what had now become the door to life itself.

As in a trance I saw the end of a rope hitched to a bulwark stay and leading over the side of the ship. Attached to the outboard end would be a cork fender. If I could get that fender inboard it would serve as a step and give the extra height I needed to reach the knob of the lock.

I crawled to the ship's side and pulled myself upright. Then began the painful haul of dragging the fender over the bulwarks. At last it came, a frozen lump that fell to the deck like a cannon ball. I rolled it to the foot of the door, then, standing on top of it, I pushed my arm through the hole once more.

At last I could reach the unlatching knob. With frost-bitten fingers I turned the sneck and the door swung open. I fell into the cabin and the door crashed behind me. Driven by the desperate need for self-preservation, I reached my goal, and all the feeling was snuffed from me like the blowing out of a candle.[24]

At the time – 1932 – the ordeal of the Blue Funnel ship *Phemius,* which survived a hurricane in the West Indies, was widely reported, and inspired James Hanley's novel *In Hazard.* Captain D C L Evans hove his ship to in the early evening.

I went down to the saloon to see for myself how things were down there. I found the saloon awash and all the rooms on the starboard side flooded, a pitiful state of affairs. I then returned to the bridge and tried to estimate the force of the wind. Putting my arm out into the wind I found that the force of the spray striking my hand was agony, and for some minutes afterwards it was numbed as if by a severe electric shock. My estimate was that the minimum force of the wind was 200 miles an hour.

At 9 p.m. the steam failed, the fire blew out with the back draught and oil ran out through the furnace doors. The ship was in total darkness. A constant, almost solid, sheet of spray, but no heavy water, continued to blow over the open hatches throughout the night [these hatch covers had been blown off] and I estimated that ten tons an hour went down the open Number 3 hatch and five tons an hour down Numbers 5 and 6 hatches. We were now without fresh water.

The *Phemius* was carried over 200 miles by the hurricane and went through the dead centre several times. Early on the third day the ship sent out an SOS for assistance. On the fourth day the crew began to pour oil from the latrines onto the sea, which was threatening to engulf the ship.

> The effect of the oil was almost beyond belief. Towering seas tearing along towards our exposed and listed side crumpled up within ten feet of the ship and, although we could not escape entirely, they landed on board in heavy volumes of dead water. The ship would have foundered had we not poured oil continuously.[25]

By the fourth day Evans estimated that there was over 1000 tons of water in the holds and engine room. On the eighth day the battered *Phemius* was towed into Kingston, Jamaica.

The interwar period for shipping was one long slump and in the 1930s many qualified mates sailed as seamen for the lack of officers' berths. One seaman recalls in 1934,

Hundreds of ships laid up. I was on the beach. A shipmate wrote of a job going on a tanker at Thameshaven, if I could get there in time to sign on. I was on the dole. The wife pawned a few things to raise my train fare.

I got to King's Cross and had to beat my way through London to Fenchurch Street, humping a sea-bag and donkey's breakfast. I arrived at Stanford-le-Hope late at night. It was raining and snowing; no buses; a taxi was out of the question. It was walk it, with donkey's breakfast and sea-bag on my back. I walked through the sleet and the rain for hours, till I reached the jetty and found her.

A steel workhouse, a coal-burning tanker about 5000 tons deadweight and over forty years old. I do not think now that anything related to the sea could be so repulsive. A downstairs fo'c'sle, under the water-line, and nine seamen in the fo'c'sle – not so big as the room I have to myself in this ship [in the 1950s]. A coal bogey belching out smoke, the stink a conglomeration of smells, coal fumes, hot oil, foul air, human sweat and urine. A small table covered with gear, rusty kits, tin mugs, tin plates, beer bottles, hand-rags, sweat-rags, cockroaches, bugs, flies and rats.

A few drunks sprawled in the bunks. It was three o 'clock in the morning and the fo'c'sle was quiet. I hadn't had a bite to eat since leaving Shields, so I fished in a rusty kit for a few hard biscuits and a lump of salt-junk.

'Hi, mate!' A drunk muttered, 'That's slops.' [Ship's property; crew issue.]

'To hell with him,' I answered. 'He ought to have been on board by now'.

I shared a piece of salt-junk with a couple of rats running round the table. With this wholesome meal resting as comfortably as a fire-bar on my stomach, I flopped on a low bunk. A drunk got up and used a bucket near my head; the bucket was for washing up plates, kits, etc., but also for slushing down the lavatory and bathing in.

I signed on her – Mexico and back. Homeward bound, my

old watchmate fell sick. He was accused of malingering. He staggered on watch. Then, one morning, he was found dead in his bunk. Two or three hours later, sewn up in a waste-bag (there was no canvas on board), the old sea-dog was slung over the side.

I was glad to get out of her, paid off. My train fare took what was left of my pay. Back in Shields. On the dole again.[26]

CHAPTER 23

War and Peace

1935–1960

In 1935 the world tonnage of shipping was close to 64 million gross tons and the United Kingdom still owned rather more than a quarter of this total. The motor ship, powered by diesel engines, was by this time making encroachments upon steam tonnage, and the carriage of oil in tankers was becoming an increasingly significant part of world trade. Sailing ships had become insignificant, though a dozen or so were still carrying grain from Australia to Europe. The last race between this remnant of a once great fleet took place in 1939 and Eric Newby was on board the winner, *Moshulu,* a steel four-masted barque.

> On the sixteenth day, with Madeira somewhere on the starboard beam, I opened Captain Jutsum's book on Knots and Splices and out fell a big red bug, big because he had been feeding on me. I lifted the 'donkey's breakfast', the lumpy straw mattress I had bought in London; underneath it, on the bunk boards, was a small piece of canvas folded in half. I opened it and it was full of them. I lifted the bed boards and saw that the frames were seething. Far worse, in every crack and mortice joint in the wood were thousands of eggs.[1]

Newby suffered bad weather aboard the *Moshulu* but bad weather was never the monopoly of sailing ships. Bound from Trinidad to Lyness with a cargo of fuel oil, the Royal Fleet Auxiliary *War Bahadur* suffered the worst storm its captain had ever known in fifty-three years at sea, including times when he had rounded Cape Horn. He estimated the height of the sea to be from sixty to seventy feet.

> The ship looked as if she had been subjected to a heavy bombardment. [As I have said,] the paravane which had been clamped down under butterfly screws on the starboard bow, had been wrenched adrift, carried along by the sea, and dropped on the starboard side of the lower bridge where the lifeboat had been. The for'ard trelliswork steel derrick had been forced adrift from its crutch where it was securely lashed, lifted right over to a point aft, hanging partly over the side, and with a complete turn in it. The upper and lower bridges and the houses upon them, including the saloon, had been further damaged during the night and were now a very sorry sight with wreckage everywhere. Even the saloon bulkhead had been forced back, leaving the saloon and cabins open to the sea.[2]

In August 1939, one month before the declaration of the Second World War, thirty-one members of the crew of the cargo-liner *Napier Star* were each sentenced in London to six weeks' hard labour for wilfully disobeying the commands of the master and combining to impede the progress of the ship. The prosecution had been brought by the ship's owners, the Vestey family's Blue Star Line.

> The story began in Port Elizabeth, South Africa, in May of the same year when at teatime a quartermaster complained that the food was not fit for a dog. Finding the master ashore, it seems that the ratings left the ship in a body to go in search of him, carrying a can of hotpot which was the source of their complaint. They stopped first at the ship's agent's office. The agent, on being asked to smell it, had said, 'Get it out of here, I can smell it all over the place'. When the crew found the master, he listened to their complaint and then ordered them back to the ship. They returned to the quay but refused to go back

aboard, although the ship was waiting to sail. The men eventually rejoined on the promise of bacon and eggs and no victimisation.[3]

The 13,581-ton *Athenia* was sunk by a U-boat nine hours after war was declared on 3rd September 1939. It was the first hostile act of the war. The passenger ship *Orduna* sailed from Liverpool on that same day, and Alan Peter, an able-seaman, was put to work with the carpenter.

> We were trying to free the lifeboats because, believe it or not, the boats were painted to the chocks all the way along ... They were all wooden boats and would leak like sieves.[4]

In February 1940 Leslie Harrison, who became general secretary to the Mercantile Marine Service Association, an officers' organisation, in the 1950s, noted in his diary that the Nourse Line (owned by P & O) had instructed its ship-masters verbally not to have life-boats swung out in heavy weather as they cost £50 to £60 apiece.[4]

Rodney Wilson joined the Merchant Navy at about this time and filled his mattress and pillow with straw in the basement of the Liverpool Sailors' Home before joining his ship.

> There was this great rusty lump of iron ... then you get aboard and you see the toilets ... then you go into your room and there's only a paraffin lamp. The room was full of smoke because it had been used the night before. There was only two blankets and you threw away the palliasses the feller before you had had ... There was no bathroom. You bathed out on deck out of a bucket ... To do your washing you threw your clothes over the 'wall' on the end of a line ... Hours in those days weren't regulated and the food was disgraceful.[5]

The epic convoy which met up with the German pocket battleship *Admiral Scheer* and was defended by the valiant crew of the *Jervis Bay* was in mid-Atlantic in November

1940. About this time, the *Assyrian,* at the head of another convoy, was torpedoed some 400 miles northwest of Scotland. Its chief engineer, W H Venables, was left in a sea covered by pit-props from another torpedoed ship.

For over an hour I swam with a pit-prop beneath each arm, swimming with very methodical strokes of my legs, trying to get the best out of them – anything to keep my mind from the great loneliness of the ocean. Although I was swimming in the North Atlantic in the middle of October, the water did not feel as cold as I would have imagined. But my hands lost all feeling, and my stomach felt as if it were full of ice. I feared that even if I were eventually picked up I would be a physical wreck ...

When I had been nearly three hours in the water I had given up all hope of being saved. The icy feeling in my stomach was creeping higher, and I knew that when it reached my heart I would die. I never felt fitter in my life.

The moon was lowering behind scudding clouds, and I was afraid it would go, leaving me in darkness. I seemed to be the only thing that lived on the face of the sea. I thought of the fine ships lying far beneath me on the ocean bed and of the men still in them ... In my mind's eye I could picture myself sitting with the folks at home beside the fire. I knew that was worth fighting for, and swam on. My hands ached with the cold, but I kept them clasped about my chest so that the pit-props hugged beneath my armpits formed a V about me, my head being at the apex. I swam on and on, waiting for the daylight. I wanted to see the dawn of a new day, then I would die.

When I saw the dark shape of a sloop ahead of me I could hardly believe my eyes. I believe that when I was taken aboard the *Leith* my clothes were badly torn, my life-jacket in shreds – probably due to my struggle when the *Assyrian* rolled on top of me. The sloop's petty officers took me to the galley and massaged me for an hour before I showed signs of life. Then it took two of them to hold me as I struggled to get at the galley fire. I drank a mug of cocoa which scalded my throat. But of these things I knew nothing. Only my scalded throat remained.[6]

In 1941 the ss *Parracombe* was sunk when bound for Malta. Stanley Sutherland was one of the survivors.

Thirty officers and men went down with the ship, we were seventeen survivors, one Arab died ashore later through exposure. I swam to the nearest raft to see if I could see my brother. I shouted out his name, but no answer. Later, away in the distance, I heard a shout which I didn't recognise. Leaving nothing to chance, I swam away from the raft and came upon Jimmie hanging on to a broken wooden derrick. After much trouble we made a boom defence tank on which was lying the second mate with his right arm hanging off at the shoulder, also a gunner with an ankle injury. The tank couldn't hold four of us. The second mate reckoned it was making water. In the distance I saw a raft with two persons on it. I told the men I would swim across and and try to bring it back. I misjudged the distance, and could feel a seizing at my heart. I slipped off my lifejacket as it weighed a ton, also my dungarees, and swam a bit easier. On making the raft I discovered it was my pal Andrew Starrs of Admiral Terrace, Edinburgh, also the second wireless officer. We tried to paddle the raft across to the tank, but the current was too strong. We spent a cold night with the waves lashing over the raft.

After being adrift for thirty hours we were picked up by a Vichy French seaplane, and landed at the naval base, Bizerta. Later we were shifted to Tunis and marched through the streets barefooted and spat on by the Italians. We told them 'Bye and bye we'll get you', which we did when the Eighth Army left Alamein.[7]

In this same year Captain R F McBreaty was in convoy aboard ss *Lancaster Castle* when the convoy was attacked by U-boats and the *Lancaster Castle* had to take avoiding action to pass a burning tanker.

We passed quite close to the burning vessel and could feel the raging flames. Worse still, we could hear the screams and shouts from the crew, some of whom were clustered on the poop deck as far away from the flames as they could get. It was no use jumping overboard for they would only have found themselves in a sea of burning oil. It was a sickening sight, and we could do nothing to help.[8]

R A Smith, second mate, was one of the survivors from a burning tanker. He was aboard the *Cadillac* in 1941 when she was torpedoed 300 miles northwest of the Outer Hebrides.

We waited alongside [in the boat] for about 3 or 4 minutes but there was still no sign of anybody; as the position looked serious – the sea was already a mass of flame from the burning oil running out of the ship – I gave orders to cast off. We got out the oars and tried to pull away from the flames but it was hopeless, there was a wall of flame all round us, we could hardly breathe and could see nothing. Then a tragic thing happened; most of the men in the boat jumped into the water with the oars. They were nearly mad with the heat and pain and some were calling out and others were praying; they did not know what they were doing. There was about a foot of water in the bottom of the boat, so I lay down at the bottom where I found it slightly more easy to breathe, and after a few minutes I heard someone, who I discovered was the Bosun, Combes, say, 'We are getting out of it'. There were only five of us left in the boat, we found four oars, and somehow managed to pull clear of the flames for about a mile.[9]

An hour later they were rescued, all badly burned, one dying from the severity of the burns.

Quartermaster Angus MacDonald survived five weeks in a life-boat in 1942 when his ship, the Ellerman liner *City of Cairo*, was torpedoed in the South Atlantic. Finding himself in the water after a second torpedo hit the ship,

MacDonald swam to a life-boat, organised its baling out, and took it round picking up other people, including the chief officer, Mr Britt.

When everything was settled we set sail and started on our long voyage. Our boat was now overcrowded with fifty-four persons on board – twenty-three Europeans, including three women, and thirty-one lascars. There was not enough room for everyone to sit down, so we had to take turns having a rest.

Once we were properly under way Mr Britt spoke to us all. He explained all the difficulties that lay ahead, and asked everyone to pull their weight in everything to do with managing the boat, such as rowing during calm periods and keeping a look-out at night. He also explained that as we had lost nearly half our drinking water we must start right away on short rations. We could get two table-spoonfuls a day per person, one in the morning and one in the evening. He told us there were no passengers in a lifeboat, and everyone would have to take their turn baling out as the boat was leaking very badly.

Before noon on that first day we saw our first sharks. They were enormous, and as they glided backward and forward under the boat it seemed they would hit and capsize us. They just skimmed the boat each time they passed, and they were never to leave us all the time we were in the boat.

People began to die from the fourth day onwards.

On the fifteenth morning at dawn both Mr Britt and Bob were dead, also three Europeans, and a few lascars. A few more lascars died during the day. One of the firemen said that if he couldn't get extra water he would jump overboard, and later in the day he jumped over the stern. He had forgotten to take off his lifejacket and, as we were now too weak to turn the boat round to save him, the sharks got him before he could drown. The remaining survivors voted that I should take over command. On looking through Mr Britt's papers I could see the estimated distances for each day up to about the tenth day, but after that there were only scrawls on scribbles.

When the German raider *Rhakotis* found the boat, only three were left alive – MacDonald, a steward named Jack Edmeads, and a passenger, twenty-year old Diana Jarman, who was critically ill. Although he did his best for her, Diana died under the German surgeon's knife. Two weeks later the *Rhakotis* was sunk in the Bay of Biscay by a British cruiser and Edmeads reached Spain in a *Rhakotis* life-boat, was repatriated, and subsequently lost his life in his next ship. MacDonald, in another *Rhakotis* life-boat, was picked up by a U-boat and spent the rest of the war in Milag Nord, the German prison camp for merchant seamen.[10]

In this same year – the worst in the battle of the Atlantic, a year which saw the loss of a thousand British and British-controlled ships – John Dempsey was picked up by the German raider *Atlantis* after she had sunk his ship, the *Balzac*.

It was luxury to any ship I'd been in previously, it was all new. They had linen and big thick mattresses whereas on our own ship we'd been on straw palliasses which had gone so flat we were virtually lying on the steel slats of the bunk. The accommodation and the food was better than the ship we'd just come from ... Sometimes the Dutch officers [who were also prisoners] would wine and dine with the German officers – they were all seafarers and that's the way everybody saw each other. A lot of the sailors used to come down to us and give us cigarettes. I couldn't say anything against them, they never ill-treated us in any way.[11]

The 'Queens' – *Queen Elizabeth* and *Queen Mary*, Cunard's giant passenger ships – survived the war unscathed, but they picked up no survivors.

Between Rio and New York, when we were in a position about 200 miles north of Bermuda, we sighted five lifeboats loaded with men, also a capsized boat. It was a fine day, with a moderate wind, and the boats were under sail and steering a course for Bermuda. It is a hard decision to make not to stop and pick up brother seamen in distress, but the capsized boat indicated that they were probably near the scene of the disaster and a German submarine was probably lurking around, waiting for just such a thing to happen. I made a signal slowly with a powerful morse lamp saying I would report their position by radio, and regretfully left them. On arrival in New York I got a message from the US Navy Department, thanking me for my prompt action and stating that an American ship had picked them up safely the next day.

A few weeks later our purser, Charles Johnson, received a letter from his wife in which she wrote: 'Our son was in one of those lifeboats and was chagrined to see his father go speeding by, leaving him in the lurch'.[12]

Uniquely, perhaps, Chief Officer Stanley Simpson sailed his lifeboat across the Atlantic for twenty-three days, landing in Tobago with all twenty-two aboard alive, if not entirely well. Initially, with an apprentice, he had searched the ship before leaving her, and the two of them had to swim for the boat, which was some way off.

The boy seemed to be tiring and did not speak for a long while. His next words brought the sour metallic taste of fear to my mouth.

'Oh Christ! A shark!'

I had known fear before, and was to know it often again, but never such an extremity of terror as at that moment. The sleek dark fin seemed to move very slowly through the water. The boy was by this time almost unconscious and vomiting feebly as I towed him towards the boats. There were now three sharks circling us and drawing closer, and the first attack had a nightmare illusion of slowness – no sudden quick rush, but a deliberate head-on approach of indescribable horror. I struck out with my free hand and felt the dreadful solidity of the shark's head as it swirled past, grazing the skin from my arm from waist to shoulder.

The boy was taken only ten feet from the boat. I did not see him go – a violent wrench as the body was torn from my grasp, a sudden rusty staining of the sea, a confused memory of shouting men and flailing oars as I was dragged into the boat: that was all.

Simpson took charge of his boat, aware that they were 820 miles from Tobago, the nearest land.

I talked with the men, telling them that I was quite sure we would be saved – a conviction which I truly felt, and which rarely deserted me during the long weeks ahead. The trade wind, I said, was almost constant in these seas, and set, with the current, always in our favour – and we had much to be thankful about ...

The most valuable item in the boat was a bag, containing my sextant and tables and elemental data for navigation, which I had kept always packed and ready to hand on the ship. This equipment, with a good wrist-watch that had survived the hazards and immersion of my long swim to the lifeboat, provided the tools whereby I could plot the progress of the boat from day to day – an immense practical and spiritual comfort to us all ...

In the satchel that held the sextant was a book of English verse from which I drew solace immeasurable ... I read aloud to the men one morning and they asked for more.

Rain provided water and, after twenty-two days, they saw what looked to be a cloud on the horizon but which proved to be land. The following day,

The boat turned the point and steered into the bay, which had the unreal beauty of a picture from a child's story-book. Quietly, slowly, wearily, the boat moved across the sparkling transparency of the calm water, and at last the stern was resting upon the white sand.[13]

At the other end of the Atlantic the *Empire Starlight,* a 10,000-ton tramp steamer, was in convoy to Murmansk. The convoy was bombed on the 22nd, 23rd and 24th March 1942, and encountered ice on the 25th, 26th and 27th, when the commodore ship, *Induna,* with a naval trawler short of fuel in tow, became fixed in the ice, with other ships stopped astern of her.

Empire Starlight was still navigable, and Captain Stein ordered all possible steam. Crunching and grinding through the ice, he cut his way round the convoy and, on reaching open water again some four hours later, advised the rest of the fleet to follow him. At this time he could see none of them. A blinding blizzard had blown up, the ice particles being driven by the wind like darts of steel, and conditions were almost unbearable.

The following day the *Induna* and another vessel were sunk, and there was another air attack the day after, by which time the *Empire Starlight* was alongside in Murmansk.

Discharging, which had been in progress all day, was continued after tea. Just before 9 p.m. air raid warnings sounded and a direct dive-bombing attack was made on *Empire Starlight.* In spite of the barrage of fire put up from the ship, the German plane screamed down almost to point-blank range before releasing his bombs; a 500-lb bomb burst through the deck and, with a shattering roar, filled the forehold with death and fury. This bomb was one of a stick of five, and the other four all exploded within the vicinity of the ship. While the Ack-Ack gunners were certain they had hit the plane, the chaos in the fore part of the *Empire Starlight* was evidence enough that the German pilot and bomber had made a successful sortie. Rescue and firefighting parties got to work immediately since, in addition to the physical damage caused by the explosion in No.1 hold, fire had broken out in No.2. The rescue party, fighting their way through the debris of damaged and shattered motor-trucks in the fore-hold, reported that six Russian workmen had been killed and eight motor-trucks destroyed. By midnight the fire in No.2 hold was under control, and a later examination proved that three Hurricane fighters were completely destroyed and three more seriously damaged in this hold.

The bomber had crashed half a mile away, but more than twenty further air attacks followed. Two more German bombers were shot down by the *Empire Starlight* crew but the ship was near its end. On 26th May

at 1715 hours a heavy and sustained attack was deliberately aimed at the *Empire Starlight*. Six Junkers 88s, three four-engined bombers unidentified, and three Stuka dive-bombers concerted to finish off the stricken ship. On 1st June a stick of bombs burst all along the port side during a raid, and she finally settled on the bottom with decks awash at high water. But the plane which inflicted this final indignity suffered for its temerity. For the last time the Ack-Ack team had manned their guns, and the German raider, fatally hit, crashed alongside her target.

The only casualty among the seventy-seven men who sailed in the *Empire Starlight* was a Chinese rating who was killed in a shelter ashore. Captain W H Stein was awarded the Lloyd's War Medal for Bravery and the OBE.[14]

In 1943, the year in which the British Ministry of War Transport issued, for the first time, a *Guide to the Preservation of Life at Sea after Shipwreck,* the SS *Oiltrader,* a tanker loaded with 16,000 tons of octane, was in convoy with the battleship HMS *Ramillies,* which carried Sir Winston Churchill, the British Prime Minister. The convoy was harried by 'wolf-packs' of U-boats in mid-Atlantic and some ships were torpedoed. Horned mines bobbed past the remaining ships as they neared the Western Approaches in fog. Then fire broke out in the *Oiltrader's* magazine, but was put out successfully. As the convoy met the first gulls,

> That morning four-engined bombers, wave-hopping, roared in low between the convoy columns, machine-gunning, and sometimes rising steeply to drop sticks of bombs. None of the ships dared to use their ack-ack guns because they were afraid of hitting each other.

However, the enemy planes made off, except for one which was tricked into diving into the sea by a British flying-boat, and more RAF planes appeared.

> *Oiltrader*'s cook glanced out of the galley and said to an AB, pointing his ladle skyward, 'I don't know 'ow them RAF blokes do it. Dangerous job that'.[15]

The wartime Liberty ships, built in the United States, were an improvement on prewar ships, not least in their provision for seafarers. Accommodation, in one block amidships, was better, toilet arrangements were much improved, with a number of shower cubicles and a laundry room provided. However, attitudes remained the same. Heading from the Normandy beaches in 1944, SS *Samwake* was sunk by German E-boats. The survivors were landed at Dover and sent to London in a double-decker bus.

> Old habits and traditions die hard, for in the front on the top deck sat the Captain and his officers, further back the POs and the lower ranks down below ... There were stops in the country for calls of nature and at one stage it was decided that a little liquid refreshment would go down very well, and so the driver was asked to look out for a suitable watering hole. We pulled up shortly afterwards at a large establishment surrounded by a car park. Eyes were raised when we all trooped in, officers to the saloon bar, crew to the public, and the proprietor looked at us. It was not until the orders started coming in that she spoke. No, she could not serve us, not even

with one glass each, there was only enough for her regular customers, and no way was she going to part with it. So it was back to the bus.[16]

Attitudes towards poor Jack are also illustrated by the account of a ship's carpenter's experience after the Harrison Line ship *Wayfarer* was sunk in the Indian Ocean. Suffering a dose of fever, he went down with the ship but swam to a raft.

There were four men on the raft already, and two more joined us subsequently. The first thing I did was to bring up all the salt water I had swallowed. I felt a bit better afterwards, but I had great difficulty in breathing and my heart was giving me some pain. To alleviate the pain I lay across a cork lifejacket – there were many floating about – in a semi-kneeling position, my arms folded across my chest and my head resting on the bottom of the raft. It was not very comfortable, but it was the most comfortable arrangement I could make. I had a terrible thirst and wondered if I could last the night.

A week later the raft drifted into a shallow lagoon and the survivors were found by native fishermen.

With the help of the natives and their boat we rounded up the others, now rather scattered, some on the raft, some north, some south, and the two of us on the reef. Two men had dived into the sea from the ship naked. Another, rescued from the upturned boat, had only a shirt, while the two who had been with him were wearing only bathing trunks. I was more fortunate than the rest because on the night we were hit I was dressed in vest, trunks, socks, trousers, sandals and patrol jacket. The vest I had since used, unsuccessfully, as an improvised fishing net, and I had lost the sandals while swimming for the reef. My trousers were gradually growing shorter as I kept tearing strips off the bottoms to bandage my feet which had been badly cut by the coral. We looked a poor collection and felt much as we looked.

Later on, those who lived – ten in number – were transported to the District Administrator's residence in Palma, Mozambique, where they were cared for and hospitably entertained.

> Eventually we were taken to the Rovama river where we crossed by canoe to British soil. An army truck took us to Mikandari and from there we were taken to Lindi through country where the ant-hills were as big as houses. From Lindi we went by coaster to Dar-es-Salaam, and there I had the unique experience of having my feet examined by a native house-boy. He was armed with a brass safety-pin, cotton-wool and vaseline and said he would look for 'jigger flea' that would most likely be embedded under my toes. The parasite is very common in Africa and one can quickly make its acquaintance if one is rash enough to walk anywhere barefoot.
> Eventually we reached Mombasa by way of a naval motor torpedo boat and there we joined BI's fine ship *Shirala*, leaving her at Suez. From Suez we went to Port Said where we joined the *Queen of Bermuda*, which was trooping. Aboard the *Queen of Bermuda* we were treated like criminals and our official reception in Liverpool was in no way welcoming. However, the reception I had when at last I reached home more than compensated me for the journey from Suez.[17]

Two rafts from the *Sutlej* were adrift in the Indian Ocean for forty-nine days after the ship had been sunk by a Japanese submarine in 1944. Both British and Indian sailors behaved in an exemplary fashion and two of the latter saved the lives of those on the chief engineer's raft by catching birds and fish.[18]

The crew of the tanker *British Chivalry* were not so lucky. After being torpedoed by a Japanese submarine some 500 miles northeast of the Seychelles, they abandoned ship and the master was taken prisoner aboard the submarine.

It was then noticed that the submarine had turned and was steaming towards us ... When 30 yards away the submarine opened fire with machine-guns on the boats. The men in the other boat shouted for us to slip the tow rope, in order to separate the boats as far as possible. The submarine steamed backwards and forwards, machine-gunning the boats each time she passed at very short range. I and my crew immediately jumped into the water for safety, but the men in the other boat crouched down in the bottom, consequently each time the submarine passed, he was able to fire down into the boat, killing or wounding most of the crew.

At one time the submarine steamed through the men in the water, and as he did so put his helm over and swung amongst them but fortunately no one was hurt. I decided the best course was to pretend to be dead, so I just floated, keeping one eye on the submarine all the time so that I could see on which side of the boat he was coming, and so keep out of the way. Both lifeboats were holed and filled rapidly; several men attempted to bail out the starboard boat but as they stood up, so they were shot down by the submarine. This boat contained so many dead men that it eventually sank ... Finally [after one and a half hours], the submarine ceased firing and steamed off ... Captain Hill (our Master) was made to stand on the deck of the submarine to witness the machine-gunning of the boats and the men in the water; it was observed that a camera-man was taking photographs throughout the incident.[19]

Incredibly, of the fifty-nine crew thirty-eight survived. They packed into the crudely repaired remaining lifeboat and were rescued by another British ship five and a half weeks later. Those who survived in this way were luckier than those who were taken prisoner by the Japanese. Jim Crewe of the ship *Tantalus* weighed 64 pounds when he was released after three years of camp life in Manila.

They issued you with about two ounces of rice a day and a handful of greens and there was forty pounds of meat per week for a camp of four thousand people. So what the camp cooks did was to put the meat in a pot and just boil it until there was nothing left, then they used that to boil the rice in so that nobody could say, 'I've got a piece of meat and you haven't'.[20]

At last the Second World War was drawing to a close.

As we neared the coast of Ireland the commodore signalled to tell us that, as we were the last convoy of our particular class of merchant ship, aircraft would be flying over us soon to take pictures, and instructing us to make a good show by being in our correct stations and to keep formation. The aircraft arrived, flying close over us, and along the lines of ships. We were, we realised, important news, probably for the last time in our several lives. From now on we were merchant ships without glamour, carriers of cargo for a nation at peace. A few older men commented ironically that as such we would not be photographed nor would we be news.[21]

Through the war years British merchant ships were manned by some 145,000 merchant seamen. During these years more than 50,000 of these merchant seamen died, a far higher proportion of those who served than died in the nation's armed forces. But there were compensations for the survivors when peace came.

On watch I am able to pace the full length of the bridge, unobstructed by gun-pits and ammunition lockers. Naval gunners have returned to naval vessels, and my watch below is never interrupted by a practice shoot or a frenzied dash to action stations. Numerous rivet holes and odd scars on the steelwork are all that remain to show that here was a 4-inch gun or a 12-pounder or, perhaps a 'pillar-box' with its trays of lethal rockets. Down below, in my cabin, is a certificate stating that I am proficient in the firing, cleaning and oiling of a Hotchkiss, Lewis and Martin machine-gun. I keep it for old time's sake.

Soon the crew will be painting the vessel but, when the task is done, we shall not be rewarded by a gloomy picture of unrelieved grey, as would have been the case a couple of years ago. With green boat-topping and a black hull, the superstructure will be finished a gleaming white and the masts, derricks and funnels buff-coloured. Thus the ship assumes a new personality, an individuality which somehow was lacking when she was merely another cog in a vast ocean-spanning machine.[22]

Loading iron ore, however, had not changed.

That red dust was everywhere. It got in your hair and down your shirt; it penetrated your food; and it invaded your bunk. I was six months on that ship and I left her looking like a blood brother of Hiawatha.[23]

And the captain was still expected in 1948 to know all there was to know about medicine, at least in the Pacific Ocean where the ships were out of radio touch with doctors. A rating had a gangrenous thumb and the captain decided that he must amputate it.

To deaden the pain I gave him a morphine injection in the hand and handed him a couple of stiff glassfuls of whisky which he swallowed gratefully. When I thought the injection had had time to act, I began the incision. Actually, I learnt later that morphine is not a local anaesthetic, ...

Savarino winced as the scalpel went in. But he made not a murmur. It was very sharp and in a few seconds I could feel hard bone all the way round. There was surprisingly little bleeding. Then I picked up the hacksaw. This was the part I had been dreading. Miranda [a Filipino rating] took a firm hold on our patient and I began sawing. At the first stroke of steel on bone Savarino screamed, his face twisted in agony and fear and he struggled like a tiger. But fortunately our preparations has been well made. The ropes holding him down didn't budge and little Miranda, looking as green as a Filipino can, was gripping grimly.

333

It was some time before I could pluck up courage enough to continue. I decided that the best method was to saw through quickly. So gripping the hacksaw in my right hand and the top of the thumb in my left, I started again. At first I had difficulty making our improvised instrument bite into the bone at all and when finally it began to make some headway the clumsy blade drew the flesh with it at each stroke ...

To Savarino the sawing must have lasted half an hour. In fact it was over in less than two minutes. I said to Miranda: 'For Christ's sake give him another shot of whisky'. But there was no reply. When I looked round I saw Miranda had gone. He had staggered out on deck and fainted. And then I realised that Savarino wouldn't need the whisky. He too had fainted.[24]

The seas and the world's climates, of course, had not changed with the peace. There could still be bad weather in the Mexican Bay of Tehuantepec. Aboard Wilson Money's vessel,

> After one particular spine-fracturing jolt there was an almighty crash in the alleyway outside my room and after a moment's thought I realised what it was. On both the port and starboard corridors there were recesses in which fire extinguishers were slung. One of them had jumped from its hook and was rolling about the deck outside our cabins like a primed bomb.

Those in their bunks were reluctant to rise and deal with the problem.

> Inevitably, on an exceptionally vicious roll, the madcap extinguisher slid athwartships, like a crazily computerised torpedo, and slammed head on into the Old Man's door, thereby activating the plunger in its nose.
>
> That did it! Not only did the steel drum race up and down the V-shaped alleyway, knocking paint and cobs of timber from bulkheads, but the foaming fluid from its interior

squirted furiously from its hose, whipping round and spitting CO_2 like venom from an enraged cobra. When, at one bell, the standby man arrived to call the second mate, he met it head on and was immediately smothered like a cream puff, losing his footing in the slime, and joining the cause of the disaster in sliding, skipping and skating to and fro across the accommodation. Only then did the occupants of the adjacent cabins emerge and assist in the fantastic custard-pie-flinging pantomime in the course of which four fast and furious fellows succeeded at last in capturing the runaway and lashing it back to its home base, mopping up the mess in some measure while the exhausted extinguisher still spurted faintly like some languishing Lothario.

After further mishaps in which Money cut his feet on broken glass and bruised his backside in a fall, he hung on to his washstand which was riveted to the bulkhead.

And so it went on. A thousand tons of ocean would hit the forefoot. Then would come the sickening sweep, a ride on a super figure-of-eight roller coaster with a neckbreaking swerve at the peak, though you never knew which way, followed by another bonebreaking descent to twenty thousand leagues under the sea as my lacerated feet slapped the bottom bunkboard and I stood on my heels while the ship's stem sliced into the next roller, half of which swept along the foredeck and thundered against the midship housing, shaking the vessel to her very keelson and all but flinging me head first into the window. I stared at the glass in fascination, praying that it would withstand the massive impact, and that the bolts of my washstand would take the strain of my 160 pounds of fearful flesh and blood.[25]

In another part of the world, Captain Jim Petrie and his crew were approaching the coast of northern Newfoundland with a cargo of high grade aviation spirit, but ice prevented their reaching their destination of Lewisporte.

By this time the ship was in a terrible state. Everything liquid had frozen, including the ink in our pens. To maintain fresh water for drinking and for boiler use, the chief engineer had collected all the flexible pipes he could lay his hands on and, after joining them together, wrapped them round the fresh water tanks. One end was then connected to one of the main engine steam pumps and the other end put down into the after peak boiler water tank. The steam thus forced through the pipes thawed out the fresh water. Up on deck a wire half-an-inch in diameter was now twenty-four inches thick with ice. The radio aerial between the foremast and the mainmast was so heavy with ice that it had stretched to one-and-half times its normal length and sagged to the deck, where its middle was covered with snow though the two ends were still fast to the masts.

We arrived back in Saint John's on 9th January, the rumour having gone round that we had foundered. From the Plimsoll Line it was calculated that we had shipped over 300 tons of ice. Several of the crew had to be treated for frostbite, but not one had grumbled throughout that testing time.[26]

Vermin could still be a problem, at least aboard the *Woodham Rover* in 1946.

Before we left the sulphur wharf the Port Health Authority collected over eighty rats just lying in the tween decks and on the beams. On the way to Archangel we collected 285 more of all shapes, sizes and colours as we cleaned the holds of their past cargo of sulphur and coal. Bill was the only AB on day-work, so the watches as well worked overtime during the ten-day run. The holds were filthy and strewn with dunnage. We had to work with damp kerchiefs over our mouths, but still the mixture of sulphur and coal-dust clogged our throats and nostrils. Dead rats appeared everywhere, and we kept a tally of them as we shovelled them into sack after sack. To bath ourselves we had to get our water from the pump amidships, hump it aft, and do the bucket drill. After a few days my skin broke out in a rash, mainly round the groin where my dungarees chafed the soft flesh.[27]

The ship's reception by the Russians had not changed by 1951 when the tramp steamer *Apapa* called at Murmansk on its way to Siberia to load timber.

> The pilot was accompanied by two soldiers who, after a cursory examination of the ship, stationed themselves one on each wing of the bridge, rifles at the ready. As soon as we had tied up alongside the jetty, a ladder was put over at the instigation of the pilot and another dozen soldiers and several civilians invaded the vessel.
>
> All members of the crew were then ordered to line up on deck, two of the soldiers mounting guard. Meanwhile, the rest of our visitors searched the ship thoroughly. When they returned, our identity cards were collected by an army officer who, with the assistance of our own chief officer, proceeded to identify us one by one, tallying each man against a crew list procured from the captain.
>
> As our names were called out we were obliged to pass between our armed guards and wait until the check was complete. Anyone having in his possession a private radio set, binoculars, cameras, maps or anything of a like nature was required to relinquish them into the hands of the Russian authorities. Our identity cards were also taken ashore.
>
> This whole business took the best part of four hours. During all this time we were kept on deck in the bitter cold under the watchful eyes of the guards. Having satisfied themselves that we harboured no spies or other subversive things, the searchers went ashore, leaving the ship still thoroughly guarded.

At Igarka, the loading port,

> As soon as we were tied up, the inevitable soldiers swarmed up the gangway, some to escort the pilots away, others to mount guard against the possibility of our trying to get ashore. We had one soldier at the foot of the gangway, another

at its head, while still more patrolled the decks. At the end of the jetty facing us was a machine gun tower with guns trained on the ships, and at intervals along the quay were sentry boxes, each one occupied, other troops walking up and down the wooden jetty.[28]

At sea there was little concern for pollution and, although by 1960 the coal-burning fireman had largely disappeared to give way to the rag-carrying motorship greaser, in the new giant oil-propelled tankers – they had reached 30,000 deadweight tons – any oil sludge was just thrown overboard.

Joe and I climbed wearily up the steel ladder towards the small circle of daylight that was the tank-top of just one small section of that huge oil-tanker ploughing its way through the Persian Gulf. We had been down there for two-and-half hours, working in a confined space with poor lighting, digging oil sludge with small hand shovels and heaping it into buckets to be hauled aloft and dumped over the ship's side. The thick black sludge covered us from our hands to our armpits – the sleeves of our boiler suits having been cut away for coolness. Our boiler suits were sticky with it; our rubber boots had become shapeless, clarty lumps; the muck was on our faces, smeared where we had wiped away the sweat; it was on our caps, in our hair, up our nostrils, the stench of it was everywhere. On reaching the deck we both made for the ship's rail and hung over it for a moment to catch what breeze there was; then we flopped down on the deck, exhausted.[29]

And with new cargoes came new hazards.

The worst thing I've encountered since I've been on these gas ships was when we were carrying ammonia and there were three of us putting a new runner on the derrick. The derrick was down over the manifold, and one morning as we were steaming along the mate, as usual, vented off the gas. It must have got into a down-draught eddy, because I got the full brunt of it. I couldn't breathe. I just stopped, and I felt myself going over. Fortunately my mate saw what was happening, caught me and threw me over on to the deck. When I came out of it about ten minutes later I was burnt all under my arms. The ammonia had got to the soft parts of my body where I was sweating, and I was red raw.[30]

But it was not all bad on the run from Europe to the Antipodes on a twelve-passenger ship.

There was no bars in 1955 but if the Old Man was of a generous nature we were allowed to buy six beers for Saturday night. They were stored in a bucket of cold water, and then the lads started to drift to the after hatch in ones and twos – each with his bucket. Occasionally there was a guitar on board and stories and songs swapped and sung until all the buckets held only water.

Approaching the first landfall, probably Panama or Suez, a holiday atmosphere pervaded the ship along with much letter writing activity and thoughts of incoming mail. Those who were free usually got ashore, arriving back with sore heads or with full shopping bags – sometimes both – and with enough to yarn about for the next few weeks.

Film night was a major event each week, usually screened on a hatch, with everyone grouped in front of the screen in strict pecking order: captain and passengers, senior officers and so on to the deck and galley boys who, although they could not see much at the front, at least could hear better than everyone else.

So the voyage settled into a pattern of work, sunbathing, games and social events. There was a serene air on board, a word I do not think could be applied to any ships or voyages by 1985.

After about six weeks discharging [in Auckland or Sydney] another month or so was spent loading, usually meat, butter and wool, and then off we would go to the USA and Canada where again we would spend quite a time discharging and loading before returning to the Antipodes – this time loading for home, if we were lucky.[31]

The last word in this era is given to the seaman who had very different experiences in 1934. For him and many others the 1950s were halcyon days.

I had just finished a five-month trip and, after twenty-seven days leave with pay, I reported to the Pool to ship out again.

I was sent to Bank Chambers to interview Captain Arnot for a new tanker, the mv *Sheaf Royal*, an 18,000-tonner, one of Souter's. 'The ship is not due in until Wednesday,' said Captain Arnot. 'I'll put you on pay from today, Monday. She is coming into Heysham. You will get a free railway warrant, and a car will meet you at Lancaster Castle station.'

With two other shipmates, I travelled in comfort. A car at the station took us with our suitcases to the agent's office at Heysham. The ship was at anchor in the bay.

'She is not coming alongside till three o'clock,' the agent said. 'Leave your baggage here. The car will take you to a hotel at Morecambe for lunch, pick you up at three, and take you down to the ship.'

We looked round to see what we were joining. Bathing-pool, smokeroom, library, recreation room, showers, single rooms for everyone on board, bed lights, and so on. We signed on her.

That night I took a shower all by myself. Here was something else I had dreamed of. Back in the old days, I washed in the heads, three to a bucket and so over-crowded I was never quite sure whose leg I was washing.

Then I turned in, my head on yielding pillows, stretched my legs under white linen sheets, so soft and smooth, switched on my bed light, and read the shipping reports in the *Evening News*. I had been a long time thinking of this kind of berth.

Next morning I went to the mess-room to a breakfast of cereals, curry and rice, eggs and bacon, hot rolls and marmalade, with cups of tea.

We are now bound for Singapore, then homeward via the Persian Gulf. I guess I'll hang on to the log line for a few trips.[32]

CHAPTER 24

The End of Poor Jack

1960–2000

It all happened very quickly round about 1960. With the coming of jet aircraft, passenger services on ocean routes virtually disappeared, and with them went the stewards. Large bulk carriers replaced trampships in the deep-sea trades, and the short-sea trades saw the advent of the ro-ros – the roll-on, roll-off vessels. In the ratio of about seven to one, the cargo-liners began to be replaced by container ships, otherwise known as box-carriers. Fewer and fewer seafarers could move more and more cargo, and the 'hands' did not need to be as skilled as they once were. Even so, in the United States and in Western Europe native seafarers were not all that easy to come by, and for a further fifteen years or so after 1960 the halcyon postwar years continued for those who remained.

> On my present ship I [the radio officer] have a well-appointed, air-conditioned cabin with a double bunk, a large settee, double wardrobe, knee-hole desk and plenty of drawer and cupboard space. For my entertainment the Owners have provided me (and for that matter all the officers' cabins are the same) with a Hallicrafters 'World-Wide' receiver with which I keep in touch with events from home, including the Merchant Navy programme.

The crew, also well accommodated, could call home cheaply by telephone.

Recreational facilities at sea are excellent. Most modern Norwegian ships have built-in swimming pools, which are very popular with the crew. Packs of cards, chess, Chinese checkers, dominoes and other games are provided by the Norwegian Government Seamen's Welfare Board. Libraries and movies are also provided, and among the crew concerts are occasionally arranged, especially on public holidays.[1]

Wives could often be taken to sea, paid leave was more frequent, and some owners of tankers, bulk-carriers and container ships began to employ women as navigators and radio officers – the first of the latter in British ships in 1970.

In 1971, on a North Atlantic car-carrier, the captain complained that the ship's distilled sea-water was so pure that it did not make a good cup of tea, and instant coffee had become the popular hot drink.

The living quarters are of a high standard and superior to many except the best hotels. Apart from the juniors most officers have their own dayroom with a fridge, bedroom and bathroom. The junior officers and petty officers share a bathroom between two. There are also officers' and crew bars where draught lager is served at 10p a pint and a large selection of spirits is available. Sweets, chocolates, nuts and crisps can be bought from the catering officer. Cigarettes sell at 10p a packet of 20 and whisky is 80p a bottle! In the bars are international television sets so that no matter where in the world the ship may be she can tune in to local television. Food, like the accommodation, compares well with that of a good hotel, so it is little wonder that the bill to feed the 33 crew for one month is £2,000.

On Christmas Day the company permits a generous allowance to the crew – there was a free barrel of lager, with sherry, spirits, red and white wine and liqueurs. Dinner was a full-scale banquet with soup, prawn cocktail, smoked ham, fish, minute steak, turkey, ham, Christmas pudding, fruit salad, ice cream, mince pies, Christmas cake, and some people managed a double portion of Christmas pudding.[2]

Seafarers, generally, had changed.

> The most striking metamorphosis since my first days at sea, fifty years ago, has been in the new thinking of seamen of all ranks. I am no longer surprised to find myself involved in a discussion on astro-physics or social theory developing from a casual remark to the man at the wheel.[3]

But with automation in all parts of the ship the nature of the rating's work had changed vastly since the days of sail, and even since the days of the tramp steamer. A medical officer likened a container ship to a factory in terms of space – 14 acres or more of decks – but the number of men working there might be no more than one-fortieth of the number working in a factory covering that acreage. Port turn-round times were reduced and a package holiday might offer more opportunity of seeing foreign places than a seafaring life. Not everyone was satisfied.

> In spite of improvements in living conditions, food, money and leave, our status as working men is becoming lower and lower. Speaking more of certificated men and mainly of tankers, we are fast becoming a race of sea-going 'skivvies'. Now, more than ever, ships are using the automatic pilot day and night which means that we have virtually a two-man watch, invariably of adult ratings. But now we no longer have the self-respect which comes from being at least efficient helmsmen. My last three ships have been tankers and in all I have been a watch-keeper. My duties have consisted of cleaning windows, polishing brass, scrubbing wheelhouse and chartroom decks – often on hands and knees – emptying ashtrays and waste-paper baskets, filling kettles, emptying teapots and washing up teacups.[4]

And ratings remained subject to a rigid class distinction, not merely in the fast disappearing passenger ships.

> My relationships with officers on the passenger boats were generally good. I was always industrious, so I didn't have any

problems – until I went on the Union Castle boats. There it was the full-on class distinction, and I've never seen anything like it. I remember it was in 1973 on the *Windsor Castle*, and it was like the lions and the gladiators – them being the lions and us the gladiators. They'd have you up on the bridge [ie before the Captain for possible fining] for the pettiest thing, and they'd all be up there. It seemed like twenty of them in their full regalia. Now I've never seen it but I've heard people say that they'd have the union jack on the skipper's desk! They'd go to the most elaborate lengths to get you; they'd conspire and tell lies to do you.[5]

Ships had changed and were still changing rapidly – the passenger-carrying *Windsor Castle*'s day was almost done, and the new VLCCs or very large crude carriers of oil (tankers over 100,000 deadweight tons) were more than 900 feet long. But the sea and the weather could not be changed.

Having rounded the Quoins we are in the Arabian Gulf and steaming well and truly down 'Tanker Alley'. The air is hot and bone-dry, just as if someone had opened an oven door. It dries the skin so quickly that you do not realise how much you are sweating. But fold your arms and protect a patch from the wind and it becomes wet and sticky with perspiration. It is weather to give you a tremendous thirst – requiring large doses of salt tablets ...

Loading the ship is not just a matter of sitting in air-conditioned comfort while the oil flows through the pipeline and into the tanks. The mate on watch has plenty of jobs to attend to on deck. Safety and pollution checks must be made, moorings and gangways attended to, gas vents adjusted, and the valves and gauges themselves have to be checked visually. During the course of a six-hour cargo watch the duty mate must cover a considerable distance, for it is a good three-minute walk, for instance, to the forecastle-head. This problem was not overlooked when VLCCs were a novelty. It was decided that bicycles would be necessary to cover the distance. Unfortunately, seamen proved prone to cycle accidents. Several broken limbs later, they now make their rounds on foot.[6]

Things could still go wrong, though not as often as in the days of sail.

Before I reached the compass repeater I realised something was wrong. There was a noise that shouldn't have been there. Above the wind's scream I could just pick out a shriller tone. It was steel grating on steel. My stomach turned right over as I realised the bulldozers were shifting. The seas smashing across the deck must have loosened the lashings, allowing the twenty-tonne monsters to start sliding about.

I didn't have to make a decision; the sea made it for me. As I balanced precariously on the hatch edge, only feet from those huge steel tracks, I felt the deck falling away beneath me. The ship suddenly plunged downwards, dropping like a lift into the trough in front of a huge wall of dark water. Before I'd realised what was happening, the bows dug in with a solid crash and the wave toppled over on to the ship, burying the foredeck completely. I didn't have time to grab anything before the crest of the wave plucked me off the hatch. The sea was roaring down the deck, covering the hatches, bulldozers and masthouses completely. The huge force of the water tumbled me over and over down the deck. I felt myself smashed against the ship's side rail and just managed to grab and hold on as the wave threw me overboard! I couldn't think or breathe; I didn't feel any pain. I was just holding on for all I was worth. I hung suspended over the side of the ship as the niagara pulled at me. The ship was lifting now, shedding the water from the decks. I was vaguely aware of a rumble beside me, then another force, greater even than the sea which was doing its best to break my grip, twisted and buckled the rails that I had clamped myself on to. I couldn't hold on. For one terrible moment I hovered in free space before the ship rolled into the sea and I was thrown back on the deck again. I lay there gasping, wondering what the hell had happened.

There was a huge gap in the rails, either side of which they were bent and tangled like steel spaghetti. The bulldozer had followed me down the deck and gone overboard just inches from me. I had been thrown back aboard through the gap which it had made on its way out. It was then that I started to shake with fear.[7]

Politics, like piracy, could still affect the seafarer on occasion. In 1978 there was a revolution in Iran and John Guy was alongside at Bandar Shapour in the 30,000-tonne bulk carrier *Rupert*.

At the new year things started hotting up politically. Ayatollah Khomeni sent everyone a hair from his beard and appeared to the faithful in the moon. His picture sprouted everywhere, on the truck windscreens, proudly worn badges and telegraph poles. During the discharge all the dock labour lived aboard, huddled crowds of dew-soaked poverty sleeping on the open steel decks. They washed their feet each day at the tap we provided but we saw very few performing the Muslim prayers. Just when we had become accustomed to this ever-present mass of humanity they all disappeared. Borne on invisible wings the strike message came aboard and in a gathering stream the men picked up their blankets and tea cups and slouched off along the quay.

January passed, unmourned, into a wet February, silence still upon the waiting ships ...

Suddenly, the Shah was gone and the Ayatollah made his triumphant return. The Iranians were ecstatic, puffed out with pride in their strength. People's committees mushroomed to take over from the old local governments. We saw more people now. Scornful for westerners, hating the Americans and English, they asserted themselves over us whenever they had a chance.

I acquired a badge with a picture of Khomeni and I wore it as a charm, passing myself off as French. It didn't always work. A white face was enough to get you into trouble. 'For you all Iranians are policemen.' Spit-speckled lips curled back in hate as they demanded to know where you were going. We were very careful.[8]

In Japan, though, a night ashore could still be like old times. In the bath-house in Yokohama the masseuse called her European customer Fuji-San because his long occidental nose reminded her of the mountain. After steaming and bathing him, she laid him face down upon the table and began to walk on his back.

Her feet slid expertly outwards from my spine, the balls of her heels kneading odd knots of muscle, her toes stimulating unguessed-at erogenous zones as, in a slow and meticulous promenade, she made several passes from neck to coccyx while I groaned in luxurious delight beneath her. But this was nothing to the performance to be endured lying on my back. Her strong fingers probed the tense muscles of my legs, over stood-upon in the long watches of our voyage, or cracked the tendons of my arms and gave my head a sinew-snapping twist that made me fear for my life – except that in the aftermath I felt extraordinarily revitalised. During this clinical operation my physical lassitude was such that desire seemed moribund, despite the strange intimacy. To preserve the decencies Mitsuko, her almond eyes averted in deference to my libidinous sensibilities, draped a small cotton towel across my limp penis.

But looking up at her, her breasts alive within the restraint of her brassière as she kneaded my thighs, sitting astride my lower legs, it was impossible not to respond to her presence. The little cotton towel rose like a diminutive bell-tent and Mitsuko smiled at me.

'Ah-so ... Fuji-San ... ', she laughed as she moved her hands upwards.[9]

But not every seafarer got ashore by 1980.

I think perhaps the modern ship has produced a new kind of loneliness among seafarers. You can be on the bridge for an hour or so in front of your console and not see another guy. Then there are fewer of you aboard ship. I mean, what's the average crew on, say, a 50,000 tonner – twenty-five or so? By the time you have been divided into watches and had your sleep the chances of actually meeting a shipmate are much reduced. When you're handing over watches might be just about the only time you meet anyone ... And there isn't all that time in port. And then our dock systems have gone mad, haven't they? No longer is the quayside up against Wool-worth's, and then if you're tucked up against the west wall at Seaforth it's in outer space. It's a mile and half before you see another human being, and if you're docked within the container dock itself then you have a flashing light in a helmet on your head before you're allowed to walk through the container system. You have to wait for a bus, so you don't go ashore. So there you are, on the fourteenth floor by lift, in your seagoing can with no one to talk to.[10]

Job satisfaction had disappeared for many by that same year.

Young seafarers no longer see the world in container vessels and bulk carriers as they used to in the great cargo liners and tramp ships which had character about them, as opposed to the ugly steel barges with blocks of flats perched on the stern that we see today. In such *unattractive environments*, with *quick turn rounds* and *frequent crew changes*, job satisfaction must needs be difficult and monotony a very present adver-sary, with relief day and the pay table tending to become the be-all and end-all. In addition, there is today the biggest ship-ping slump in living memory bringing a constant threat of redundancy which by no means contributes to peace of mind.[11]

The new age was described vividly by John Guy, then a Chief Officer, in 1983.

Time was, when seamen were a race apart, a people made spe-cial by the harsh demands of their calling ...

I went to sea when the general cargo ship was still the norm. Trips were long and mail uncertain but the food was reasonable. That perhaps was the time of happy ships. We were not deprived of creature comforts but neither were we detached from our environment. There was a good feeling in some of those ships. At sea we felt the elements and knew that we were special, somehow better than the shorebound. In port, we finished work, showered up and were away ashore, raucous groups letting off steam in the time-honoured way.

These cosy tinted memories are intruded upon by the sound of heavy rock music. Follow the repetitive beat down the harsh formica alleyways and enclosed stairwells and step into the softly lit, softly furnished lounge. Observe the flabby blank faces of the seafarers of today, a cluster of dead white blobs around the anonymous bar. Empty-headed, idle wives whining about some imagined slight compete for air time in their husbands' eternal discussion of cars and football. The music blankets the sound track of the tenth re-run of *Coronation Street* on the video.

This scene is unchanged at sea or in port, fair weather or foul, tanker or bulker. The world outside no longer intrudes. Massive ships, the constant icy blast of air-conditioning and passive entertainment on tap has eroded any sense of seagoing. Physical violence is largely a thing of the past, replaced by the crushing mental violence of twenty-four hour video TV, weekends at sea with nothing to do and stays in port too short to catch a cold, never mind a girl ...

We shall leave no legacy of romance to stir the blood of our island nation. Floating office boys and effete nine-to-five engineers are not the stuff of legend. Soon, when the last British seafarer is made redundant and sealife exists only in uncertain memory, this generation will be forgotten. Certainly no one will write about us: there is nothing to say.[12]

Tony Hinks was six months on the round-the-world ro-ro *Barber Perseus*, and never once had time to go ashore.

Let's take it from arriving in Norfolk, Virginia, which will be about two in the morning, previously having had a four-to-five hour stand-by coming up river. About twenty minutes after getting alongside we'll have the ramp down. On this ship we can load five decks from the stern, and we can also load on to the main deck with cranes and gantries. Now by six we've got everything ready for the shoreside men to come in. At that point we'll have about an hour's break and after that we could be loading catering, engine-room and deck stores. When that's done we might have an hour on the quay, working from our stacker truck, painting the ship's side, and soon after that it could be time to be getting the ramp up and lashing down the containers on deck ready to be off. After six hours we could be sailing again.

Three hours in Baltimore, little more in New York, and then across the Atlantic, through the Mediterranean, the Suez Canal and the Red Sea to Jeddah.

Jeddah is the longest stop, with thirty-six hours, but you never get ashore because you can't get a pass. In Dubai you'll have about five hours, and then it's Dammam. You have a day in Dammam, and then it's Bahrain, where you usually have a night. From Bahrain we'll go up to Kuwait. After that we'll have an eight-and-a-half day passage across the Indian Ocean to Singapore.

In Singapore we'll be loading as well as discharging, whereas in the Gulf ports we'll have been discharging and picking up empties. Singapore is the first loading port for the States, but we'll only be there for about twelve hours. You could arrive there at ten at night and they'll be working the ship immediately. We'll be leaving at eleven next morning, and then exactly the same could happen when you get to Hong Kong. You might have a bit longer in Hong Kong but you'll never get a day.

The next port is Keelung, in Taiwan, and then it's Kao-hsiung, and then it's off to Kobe in Japan. After Japan it's eleven and a half days across the Pacific to Los Angeles. We'll have about ten hours there, then it's down through the Panama, and at Cristobel at the Caribbean end of the canal we'll probably have a night in. Our next port is Palm Beach in Miami, and then we'll go up to Savannah, Baltimore and New York, and then we'll go back round the coast to New Orleans, Houston, Norfolk, Baltimore, New York, and then off to Jeddah again.[13]

As the second millennium drew to its close, after 1980, the whole world shipping scene changed. 'Flags of convenience', countries which hitherto had few maritime connections, if any, countries such as Liberia, Panama, Cyprus and Costa Rica, were virtually unknown when the Second World War ended in 1945. Thereafter, these flags proved convenient because they were mainly free of taxation on shipowners' profits, and ships on their registers were not subject to government regulations, many of them relating to the safety and welfare of seafarers, imposed on their shipping by traditional maritime countries. By 1957 flag of convenience fleets accounted for about 13 per cent of world tonnage. By 1988, when the world fleet had risen nearly fourfold to some 400 million gross tons, they accounted for more than 40 per cent. From Europe the merchant fleets 'flagged out' to flags of convenience, where seafarers could be employed at Third World wages, and by 1988 the United Kingdom had sunk to twelfth place in the world list of maritime nations.

Many of the officers 'flagged out ' too because redundancy was rife at home; and 'poor Jack', the ocean-going Western rating, virtually disappeared, to be replaced, where he needed to be replaced in the automated ships being built, by the world's poor. Filipinos, Chinese, Bangladeshis, Kiribatis, even Zulus, became the remnants of a dying race. 'It is poverty that drives men to sea', said Aristotle Onassis, a Greek shipowner who ought to have known, since he made enormous sums of money out of poor sailors. 'Otherwise', he went on, 'no one would bear the hardships and deprivations, the separation from hearth and home and country of the sailor's life'.

> In the last ten years [wrote one British shipmaster in 1985] I have not entered a British port and on only one ship have I ever served for more than one consecutive voyage. I have received my wages from six different employers and in one case counted myself lucky to have received them at all. I have twice resigned and twice been made redundant. I am unknown man, an itinerant master, working where and when I can.[14]

Another shipmaster wrote,

> The prospect of unemployment does tend to concentrate the mind wonderfully when faced with decisions on whether or not to join a ship bound for Kharg Island and similar war zones [Iran and Iraq were at war]. What's death to unemployment?[15]

A young rating who had recently acquired his third mate's certificate was hoping, in 1982, to secure employment as an officer with a British company employing British seafarers.

> To go foreign flag was not my original intention but, after writing to over 100 British companies and receiving refusals because of the present economic recession, I was desperate for a job.

He joined a ship at anchor off southern Cyprus.

> My worst fears were realised on my first night on board. When I went down to turn in I pulled back the top sheet, which somehow had tyretreads across it, and there in the middle of my bunk were ten very large cockroaches holding a party.
> I do not have enough paper to write about all the faults of the ship, but here are a few: cockroaches everywhere; rats in

the galley; an engine room where it was difficult to breathe without apparatus; language difficulties due to the international complement, which results in breakdown of communication; inedible food; chronic lack of fresh water; showers which tended to spray fuel oil without warning; and total apathy towards safety. Examples of the latter were people smoking on deck while loading petrol, a dangerous loading plan caused by inexperienced planning; no boat or fire drills, nor up to date muster lists.

I have since resigned from that foreign company and I sometimes think that I would rather be unemployed than ever go foreign flag again. But they tell me on the British pool that I cannot ship out, even if a job comes up, because I have served foreign.[16]

There were other problems, too, with some flag of convenience ships. Made redundant by a Glasgow company, a very experienced shipmaster found himself running contraband.

This ship is a small multi-purpose carrier running contraband – 'stuffed' containers from the Far East to Lagos and Port Harcourt. What appears on the manifest is totally irrelevant regarding the container's true contents, which has been proven when inspecting the odd broached unit in Nigeria.

Facilities and living standards aboard are appalling. Soap is not supplied, linen changed fortnightly, and the feeding rate a meagre DM7 a day which at the current exchange rate is about £1.50. Meals are one-course affairs with maybe once a week a sweet of tinned fruit or ice cream. Filipino cooks do not help as nothing is put in the oven. Everything is fried, even carrots, cauliflower and tinned French beans. One thing is certain; this has been a mistake. But when on the dole anything seems an improvement.[17]

Running contraband unknowingly was not the only problem. A chief officer joined a Panamanian ship with a Filipino crew.

The total crew numbers 24, which I think is not enough to man this ship which originally had a crew of around 40. When I joined the ship I found it badly neglected. It had been owned by Greeks for some time and they 'let it go' rather badly. I have been working hard to get it safe and clean again. The ship is actually owned by a Chilean, managed by a German company from Cyprus and is on charter – hired out – to a Danish company.

In Lagos gangs of robbers steal openly from ships. The day we arrived there were gunshots on the ship a few yards away from us, and another container ship was boarded by robbers, armed with guns and knives, who knew where to look for a particular container, indicating that they had assistance or guidance from authorities ashore who would know what the ship was carrying.[18]

Theft and piracy were also common in the Malacca Straits.

While we were coming down the Malacca Straits at reduced speed to arrive at the Singapore pilot by daybreak, we were boarded in the early hours of the morning by thieves who broke into the ship's office and removed typewriters, an adding machine, a duplicator and a photocopying machine. They also entered a couple of cabins and stole money and other odds and ends. The cabins were empty at the time as the people living in them were on watch.[19]

Other problems as old as seafaring still materialised from time to time.

We have a 62-year-old steward with a bladder blockage. We put him in a bath and gave him a shot of morphine but this did not work so I whacked tetracycline into him. [Neither likely to do the sick man any good.] Right in the middle of the ocean there is not much choice – no ships anywhere with a doctor, 3 days to Walvis Bay, 2½ days to St Helena (where there are no helicopters), 4 to Cape Town, 5 to Brazil, 2 to Tristan da Cunha (no helicopters and a very heavy swell).

When I joined the morphine was two years out of date and I'd fortunately seen it and replaced it, but this catheter game is enough to drive one up the wall, particularly getting out of bed at 2 am, measuring what goes in and what comes out.

I hope to get the sick man off shortly. At least he's still alive.[20]

In desperation, a British radio officer, made redundant after twenty years with the Blue Funnel Line – which was famed on the high seas for a hundred years – shipped out in a foreign flag ship at Filipino wages. What follows is extracted from his 1984 diary.

Day 1. Sailed for Beirut aboard this 6400-ton ship which now carries containers. The crew number 14: Master (Brit), Mate (Chilean), Chief Engineer (Polish), Second Engineer (Filipino), Radio Officer (Brit), Cook and Steward (Filipino), Bosun, Leading Seaman and five Seamen (Kiribati). We trade world wide. My pay is US $800 a month – £5,700 a year.

I found the following defects: 1. Neither radar working. 2. Echo-sounder not working. 3. Main transmitter on half power only. 4. Two aerials unserviceable. 5. Auto-alarm giving no signals. 6. No spares. 7. No testmeter.

Day 4. Since we carry no Second Mate and no Purser the Master asked me to correct the charts and to check the provisions for an inventory at the end of the month. If the Chief Engineer can't cope he also wants me to act as Electrical Officer.

Day 5. The food is diabolical: the allowance is DM7 (less than £2) per man per day. We eat what we are given; there is no choice. The Cook is Filipino and has never seen a galley before.

Day 56. The Master has had a large cyst removed [in port]. I have to dress it daily, so now I am Doctor.

Day 81. Master discharged seriously ill. Could not diagnose condition. He was very weak and unable to eat. New Master is Yugoslav.

Day 111. After discharging half the crew we sailed out to anchorage, 15 miles from shore, to lay up. Seven of us are left: Master, Mate, Chief Engineer, Second Engineer, Radio Officer and two Seamen. Now we make up our own beds, clean the cabins and take turns at cooking. As Second Mate I went aft and berthed at the bunker jetty and then unberthed for sea. One foreign seafarer said to me, 'You British will all be out of a job soon.'

Day 120. We are still at anchor 15 miles from land. We understand the vessel is up for sale.

Day 121. There has been no clean linen since the Steward left and today the water is on ration.

Day 133. Still at anchor. Still no sign of employment or sale. Now the Captain is going to ration the coffee and the toilet paper has run out.[21]

Towards the end of the millennium the Third World crews of some flag of convenience ships sailed under conditions which were as bad as they had ever been. In 1985 the 11,715-gross ton freighter *Frusa,* registered in Gibraltar, made an unscheduled visit to Bermuda for water and fuel.

As the pilot was leaving, a seafarer bolted down the gangway ... According to the seafarer, the crew on board had virtually been prisoners for the past four months and had been treated like 'animals'. He said the crew had been deprived of adequate water, had not been properly fed for the past fifteen days and were sick from the poor diet, and were owed four months' back pay ...

The Yugoslav captain of the vessel made every effort to sail away before the authorities in Bermuda could intervene, and the same day the ship pulled into port, he told the twenty-six Yugoslavian, Moroccan, and Sri Lankan crew members to cast off for Texas. When they flatly refused, he accused them of mutiny. The Bermuda authorities sided with the crew.

Investigations revealed that the meat had been on board for ten months and was rotten. The canned food tins were rusty and had been bought after the expiration date. The port inspector, Ron Ross, estimated that there was only enough food for ten men for two days, yet the crew of twenty-six men had been ordered to depart for a destination several days away. There was only one tin of milk on board, and in the last port, Safi, Morocco, only sixty tons of water had been loaded, not nearly enough for an Atlantic crossing. According to the crew, 'The taps were kept closed for four days after leaving port, and after that they were opened only half an hour every two or three days'.[22]

Notes

Chapter 1
1. A Erman, *The Literature of the Ancient Egyptians* (1927), London, pp29–35.
2. Cf P Jay (ed), *The Greek Anthology* (1973), London.

Chapter 2
1. L Casson, *Ships and Seamanship in the Ancient World* (1971), Princeton, New Jersey, pp235–6.
2. A S Hunt & C C Edgar, *Select Papyri*, Vol 1. Loeb Classical Library (1932), Letter No 112, London, pp305–7. See also Casson, *op cit*, p212.
3. Cf M Heseltine (ed), Petronius, *Satyricon* (1913), London, p177.
4. A Courtauld, *From the Ends of the Earth* (1958), London, pp8, 9–10, 16.
5. N Beamish, *The Discovery of America by the Northmen* (1851), London. See also Courtauld, *op cit*, pp25–6.
6. R Hakluyt, *The Principal Navigations, Voyages, Traffics and Discoveries of the English Nation* (1927), London, Vol 1, p105.
7. G F Golding, *Records and Songs of Saxon Times* (1932), London, p98.
8. Cf *ib*, pp126–8.
9. Courtauld, *op cit*, pp29–31.
10. Golding, *op cit*, pp73–4.
11. Courtauld, *op cit*, pp33–4 (from the Icelandic Saga of Eric the Red).
12. *The Vinland Sagas* (1965), Harmondsworth, pp55, 58–9.
13. *Ib*, pp67–70.
14. *Ib*, pp103–4.

Chapter 3
1. W O Hassall, *How They Lived* (1962), Oxford, pp87–8. See also J Stevenson, *The Church Historians of England* (1855), Vol 3, Pt 2, p560 (from Simeon of Durham).
2. W McFee, *The Law of the Sea* (1951), London, p62. McFee refers to the antiquarian tomes of Francis Grote.
3. See C E Fayle, *A Short History of the World's Shipping Industry* (1933), London, p75.
4. *Ib*, p72.
5. Cf Hassall, *op cit*, p85. T Twiss (ed), *The Black Book of the Admiralty*, Vol 1, Rolls Series (1871), p105 (the major source on the Laws; this passage relates to 1337–51).
6. Fayle, *op cit*, pp96–7.
7. Hassall, *op cit*, p86. W Dugdale (trs), *Monasticon Anglicanum – A History of the Abbies and other Monasteries, Hospitals, Friaries and Cathedral and Collegiate Churches* (1830), Vol 6, Pt 1, p704.
8. *The Black Book of the Admiralty*, Vol 1, Rolls Series (1871), pp13–19.
9. Hakluyt, *op cit*, Vol 1, p100.
10. Cf Hakluyt, *op cit*, Vol 1, pp175–94.

Chapter 4

1. C E Fayle, *A Short History of the World's Shipping Industry* (1933), London, p101.
2. H H Hart, *Sea Road to the Indies* (1952), London, pp16–7 (quoted from Gomes Eannes de Azurara, Chronicles).
3. A L Salzman, *English Trade in the Middle Ages* (1931), Oxford, pp274–5 (trs Devon Assoc, xlvii, p202).
4. Hart, *op cit*, p22 (quoted from G R Crone, *Voyages of Cadamosto*, etc [1937], London)
5. D Burwash, *English Merchant Shipping 1460–1540* (1947), Toronto, p24 (modernised).
6. *Ib*, p39.
7. *Ib*, p39.
8. S E Morison, *Christopher Columbus Mariner* (1956), London, pp69–70.
9. *Ib*, pp251–6.
10. *Ib*, pp216–7.
11. J A Williamson (ed), *The Cabot Voyages and Bristol Discovery under Henry VII* (1962), Cambridge, pp201–2.
12. Morison, *op cit*, p150.
13. Williamson, *op cit*, pp209–10.
14. *Ib*, p269.
15. Hart, *op cit*, p149.
16. *Ib*, p187.
17. *Ib*, p41.
18. *Ib*, p227.
19. Morison, *op cit*, pp187–8.
20. *Ib*, pp200–1.
21. Hart, *op cit*, p232.
22. *The Mariner's Mirror* ('The Carriera da India 1650–1750'), Vol 46, No 1, pp39–40.

Chapter 5

1. Antonio Pigafetta et al, *First Voyage round the World by Magellan* (1874), London (Hakluyt Society). See also Mairin Mitchell, *Elcano: the First Circumnavigator* (1958), London, pp60–6.
2. E C B & K Lee, *Safety and Survival at Sea* (1971), London, p103.

3. M Mitchell, *op cit*, pp87–9.
4. H H Hart, *Sea Road to the Indies* (1952), London, p253.
5. *Le discours de la navigation de Jean et Raoul Parmentier de Dieppe. Voyage à Sumatra en 1529.* (Reported in H M Lydenberg, *Crossing the Line* [1937], New York, p15 [trs R Hope].)
6. Slightly modernised from D Burwash, *English Merchant Shipping 1460–1540* (1947), Toronto, pp33–4. Burwash cites High Court of Admiralty 24, File 5, large bundle, by John Aborough contra John Andrewes.
7. E S Dodge, *North-West by Sea* (1961), New York, p33.
8. Modernised from Burwash, *op cit*, pp78–9.
9. 32nd Henry VIII 1540, quoted in H C Hunter, *How England Got Its Merchant Marine* (1935), New York, p51.
10. A L Salzman, *English Trade in the Middle Ages* (1931), Oxford, p282.
11. R Hakluyt, *The Principal Navigations, Voyages and Discoveries of the English Nation* (1927), London, Vol 1, pp235–6.
12. Richard Eden's 'Preface to the Reader' in his translation of *The Decades of the newe worlde of Peter Martyr* (1455–1526), the third book on America to be printed in English (Londini, *In aedibus Guilhelmi Powell* [1555]).
13. Hakluyt, *op cit*, Vol 1, p345.
14. *Ib*, p378.
15. C R Boxer (ed), *Further Selections from the Tragic History of the Sea, 1559–1565* (1968), Cambridge (for the Hakluyt Society), pp64, 72–3, 106.

Chapter 6

1. J A Williamson, *Sir John Hawkins, the Time and the Man* (1927), Oxford, pp94–5.
2. *Ib*, p100.
3. *Trial of Miles Phillips*, Mexican National Archives, *Inquisition*

Records, Vol 54, evidence of William Collins, 12–13 of transcript by G R G Conway. Quoted by J A Williamson, *Hawkins of Plymouth* (1948), London, pp71–2.

4. Fronde, Da Silva to Eliz.; 6 Oct 1567, Spanish MSS, Rolls House. Quoted by W S Lindsay, *History of Merchant Shipping* (1876), London, p128.

5. T S Willan, *Studies in Elizabethan Foreign Trade* (1959), Manchester, p14.

6. J Hampden (ed), *Francis Drake Privateer: Contemporary Narratives and Documents* (1972), London, pp37–9. (See Sir John Hawkins' account in Hakluyt.)

7. J J Keevil, *Medicine and the Navy*, Vol 1, 1200–1649 (1957), London, p122. From Hakluyt.

8. Hampden, *op cit*, pp66–7. From *Sir Francis Drake Review* (1626), London.

9. *Ib*, p68.

10. J A Williamson, *Hawkins of Plymouth* (1949), London, pp154–5. From G R G Conway, *An Englishman in the Mexican Inquisition* (1927), Mexico City, pp155–62.

11. E G R Taylor (ed), *A Regiment of the Sea* (1963), Cambridge, pp170–1.

12. G Cawston & A H Keane, *The Early Chartered Companies* (1896), London, pp196–7.

13. *The Three Voyages of Martin Frobisher in Search of a Passage to Cathaia and India by the North-West, Ab 1576–8* (1847), London, Hakluyt Society, pxxvi.

14. R Hope, *The Merchant Navy* (1980), London, pp12–13.

15. F Drake (G E Hollingworth [ed]), *The World Encompassed* (1935), London, p8.

16. *Ib*, pp51–2.

17. *Ib*, p64.

18. *Ib*, pp84–5.

19. *Ib*, p117, 119–21.

Chapter 7

1. T S Willan, *Studies in Elizabethan Foreign Trade* (1959), Manchester, p7 (HCA Examinations, 24 [1582]; *Libets* 52, No 37).

2. E G R Taylor (ed), *The Troublesome Voyage of Captain Edward Fenton*, 1582–3 (1959), Cambridge, Hakluyt Society, 66–7.

3. *Ib*, pp166–7 (modernised).

4. *Ib*, pp273–5 (modernised).

5. *Ib*, p166 (modernised).

6. *The Voyages and Colonising Enterprise of Sir Humphrey Gilbert* (1940), London, Hakluyt Society, p438.

7. D W Waters, *The Art of Navigation in England in Elizabethan and Early Stuart Times* (1958), London, p179.

8. *The Roanoke Voyages*, 1584–90, Vols I & II (1955), London, Hakluyt Society, pp219–20.

9. J J Keevil, *Medicine and the Navy*, Vol 1, 1200–1649 (1957), London, p11.

10. P Kemp, *The British Sailor* (1970), London, pp10–11. From Add MSS 12, 505, f241, BM.

11. *Ib*, pp8–9. From S P Dorn. Elizabeth, ccxiv, 66, PRO. Printed in *Defeat of the Spanish Armada*, NRS, 1894, Vol II, pp96.

12. *Ib*, p12. From *Defeat of the Spanish Armada* as above.

13. Pinkerton, *A General Collection of the Best and Most Interesting Voyages and Travels in all Parts of the World* (1808), London, p815. (Cumberland's Voyage to the Azores.)

Chapter 8

1. K R Andrews (ed), *English Privateering Voyages to the West Indies 1588–95* (1959), Cambridge, pp54–5. (Modernised from HCA 13/28, 29 January 1589/90.)

2. *Op cit*, pp66–7. (Modernised from William Magoth's account in *Principal Navigations* III [1600], pp839–42; XI [1904], pp381–4.)

3. C Lloyd (ed), *The Englishman at Sea* (1946), London, p118. (From Linschoten's Itinerary, Eng trs 1598.)

4 *The Roanoke Voyages, 1584–1590*, Vols I & II (1955), London, Hakluyt Society, p598.

5. J J Keevil, *Medicine and the Navy*, Vol 1, 1200–1649 (1957), London, pp98–9.

6. D W Waters, *The Art of Navigation in England in Elizabethan and Early Stuart Times* (1958), London, pp233–4.

7. P Kemp, *The British Sailor* (1970), London, p17.

8. C R Markham (ed), *The Voyages of Sir James Lancaster, Kt, to the East Indies*, Burt Franklyn, New York, originally (1877) Hakluyt Society, p11 (Edmund Barker's account).

9. *Ib*, p29 (Henry May's account).

10. Andrews, *op cit*, pp197–9. (HCA 13/30, 4 December 1592.)

11. C R Boxer (ed), *The Tragic History of the Sea, 1589–1622* (1959), Cambridge, Hakluyt Society, pp115–7.

12. *The Observations of Sir Richard Hawkins, Knt. in his voyage into the South Sea in the year* 1593 (1847), London, Hakluyt Society, p26. (Reprinted from the edn of 1622.)

13. *Ib*, pp65–6.

14. *Ib*, pp56–7, 60, 82, 86.

15. Keevil, *op cit*, pp115–6.

16. Hawkins, *op cit*, p143.

17. *Ib*, p153.

18. G F Warner (ed) *The Voyage of Robert Dudley, etc., 1594–5* (1899), Hakluyt Society, p14

19. Keevil, *op cit*, pp107–9.

20. *Ib*, pp109–10. (Spelling modernised.)

21. J S Corbett, *Drake and the Tudor Navy* (1988), Aldershot, p399.

Chapter 9

1. H Weinstock (trs), *Francesco Carletti: My Voyage Around the World* (1965) London, pp70–1.

2. *Ib*, pp127–8.

3. *Ib*, pp185–6.

4. C R Markham (ed), *The Voyages of Sir James Lancaster, Kt, to the East Indies*, New York, originally (1877), London, Hakluyt Society, pp61–2.

5. H H Hart, *Sea Road to the Indies* (1952), London, pp136–7. (From Jean Moquet, *Voyages en Afrique, Asie, Indres Orientales et Occidentales* [1830], Paris.)

6. L Gardiner, *The British Admiralty* (1965), Edinburgh, p61.

7. P L Barbour, *The Three Worlds of Captain John Smith* (1964), London, pp215–6.

8. E G R Taylor (ed), *A Regiment of the Sea* (1963), Cambridge, passim.

9. W Raleigh, *The English Voyages of the Sixteenth Century* (1910), London, pp181–2.

10. M Strahan & B Penrose (eds), *The East India Company Journals of Captain William Keeling and Master Thomas Bonner, 1615–1617* (1971), Minneapolis. (The quotations are to be found in pp63–153, except for the last which is on p44.)

Chapter 10

1. C Lloyd, *The Englishman and the Sea* (1946), London, pp76–7. (From *Diary of Governor Bradford*.)

2. C R Boxer (ed), *The Tragic History of the Sea 1589–1622* (1959), Cambridge, Hakluyt Society, p194.

3. C Lloyd, *The British Seaman* 1200–1860 (1968), London, p60.

4. J Smith, *A Sea Grammar* (1970), London, pp45, 49, 79–80, 96–7.

5. P Kemp, *The British Sailor* (1970), London, p24. (From J.R.Tanner [ed], *Hollond's Discourses of the Navy* [1896], NRS, pp178–9.)

6. M Oppenheim, *A History of the Administration of the Royal Navy* 1509–1660 (1988), Aldershot, p233.

7. C Lloyd, *The British Seaman*, pp73–4.

8. L Fox, *North-West Fox, or Fox from the North-west Passage* (1635), London.
9. W G Perrin (ed), *Boteler's Dialogues* (1929), NRS, pp17–19.
10. E K Thomson, *The Mariner's Mirror*, Vol 48, No 1, p77.
11. Perrin, *op cit*, p65.
12. C Lloyd, *The Englishman and the Sea*, pp85–6. (From Nathaniel Knott, *An Advice of a Seaman* [1634].)
13. *Ib*, p64.

Chapter 11
1. E H W Meyerstein (ed), *Adventures by Sea of Edward Coxere* (1946), Oxford, pp26–8.
2. *Ib*, pp38–9.
3. *Ib*, pp41–2.
4. *Ib*, pp81–2.
5. *Ib*, p90.
6. *Ib*, pp119–20.
7. *Ib*, pp126–7.
8. B Lubbock (ed), *Barlow's Journal*, 2 vols (1934), London, p60.
9. *Ib*, p68.
10. *Ib*, p89.
11. J Esquemeling, *The Buccaneers of America* (1898), London, pp2–3.
12. Barlow, *op cit*, p146.

Chapter 12
1. J Baltharpe, *The Straights Voyage or St David's Poem* (1959), Oxford, pp23–4.
2. *Ib*, p39.
3. *Ib*, p42.
4. *Ib*, p45.
5. *Ib*, p63.
6. *Ib*, pp65–6.
7. *Ib*, p75.
8. *Ib*, pp94–5.
9. B Lubbock (ed), *Barlow's Journal*, 2 vols (1934), London, p213.
10. C Fryke & C Schweitzer, *Voyages to the East Indies* (1929; originally 1700), London, p172.
11. *Ib*, p273.
12. *Ib*, pp177–8.
13. *Ib*, pp178–9.
14. E D Ross & E Power (eds), *The Diary of Henry Teonge* (1927), London, p233.
15. Fryke & Schweitzer, *op cit*, p24.
16. *Ib*, p25.
17. *Ib*, pp49–51.
18. *Ib*, pp 86–7.
19. *Ib*, pp93–4.
20. *Ib*, pp108–9.
21. *Ib*, pp115–6.
22. *Ib*, p127.
23. *Ib*, p146.
24. *Ib*, pp155–6.

Chapter 13
1. T Phillips, *A Journal of a Voyage in the Hannibal of London* (1693–4).
2. N Uring, *The Voyages and Travels of* (1726, reprinted 1928), London, p3.
3. *Ib*, pp6–7.
4. *Ib*, p8.
5. J Eaden (trs), *The Memoirs of Père Labat, 1693–1705* (1931), London, p174.
6. Uring, *op cit*, pp22–3.
7. *Ib*, pp48–9.
8. *Ib*, p50.
9. Eaden, *op cit*, p259.
10. Uring, *op cit*, p66.
11. *Ib*, pp66–7.
12. *Ib*, p66.
13. Woodes Rogers, *A Cruising Voyage round the World* (1712, reprinted 1928), London, p5.
14. *Ib*, p6.
15. *Ib*, pp9–10.
16. *Ib*, pp17–8.
17. *Ib*, pp22–3.
18. *Ib*, p78.
19. *Ib*, pp91–4.
20. *Ib*, p131.
21. *Ib*, p167.
22. *Ib*, p168.
23. *Ib*, p185.
24. *Ib*, p187.
25. *Ib*, pp214–5.

Chapter 14
1. G Shelvocke, *A Voyage Round the World* (1726, reprinted 1928), London, p29.
2. *Ib*, pp40–1.

3. *Ib*, pp99–100.
4. *Ib*, pp116–7.
5. *Ib*, p138.
6. *Ib*, p144.
7. *Ib*, p194.
8. *Ib*, p239.

Chapter 15
1. *The Wreck of the Wager* (1983), London, pp228–9.
2. *Ib*, p91.
3. *Ib*, p94.
4. *Ib*, pp98–9.
5. *Ib*, p109.
6. *Ib*, p109.
7. *Ib*, p111.
8. *Ib*, pp145–6.
9. G Anson, *A Voyage round the World* (1974), London, pp105–7.
10. *Ib*, pp338–341.
11. G P Stewart & D Guthrie (eds), *Lind's Treatise on Scurvy: A Bicentenary Volume* (1953), Edinburgh.
12. H S Vaughan (ed), *The Voyages and Cruises of Commodore Walker* (1928), London, p2. First published 1760.
13. *Ib*, p20.
14. *Ib*, p97.
15. *Ib*, pp41–2.
16. *Ib*, pp62–4.

Chapter 16
1. B Martin & M Spurrell (eds), *The Journal of a Slave Trader 1750–1754 by John Newton* (1962), London, pxiii.
2. *Ib*, ppxiv–xv.
3. *Ib*, p75.
4. *Ib*, p103.
5. *Ib*, pxiv.
6. *Ib*, p102.
7. *Ib*, pxiv.
8. L A de Bourgainville, *Voyage autour du Monde* (1771), Paris, pp189–91. See also L D Hammond (ed), *News from New Cythera: A Report of Bourgainville's Voyage 1766–1769* (1970), Minneapolis.
9. *An Account of the Voyages: Discoveries in the Southern Hemisphere. Commodore Byron, Captain Wallis, Captain Carteret, & Captain Cook* (1773), London, p481.
10. J C Beaglehole (ed), *The Journals of Captain James Cook on His Voyages of Discovery*, Vol 1 (1955), Cambridge, p138.
11. *Ib*, Vol II (1961), pp443–4.
12. *Ib*, Vol III (1967), pp265–6.
13. G Robertson, *The Discovery of Tahiti: A Journal of the Second Voyage of HMS Dolphin round the World 1766–1768* (1948), London, pp64–5.
14. *Ib*, p99.
15. H Wallis (ed), *Carteret's Voyage Round the World 1766–1769* (1965), Cambridge, p151.
16. Beaglehole, *op cit*, Vol II, p64.
17. *Ib*, pp72–3.
18. A G Price (ed), *The Explorations of Captain James Cook in the Pacific* (1971), New York, p108. (First published 1957.)
19. *Ib*, p188.
20. Beaglehole, *op cit*, Vol III, p479.
21. P Quennell (ed), *Memoirs of William Hickey* (1960), London, pp105–6.
22. *Ib*, pp267–9.
23. *Ib*, p261.
24. *Ib*, p106.
25. *Ib*, p106.
26. *Ib*, pp91–2.
27. *Ib*, pp134, 142.
28. *Ib*, pp150–2.
29. *Ib*, pp370–6.
30. *Ib*, pp184–6.
31. D C Harvey (ed), *Journeys to the Island of St John* (1955), Toronto, p20.
32. G L Lowis, *Fabulous Admirals* (1957), London, p64.

Chapter 17
1. G Grant, *The Life and Adventures of John Nicol* (1822), London, p63.
2. *Ib*, pp134–53.
3. *Ib*, pp167–8.
4. *Ib*, pp173–4.
5. *Ib*, pp193–5.

6. *Ib*, pp203–4.
7. W Bligh, *A Voyage to the South Sea* (1969), Victoria, Australia. (A facsimile reprint of the original London edition, 1792.)
8. *Ib*, p259.
9. S Childers (ed), *A Mariner of England: An Account of the Career of William Richardson from Cabin Boy in the Merchant Service to Warrant Officer in the Royal Navy* [1780 to 1819] as told by himself (1970), London (first edn, 1908), p44.
10. *Ib*, p47.
11. *Ib*, p50.
12. *Ib*, p51.
13. *Ib*, p90.
14. *Ib*, p91.
15. *Ib*, pp173–4.
16. *Ib*, pp292–3.
17. H Compton (ed), *A Master Mariner, being the Life and Adventures of Captain Robert Eastwick* (1891), London, p25.
18. *Ib*, p60.
19. *Ib*, pp76–7.
20. E Fanning, *Voyages and Discoveries in the South Seas, 1792–1832* (1924 & 1989), New York, p60.
21. *Ib*, pp175–6.
22. *Ib*, pp197–8.
23. P Woof (ed), *The Grasmere Journals* (Dorothy Wordsworth) (1991), Oxford, pp50, 78–9.
24. M D Hay (ed), *Landsman Hay: The Memoirs of Robert Hay, 1789–1847* (1958), London, pp70–3.
25. *Ib*, p190.
26. C S Forester (ed), *The Adventures of John Wetherell* (1954), London, p61.
27. *Ib*, p176.
28. W Robinson, *Jack Nastyface: Memoirs of a Seaman* (1973), London, pp87–9.

Chapter 18
1. E Fanning, *Voyages and Discoveries in the South Seas, 1792–1832* (1989), New York, pp288–9.
2. *Ib*, pp291–2.

3. *Ib*, pp298–9.
4. *Narratives of the Wreck of the Whale-Ship Essex* (1989), New York, p38.
5. *Ib*, pp49–50.
6. *Ib*, pp68–9.
7. *Ib*, p87.
8. *The Seafarer*, Autumn 1983, p84. (From an unpublished MS in the possession of J de Coverly.)
9. From the unpublished MS referred to above.
10. *Ib*.
11. *Ib*.
12. *Ib*.
13. *Ib*.
14. D C Harvey (ed), *Journeys to the Island of St John* (1955), Toronto, p89.
15. R H Dana, *Two Years before the Mast* (1911), London, p34.
16. *Ib*, pp74–5.
17. *Ib*, pp92–3.
18. *Ib*, pp111–2.
19. *Ib*, p125.
20. *Ib*, p249.
21. *Ib*, pp253–4
22. *Ib*, pp363–4. Cf E O'Neill, *Long Day's Journey into Night* (1966), London, p134.

Chapter 19
1. Anon, *Seafarers and Their Ships* (1955), London, pp26–7.
2. W Runciman, *Collier Brigs and Their Sailors* (1926 & 1971), London, pp272–3.
3. *Ib*, pp36–7.
4. *Ib*, pp86–7.
5. *Ib*, p89.
6. *Ib*, pp209–10.
7. H A Gosnell, *Before the Mast in the Clippers. The Diaries of Charles A. Abbey* (1937 & 1989), New York.
8. *Ib*, p49.
9. *Ib*, pp52–3.
10. *Ib*, pp121, 132–3.
11. *Ib*, p144.
12. *Ib*, p211.
13. *Ib*, p221.
14. Stan Hugill, *Sailortown* (1967), London, pp102–3.

15. Charles Dickens, *Household Words*, 22 March 1851.
16. Stan Hugill, *Shanties and Sailors' Songs* (1969), London, pp212–3.
17. *Ib*, p98.
18. Hugill, *Sailortown*, pp207–8.
19. *Ib*, p214.
20. Anon, *Great Shipwrecks* (1877), London, pp339–40.
21. Hugh Falkus, *Master of Cape Horn* (1982), London, pp102–3.

Chapter 20
1. F W Wallace, *Under Sail in the Last of the Clippers* (1936), Glasgow, p173.
2. *Ib*, pp78–9.
3. L A Woollard, *The Last of the Cape Horners* (1960), Devon, pp??.
4. J W Holmes, *Voyaging* (1965), London, p37.
5. *Ib*, pp36–7.
6. *Ib*, pp72–3.
7. Sir James Bissett, *Sail Ho!* (c1952), Sydney, pp117–9.
8. W Runciman, *Collier Brigs and Their Sailors* (1926 & 1971), London, pp245–7.
9. Don Aldus, *Coolie Traffic and Kidnapping* (1876), London, pp189–90.
10. J Havelock Wilson, *My Stormy Voyage through Life*. Vol I (no date), London, pp31, 32, 35.
11. *Ib*, p112.
12. *Ib*, pp151–2.
13. *Ib*, pp54–6.
14. *Ib*, pp59–60.
15. S Hugill, *Sailortown* (1967), London, p108.
16. S Hugill, *Shanties and Sailors' Songs* (1969), London, p43.
17. S Hugill, *Sailortown* (1967), London, pp240–1.
18. F W Wallace, *op cit*, pp136–7.
19. *Ib*, p194.

Chapter 21
1. Jan de Hartog, *A Sailor's Life* (1956), England, p107.
2. Sir James Bisset, *Sail Ho!* (c1952), Sydney, p46.

3. *Ib*, p51.
4. James S Learmont, *Master in Sail* (1950), London, p31.
5. *Ib*, p36.
6. *Ib*, p217.
7. Hugh Falkus, *Master of Cape Horn* (1983), London, p125.
8. *Ib*, p137.
9. Learmont, *op cit*, p58.
10. *Ib*, pp67–8.
11. *Ib*, p113.
12. *Ib*, p171.
13. *Ib*, pp190–3.
14. *Sea Breezes* (October 1947). Quoted by Learmont, p120.
15. William H S Jones, *The Cape Horn Breed* (1956), London, pp41–2.
16. *Ib*, pp54–5.
17. *Ib*, pp73–5.
18. *Ib*, pp86–7.
19. *Ib*, pp115–6.
20. James P Barker, *The Log of a Limejuicer* (1934), London, pp241–2.
21. Jones, *op cit*, p133.
22. *Ib*, pp747–8.
23. Barker, *op cit*, p35.
24. *Ib*, pp181, 204 and 211 respectively.
25. J W Holmes, *Voyaging* (1965), London, p138.
26. *Ib*, p141.
27. *Ib*, pp139–40.
28. *Ib*, p146.
29. J Bisset, *op cit*, pp50–1.
30. *Ib*, pp198–9.
31. *Ib*, pp210–1.
32. Holmes, *op cit*, p120.
33. Bisset, *op cit*, pp98–9.
34. Captain Frank H Shaw, *Seas of Memory* (1958), London, pp72–6.
35. *Ib*, pp77–8.
36. Captain A G Course, *The Wheel's Kick and the Wind's Song* (1950), Newton Abbot, pp99–100.
37. 'Shalimar', *True Tales of Sail and Steam* (1943), London, p33.
38. D Bone, *Merchantmen-at-Arms* (1936), London, p15.
39. H Grattidge, *Captain of the Queens* (c1954), London, pp103–4.
40. S Hugill, *Sailortown* (1967), London, pp158–9.

Chapter 22

1. J C Healey, *Foc's'le and Glory Hole* (1936), New York, p106.
2. Marshall Everett (ed), *The Wreck and Sinking of the Titanic* (1912), Chicago, p99
3. F Pietraroia, *The Seafarer* (1934), p20.
4. Healey, *op cit*, p57.
5. Frank T Bullen, *The Men of the Merchant Service* (1900), New York, p253.
6. R Hope (ed), *Seamen and the Sea* (E Morris, 'Small Boat to Paradise') (1965), London, pp194–5.
7. A G Course, *The Wheel's Kick and the Wind's Song* (1968), Newton Abbot, p135.
8. *Ib*, pp153–4.
9. J W Holmes, *Voyaging* (1965), London, p157.
10. *Ib*, pp175–6.
11. Hope, *op cit* (W E How, 'In the Antarctic'), pp80–1.
12. W J Slade, *Out of Appledore* (1959), London, p48.
13. Course, *op cit*, pp87–8.
14. Hope, *op cit* (S Gorrell, 'Second Mate'), pp101–2.
15. *The Seafarer*, January 1957, p3.
16. R Hope (ed), *Sea Pie* (J B Maguire, 'Doctor at Sea') (1984), London, p70.
17. R Hope (ed), *The Seaman's World* (J Moody, 'Today and Yesterday') (1982), London, pp76–7.
18. *The Seafarer*, October 1937 (J L Dickinson, 'Bound for Shanghai'), pp117–8.
19. *The Seaman's World* (D Chadwick, 'Cargoes'), pp19, 22.
20. *Sea Pie* (F Goodall, 'Fifty Years at Sea'), p104.
21. *The Seaman's World* (S Algar, 'Conrad Country'), pp17–8.
22. *Seamen and the Sea* (D Graves, 'The Loss of the Egypt'), p97.
23. *The Seaman's World* (A D Blue, 'Captured by Chinese Pirates'), pp29–33.
24. *Ib* (John Aldiss, 'Pump Ship'), pp94–6.
25. *Ib* (D L C Evans, 'Hurricane'), pp24–6.
26. *Sea Pie* (A Robson, 'Steel Workhouse'), pp1–2.

Chapter 23

1. E Newby, *The Last Grain Race* (1948), London, p85.
2. R Hope (ed), *Sea Pie* (D A Rees, 'Storm') (1984), London, p9.
3. T Lane, *The Merchant Seaman's War* (1990), Manchester, p98.
4. *Ib*, pp224–5.
5. T Lane, *Grey Dawn Breaking* (1986), Manchester, p49.
6. J L Kerr, *Touching the Adventures* (W H Venables, 'The Torpedoing of the Assyrian') (1953), London, pp29–31.
7. *Ib* (Stanley Sutherland, DSM, 'Blockade-Runner'), pp144–5.
8. R F McBreaty, *Seafaring as I saw it, 1939–45* (1995), Durham, p33.
9. T Lane, *The Merchant Seaman's War*, pp237–8.
10. Kerr, *op cit* (A MacDonald, 'Ordeal'), pp32–50.
11. *The Merchant Seaman's War*, p196.
12. R Hope (ed), *The Seaman's World* (J Bisset, 'The Queens in Wartime') (1982), London, p46.
13. *Ib* (S Simpson, 'Voyage to Tobago'), pp59–65.
14. Kerr, *op cit* (S C Whitehead, 'The SS Empire Starlight'), pp85–92.
15. *The Seaman's World* (F Goodall, 'Atlantic Convoy'), p39–41.
16. McBreaty, *op cit*, pp145–6.
17. *Sea Pie* (T Allen, 'Survival from Shipwreck'), pp39–43.
18. *The Merchant Seaman's War*, pp179–80.
19. *Ib*, pp242–3.
20. *Ib*, p203.
21. *Touching the Adventures* (E W Stedmond, 'The Last Convoy'), p249.
22. *Sea Pie* (G N Howe, 'The Coming of Peace'), p46.
23. R Hope (ed), *Seamen and the Sea* (T Grout, 'First Ship') (1965), London, p11.

24. K Ainslie, *Pacific Ordeal* (1956), London, pp108–9.
25. *The Seaman's World* (W Money, 'The Deaded Bay'), pp111–2.
26. *Sea Pie* (J Petrie, 'Playing it Cool'), p48.
27. *The Seaman's World* (A Collinge, 'Archangel for Orders'), p79.
28. *Sea Pie* (C Bowness, 'Trip to Russia'), pp58–9.
29. *Ib* (N Hearn, 'Tar Wash'), pp81–2.
30. T Lane, *Grey Dawn Breaking* (1986), Manchester, p117.
31. *The Seafarer* (G Lazarus, 'The Good Old Days') (Spring 1985), pp4–5.
32. *Sea Pie* (A Robson, 'The Palmy Days'), p67.

Chapter 24
1. *The Nautical Magazine*, January 1964, pp17, 19.
2. R Hope (ed), *The Seaman's World* (B McManus, 'North Atlantic Car-Carrier') (1982), London, p115.
3. The late Captain J MacRae, c1970.
4. Letter in *The Seaman*, June 1964, p127.
5. T Lane, *Grey Dawn Breaking* (1986), Manchester, pp154–5.
6. *The Seaman's World* (R Hawkins, 'Down Tanker Alley'), pp126, 131.
7. *The Seafarer*, Winter 1985 (J H Guy, 'The Lesson'), pp113–5.
8. R Hope (ed), *Sea Pie* (J H Guy, 'End of the Shah') (1984), pp132–3.
9. R Woodman, *Voyage East* (1988), London, pp134–5.
10. Lane, *Grey Dawn Breaking*, p44.
11. *The Seafarer*, Winter 1985, p147.
12. *Ib*, Summer 1983, p60.
13. Lane, *op cit*, pp133–4.
14. *The Seafarer*, Autumn 1986, p86.
15. *Ib*, Autumn 1984, p101.
16. *Ib*, Spring 1982, p18.
17. *Ib*, Autumn 1982, p98.
18. *Ib*, Spring 1981, p18.
19. *Ib*, Spring 1982, p23.
20. *Ib*, Summer 1983, p62.
21. *Ib*, Autumn 1984, p97.
22. P K Chapman, *Trouble on Board: The Plight of International Seafarers* (1992), Ithaca, New York, ppix, x.

The Seafarer is the quarterly magazine of the Marine Society, London. The author was responsible for its production from 1947 to 1986.

For further background to the content of this book see Ronald Hope, *A New History of British Shipping* (1990), London.

Index

Abbey, Charles, 245-9 *passim*
Aborough, John, his navigating
    equipment, 53
Abraham, Captain, of brig *Pioneer*,
    260-1
Acapulco, 103, 181
accommodation, elegant cabin, 198;
    295; Liberty ships, 328; 341-2
Achin, 112
Adam de Moleyns, 32
advance pay, 230, 249; 'flogging the
    dead horse', 251
Aelfric, 17
American War of Independence, 188,
    202-3
ammonia, as cargo, 338-9
Anarcharsis, 6
Anson, Commodore George, 174,
    179-82 *passim*, 190
Antarctic skies and seas, 275-6
Antipater of Thessalonia, 7
Alaric the Goth, 12
albatross, 167, 257
Aldiss, John, 310-12 *passim*
Alfred, King, 16
Aphrodite, 28, 33
Aplin, Frank, 257
Apollonius of Rhodes, 4
apprentices, 272-3, 278-9, 304,
    310-2
Argonauts, 4-5
Armada, 81-3, 86
Arthur, King, 29
Atlantic liners, 292, 294-6, 305
Auden, W H, 110

Balboa, conquistador, 50

Baltharpe, John, 137-40 *passim*
Banks, Sir Joseph, 192
Bannister, surgeon, 75-7
Bantam, Java, 144
Bantry Bay, 90
Barbary Coast, 252-3
Barker, Captain James P, 276-284
    passim, 286
Barlow, Edward, 131-6 *passim*, 140-1
Barnaby, Thomas, coal trade, 54
Batavia (Jakarta), 209
Battle of the Nile, 206-7
Battle of Trafalgar, 221
Beare, James, epitaph, 110
Betagh, William, 168, 173
bicycles on board, 344-5
Bight of Benin, 150
bilge water, 36, 57
Binyon, Lawrence, 16
biscuits (ship's), 231, 233, 246;
    'Liverpool pantiles', 276; weevilly
    hard tack, 309
Bisset, Commodore Sir James, 271, 285,
    287
Black Book of the Admiralty, 29
'Black Sam', 198
Bligh, Captain William, 207-10 *passim*
Blue, Chief Engineer A D, held to
    ransom, 310
Blue Funnel, 312, 355
Board of Trade, marine department,
    241; compulsory examinations,
    242; scale of food, 242;
    'a burlesque', 262; 283
Boca, La, 267-8
Bone, Sir David, going into steam,
    291-2

books, no use for, 122
Borough, Stephen, 56
Boteler, Captain, 123-4
Bougainville, Louis Antoine de, 191
Bourne, William, 66, 110
boys at sea, 246-7, 255-7, 304
Bradford, William, leader of Pilgrims to
    New England, 115-6
Braithwaite, Richard, 120
Bremen, 37
Bristol, 38, 42-3
British Columbia, Drake in, 70
British merchant shipping at peak, 270
British Ministry of War Transport, 327
British seamen killed in World War II,
    332
Brittany, 32
buccaneers, 153
'bucko mate', 245-6, 298-9
bulcao, wind, 45
bulk carriers, 341, 346
Bulkeley, John, 176-7, 179, 205
bulldozers shifting, 345-6
Bullen, Frank, 296
bum-boats, 138-9, 221
bunkering coal, 308
Burrough, Sir John, 91
burying the dead, 117, 140, 292,
    299-300, 315
Byron, Hon. John, 174-6, 179, 191

cabbage-trees, 160
Cabel, John, 184-6 passim
Cabot, John, 43
Cabot, Sebastian, 43-4, 54
Cabral, Pedro, 45
Cadamosto, Alvise, 38
Caesar, Julius, 7
Calicut, 45, 51
Callao, 299
Cambrensis, Giraldus, 29
cannibalism, 227-8
Canterbury Tales, 31-2
Canton, 198
Cape Finistère, 32
Cape Horn, first rounded, 114; 159,
    167, 174, 179, 255, 257; 1905, 266;
    270-1, 277-8, 291, 317
Cape of Good Hope, 40, 206
Cape Verde, 38
Caple, Thomas, 176
careening, dangers of at sea, 95

Carib Indians, 42-3
Carletti, Francesco, 5, 103-5 passim
carracks, 24, 33
Carteret, Captain Philip, 191, 195
cassava, 93, 166, 170
cattle, carriage of, 289-90
Cavendish, Sir Thomas, 80-1, 89-90
Celtic saints, 12-15 passim, 37
chain-locker, 244
Chancellor, Richard, 55-6
Channels, the, 4
Charles II, King, 131
chartered companies, 103
Chase, Owen, 226-8 passim
Chatham Chest, 29, 108
Chaucer, Geoffrey, 30-2, 294
Cheap, Captain, 174-7 passim, 179
Chidley, John, 87-8
Christian, Fletcher, 207-8
Christmas at sea, 132-3, 143, 342-3
Churchill, Sir Winston, 327
class distinction, 328, 343-4
clippers, 255
Clipperton, Captain John, 166, 168, 171
coal-burning tanker, conditions on
    board (1934), 314-5
cod, 24; stock fish, 33; bears eating, 44;
    82; Poore John, 100; backalew, 112;
    119, 130-1, 246
coffin ships, 262
Coleridge, Samuel Taylor, 167
Columbus, Christopher, 40-43 passim,
    46-48 passim
compass, 33
conditions on board ship, 133-4, 285,
    318, 340, 353, 355-7
Conrad, Joseph, 2
container ships, 341, 343
Cook, Captain James, 191-3, 196, 202
corposants, 300
corrupt officials, 119
'Count Douglas', third mate, Plassey,
    198
'country ship', 211, 213-4
Course, Captain A G, 298-9
Coverly, Edward, 228-32 passim
Coxere, Edward, 126-31 passim
crew, marrying in Cork, 156; mixed
    nature, 157, 353, 355
crimps, 141, 230, 249-50, 252,
    265-6, 273
crossing the line, 52-3; Pointe du Raz,

134; Tropic of Cancer, 157-8
crusade, 13th century, 28
Crusoe, Robinson, 156; Alexander
    Selkirk, 159, 161
Cumberland, Earl of, 83-5, 101
Cummins, John, 176
Curtis, Thomas, 201

da Gama, Vasco, 44-6, 48, 52
Dampier, Captain, 159-60
Dana, Richard, 233-40 passim
Dauber, Masefield poem, 137
Davis, John, 80, 89-90, 113
decay of shipping, 54
Dee, John, 42
de Quiros, discovery of Tahiti, 191
de Ruyter family, 144
Descent into the Maelstrom, 29
Dias, Bartholomew, 40, 43
Dibdin, Charles, 3, 28
Dickens, Charles, 250
Dicuil, 14
Discovery of the Bermudas, The, 110
Disraeli, Benjamin, 270
donkey's breakfast, 314, 316, 318
Dow, Captain, 247-8
Downs, The, 140; hurricane, 201
Drake, Sir Francis, 5, 29, 62-5, 68,
    69-75; sonnet, 77; 80-3; last
    expedition, 99-102; Chatham
    Chest, 108
Drake, John, 64, 75
drink, 98, 124, 127-8, 237, 258-9, 271,
    273
Dudley, Robert, 98-9
Dutch courage, 144
Dutch East India Company, 103, 141,
    143, 148
Dutch Wars, 126

Earswick, Richard, merchant, 74
East India Company, 103, 106, 197-201,
    213, 215
East Indies, Lancaster's voyage, 91-2
Eastwick, Captain Robert, 213-4
Ebesham, William, 39
Eden, Richard, 56
Edward I, King, 28
Edward III, King, 32
Effingham, Lord Howard of, 82
Elcano, Juan Sebastian de, 51-2
Eliot, Hugh, 42

Elizabeth I, Queen, 60, 68; knights
    Drake, 73; country's economy, 74;
    profit from privateering, 81, 91
Eric the Red, 18, 20
eskimoes, 68
Esquemeling, John, 134
Eusden, Laurence, Poet Laureate, 165
Evans, Captain D C L, 312-3
expedition rules, 55, 57

Fairbourn, Sir Stafford, 154
Fanning, Captain Edmund, 214-6,
    223-6 passim
Fenton, Captain Edward, 75
Fiddler's Green, 3, 267-9
Finnbogi, 20-1
fire at sea, 132, 146, 151-2, 253, 277-8,
    296-7
fireworks, 304-5, 307-8
fishing at sea, 153
flags of convenience, 351-7
Fletcher, Francis, 69
flogging, 65-6, 111, 189, 203-4, 210-3,
    220, 236-7
Flores in the Azores, 88
food, 50, 53, 60-1, 139, 143, 212, 239,
    246, 272, 276-7, 306, 317; see also
    provisions
fool's gold, 68
Fox, Captain Luke, 121-2
freebooters, 39-40
Freshwater Bay, 177
Freydis, 19-21
Friendly Islands (Tonga), 194, 209
Frobisher, Martin, 67-8
frost-bite, 279-80
Fryke, Christopher, surgeon, 143-9
    passim

galleys, 24, 33
Gilbert, Sir Humphrey, 78-9
Gillies, Jack, 218-20 passim
'glory hole' (crew quarters), 295, 305
going aloft, 256
Gore, Captain Arthur, 198
Gorges, Captain Sir Ferdinando, 119-20
Gorrell, Captain Syd, from Appledore,
    303-4
Graves, Radio Officer Dorrington, 310
Greenland, 18-22, 24
Grenville, Sir Richard, 79-80; death,
    88-9

Grimolfsson, Bjarni, 22-3, 25
guano, loading, 285-6
Guide to the Preservation of Life at Sea after Shipwreck, 327
Gulf of St Lawrence, 201
Gunn, Captain Simon, 282
Guy, John, 346-7, 348-9

Hakluyt, Richard, 29, 63, 67
Hamburg, 37
Hamlet, performed at sea, 111
hammocks, 243-4
Hanley, James, 312
Hanno of Carthage, 6, 37
Hanseatic League, 37-8
happy ship, 248-9, 274, 284-5, 339, 340
Hare, Captain Stephen, 74
Harriet Lane, 263
Harrison, Leslie, 318
Hartog, Captain Jan de, 271
Harvey, Thomas, 177
Hatley, Captain, 166-8
Hawaii, 193, 204, 207
Hawkins, Sir John, 60-2, 65, 99-100, 108
Hawkins, Richard, 95-8 *passim*
Hawkins, William, 53, 60
Hawks, Henry, 63
Hay, Robert, 218-20 *passim*
Helgi, 20
Henry V, King, 32
Henry the Navigator, 37, 39
Herodotus, 6
herrings, 24; red, 127
Hickey, William, 197-201 *passim*
Himilco, 6
Hinks, Tony, 349-51
Hispaniola, 93
Hobbes, Thomas, 2, 148
Holmes, Captain J W, 257-9, 284-7, 300
holy relics, 162
Homer, 4
Hoorn, 114
Hore, Captain Robert, 53
hurricane in Deal, 201
Hylton, Sir William, Admiral of the Humber, 29

ice-box, 306
Iceland, Celts in, 14; 33
ice on ship, 336
In Hazard, 312

international crews, 353, 355
Isidorus of Aegae, 8

Jackson, Bill, Dana's 'thoroughbred' English sailor, 235-6
James I, King, tastes a pineapple, 108
Japanese machine-gunning of seafarers in boats, 331
Japanese massage, 347
Japanese treatment of POWs, 331-2
Jenkinson, Anthony, 57
jet aircraft, 341
'jigger-flea', 330
'Jimmy the Drummer', 266
job satisfaction, disappears, 348
Jones, John Paul, 202
Jones, W H S, apprentice, 276-82 *passim*
Jourdain, Sylvester, 110
Juan Fernandez, 159, 168-70, 179, 181

Karlsefni, 20
Kedgell, Captain, 94
keelhauling, 123
Keeling, Captain William, 111-4 *passim*
Kidd, Captain William, 153
Knox-Johnston, Sir Robin, 182-3

Labat, Father, 152-3; dancing on board, 155
Lancaster, Sir James, 91-2, 106
Land of Cockaigne, 5, 105
Lascar seamen, 105
latrines, 148, 243
law of the sea, 1, 7, 26-7, 29
Layfield, Dr, chaplain, 101
leaky ships, 132
Learmont, Captain James, 272, 274-6
Leicester, Earl of, 76
Leif the Lucky, 19-20
Leviathan, 148
Libel of English Policy, 32
liberty day, 238
Liberty ships, 328
lifeboats, 253; *Titanic*, 294; 318
Lind, Dr James, 182-3
loading iron ore, 333
Lob Lob Creek, 199-200
loneliness in modern ships, 347-8
Longfellow, Henry Wadsworth, 79
Lübeck, 37
Lucian, 11

Macao, 172, 181
macaroni, 100
MacDonald, Angus, 321-3 *passim*
Maclean, Thomas, 178
Madox, Richard, 75, 77
Magellan, Ferdinand, 50-1
Magellan Strait, 50, 69, 87-8, 90, 176,
    194-5
Manila, 103
Manila ship, 156, 163-4, 181, 190
man overboard, 247, 283
Mansel, Sir Robert, 108
Marchaunt, Captain, 81
Martinique, 212
Martyr, Peter, 44
Masefield, John, 137, 270-1
McBreaty, Captain R F, 320-1
mercantilists, 33
mercantile marine becomes Merchant
    Navy, 305
Mervyn, Sir Henry, 124-5
middle passage, 150, 153
Milag Nord, 323
missionary societies, 223, 253, 264-5;
    burial, 299-300
Moby Dick, 226
Mocquet, Jean, 106-8
Mombasa, 44-5
Money, Wilson, 334-5 *passim*
monsoon, sailing with, 12
Moone, Thomas, 64, 68
mortality of seamen, on slave-ships,
    190; *circa* 1900, 294
music on board, 69, 155, 183, 267,
    349
mutineers, 157, 207

Nagasaki, 104
Napoleonic Wars, 212, 223
National Amalgamated Sailors' and
    Firemen's Union of Great Britain,
    264
National Union of Seamen, 263
navigation, taught in London, 151
Neptune in Whampoa, 229
Newby, Eric, 316
New Cythera, 192
Newfoundland, 42, 43, 53, 67, 78, 130,
    335-6
Newport, Captain Christopher, 92, 94
Newton, Captain John, 188-90
Nicol, John, 203-7 *passim*

North Cape, 16
north-east passage, 55
north-west passage, 67
Norway, 20, 25, 29, 30
Nourse Line, 318

Ogygia, 5
Ohthere, 16
oil-lamps, 306-7
Oléron, Judgments of, 1, 26-7

Pacific Ocean, 50, 103, 171
packet-boat, 155
'palmer of ferula', 96
passenger services, disappearance of,
    341
Peckham, Sir George, 77
penguins, 87, 90; eggs, 214-5; 225
Pentland Firth, 30
Pepys, Samuel, 134-5
Periplus of the Erythraian Sea, 45
pests, ants, 211; bugs, 129, 316;
    cockroaches, 306, 352; lice, 90-1,
    129, 175; mosquitoes, 63; rats, 50,
    107, 113-4, 160, 211-2, 275, 336-7,
    352; smoking ship, 339
Petrie, Captain Jim, 335-6
Petronius, 12
Philip of Thessalonika, 8
Phillips, Captain Thomas, 150-1
Phoenicians, 6, 26
Pigafetta, Antonio, 50
pigs at sea, 143; cochon boucanné,
    152-3; loss of, 201-2; 229
pilgrims, 34-6; moslem, 46; to New
    England, 115
pilot book, 39
pineapple, 108
piracy, 148, 215-6, 354
Pisagua, nitrate port, 273, 281
Platt, Sir Hugh, surgeon, 99-100
Pleiades, 7
Plimsoll, Samuel, 262
Poe, Edgar Allen, 29
Pollard, Captain George, 228
pollution, oil, 338
Pope, the, division of world, 52; bulls,
    161-2
Port Famine, 87-8
Portofarino Castle, Tunis, 129-30
Portugal, 32, 45, 57; sailors, 205
Pott, Bob, 198-200

press-gang, 96, 126, 135-6, 154, 205-6, 211, 213, 222
Prince William, 25
prisoner-of-war, 218, 220-1
privateering, 74-7, 79-81, 83-94, 151, 156-64, 166-87
proas, 144, 215-6
prostitution, 104-5, 146, 199, 204, 221, 250-3, 266-8
provisions, 123-4, 166, 195, 261-2; see also food
Puerto Rico, 93
pumping ship, 260
pyrites, loading, 308-9
Pytheas, 6, 37

radio officers, 305
Raleigh, Sir Walter, 79, 89, 91, 99, 115
Ranletts, Captain 'Bully', 246
Rapa, South Sea island, 297-8
Ratcliffe Highway, 250-1
redundancy, 351-2
Regiment for the Sea, A, 66, 110
religious services at sea, 40, 61, 116, 118, 147, 149, 178-9, 189, 231, 292
revolution in Iran, 346-7
Rhodes, 1, 7, 26
Richard II, King, 29
Richard II, performed at sea, 111
Richard Lion Heart, 25
Richardson, William, 210-3 passim
Robertson, George, 194
Robinson Crusoe, 218
Robinson, William, 221
ro-ros, 341, 349-51
Rossetti, Dante Gabriel, 25
Rousseau, Jean-Jaques, 192
Royal Navy, 2
rules in privateering, Woodes Rogers, 158-9, 161, 163
Runciman, Walter, 243-5
running contraband, 353
Russia, trading route to, 56-7
Russian reception, 337-8

St Brendan, 12-13
St Helena, 92
St James of Compostella, 33-4
St Malo, 32
St Nicholas, 57
St Paul, 8, 11-2
salt meat, 212, 246, 262-3, 277, 309; see

also food and provisions
San Francisco, Drake in, 70-1; Barbary Coast, 252-3; 273
San Juan de Ulua, 62, 64
sarang, 105
Saxons, 15-18
scallop shell, 33
Schouten, Willem, 114
Schweitzer, Christopher, 141-2
scurvy and suggested cures, 63, 76, 81, 90, 96-7, 106-7, 111-3, 162, 172, 180-2, 194-8, 204, 242
seafaring epics, 208-9, 296-7, 321-3, 324-5, 329-31
Sea Grammar, A, 117-9
seals and seal-skins, 169, 176-8, 214, 224
seamen, begging, 216-8; burnt, 224-5, 321; in gaol, 273-4, 285; in short supply, 116-7, 184; scalded, 223-4; struck by lightning, 225-6; treatment of, 120, 122-3, 189, 259-61, 317; see also flogging
seamen's character, 120, 190, 197, 249, 263-4, 271, 295-6, 343, 348-9
seamen's clothes, 53, 83, 124-5, 128, 151, 196, 218-9, 238
seamen's gild, 38
seamen's hospital, Batavia, 209-10
seamen's illnesses (other than scurvy), 63, 76-7, 81, 82-3, 90, 92, 100-1, 112, 142, 145, 150-2, 194-5, 211-2, 243, 287-9
seamen's language, 271
seamen's missions, 223, 250, 253-4, 264-5, 299-300, 318
seamen's pay stopped, 133, 136
seamen's protests, 81-2
sea-pie, 263
Selkirk, Alexander, 156, 159-61
Serisen, Captain, 288-9
Seven Years War, 203
Shackleton, Ernest, 301-2
Shakespeare, William, 110
shanties, 110, 250-1, 266-8
sharks, 142, 232, 297, 322, 324-5
Shelvocke, Captain George, 166-73 passim
ship as she, 8
Ship Captain's Medical Guide, 283, 286-7
ship losses, 241, 323

shipmaster as doctor, 280, 333-4, 354-5
shipmaster's character, 66-7, 188-9, 202, 241, 259, 262, 272, 282-3, 292
ships: *Active*, 211; *Alert*, 237-40; *Apapa*, 337-8; *Archibald Russell*, 300; *Asia*, 141-2; *Assyrian*, 319; *Athenia*, 318; *Atlantis*, 323; *Barber Perseus*, 349-51; *Barwell*, 213; *Betsey*, 214-6; *Blair Atholl*, 257-9; *Bona Esperanza*, 56; *Bonaventure*, 91; *Bounty*, 207; *British Chivalry*, 330; *British Isles*, 276-84; *Buckinghamshire*, 228-32; *Cadillac*, 321; *Cadogan*, 172; *Canning*, 228-9; *Centurion*, 179, 181-2; *City of Cairo*, 321, *Conway*, 273; *Cruttenden*, 198-9; *Cumbrian Chieftain*, 290-1; *Dainty*, 95-8; *de Conception de Recova*, 171; *Dee*, 131; *Delight*, 1748; *Desire*, 80, 89-90; *Diana*, 232-3; *Dog*, 86-7; *Dolphin*, 191, 194-5; *Dragon*, 106, 111-14; *Dutchess*, 163; *Egypt*, 310; *Elizabeth Jonas*, 82-3; *Empire Starlight*, 326-7; *Endurance*, 301; *Essex*, 226; *Garland*, 100; *Golden Dragon*, 92-3; *Golden Hind*, 68, 72-3; *Golden Lion*, 81; *Goliath*, 206; *Grand Duchess*, 256; *Harve de Grace*, renamed *Marquiss*, 161; *Hussar*, 220; *Jervis Bay*, 318; *Jesu Maria*, renamed *Happy Return*, 171; *Kingsport*, 259-60; *Lady Julian*, 204; *Lancaster Castle*, 320; *Leicester*, 75-7, 89; *Madre de Dios*, 91-3; *Magdalen*, 32; *Marchant Royal*, 91; *Margaret*, 93-4; *Mauritania*, 294; *Mayflower*, 115; *Moewe*, 302-3; *Monkbarn*, 300; *Moshulu*, 316; *Napier Star*, 317; *Nassau*, 198; *Nazaré*, 49; *New Shoreham*, 201; *Nostra Seniora de la Incarnacion Disengagio*, 164; *Nottingham*, 205-6; *Nuestra Senora de Covadonga*, 181-2; *Oiltrader*, 327-8; *Olympic*, 294; *Orduna*, 318; *Parracombe*, 320; *Penelope*, 91; *Phemius*, 312-3; *Pilgrim*, 233-7; *Plassey*, 197, 199; *Prince of Kaunitz*, 211; *Prudence*, 92-3; *Queen Elizabeth*, 323-4; *Queen Mary*, 323; *Recovery*, built from *Speedwell*, 170; *Revenge*, 88-9; *Rhakotis*, 323; *Russian Merchant*, 183; *St David*, 137-40; *St Tubas*, 178-9; *Sacra Familia*, renamed *Holy Family*, 171; *Samwake*, 328; *Santo Alberto*, 94-5; *Sao Joao Baptista*, 116; *Sao Paulo*, 57-9; *Searchthrift*, 56; *Speedwell*, 166-9; *Squirrel*, 78-9; *Success*, 166, 171; *Surprise*, 245-6; *Sutlej*, 330; *Swallow*, 195; *Swan*, 64, 68; *The Spy*, 210-1; *Titanic*, 294; *Victory*, 83-5; *Volunteer*, 223-5; *Wager*, 174, 205; *War Bahadur*, 316; *Wayfarer*, 329; *W. D. Potts*, 302; *William*, 183; *Windsor Castle*, 343-4; *Worcester*, 273
ships at sea in doing of rail, 191 3
ship's nails, removal of, 192
ships of reprisal, 86
ship's rules, 117
ships' salutes, 112-3
ships' sanitary arrangements, 148, 243
shipwrecks, select committee enquiry, 241
Simpson, Chief Officer Stanley, 324-5
slaves and slave trade, 37-9, 60, 63, 93, 146, 150-3, 162, 165, 188-90, 210-1
sleeping on watch, 244, 246
slop chest, 55, 283
slump, 313-5
Smith, Captain John, 108-9, 117-9
Smith, R A, 321
smuggler, 200-1
sodomy, 142
Soncino, Raimondo de Raimondi de, 43
South Sea Company, 165
South Street, NY, 292-3
Spanish Inquisition, 53, 65
Spens, Sir Patrick, 30
starvation, 286, 300, 322
steamships, 242, 304
Stein, Captain W H, 326-7
Stella Maris, 28
steward's life, 295
storm at sea, 98-9, 291, 312-3, 316-7, 334-5, 345-6
Strabo, 6
surgeons, 80, 99, 101, 111, 140
survivors, treatment of in World War II, 328-30

Sutherland, Stanley, 320
Swiss Family Robinson, 215

Tahiti, 191-2, 207
Taino Indians, 42
Talamanca Indians, 46-7
'Tanker Alley', 344
tankers, 316; burning, 320-1
tea, smuggling of, 200-1
Tennyson, Lord Alfred, 89
Teonge, Rev Henry, 143
Teredo navalis, 22
The Seafarer, Saxon poem, 15-16
The Tempest, 110
Third Crusade, 25-6
Thorne, Robert, 42
Thorvald, 19-21
Thread, Captain Robert, 93-4
Timor, 209
Tiresias, 6
Tobago, 324
Tonga, 194, 209
Trimalchio, 12
tropical weather, 239-40, 267, 284-5
Trujillo, 94
Turgot, 'first' stowaway, 25
'two-mate' ships, 309

Ulysses, 5-6, 11, 44
Uring, Captain Nathaniel, 151-6

Venables, Chief Engineer W. H., 319-20
venereal disease, 42, 138, 162, 193-4, 251
Veneti, 7
Venus, transit of, 191
Vespucci, Amerigo, 45
Vestey's Blue Star Line, 317
Victoria, Queen, 270
Vikings, 13, 15, 18-23
Vinland, 13, 19-21
Virginia Dare, 110
Virgin Mary, 28, 116
VLCCs, 344-5

Waddell, Captain, 197, 200-2

Walker, Commodore George, 183-7 passim
Wallis, Captain Samuel, 191-2
Walter, Archbishop Hubert, 26
Walton, William, 87
Wapping, 205
War of Jenkins' Ear, 183
water, distilled, 97, 196; filtered through sand, 81; shortage of, 84-5, 107-8, 147, 171, 262, 279, 286, 306-7, 353; sucked through musket barrel, 170, 210
wedding party in Banda, 309
Welladvice, Captain John, 213
West, Paddy, 249
Wetherell, John, 220-1
Whampoa, 172, 198-9, 229, 245, 247
whirlpool, 29
White, Captain John, 110
Whitelam, Sarah, 204-5
White Sea, 16, 57
White Ship, The, 25
Whittington, Dick, 32
Wilberforce, William, 189
Wilkinson, Captain, 220
Willoughby, Sir Hugh, 54-6
Wilson, Havelock, 262-3, 266
wine trade, 26, 31
Winnington, Robert, 38
wireless operators, 305
wives on board, 105, 342
'wolf-packs' of U-boats, 327
women, and children first, 58; at Battle of the Nile, 206; employed as officers, 342; on board ship, 52; waiting for husband's pay, 135
Woodes Rogers, Captain, 156-164 passim
Wood, James, surgeon, 99, 101
Wordsworth, Dorothy, 216-8
Wordsworth, William, 167, 216-8
working hours, 1914, 295
world tonnage, 1935, 316
Wyatt, Captain, 98-9
Wynkyn de Worde, 13